The Central Wales Line

Dedication
To Rose and Didi

Llandrindod Wells c1905. Two Webb tank engines head a Euston express. (LNWR Society collection)

Half title: *A double-headed steam excursion with BR Standard 2-6-4Ts Nos 80080 and 80079 works south from Llandrindod on 9 October 1993.* (Roy Palmer)

As part of our ongoing market research, we are always pleased to receive comments about our books, suggestions for new titles, or requests for catalogues. Please write to: The Editorial Director, Oxford Publishing Co., Sparkford, Near Yeovil, Somerset, BA22 7JJ.

The Central Wales Line

AN ILLUSTRATED HISTORY OF THE SHREWSBURY TO SWANSEA RAILWAY

A. Doughty

OPC

Oxford Publishing Co.

First published in 1997

A catalogue record for this book is available from the British Library.

ISBN 0 86093 516 7

Oxford Publishing Co. is an imprint of Haynes Publishing, Sparkford, Nr Yeovil, Somerset BA22 7JJ

Printed in Hong Kong

Typeset in Times Roman Medium

Acknowledgements

City of Swansea Archives
R. A. Cooke
John Horsley Denton, Shropshire Railway Society
GWR Society Ltd
Historical Model Railway Society
The Late G. A. Hookham
LNWR Society
HOWLTA
National Museum of Wales (Welsh Industrial Maritime Museum)
Newton Abbot Railway Studies Centre
Powys County Archives Office
Powys County Library
The Quail Map Company
Railway Magazine
Shrewsbury Local Studies Centre
Jim Smout
G. L. Spencer
Dr P. A. Stewart
Swansea Museum
Nigel Wassell
Glyn Watson
Welsh Railways Research Circle
Tony Williams
University College of Wales

With special thanks to Mike Watson who also read the chapters.

Plans and Track Diagrams reproduced by kind permission of the following:

34 Line – General Map – R. A. Cooke
35 Central Wales Line Craven Arms–Pontardulais. Gwaen-cae-Gurwen–Abernant Branches Track diagram. Quail Map Co.
38 Gwaen-cae-Gurwen Track 1848-1966 – R. A. Cooke
39 Garnant to Gwaen-cae-Gurwen Track 1876-1916 – R. A. Cooke
39 Brynamman West Track Diagram. Courtesy D. T. Davies
39 Garnant Track Diagram. Courtesy D. T. Davies
43 Map of proposed line. Llandeilofawr–Carmarthen and Pontarddulais–Swansea. Nigel Wassell.
44 Penclawdd Track c1878-1915 – R. A. Cooke
45 Llanmorlais Track c1878-1915 – R. A. Cooke
46 Mountain Branch Track 1 – R. A. Cooke
46 Mountain Branch Track 2 – R. A. Cooke
47 Mountain Branch Track 3 – R. A. Cooke
47 Mountain Branch Track 4 – R. A. Cooke
48 Mountain Branch Track 5 – R. A. Cooke
55 Swansea–Llandilo map – R. A. Cooke
57 Swansea Victoria Track c 1880 – R. A. Cooke
57 Swansea Victoria Track 1898 – R. A. Cooke
58 Swansea Victoria Track 1928 – R. A. Cooke
62 Gorseinon Track 1935 – R. A. Cooke
63 Pontarddulais Track 1915 – R. A. Cooke
64 Pontarddulais Track 1876 – R. A. Cooke
T2 Branch Line Map – R. A. Cooke
67 Pantyffynnon Track 1892 – R. A. Cooke
67 Pantyffynnon Track c1876 – R. A. Cooke
68 Pantyffynnon Track 1955 – R. A. Cooke
T2 Branch Line Map – R. A. Cooke
67 Pantyffynnon Track 1892 – R. A. Cooke
67 Pantyffynnon Track c1876 – R. A. Cooke
68 Pantyffynnon Track 1955 – R. A. Cooke
70 Llandilo Track 1961. Chief Civil Engineer's Office BR.WR Paddington
74 Llandovery Track 1961. Chief Civil Engineer's Office BR.WR Paddington
81 Builth Rd Track 1961. Chief Civil Engineer's Office BR.WR Paddington
82 Llandrindod Track 1961. Chief Civil Engineer's Office BR.WR Paddington
88 Knighton Track 1961. Chief Civil Engineer's Office BR.WR Paddington
92 Central Wales Track 1960's. Eric Williams
92 LNWR Plan of additional Land – proposed purchase 1877 Craven Arms – John Horsley Denton

Contents

Introduction

The Central Wales Line runs between Swansea and Craven Arms and on to Shrewsbury – nowadays covering the 121½-mile journey in about four hours. It is in as direct a fashion as one can reasonably expect of a route originally designed to answer the transport demands of a once-flourishing industrial area, the needs of a sparsely populated rural community and which crosses difficult and mountainous terrain.

1828 Llanelly Railway Company founded.
1835 Llanelly Railway Co. merged with Dock Co. to become Llanelly Railroad & Dock Company and subsequently, Llanelly Railway Co.
1839 (June) Llanelly Dock to Pontardulais line opened.
1841 (May) Pontardulais to Duffryn Lodge (later known as Tirydail & Ammanford) opened.
1846 (August) Shrewsbury & Hereford Railway Company formed.
1851 Shrewsbury & Hereford Railway line reached Craven Arms and Stokesay.
1853 Llanelly Railway Company permitted to run line into South Wales Railway Llanelly Town passenger station.
1854 (July) Formation of Vale of Towy Railway (Llandilo to Llandovery).
1857 (January) Llanelly Railway Co. – Duffryn to Llandilo opened (freight).
1857 (July) Llanelly Railway Co. – Duffryn to Llandilo opened (passenger).
1858 (April) Llanelly Railway Co. (Vale of Towy leased to Llanelly).
Llandilo to Llandovery opened.
1858 (May) Formation of Knighton Railway – Craven Arms to Knighton.
1859 (August) Formation of Central Wales Railway to construct Knighton to Llandrindod.
1860 (July) Formation of Central Wales Extension Railway – Llandrindod to Llandovery – project formed.
1860 (October) Knighton Railway. Craven Arms to Bucknell opened.
1861 Knighton Railway. Bucknell to Knighton opened.
1861 Central Wales Railway. Knighton to Knucklas (freight) opened.
1862 LNWR/GWR joint lease of Shrewsbury–Craven Arms (Hereford) route.
1862 Central Wales Railway passenger traffic to Knucklas opened.
1864 Central Wales Railway. Knucklas to temporary terminus at Crossgates (Penybont) (goods only) opened.
1865 (October) Central Wales Railway extended to Llandrindod.
1866 (January) Llanelly Railway Co. Pontardulais to Swansea Dock (freight traffic only) opened.
1866 (November) Central Wales Extension Railway section between Llandrindod and Builth Road (High Level) opened.
1867 (March) Central Wales Extension Railway Builth Road to Garth opened.
1867 (May) Central Wales Extension Railway Garth to Llanwrtyd opened.

Construction was nothing like as direct, however; it was in fact a very piecemeal affair so that, although the following are, for purposes of reference, in chronological order, they do not represent the whole picture of the line's development.

(The spelling in this list is that which was originally applicable. Subsequently, the spelling in present usage is used for stations and places.)

1867 December) Llanelly RDC. Pontardulais to Swansea Victoria (for passengers) opened.
1868 (June) Central Wales Extension Railway Llandrindod to Llandovery opened.
1868 Knighton Railway, Central Wales Railway and Central Wales Extension Railway absorbed by London & North Western Railway.
1868 Llanelly Railway's lease on Vale of Towy Railway shared by LNWR.
1870 LNWR/GWR joint ownership Shrewsbury–Craven Arms (Hereford).
1871 Llanelly Railway line Pontardulais to Swansea transferred to separate company owned by LNWR.
1873 (January) Remainder Llanelly RDC's responsibilities leased to GWR.
1889 The Llanelly Railway & Dock Company absorbed by GWR.
1923 LNWR absorbed into London Midland & Scottish Railway.
1948 (January) Nationalisation. Whole route under control of British Railways Western Region (but was for a short period, under London Midland Region operating area).
1962 (June) BR closure threat.
1964 (June) Pontardulais to Swansea Victoria route closed (BR) Diesel multiple units operated Llanelli to Shrewsbury.
Through freight re-routed.
1967 (November) Second BR closure threat.
1970 Through trains between Shrewsbury (via Llanelli) to Swansea High Street Station commenced.
1972 Pantyffynnon to Craven Arms classified as Light Railway.
1980 Heavy main line locomotives banned on line – excursion traffic ended.
1981 (November) Heart of Wales Line Travellers' Association formed.
1985 Announcement of £644,000 investment scheme.
1987 (October) Collapse of Glanrhyd Bridge. Section between Llandeilo and Llandovery closed.
1988 (October) Resumption of through service after new bridge completed.
1989 (February) Return of first of excursion trains.
1994 Commencement Privatisation process. CWL under Regional Railways South Wales and West Train Operating Company. Railtrack plc responsible for stations, infrastucture etc.
1996 Rolling stock bought by ROSCO.
Prism Rail plc won franchise to operate line. 24-hour recorded telephone information service on line available.
Through freight trains on CWL in the spring due to repairs on South Wales main line (first since 1965).
1997 £300,000 to be spent by Railtrack on repair of stations.

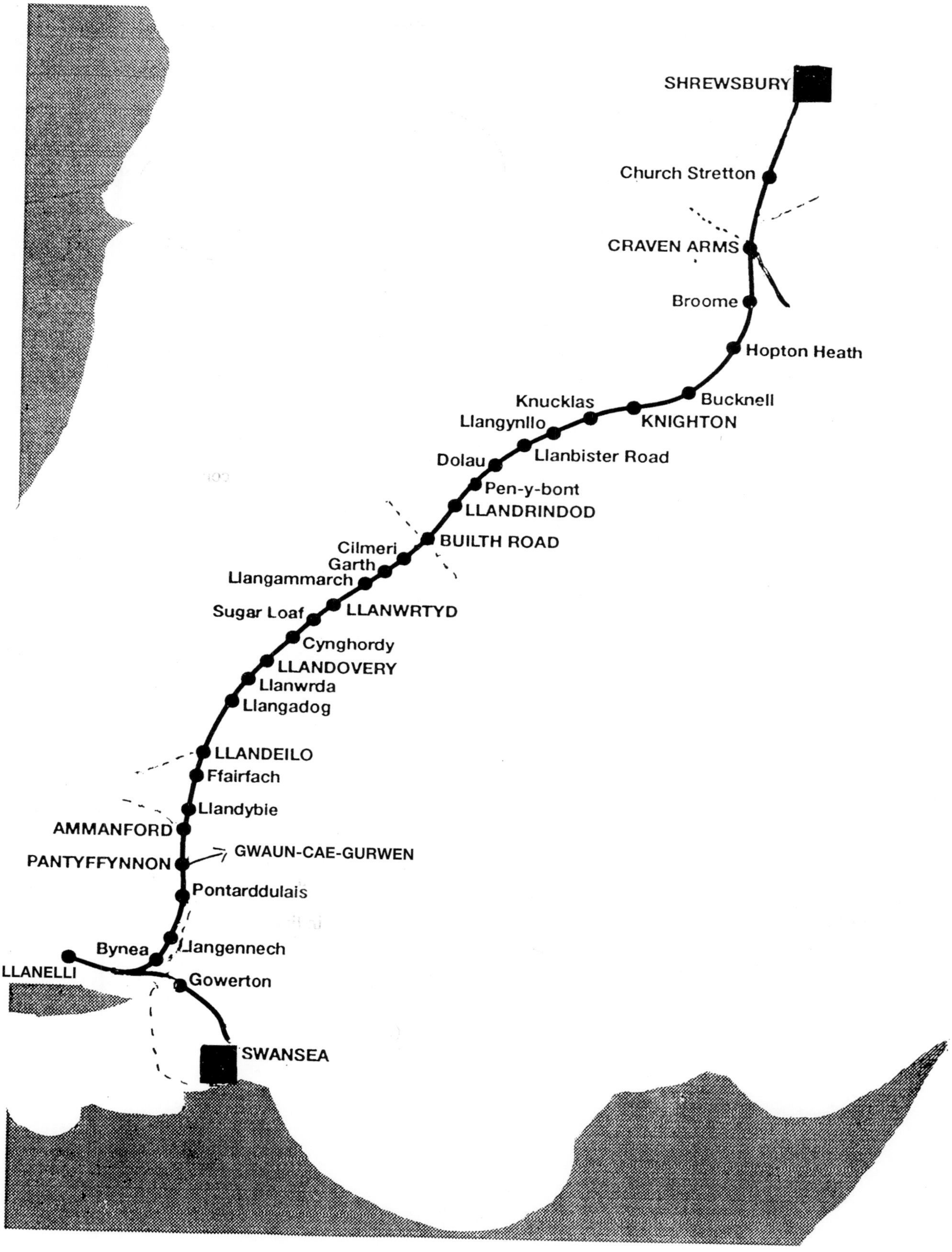

The Central Wales Line

1

The Route – Swansea High Street to Shrewsbury

Leaving Swansea (High Street), Maliphant carriage sidings and Landore depot can be seen below on the right side. The train then ascends at 1 in 52 to enter Cockett Tunnel (789 yards) and descends to Gowerton (1 in 50) after which comes a fine view over the Loughor estuary, crossing the 18-span Loughor Viaduct, constructed of steel and supported by timber piles.

The route continues to Llanelli from where. after reversal, it leaves the main line at Llandeilo Junction, passing Genwen Junction, where there is a loop connecting British Steel Trostre Tinplate Works, and then crosses marshlands to Bynea, 1m 7 ch (from Llandeilo Junction) and Llangennech, 3m $0^{1/2}$ch.

There is a continuing vista of the Loughor estuary before leaving the Swansea District Line (Llandeilo Junction to Court Sart Junction) at Morlais Junction, then via the 88-yard Pontarddulais Tunnel, which now has a continuous slab concrete base (relaid in 1983), over the Loughor once more and into Pontarddulais, 5m 25ch. There was a junction (right) with the original LNWR route from Swansea Victoria and from Pontarddulais to Llandeilo, the 'Premier Line' ran over GWR track.

The Loughor is joined by the River Amman just before Pantyffynnon station, 10m 7ch where the signal box controls the 79-mile long single-track between Pantyffynnon and Craven Arms. The junction which precedes the station serves the Gwaun-cae-Gurwen anthracite washery. The line (right) now extends only $6^{3/4}$ miles on its original course to Brynamman and Abernant.

Once past Ammanford, 11m 21ch, – which was once known as 'Tirydail' and before that 'Duffryn', (the trackbed of the Llanelly Company's mineral branch to Cross Hands was just beyond the station), the industrial area is replaced

A view from a passing train of British Steel's Trostre Tinplate Works illustrates part of the present-day industrial section of the line.
(Courtesy John Horsley Denton)

The view from the train across Loughor Estuary.
(Courtesy John Horsley Denton)

The exterior of Pontardulais station, c1964.

(Bernard Matthews collection)

by the agricultural scene and so begins the gradual approach to the mountains of Mid Wales.

On to Llandybie, 14m 5ch, and over Cilyrychen Crossing which was opened by the Llanelly Co. on 1 January 1858 situated north of Pentregwynlais and Pistill limestone branches with a view of the old Cilyrychen lime kilns on the left. A new siding was built for the Cincoed Lime Co. in 1924. The crossing had a loop but, like many others on this section, passenger trains could not pass here. The line was singled in 1965 and the signal box, opened in 1913, became a ground-frame on 13 January 1966. The crossing is situated on the busy A483 road which runs from North to South Wales.

The line now ascends to 250ft above sea level passing the site of the former Derwydd Road station, 14m 46ch, through meadowland and descending at 1 in 105 to Ffairfach, 17m 18ch. The old trackbed of the Carmarthen line is on the left and after crossing the River Tywi, the line runs into Llandeilo, 18m 2¾ch, where there is a passing loop, the town crowning the heights on the 'up' side.

There follows straight track through Talley Road and Glanrhyd stations, both closed in 1955, and an ascent of 1 in 100 to traverse Glanrhyd Bridge, 8 metres high and 65 metres long, built in 1988 700mm higher than its predecessor which collapsed into the flooded River Twyi the year before with tragic consequences (See Chapter 6, Stations).

Making an equal descent of 1 in 100 and passing an old milk siding on the 'up' side, the next station is Llangadog, 23m 59¼ch, then over the River Tywi Viaduct and on to Llanwrda, 25m 47ch. The straight section which follows crosses Llwynjack Bridge (a four-span plate girder construction) to arrive at Llandovery, 29m 20ch. Here, there is a passing loop and a crossing north of the station which is operated by train staff.

After the driver has obtained the token for the next section to Llanwrtyd Wells the train curves through woodlands and climbs to Cynghordy, 54m 55¼ch, and the spectacular Cynghordy Viaduct (18 spans of 36ft 6in) over the River Bran. The line is now 93ft above ground level.

Between Cynghordy and Llandovery there is a change of mileage posts (0 – 59 miles 13.7 chains from Craven Arms and 0 – 29 miles 40 chains from Llandeilo Junction) reflecting the old LNWR and GWR days. The 1 in 60 ascent to the summit (climbing 550ft in 7 miles from Llandovery) now commences with awe-inspiring views across the Brecon Beacons and Black Mountain (singular, and not to be confused with the Black Mountains to the east of the

The impressive lime kilns at Cilyrychen – once served by the CWL – tower over the machinery of the present occupants of the site (McAlpines) who keep a diesel storage tank on top of them. The kilns were designed by R. K. Penson (1816-86), brother of the architect of Shrewsbury station.

(Rose Coleman)

An enthusiasts' visit to Llandeilo station in the mid 1960s.
(Nigel Wassell collection)

The view from the cab of the new Glanrhyd Bridge in late 1988.
(Roy Palmer)

Cynghordy Viaduct.
(HMRS/G. M. Perkins collection)

Approaching Llandovery, 19 May 1986. The 2-car unit that was due to be crossed here can be seen approaching the station.
(Courtesy John Horsley Denton)

The view across Llwynjack Bridge over the River Towy, south of Llandovery in 1932.
(Dorothy Bound)

Looking south towards Cynghordy in the early 1930s. The gradient here is 1 in 60.
(Dorothy Bound)

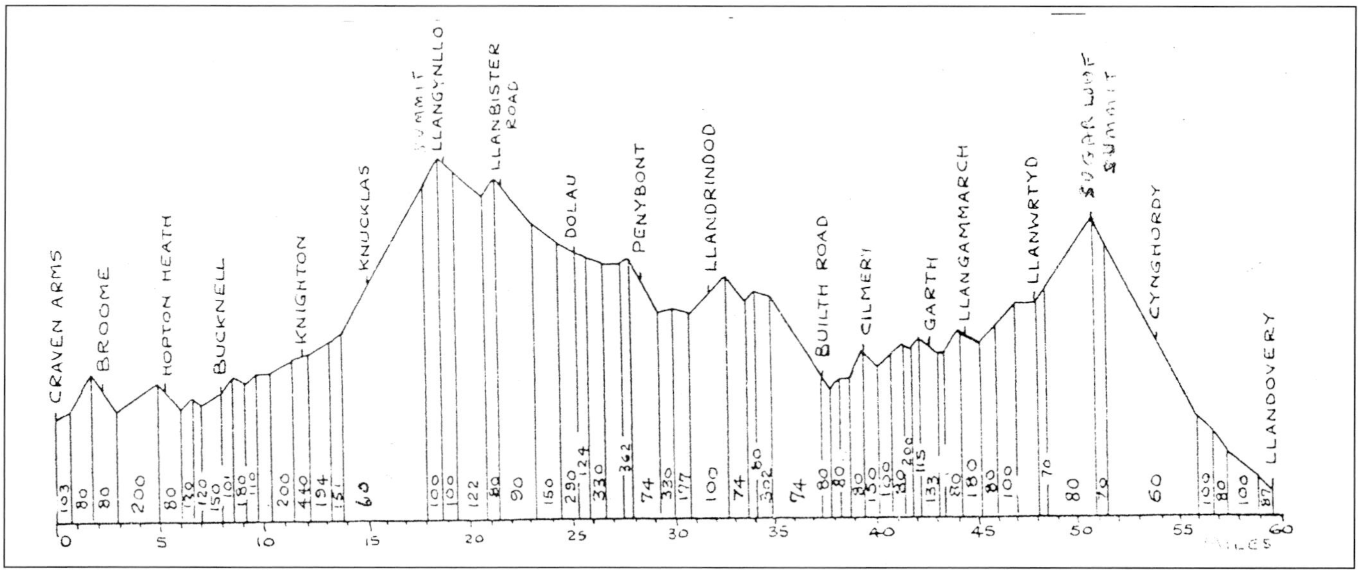

Gradient profile, Craven Arms–Llandovery.

Beacons) to the rear: the conical Sugar Loaf rises ahead and the track seems to be glued somewhat perilously to the hillside above the Bran Valley.

Passengers suffering from vertigo remain on the left hand side of the carriage while others twist themselves into extraordinary contortions in an attempt to take photographs. Increased tree growth has rather lessened the impact for either, although a certain amount of felling has taken place in the last few years. (The species of trees in this area was particularly prone to the effects of acid rain and when re-planting took place, a different variety was used.)

This part of the route was not only difficult to construct but was also to present problems for the engines which had to run over it after the long ascent, as the track had a tendency to be greasy which sometimes made for difficult grip. Not for nothing did a publication by the Swansea Railway Circle describe the Sugar Loaf as 'a truly fearsome obstacle; seven miles of continuous climbing without any sort of respite'. There was a serious derailment in 1939 when a Super D 0-8-0 heading a freight train of 26 wagons ran out of control from Sugar Loaf on the 1 in 60 gradient towards Cynghordy, at which point the signalman turned it into the sand drag. The driver died from his injuries a few days later but the fireman, who had jumped from the footplate as the runaway tore through Cynghordy, survived. Most of the wagons ended up in a field and, because of the length of the sand drag, there was no blockage of the line.

The route now continues through the Sugar Loaf Tunnel which is 110ft below ground at the midway ventilation shaft. For nearly all of its 1,000 yards the tunnel is situated under a geological fault and is always extremely damp as a consequence of the seepage from the streams which run above it. Some rebuilding took place in 1947 when part of the tunnel collapsed and in November 1949, loose keystones in the roof required attention, necessitating it being closed for nearly two months, reopening again on 10 January 1950.

Five years later it was closed again, from 2 May 1955 until 22 July 1955 and then again for drainage work in May of the following year. By 1991 the geological fault had shifted slightly resulting in a bulge in the roof and regular inspections had shown that mortar was also being leached out from each side of the previous repair.

Strengthening of the bulge was effected by spraying on concrete to reinforce the wall and the roof and was carried out by BR's labour force. The problem of leaching mortar was tackled by Tunneline of Cheshire who lined the roof

The impressive view of the south west approach to Sugar Loaf.
(HMRS/G. M. Perkins collection)

Repairs to Sugar Loaf Tunnel, 9 December 1949.
(Welsh Industrial & Maritime Museum)

with concrete by a patent process used on a railway tunnel for the first time in the UK and which was speedier and less costly than normal methods. The tunnel was only closed for a month and the total costs amounted to £150,000.

In December 1992, a landslip – brought about by atrocious wet weather across the southern half of the country – blocked the line for a short time. After heavy storms in June 1993, there was another landslip near the northern entrance to the tunnel with the result that water poured through and caused erosion of ballast and earthworks beyond the southern end. This was put right within three weeks. Regular checks are carried out on this dank gloomy hole to ensure that it is in good repair.

Beyond the summit, which is 820ft above sea level, is Sugar Loaf Halt, 50m 68½ch, at which point in steam days, the guard carried out a check on freight trains and handbrakes were pinned down to control speed on the descending gradients. The maximum load of coal unbanked on the 'up' line up the Sugar Loaf gradient was 16 12-ton wagons. Originally opened for railway staff who were housed in cottages long since demolished, the halt is now in use, via the steps on the 'up' side, for those travelling on summer Sunday services including ramblers bent on exploring this beautiful area.

The descent to Llanwrtyd Wells, 48m 4½ch, and the River Irfon via Berthddu Crossing is 1 in 70. Llanwrtyd, with the Abernant Hotel visible and close to the station on the 'down' side, has a passing loop. After the next station, Llangammarch, 44m 40ch, comes the 55-yard brick arch tunnel of the same name, followed by a cutting, an embankment and several bridges before reaching Garth, 42m 69ch, which once had a passing loop but is now reduced to a single platform on the 'up' side.

The line proceeds to Cilmeri, 39m 38ch, from which can be seen (left) a monument marking the place where Prince Llewelyn the Last was slain by the English in 1282. With the Irfon Valley on the right the route continues through Cilmeri and Rhosferig tunnels (115yd and 64yd).

There follows another two bridges before Builth Road, 37m 40ch, is reached. The first bridge (39ft high) is of wrought iron and traverses the River Wye and the second (32ft steel girder), crosses the old Cambrian Railways Mid Wales line which closed in 1962.

The route now exchanges the Wye Valley for that of the Ithon, passing Howey where there was a loop at which point 'up' banking engines returned to Builth Road, but no station – although there has recently been some lobbying from the increasing local community for a halt and not for the first time. The Disserth Parish Book 1825–1865 records a resolution on Easter Monday 1865 to 'memorialize the Central Wales Railway Directors to place a Station House at or near Howey Village for the general benefit and trade of

Llanwrtyd Wells looking north in the BR period.
(Bernard Matthews collection)

the inhabitants of this neighbourhood'. This request was not so unreasonable as it might appear today because at that time, the village was more important than Llandrindod which was just about to flourish as a spa; the postal address of the latter being 'Llandrindod Wells, near Howey'.

The pass in the hills through which the River Wye runs from its source in distant Plynlimon is visible on the left, as at 1 in 74 the line reaches Llandrindod Wells, 31m 72ch, the next block post and a place of large Victorian buildings very much in contrast with its surrounding rural scenery.

The route then proceeds under a bypass, constructed in 1994 north of Llandrindod level crossing to avoid congestion of road traffic on the latter when gaining access to the industrial estate on the 'up' side. The next halt, after glimpses of the hilltops of Radnor Forest on the right, is Penybont, 26m 21ch, followed immediately by Penybont Tunnel (404yd) the line slewing to the 'down' side (See Chapter 6 Stations) and continuing through a wild area of common through Dolau Halt, 25m 27ch (the deserving recipient of many awards).

The line briefly joins the River Aran through gently undulating landscape and then climbs to Llanbister Road, 21m 25ch – an isolated halt at 848ft above sea level. Passing Maylords and Troedyrhiwfedwen crossings, it runs above the valley of the River Lugg – an especially impressive section on a route which seldom lacks outstanding scenery and where on wet days, the lanes which streak out into the hills on the right look like so many glistening rivers.

A descent to Llangynllo station, 18m 58ch, at 1 in 80 is followed by a climb to the summit of the line (980ft above sea level) and into Llangynllo Tunnel (647yd, constructed of brick and masonry and 82ft deep at its central ventilation shaft). A descent 1 in 60 follows, passing a strange conical hill and Heyope Church on the right, to cross the spectacular Knucklas Viaduct (69ft above ground with 13 x 35ft 9in arches) curving left into the station of that name at 14m 68ch.

Following the River Teme with Offa's Dyke running high on the left hand side and crossing Panpunton Bridge, the line reaches Knighton, 12m 23ch, where the last token for the 'up' journey is collected. Leaving the station (which is in England although the town itself is in Wales) the route crosses the border following the River Teme (right) to Bucknell, 8m 0ch, with Clun Forest in the distance and following a straight section to Hopton Heath, 5m 9ch.

After passing through flat meadowland and crossing the River Clun, the next station is Broome, 2m 46ch, after which the track curves north east to Craven Arms, 0m 0ch. This was once known as 'Craven Arms and Stokesay' and the 13th century castle of the latter name can be seen on the right before arriving, and the Craven Arms Hotel is visible (also right) as the train approaches the station.

Builth Road refreshment rooms were situated on the Low Level station and served passengers from both lines. The premises are now the Cambrian Arms and are visible from the 'down' side of the Central Wales Line. The Mid Wales Line to Moat Lane Junction ran under the bridge which is still used by the CWL, as seen here in 1994.
(Rose Coleman)

Llangunllo Tunnel, viewed from the north.
(HMRS/G. M. Perkins collection)

This is the end of the long 79-mile single track section from Pantyffynnon and the final token is relinquished at the signal box here. The train now joins the Cardiff–Manchester route (right) – once the Shrewsbury & Hereford Railway – passing on the left, beyond the signal box and overbridge at the site of Stretford Bridge Junction, the one-time junction with the old Bishops Castle Railway which closed on 20 May 1935. The A49 road is now visible for a while on the right with hilly terrain ahead, then we pass the site of Winstow Halt, through charming little Marsh Brook station (closed in the 1950s), on over the crossing controlled by semaphore signals and proceeding to Church Stretton situated in the shadow of the Long Mynd (nearly 1,700ft at its peak). The hotel of the same name is lodged in the hillside on the left at its approach and Caer Caradoc is visible high on the right as the train leaves.

Some miles ahead, as the line descends from Church Stretton through the sites of Leebotwood, Dorrington (another signal box) and Condover stations (closed 1958), the Wrekin, the last hill of any height, is visible across the flat terrain ahead on the distant right. At the approach to Shrewsbury, the train enters the junction operated by the fine old LNWR Sutton Bridge Junction box (right) and the route is joined on the left by the line from Aberystwyth.

Thus, via Coleham Viaduct and passing the impressive Severn Bridge Junction box (BR's largest manually operated box) on the right, the line arrives in Shrewsbury where the station seems to be almost jammed under the castle walls of this charming historic town, and the northern terminus of the Central Wales Line is reached. The distance from Swansea High Street to Shrewsbury is 121½ miles.

Knighton station in 1994.
(Rose Coleman)

Knucklas Viaduct, viewed from a southbound train.
(Courtesy John Lloyd)

Sutton Bridge Junction, Shrewsbury, looking south. The line on the right is to Welshpool and the main line to Hereford is in the centre with Coleham shelf sidings on the left. Sutton Bridge starter signal is on top of the Coleham distant.
(HMRS/G. M. Perkins collection)

Church Stretton looking north, January 1995.
(Rose Coleman)

Broome station looking south, January 1995.
(Rose Coleman)

Swansea Victoria to Pontarddulais (LNWR) 1867–1964

(Mileages LNWR from Craven Arms)

After leaving Swansea Victoria, 95m 48ch, the original LNWR line ascended 1 in 45, passing South Dock and Paxton Street shed on the left to Swansea Bay station, 94m 56ch, whence it followed the shoreline running parallel with Oystermouth Road and the Swansea & Mumbles Railway until it crossed these via Blackpill Bridge, to run slightly inland to Mumbles Road station, 92m 65ch.

The track between Swansea Bay and Mumbles Road stations was almost continuously covered with sand, running as it did alongside the dunes. Even a specially erected fence failed to solve the problem which played havoc with the locomotives, resulting in hot bearings and, when conditions were severe, entailing the sending out of special trains to clear the line.

Killay, 90m 2½ch, was reached via Clyne Woods, crossing the River Clyne and ascending at 1 in 70 to reach Dunvant, 89m 76ch, descending to Gowerton South, 88m 26ch.

Passing the junction with the Llanmorlais branch, it then crossed the GWR line (London Paddington to West Wales) and, following over a mile of level track, reached Gorseinon, 86m 67ch, thence ascending through the well-worked Grovesend Colliery area to Grovesend station, 85m 27ch, and turning north west to Pontarddulais, 83m 28ch. The distance from Swansea Victoria to Shrewsbury was 115½ miles.

Mumbles Road station in pre-Grouping days.
(Bernard Matthews collection)

The view north eastwards from Slip Bridge to Trafalgar Arch, including the park on the left and the baths, centre distant.
(City of Swansea Archives)

Swansea Bay – the ever-present threat of sand covered track. The track on the left is the Mumbles Railway track which closed on 5 June 1960.
(Welsh Industrial & Maritime Museum)

Gowerton Crossing in Edwardian times when the crossing gates were kept closed against the road as there were more trains than road traffic.
(Nigel Wassell collection)

Scars of the past remain as is shown by this view of the derelict tinplate works near Pontarddulais, August 1962.
(Courtesy John Horsley Denton)

2

Origins and Development

The name of Llanelli (note modern Welsh spelling) is the first to appear on the list and it was with the Llanelly Railway Company that the line began.

Incorporated by Act of Parliament 19 June 1828, its capital was £14,000 with £6,000 available on loan. By 1833, the company's aim to build a tramroad to take horse-drawn traffic between the docks and Gelly Gille Coal Mine – a distance of some two miles – was achieved and in 1835 it merged with the Dock Company to become the Llanelly Railway & Dock Company.

The abundance of anthracite in the Amman Valley soon provided considerable incentive for development and by 1839, new track had been laid as far as Pontarddulais and the company acquired its first two steam locomotives.

With firms like the Cwm Amman Company planning to smelt iron alongside the line and with the prospect of being able to take the finished product by rail direct to the docks, there were substantial profits anticipated, reinforcing the Llanelly Company's aim to push forward to Llandeilo and the 2,000 £100 shares mentioned in the company's January 1839 report were soon allocated. With some 750 tons of anthracite being produced daily, they were thought to be a sound investment.

ANNO NONO

GEORGII IV. REGIS.

****

Cap. xci.

An Act for making and maintaining a Railway or Tramroad from *Gelly Gille Farm,* in the Parish of *Llanelly* in the County of *Carmarthen,* to *Machynis Pool* in the same Parish and County; and for making and maintaining a Wet Dock at the Termination of the said Railway or Tramroad at *Machynis Pool* aforesaid. [19th *June* 1828.]

WHEREAS the making and maintaining a Railway or Tramroad for the Passage of Waggons and other Carriages from or from near a certain Place called *Gelly Gille* or *Gelly Gele Farm,* in the Parish of *Llanelly* in the County of *Carmarthen,* to or to near a certain Place called *Machynis Pool* in the said Parish and County, and the making and maintaining a Wet Dock or Bason for Ships and other Vessels of Three hundred Tons Register Measure, with the necessary Works, at the Termination of the said Railway or Tramroad at or near the said Place called *Machynis Pool,* to communicate with the Sea, will be of great Advantage to the Town and Port of *Llanelly,* and to the Proprietors of divers Estates, Lands, and Hereditaments in the Neighbourhood thereof, by providing an additional and easy Communication for the Conveyance of Mineral and other Produce, and of Goods, Wares, and Merchandizes, to the Sea, and for

[*Local.*] 21 *Z* the

Llanelly Railway & Dock Co. (Railway or Tramroad from Gelly Gille Farm) Act 19 June 1828.

The *Cambrian Newspaper* dated 15 June 1839 commented:

'LLANELLY RAILWAY AND DOCK COMPANY – The annual general meeting of the shareholders in this undertaking was held on Monday, the 3rd inst., at the London Tavern, Robert Biddulph, Esq. in the chair. John Bigg Esq. (the secretary) read the report of the committee of management, which gave a very favourable account of the company's affairs. A considerable portion of the new line will be opened in September next, in addition to six and a half miles opened on the 1st inst. From the dock and the old line (two miles in length) the returns had been such during the past year as to authorise the payment of a dividend at the rate of 3 per cent. A very gratifying fact was stated with respect to the construction of the new line which it appears will be executed in the best possible manner for £150,000 less than the Parliamentary estimate.'

It goes on to state that although demand was great, the 480 shares of the capital stock still available, would be issued to existing holders. Also that, 'It was stated by one of the directors that every inch of ground on the line was mineral, the whole of which must pass along the railway to the sea.'

By May 1841, the line had reached Duffryn Lodge (later known as Tirydail & Ammanford). Tantalisingly near its goal with only a few miles to go, the work was stopped, due, it appears, to a lack of efficient management and the locomotives being overworked and undermaintained so that it was not until January 1857, after a period of financial difficulties, that the final section to Llandeilo was completed.

(During the 1840-42 period, the Llanelly Railway Co. was busy in other directions; opening the Cwmamman branch with extensions to Gwaun-cae-Gurwen, another to Brynamman and the Tirydail to Cross Hands 'Mountain' branch worked mainly by rope haulage – one gradient was 1 in 12.)

In the interim, efforts to sell off the company having failed, Messrs Ianson, Fossick & Hackworth were contracted to undertake the servicing and maintenance which they did for five years of the original seven year agreement which was terminated by mutual consent.

In the following year (1858) the stretch of line from Llandeilo to Llandovery was opened. This was owned by the Vale of Towy Company (incorporated in 1854, its capital £60,000 with further borrowing powers of £18,000) but once the service commenced, it was administered by the Llanelly Company to whom it was leased for a ten-year period

By this time, the Llanelly Company had obtained permission, in 1853, to run a line into the South Wales Railway's Llanelly Town passenger station. Although no direct connection could be made between the Llanelly Company's standard gauge system and that of the South Wales Railway which was broad gauge, a mechanical device was contrived to lift and transfer coal from one to the other on a second branch which was opened in 1858 to service the docks. Passengers were first carried in 1841.

During the period of frustrating delays in the south, developments were taking place at the northern end of what eventually became the present Central Wales Line.

With an eye on the possible advantages of through

transport between the Midlands and Bristol, the Shrewsbury & Hereford Railway had commenced work upon the first section which reached 'Craven Arms and Stokesay' in 1851. Its arrival was the cue for a proposal to build a connection between this station and Knighton, the Knighton Railway Company, incorporated in May 1858, considering the probability of its eventual link up with Llandovery and South West Wales to be strong enough to warrant such a venture. (The cost of the Knighton Railway project was estimated at £66,000 which was raised from shares and there was also borrowing power of £22,000.)

The Knighton Railway was not the only one to hold this view and for a while there was strong competition from a rival scheme put forward by the Mid Wales Company whose proposed line, via Llanidloes and Builth, would have run very close to that envisaged by the Knighton Railway. It was considerable relief to the latter when the opposition's Bill was not accepted by Parliament and a great deal of celebration followed the announcement.

The cutting of the first sod was attended by elaborate ceremony and the *Shropshire Chronicle* dated 20 August 1858 devoted three long wide columns of purple prose to the event, a part of which stated:

> 'Arrived at the ground, which was admirably adapted for the purpose not less from its amphitheatrical shape, by which a large number of persons easily obtained a view of the ceremony than from its picturesque situation, Lady (Jane) Walsh was escorted to a platform by H. Robertson Esq., and in a few graceful sentences he there presented her ladyship with the spade and wheelbarrow. The latter is made of mahogany, is elaborately carved. and altogether a very fine specimen of workmanship.'

More descriptions follow but we are told that the culminating point was when 'Lady Walsh had thrown out the earth with which she had freighted the wheelbarrow. Mr Hay's band then struck up 'See the Conquering Hero' and the cheering was most enthusiastic.' Readers were treated to details of the luncheon for 500, the speeches, toasts and presentations and a list of banners and mottos with which the tent was adorned, one such being, 'Onward speed we, onward still, what can conquer Brassey's skill, what resist his iron will, pierce the mountain, scale the hill'.

Some space was devoted to the line itself in which the *Cambrian* states that:

> 'The history of the Knighton railway is soon told. In 1854 a number of influential gentlemen projected the Central Wales Railway from Shrewsbury and Hereford Railway, near the Craven Arms Station, via Knighton, Penybont, Llandrindod and Llanwrtyd Wells (passing near to the towns of Builth and Rhayader) to Llandovery, being a distance of fifty-three miles, and thence down the Vale of Towy so as to connect Milford Haven with Manchester and the North of England on the westward by a junction with the South Wales Railway, near Carmarthen (fourteen miles) and likewise to connect Swansea and its Copper Smelting Works with Liverpool and the manufacturing districts, by a junction with the Llanelly Extension Railway at Llandilo; thus offering one direct and unbroken line of traffic from the German Ocean to the Atlantic. across the centre of England and Wales.'

(However, in spite of 'warm support of the landed proprietors through whose estates it was intended to pass' due to financial pressures on those concerned, the project was held in abeyance for nearly four years and the Act was finally obtained on 21 May 1858.)

Mr H. Robertson, 'the able engineer of the line', said that there was no reason why it should not be opened in 18 months and Brassey & Field, 'the eminent contractors', were the 'best possible guarantee' that the line would be completed speedily and well.

The cost, 'including land and everything else', would not exceed £6,500 a mile and permanent way would not cost more than £5,000 a mile. However, progress proved from the start to be slow and, although the company was incorporated in May 1858, it was not until October 1860 that substantial headway was made when the line was opened to run as far as Bucknell – a distance of 9 miles. Six months later, in 1861, it reached Knighton. The following year the line became the responsibility of the London & North Western Railway.

By this time, in the haste to open up through traffic between the Midlands and the South Wales ports, two other companies had been formed. The first was the Central Wales Railway, incorporated in 1859 for the purposes of extending the line from Knighton to what was later to become known to the locals as 'Llanerch Halt' at Llandrindod Wells. The company had a capital of £160,000 with loan facilities of £53,000. Many holders paid 'in kind' in the form of land for their shares and there were several local investors who had interest in both the Knighton and Central Wales companies.

By 1861, the line was opened for mineral traffic as far as Knucklas, but it was not until October 1865, having had to negotiate a loan of £30,000 from the LNWR (which, with its interest in securing a route to link up with the Llanelly Company's standard gauge track to the South Wales ports, was never very far away) that the project was completed and the first official passenger train arrived in Llandrindod to all the customary pomp attendant on such occasions.

Not only were there the usual speeches and brass bands but a special double-headed train of 18 carriages went down the line from Shrewsbury, halting at Craven Arms where it was decorated with flags and bunting and continuing to Knighton where a large party joined it to proceed to Llandrindod. The band of the Radnorshire Rifle Volunteers travelled on the train, played during the journey and upon arrival headed a procession from Llandrindod station to the site of 'the luncheon' at which guests toasted not only the Central Wales Company but the 'Premier Line' as well. (This appears to have been a slightly less ambitious affair than that at Knighton's 'Cutting of the First Sod Ceremony'.)

According to the *Hereford Journal* on 21 October 1865:

> 'A splendid banquet was served up in a marquee upon the piece of elevated ground at the rear of the Rock House, by Mr Roberts, proprietor. Tables were laid out for 200 but only 150 attended, including Sir Charles Rouse Broughton, Bart., the Chairman of the Company, who presided. Mr R. Green-Price, MP of Norton Manor. Lt. Col. J. B. Ward, RA, Welwyn, Herts, Sir John Walsh, Bart, MP, Mr Brown Westhead, Vice Chairman of the LNWR, Mr Henry Robertson, the Engineer of the line, Mr Fowler, Vice Chairman of Llanelly Railway Mr Clarke, Engineer of Shrewsbury & Hereford Railway, Messrs Hattersley & Morton, contractors and Mr Morton, junior, Mr Joshua Dean, the Secretary etc.'

Praise was given to all concerned, the Chairman saying that they had not known the difficulties at the outset and that at one time thought work would have to be temporarily abandoned. Mr R. Dansey Green-Price toasted the contractors, 'whose perseverence in the face of the many difficulties that beset them in the construction of the line', he highly eulogised. But successful as they had been, their work was not completed. 'Let them push on to Llandovery.'

(During this period, in May 1863, Parliament gave authority for the amalgamation of the Knighton and Central Wales railways.)

The next company to be involved was the Central Wales Extension Railway (founded in 1860 with a capital of £208,000 and borrowing power of £69,333) which was formed to construct the 26¼-mile single track between Llandrindod and Llandovery, there to link up with the Vale of Towy Railway from the south.

The work was carried out in several independent sections and the first of these – at Sugar Loaf Mountain and at Llandovery – commenced as early as November 1860 preceded by some extraordinarily elaborate celebrations in the latter town on the 15th of that month.

The procession was headed by the Band of the Llandilo Rifle Volunteers followed by a great many flags and banners, the first of which displayed the slogan 'Success to the Central Wales Railway'. Representatives of Friendly Societies, shareholders, navvies and workmen followed the Llandovery Town Band and the Mayor and Corporation marched in front of Mr Batty's Menagerie and Circus Band. At the rear walked officials of the company and finally, in an open carriage, escorted by other similar vehicles and mounted escorts, came Mrs Crawshaw Bailey (the wife of the Chairman of the Vale of Towy Railway) who was to cut the first sod.

The lady carried out her duties in 'capital style' during the playing of 'God save the Queen' using a suitably inscribed shovel and tipping the earth from a mahogany wheelbarrow. The luncheon was held in the Town Hall.

Optimistically scheduled, at one stage, for completion in 1862, the work on the Central Wales Extension Railway was finally completed in June 1868.

The official public opening took place on 8 October 1868 with yet more ceremonies – military parades, music and a grand dinner attended by LNWR officials among whom was its Chairman, Richard Moon. The ceremony at Llandovery represented the completion of the through route between Shrewsbury, Craven Arms and Llanelli/Swansea.

The development of the line had been monitored by *The Illustrated London News* which, in 1865, commented enthusiastically.

> 'The opening of the Central Wales Railway from Knighton to Llandrindod in October with the approaching completion of the extension line from Llandrindod to Llandovery, bringing the Midlands counties of England into more direct communication with the mineral districts of South Wales and making pleasant watering places and picturesque scenery of South Wales more accessible than they have hitherto been, is an event of general importance to the whole country'

During this time, the Llanelly Railway & Dock Company had extended its interests in the south west.

The failure of the Dunvant Valley Railway to obtain a Bill to build a line from Swansea South Dock to Pontarddulais via Killay, Dunvant and Gorseinon, was followed in 1860/1 by two proposals for lines over a similar route. One was that of the Central Wales Extension Railway (sponsored, it is thought, by the LNWR) with a branch to the Mumbles from Blackpill and the other by the Llanelly Railway with a branch to Salthouse Pill and Penclawdd from Gower Road.

The latter was successful (Llanelly Railway (New Lines) Act 1 August 1861) and, as well as being authorised to construct a line between Swansea and Pontarddulais – which, because of the previous application was often referred to as the Dunvant Valley Line – the company also received permission within the Act to build the Llandeilo to Carmarthen branch.

The line to Carmarthen opened in 1865 and joined the Central Wales Line just south of Llandeilo, the other, from Gowerton to Penclawdd opened in 1867 and extended to Llanmorlais in 1877.

In January 1866, a line for mineral traffic from Pontarddulais to Swansea Docks finally opened and, on 14 December 1867, a passenger route into Swansea Victoria, the Llanelly Company having received a loan from the LNWR in exchange for granting the latter running rights over LRDC metals. (See Chapter 2, 'Construction, delays and difficulties'.)

By 1871, the Llanelly Company was serving about 40 collieries, nearly as many tin plate works, as well as lime and brick works. (Almost a century later, in June 1964, Swansea Victoria station fell victim to the Beeching axe.)

The original five companies involved in the construction of the Central Wales Line were absorbed at its completion in 1868. The London & North Western Railway, having provided considerable financial support and expertise, controlled Craven Arms–Llandovery, thus taking over the

DIGEST OF CASES (1)

Relating to Railway and Canal Traffic, and also to the Rating of Railways, decided by the Courts of Common Law and Equity.

AGREEMENT.]—1. Entered into by the provisional committee of a contemplated railway company to lease the line. *Held*, not binding upon the company, afterwards incorporated by act of parliament. *Monklands Ry. Cos.* v. *Glasgow, Airdrie and Monklands Junction Ry. Co.*, 11 Scotch Sess. Ca., 2nd Ser. 1395.

2. The Llanelly Ry. Co., being in want of money to complete an extension line, applied to the North Western Ry. Co. for a loan of 40,000*l.*, and it was agreed that the North Western Co. should lend the money, and have running powers over the lines of the Llanelly Co. An agreement under seal as to running powers was entered into and acted upon for some time, but afterwards the Llanelly Co. gave three months' notice to determine it, and after the expiration of that period, the latter company having refused to admit the right of the former to terminate the agreement, the Llanelly Co. filed their bill, praying for a declaration that the agreement was determined, and that an injunction might be issued against the North Western Co. to restrain them from running their trains over the Llanelly Co.'s line. The agreement contained no stipulations as to its duration or as to the terms on which it might be put an end to. *Held*, that an agreement of that character which contained no stipulations as to its duration, or as to the terms on which it might be put an end to, was one having a permanent and continuing operation, determinable only by mutual agreement. *Llanelly Ry. and Dock Co.* v. *London and North Western Ry. Co.*, L. R., 8 Ch. App. 942; affirmed in House of Lords, April 9th, 1875.

3. For exercise of running powers. *Id.*

4. For use of joint station. See *Station*.

5. Working. See *Working Agreement*.

ARBITRATION.]—Where, under an agreement confirmed by act of parliament, the parties were bound to settle by arbitration all differences that might arise between them as to the meaning and effect of the agreement, or as to the mode of carrying it out. *Held*, that the jurisdiction of the courts was by this agreement excluded, and that all disputes arising under it must be settled by arbitration. *Caledonian Ry. Co.* v. *Greenock and Wemyss Bay Ry. Co.*, L. R., 2 Sc. App. 347.

(1) This Digest is in continuation of the Digest in Vol. I. (pp. 15—25).

Page 8 'Digest of Cases' Agreement – £40,000 loan to Llanelly Company by LNWR. 29 November 1867.

An Agreement made this 29th day of November, 1867, between the LLANELLY RAILWAY AND DOCK COMPANY of the one part, and the LONDON AND NORTH WESTERN RAILWAY COMPANY of the other part.

It is hereby agreed between the parties hereto that

1. Subject to such Bye Laws and regulations of the Llanelly Railway Company as may be in force from time to time the London and North Western Railway Company shall have power to run over and use with their Engines Carriages Vehicles and Servants the Railways of the Llanelly Company and the Stations Sidings and Conveniences connected therewith.

2. The Receipts from the through Traffic shall be apportioned between the two Companies (after deducting Clearing House Terminals and Government duty) according to their mileage proportions with an allowance to the London and North Western Company out of the Llanelly Company's share of twenty per cent. on Passengers and twenty-five per cent. on Goods for working expenses.

3. The London and North Western Company to be at liberty to have their own Staff at the Stations on the Llanelly Company's Lines and to be allowed (out of the Terminals) a reasonable sum for the cost of cartage clerkage and other work done by them at such Stations the same in case of difference to be settled by Arbitration as hereinafter mentioned.

4. Whether the said running powers be exercised or not there shall be a complete system of through Booking and through Rates and Fares for all traffic to and from the Stations of each Company by the Lines of each other the receipts to be divided (after deducting the usual Clearing House terminals and Government duty) by mileage such Rates and Fares if not agreed upon to be settled by Arbitration.

5. In the event of the North Western Company exercising their running powers the Rates and Fares to be fixed by the London and North Western Company but if the Llanelly Company object to any such Rates and Fares then after one week's notice the same shall be referred to Arbitration as hereinafter provided.

6. The local traffic on the Llanelly Lines shall not without the consent of the Llanelly Company be carried by the London and North Western Company but the last named Company shall when required by the Llanelly Company carry Local Passengers by their Trains between any Stations at which they stop receiving Fifteen per cent. of the Local Fares for so doing.

7. The two Companies shall send by each other all Traffic not otherwise consigned to and from Stations on the Lines of each other whenever such Lines form the shortest Route.

8. Any difference under this Agreement to be settled by Arbitration as provided by the Railway Companies' Arbitration Act 1859.

As witness the Seals of the Companies.

L.S. of the L. R. & D. Co.

L.S. of the L. & N. W. R. Co.

Agreement Llanelly Railway & Dock Co. and LNWR 29 November 1867.

Knighton, Central Wales and Central Wales Extension railways and, by means of a joint line agreement with the Llanelly Company, shared ownership of the Vale of Towy Railway's section between Llandovery and Llandeilo.

After a legal claim upheld in the House of Lords in 1871 against the Llanelly Company who had had second thoughts about the lease, the LNWR exercised its rights to operate from Swansea Victoria to Carmarthen as well as Llandovery to Llandeilo. The Great Western Railway had responsibility for the Llandeilo to Llanelli section but over which the LNWR also had running powers from Pontarddulais to Llandeilo and also to Llanelli.

With the absorption of the Shrewsbury & Hereford Railway, the whole of the Central Wales Line was operated by the two large companies, GWR and LNWR, the latter, by dint of a far-seeing policy, having the 'lion's share' of some four-fifths of the route.

The powers of the Llanelly Railway & Dock Company which had seen the commencement of the Central Wales Line in 1839, were considerably reduced until, half a century later, in 1889, it was totally absorbed by GWR. The latter had actually taken over what was left of the system in 1873, including colliery branches, locomotives and stock.

After this time, the running of the line was apportioned thus:

Swansea Victoria to Pontarddulais – LNWR
Llanelli and Pontarddulais to Llandeilo – GWR (LNWR running powers)
Llandeilo to Llandovery – LNWR/GWR joint
Llandovery to Craven Arms – LNWR
Craven Arms to Shrewsbury – LNWR/GWR joint

In 1923, the control of the major part of the line was taken over by the newly formed London Midland & Scottish Railway including that part in the south, which was originally the responsibility of the LNWR. The Llandeilo/Pontarddulais/Llanelli section remained in the hands of the GWR.

Nationalisation in 1948 placed the Central Wales Line within the control of the Western Region of British Railways which, on 7 June 1962, made application to close it. The National Transport Users Consultative Committee (TUCC) arranged meetings in Llandrindod Wells on 30 and 31 October of that year with Professor Beacham as Chairman and a local working party was formed to fight the cause. This was chaired by Alderman Tudor Watkins MP. The Ministry of Transport did not agree to the closure proposal in total but in 1964, to cut costs, services from Swansea Victoria to Pontarddulais were terminated and the section between Llanelli and Shrewsbury was serviced by diesel multiple units with four trains (instead of five) in each direction daily. Just previous to this, the original Llanelly Railroad & Dock Co. line (Llanelly–Dock Dafen to Gelly Gille Farm Coal Mine, which opened in 1833) was closed.

Through freight was re-routed via Hereford but local freight continued throughout the line for a short period. Llandrindod closed to freight in May 1967 by which time only Llandovery and Llandeilo had facilities for goods.

Closure was again theatened in November 1967 and, after a public hearing chaired by Mr R. P. Roberts on 14 and 15 May 1968 at Llandrindod Wells, was again averted due to the line being considered as a social necessity and thus qualifying for an annual government grant of £370,000 for two years. However, local people had to wait until October 1969 for the official announcement.

To minimise running costs, Pantyffynnon to Craven Arms was designated a Light Railway and operated as such from 1972. Light Railway Orders were originally introduced by an Act in 1896 'to simplify and reduce cost of authorisation to operate'. In the case of the Central Wales Line this involved a section of 78¾ miles over which simpler and more economical signalling systems, station lighting and level crossing operation were permitted, only confirming the legality of drastic economies which had already been put into effect. It was anticipated that annual losses would be reduced by £146,000, to £30,000. (In 1962, it had been estimated that closure would mean a saving of £202,000.)

Meanwhile, in May 1970, after pressure via the Ministry of Transport, the number of trains running daily in each direction from Mondays to Saturdays, was increased from four to five and the service extended to Swansea High Street, the train reversing out of Llanelli, this forming the route of the Central Wales Line as it exists today. Passenger figures doubled during the year that followed.

In 1976, British Rail appointed Mike Tedstone as Central Wales Line Development Officer. This seemed to bode well for the future but at the end of 1980, further economies in connection with the condition of the track meant that use of heavy main line locomotives on passenger trains was banned, thus eliminating the large excursion trains which were an important source of revenue to Llandrindod and Llanwrtyd Wells.

To help promote the 'Central Wales' as a tourist attraction it was given a second name, 'The Heart of Wales Line', and

(209)

Heads of Agreement *made this 5th day of December 1867, between The LLANELLY RAILWAY & DOCK COMPANY of the one part, and the CENTRAL WALES and the CENTRAL WALES EXTENSION RAILWAY COMPANIES (hereinafter called the CENTRAL WALES COMPANIES) of the other part.*

Whereas the Companies, parties hereto, have agreed to Lease the VALE OF TOWY RAILWAY, **Now it is hereby Agreed,**

1. The LLANELLY COMPANY having (as they allege) laid out money upon the Vale of Towy Line, and also lost large sums of money in working the same, developing the Traffic, and paying to the Towy Company rent which was not earned upon the Line, the Central Wales Company, in consideration thereof, agree to pay the Llanelly Company the sum of £5,000, with Interest at the rate of £5 per cent. per annum, payable half-yearly until the Principal is paid off, which is to be paid after the completion of the Vale of Towy Lease and within Six months after the opening of the Central Wales Lines to the Vale of Towy. The Vale of Towy Railway to be taken as it stands.

2. The Rent to be paid for the Vale of Towy Railway shall be the Interest upon the borrowed Capital of the Company, and a sum equal to £5 per cent. upon the Share Capital of the Vale of Towy Company, the said borrowed Capital being £18,000 and the Share Capital £60,000.

3. The Vale of Towy Railway shall be managed by a Joint Committee of two Directors of the Llanelly and two persons appointed by the Company working the Central Wales Lines, *videlicet*, the London and North Western Railway Company.

4. The staff of the Vale of Towy Line as it shall stand at the time of this Agreement taking effect shall be taken to by the Joint Committee, who shall thereafter deal with it as they think proper.

5. The Joint Committee shall forward all Through and Local Traffic over the Vale of Towy Line by the trains of the Lessees without delay and without distinction, but the Committee shall have the power of appointing local trains to be run for local accommodation.

6. The Companies agree to book through and invoice Goods, Minerals, and Cattle to and from their respective Lines, as well as to and from the Vale of Towy Railway, so as to the fullest extent develop the Traffic of the Vale of Towy Railway—the proportion of the Receipts payable to the Vale of Towy Company arising on Through Traffic to be calculated by mileage in accordance with the Regulations of the Clearing House, with the usual terminal allowances; but in the case of Coal Traffic, the terminals are hereby fixed at Three pence per ton. The Local Rates on the Vale of Towy Railway to be settled by the Joint Committee, and in case of difference, by Arbitration.

7. The Companies, parties hereto, agree to forward all Through Traffic under their control to and from their respective systems wherever the Lines of the ...

8. The Fund out of which the Rent to the Vale of Towy shall be paid is agreed to be as follows:—

(The said Fund shall be carried to a Joint Banking Account, and drawn upon by the Joint Committee.)

A.—The Local Receipts arising on the Vale of Towy Railway, whether from Passengers, Parcels, Mails, Goods, Minerals, or Cattle, arising on or passing from one Local Station to another.

B.—The Mileage Receipts of Through Traffic with the terminals accruing at the Vale of Towy Stations.

C.—The Rents for Lands, Cottages, Buildings, Wharfs, or from any other source whatsoever.

9. The Joint Committee shall pay all Charges for Maintenance, Repairs, Working Expenses, Staff, Rates and Taxes, Government Duty, and other outgoings properly chargeable to the working of the Line.

10. The Balance of Profit or Loss, after payment of the guaranteed Dividend, to be divided in equal moieties by the Companies.

11. Any additional Works, Sidings, Stations, Engine-houses, Roads, &c., which may be necessary on the Vale of Towy Railway, (or at the Terminal Stations of Llandilo and Llandovery) to be provided at the joint expense of the leasing Companies, one half part being borne by the Llanelly Railway and Dock Company, and the other half by the other Companies.

12. It is agreed for all Vale of Towy Railway Traffic that the Llandilo Station of the Llanelly Company shall be considered the Terminal Station of the Vale of Towy Company, and that the Llandovery Stations of the Vale of Towy Railway and the Central Wales Railway shall be considered a Joint Station. That the Expenses of working and maintaining the Llandovery Stations shall be paid by the Joint Committee, and the Joint Committee shall also pay the Llanelly Railway a share of the Expenses of working and maintaining the Llandilo Station according to Traffic. The Central Wales Company to take the Terminals on its own merchandize, and Mineral Traffic at Llandovery Station paying into the Joint Fund a proportion of the cost of working the same according to the amount of Traffic.

13. This Agreement to take effect on the 1st of April 1868, when the existing Lease of the Vale of Towy Railway to the Llanelly Company expires, and shall be in force during the term of the intended Lease.

14. A standing Arbitrator to be appointed in the month of March of every year to act for the succeeding year, commencing 1st April then next, between the Companies in all points of difference which may arise between them in giving effect to this Agreement, and on any points of difference which may arise in the Joint Committee; and in case of difference as to the selection of an Arbitrator, then the Board of Trade to appoint one.

In Witness whereof, the said Companies have hereto affixed their respective Common Seals the day and year first above written.

Agreement Llanelly Railway & Dock Co., Central Wales Railway and Central Wales Extension Railway to lease Vale of Towy Railway 5 December 1867.

IMPORTANT TO LLANELLY!

LONDON AND NORTH WESTERN RAILWAY (ADDITIONAL POWERS &c.) BILL.

This Bill came before the Select Committee of the House of Commons on Thursday, and was opposed by the Great Western Railway Company and the Llanelly Railway Company.

Mr. Pope said that the Bill proposed to make a line 2 furlongs and 7 chains long, in the parish of Llanelly, to be called the Llanelly Station Railway. The great object of the leading lines was to get to Swansea. The London and North Western got there by Shrewsbury and Knighton to Llandovery, going over the line of the Llanelly Railway to Llanelly, and over another line over which they had running powers, to Swansea. Their running powers over the Llanelly Railway were ceded by agreement. But the Great Western Railway Company made that line their own, and tried to break the agreement. The Court of Chancery, however, upheld it, and now the Great Western Railway Company were doing all they could to obstruct the London and North Western Company from enjoying all the privileges which it conferred. The North Western, therefore proposed to make this little line, which would enable them to complete a station of their own, and to employ their own servants. The real reason of the opposition was that the Great Western wanted to block the North Western out, the professed reasons given in the petition being that a level crossing which it was proposed to make, was dangerous, and that to make the line was contrary to an agreement, dated 1863. As to the level crossing, if there were any that were dangerous, they belonged to the Great Western, and, as to the agreement, he did not understand what it meant.

Mr. Cawkwell gave evidence on behalf of the London and North Western Railway.

Mr. J. S. Tregoning, of Llanelly, said that his firm were acquainted with the railway facilities of the district. They sent away 500 boxes of plates every week. Those boxes would represent 90 tons weight. There was not sufficient warehouse accommodation at Llanelly, and it was of great importance that the London and North Western should have a station of their own.

Cross examined by Mr Michael: You have no complaint to make of deficient accommodation for your own traffic?—No.

Mr. Benjamin Jones, Caeffair, Llanelly, said that the present state of affairs was unsatisfactory. He had been chairman of the Local Board of Health for a great many years, and the views of the public of Llanelly were that the London and North Western should have a station there.

Mr. Bidder: The Local Board is concerned with sanitary matters?—Yes.

Will this station improve the sanitary condition of Llanelly? (Laughter.)—We are not in the forward condition in sanitary matters at Llanelly that we should wish, but I don't think the station would affect our drains. (Laughter).

You, as ex-chairman of the Local Board would be very sorry to see anything done that would endanger the lives of the good people of Llanelly?—Yes.

The level crossings might be apt to kill people?—It could not be worse than it is now. (Laughter).

Is it very bad now?—Yes, but that is not the fault of the London and North Western Company.

Charles Cook, brickmaker, Llanelly, said that it was of advantage and importance to the town that the London and North Western Company should have separate station accommodation in the town. On the 11th of February last he instructed the North Western to place two waggons in his siding, and next morning a consignment form was filled up by his clerk, Mr. Ridley. It was taken to the weighing machine in the usual course. Then an official of the Great Western Railway brought the note back, and it was altered. Afterwards the Great Western carried witness's goods away in their trucks.

Mr. Ridley, cashier of Messrs. Morgan and Co., and acting clerk to the last witness, said that he made out the consignment note, and give other corroborative evidence.

Mr. Jones, was in the employ of South Wales Smelting Company. Last February he made out a consignment note at Llanelly in the presence of a captain of a vessel, and he consigned certain goods by the London and North Western Railway Company. Afterwards he found there were two invoices—one from the North Western and the other from the Great Western. He could not tell how the Great Western got a consignment note.

Mr. John Logan was in the service of the London and North Western. On the 10th February he was instructed by Messrs. Nevill to put four North Western waggons in the sidings. This was done. The next morning the consignment note was given to witness, and proper labels were put on the waggons. He then saw a Great Western man tear the labels off. His name was Henry Davies; and he put on a Great Western label. Witness told the Great Western foreman that he had the consignment note, but notwithstanding that, they took the wagons away.

Mr. Wm. Rosser, civil engineer, Llanelly, said that the level crossing was not dangerous, and except the general principle that all level crossings are bad, there was no engineering objection to it.

Mr. Brunlees, C.E., approved to the level crossing, and this closed the case for the promoters.

Mr. Richard Glascodine, secretary of the Llanelly Railway Company, said that the consideration in the agreement was the benefit which they expected to derive from the North Western traffic, but they were grievously disappointed. The North Western acted in this way towards the Llanelly Company—they ran twelve trains over the line when two would accommodate the traffic.

Mr. Noel: They did that then at a great loss to themselves?—Yes, but at a great loss to us.

Mr. Bidder: The London and North Western can often affo d to run at a loss.

The committee adjourned till Monday.

The Select Committee to consider and repot upon this Bill met again Monday morning. Sir J. Kennaway presided, and the other members of the committee present were Mr. Noel, Mr. Elliott and Mr. Barclay. The promoters were represented by Mr. Pope, Q.C., Mr. Littler, Q.C., Mr. Chandos Leigh, and Mr. Wilberforce; while for the petitioners against the Bill—the Great Western Railway and the Llanelly Railway Companies—there appeared Mr. Bidder, Q.C., Mr. Michael, Mr. Sanders, and Mr. Dillwyn.

After much questioning and cross-questioniag, Mr. Michael and Mr. Pope addressed the Committee.

Mr. Grierson, at the suggestion of the Chairman, reduced to writing what the Great Western Company were prepared to do. They were prepared to construct, near the existing goods station at Llanelly, sheds, warehouses, and offices for the exclusive use of the London and North Western Railway Company, together with sidings, junctions, and other accommodation for the purpose of the goods traffic at Llanelly, "all upon such rent, terms, and conditions as shall be agreed upon, or in case of difference decided by arbitration."

The room was then cleared, and on the re-admission of the public the Chairman announced that "the Committee are of opinion that upon satisfactory evidence being shown of the ability of the Llanelly Company, as regards space and convenience, to afford the accommodation necessary for the purpose of the London and North Western Railway Company, the proposal sketched by Mr. Grierson affords the best form of arrangement between both parties, and the Committee submit it to them for consideration before coming to a decision on this part of the Bill."

Mr. Pope: The best thing would be to let it stand over until the adjournment, and then, no doubt, we shall be able to come to some arrangement.

Accordingly the Committee adjourned till the 9th of May.

Llanelly Guardian 13 April 1876 gives a sometimes amusing account of LNWR *and* GWR efforts to acquire supremacy.

The Llanelly Guardian.

THURSDAY, DECEMBER 26, 1872.

THE LLANELLY RAILWAY & DOCK CO.

REFERRING to the above old company, we are sorry to record that by the closing of the eventful year of 1872, the Llanelly Railway, as far as its name goes, will terminate and cease to exist with the closing of the year, and most probably its appellation will for ever be erased from the life and progress of Llanelly and its trade.

The public have for years anticipated a radical change, its "still small voice" and the beating of its pulse indicated that sooner or later it was bound to take place, and that the death knol of its existence was not far distant. But the direction in which it drifted has taken the people with the greatest surprise. Referring to the after-dinner speech recently delivered by the Chairman of the Company to the contrary, it was well understood that both the London & North Western Railway Company and the Great Western Company were negotiating for the property, and no doubt its transfer to either of them would be advantageous to their respective shareholders. It is evident that the competitive management of Mr. W. D. PHILLIPPS, and the unflinching co-operation of his subordinates at Carmarthen, Llanelly, and Swansea, since the opening of the Central Wales Railway was keenly felt by the Great Western Railway Company, and the spurring then inflicted was the means to agitate that Company to speculate, and give the best offer to the Llanelly Railway shareholders. Hence we have the authority to state that the latter Company will henceforth be part of the Great Western narrow gauge system from the 1st of January next; and it is evident that Llanelly will feel the result one way or the other. The Great Western Railway Company are no doubt able to do the place some good—the advantages of both Railway and Dock will give them that freedom of action that is denied them in other ports in this channel; and we trust that they will thoroughly take the advantage of the position they have acquired, and that the result will be a boon to the town and port of Llanelly, and remunerative to all concerned in the step so unexpectedly taken by the Company.

Llanelly Guardian *26 December 1872. The end of the Llanelly Railway.*

1981 saw the formation of the HOWLTA (Heart of Wales Line Travellers' Assocation), a group whose aims are to further the interests of the line.

In 1985/86, local authorities, Mid Wales Development, and the Wales Tourist Board, contributed a total of £212,000 to an overall £644,000 investment scheme by British Rail and the introduction of NSKT (No Signalman Key Token) system on the CWL at a cost of £473,000, commenced at the beginning of 1986.

A limited Sunday service of one train to and from Llandrindod Wells was introduced on 6 July 1986 and May 1987 saw one Sunday through service in each direction with a new weekday timetable. The first of the Sunday 'Recreation Rambler' trains between Swansea and Llandrindod Wells commenced on 21 June 1987, sponsored by the Sports Council for Wales, Dyfed and Powys County Councils (See Chapter 9 'Passenger Traffic').

Disaster struck on 19 October 1987 when, due to severe flooding, the Glanrhyd Bridge, south of Llangadog, collapsed while a train was in the process of crossing. This not only caused concern for the tragic loss of life but also fears that it would provide an excuse for closing the line. Although assurance that the bridge would be rebuilt was given the following day by Hugh Gould, British Rail's Manager for Wales, the Heart of Wales Line Travellers' Association, ever vigilant, sought confirmation and in answer to a letter of 5 January 1988, the secretary received a reply to this effect from John Davies, British Rail's Provincial Manager for Wales.

> 'I think I need to explain the position regarding the Glanrhyd bridge to alleviate any fears you may have regarding its future. The position is that after thorough examination, it is clear that the costs of reinstating the bridge are considerably higher than at first estimated and, for this reason, it has now been decided to go out to competitive tender for the repairs to the bridge. Consequently, there will be some further delay whilst the tender is prepared and the bids examined and then the speed at which it is replaced will depend on a number of features, particularly the availablility of major components etc. In any event, it seems clear that it will not be available until at least well into the summer service and for this reason it is not sensible to plan for special movements until we know more definitely what the situation will be. Whilst I am sure you will be disappointed by the delay, be assured that I am also very disappointed because of the effects on revenue and at a time when the line would be at its busiest. I must reassure you though, that there is absolute commitment to restoring the facility as early as possible and that it is intended to implement the radical service improvements that had originally been intended for May as soon as the line has been opened for through traffic.'

After preliminary chaotic attempts to find a workable arrangement, a bus service was introduced between Llandeilo and Llandovery until Llangadog and Llanwrda stations were re-opened and through rail services resumed in October 1988.

The re-introduction of the through service saw considerable problems. 'Sprinters', which had been used for some journeys during the interim were removed and the DMUs operating on the northern part of the line were in a very poor state of maintenance, constantly breaking down and even running out of fuel, resulting in severe disruptions to the service and considerable inconvenience to passengers.

Even HOWLTA, well known for its untiring efforts and patient cooperation with British Rail in the interests of the line, was moved to justifiably strong criticism in its March 1989 Newsletter. Excursions began running over the track again in February 1989 and in June 1989, the 'Recreation Rambler' was re-introduced, with 1992 seeing the commencement of the regular use of 'Sprinters'.

The Sunday service still operates in summer only with one through train in each direction commencing in May, with the addition of the 'Ramblers' which are limited to mid summer.

DEPARTMENT OF THE ENVIRONMENT

JANUARY 1971

THE BRITISH RAILWAYS BOARD (CENTRAL WALES RAILWAY) LIGHT RAILWAY ORDER

1 NOTICE IS HEREBY GIVEN that application is intended to be made in the present month of January by the British Railways Board (hereinafter referred to as "the Board") to the Secretary of State for the Environment for an Order under the Light Railways Acts 1896 and 1912 and the Railways Act 1921 for the following purposes :-

To enable the Board to work as a light railway under the provisions of the Light Railways Acts 1896 and 1912 as amended by the Railways Act 1921 such part of the Central Wales railway of the Board as comprises (a) the railway described in and authorised by the Knighton Railway Act 1858 together with the extension thereof to its junction with the Board's Shrewsbury and Hereford railway immediately south of Craven Arms station in the parish of Stokesay in the rural district of Ludlow in the County of Salop, the Central Wales Act 1859, the Central Wales Extension Railway Act 1860, and the Vale of Towy Railway Act 1854 (b) the railway firstly described in and authorised by the Llanelly Railway and Dock Act 1853 and (c) so much of the railway secondly described in and authorised by section 1 of the Act 5 & 6 William IV c.xcvi as extends from its junction with the said railway firstly described in and authorised by the said Llanelly Railway and Dock Act 1853 to a point 330 yards north of the signal box at Pantyffynnon Station in the urban district of Ammanford in the County of Carmarthen.

A copy of the draft Order will be deposited for public inspection on or before the 31st January 1971 with the

17.

Power to work railway as a light railway.

3. Subject to the provisions of this Order—

(1) The Board may work as a light railway under the principal Act the railway more particularly described in Schedule 1 hereto.

(2) Such of the enactments set out in the Second Schedule to the Light Railways Act 1896 as are still in force (except section 22 of the Regulation of Railways Act 1868 ([a]) and sections 1, 5 and 6 of the Regulation of Railways Act 1889 ([b])) shall cease to apply to the railway.

Provisions as to working.

4.—(1) The Board shall not without the previous consent in writing of the Minister use upon the railway any engine, carriage or truck bringing a greater weight than 20 tons upon the rails by any one pair of wheels.

(2) The Board shall not run any train or engine upon any part of the railway at a rate of speed exceeding at any time that fixed by the Minister for such part.

(3) Where the railway is carried across any public road on the level the Board shall not unnecessarily allow any engine, train or truck to stand across the level crossing.

(4) The Board shall not without the prior approval in writing of the Minister run on a regular daily basis more than six passenger trains and one goods train in each direction over the railway.

(5) The motive power shall be diesel or steam or such other motive power as the Minister may approve provided that nothing in this Order shall authorise the Board to use electrical power as motive power on the railway unless such power is obtained from storage batteries or from a source of generation entirely contained in and carried along with the engines or carriages.

(6) The Board shall provide all engines and multiple unit trains running over the railway with a suitable electric headlamp which shall during hours of darkness be lit on the approach to all open level crossings.

(7) The Board shall comply with the requirements prescribed for the safety of the public using the railway and set out in Schedule 3 hereto.

(8) If the Board act in contravention of any of the provisions of this section they shall for each offence be liable on summary conviction to a penalty not exceeding twenty pounds.

As to Pantyffynnon Level Crossing.

5. The Board shall at the level crossing referred to in Schedule 2 hereto maintain gates and shall employ proper persons to open and shut such gates and such gates shall when closed

(a) 31 & 32 Vict. c. 119. (b) 52 & 53 Vict. c. 57.

The Light Railway Order 1971.

across the road fence in the railway but such gates when open to road traffic may open away from the railway. The Board may keep the said gates open to road traffic (instead of closed across the road) except when engines or vehicles passing along the railway have occasion to cross the road.

6. Any penalty under this Order may be recovered in manner provided by the Magistrates' Courts Act 1952([a]). Recovery of penalties.

7. All costs, charges and expenses of and incident to the preparing for, obtaining and making of this Order or otherwise in relation thereto shall be paid by the Board and may in whole or in part be defrayed out of revenue. Costs of Order.

SCHEDULES.

SCHEDULE 1

Such part of the Central Wales Railway of the Board as comprises—

(*a*) the railways described in and authorised by—

The Knighton Railway Act 1858 ([a]) together with the extension thereof to its junction with the Board's Shrewsbury and Hereford Railway immediately south of Craven Arms Station in the parish of Stokesay in the rural district of Ludlow in the County of Salop;

The Central Wales Railway Act 1859([b]);

The Central Wales Extension Railway Act 1860([c]);

The Vale of Towy Railway Act 1854([d]):

(*b*) the railway firstly described in and authorised by The Llanelly Railway and Dock Act 1853([e]):

(*c*) so much of the railway secondly described in and authorised by the Act 5 & 6 William IV c. xcvi as extends from its junction with the said railway firstly described in and authorised by the said The Llanelly Railway and Dock Act 1853 to a point 330 feet north of the signal box at Pantyffynnon Station in the urban district of Ammanford in the County of Carmarthen.

SCHEDULE 2

The level crossing known as Pantyffynnon crossing whereby Pantyffynnon Road is crossed by the railway at Pantyffynnon Station.

SCHEDULE 3

Permanent Way.

The rails used shall weigh at least 85 pounds per yard when laid in. Check rails shall be provided on curves where the radius is 10 chains or less.

If flat-bottomed rail and wooden sleepers are used suitable bearing plates shall be provided secured to the sleepers by fang or other through bolts or by coachscrews.

The running lines shall be kept ballasted with stone throughout.

Block System.

A train staff and ticket system shall be employed for the control of single line working.

The communication system for maintaining an adequate interval of space between following trains shall be some form of telephone instrument. No other form of electrical communication will be required.

([a]) 21 Vict. c. xix. ([b]) 22 & 23 Vict. c. cxxi.
([c]) 23 & 24 Vict. c. cxli. ([d]) 17 & 18 Vict. c. cl.
([e]) 16 & 17 Vict. c. clxix.

Signalling.

At places where trains are required to cross or pass one another under the system of working for the time being in force there shall be a home signal for each direction at or near the entrance points. Starting signals will also be required. Signals may be worked from the signalbox or ground frame by wires or otherwise and shall be so weighted as to fly to and remain at Danger on the breaking of any part of the connection between the arm and the lever working it. Distant signals which need not be worked shall be provided at a suitable braking distance for the fastest trains to use the line. All facing points shall be provided with a locking device. An economical facing point lock operated by the point lever will be acceptable.

Maximum Permitted Speeds.

Except on those parts of the railway where a lower maximum rate of speeds has been fixed by the Minister the maximum rate of speed on any part of the railway shall not exceed at any time 60 m.p.h. for passenger trains composed entirely of diesel multiple-unit vehicles, 45 m.p.h. for locomotive-hauled trains provided with continuous brakes throughout, and 25 m.p.h. for all other trains.

Platform, etc.

Platforms shall be provided to the satisfaction of the Minister at all stopping places.

This Order shall impose no obligation on the Board to provide shelter, conveniences or lighting at any stations or stopping place, but where lighting is not provided a white painted strip four inches in width shall be maintained along the platform edges.

BRITISH RAIL PRESS RELEASE

A £644,000 investment programme for the Shrewsbury-Swansea Central Wales Line has been authorised by British Rail Western Region.

The major outlay will be by BR, but £170,000 will be contributed jointly by Mid Wales Development, the Shropshire, Powys, Dyfed and West Glamorgan County Councils, and Shrewsbury-and-Atcham and Brecknock Borough Councils and the Radnor District Council. Discussions on funding are also in hand with the Wales Tourist Board and South Shropshire District Council.

BR welcome this financial involvement, which is seen as recognition of the need for the line which — known for marketing purposes as the "Heart of Wales Line" and served by five weekday passenger trains in each direction — traverses a sparsely populated but highly scenic area, and caters for tourists, local travellers and people requiring access to and from the main line network.

The objectives of the investment are to cut operating costs, in line with BR's commitment to increase cost effectiveness and reduce taxpayers' support, and to increase the line's potential for special tourist trains.

The investment will fall under three headings:

SIGNALLING

By October 1986 the movement of trains over the key 79 miles of single-track between Craven Arms and Pantyffynnon will be supervised from one signalbox at Pantyffynnon, with the signalboxes and existing signalling at the Llandrindod, Llanwrtyd, Llandovery and Llandeilo passing loops removed.

The loops which enable trains in opposite directions to pass one another at these four places will be retained, but hydro-pneumatic self-acting points, one of the most recent and up-to-date developments in railway engineering, will route trains to the track appropriate to the direction of travel.

Indicators will confirm the correct setting of points, and points will be equipped with electric heaters to assist operations in freezing temperatures.

The Craven Arms-Pantyffynnon section will also be equipped with the standard BR in-cab Automatic Warning System for train drivers.

As on many other BR single-track lines, the authority for drivers to take trains on to each single-track section will be a metal "token". Instruments housing the tokens, and linked by sophisticated electronics to ensure that only one token for any one section is in use at any one time, will be operated by signalmen at Craven Arms and Pantyffynnon, but at the intermediate passing loops instruments will be at the stations, and train drivers will deposit and withdraw tokens under the supervision of the Pantyffynnon signalman.

The Department of Transport has only recently approved in principle the concept of this "no-signalman token" system on successive sections of single-track passenger lines.

In addition to reducing costs, the new signalling will permit more flexible train operation than the present restrictive "staff and ticket" system of single-line control, and will enable the line to be opened for special trains on Sundays more cheaply.

LLANDRINDOD PASSING LOOP

By May 1986, in time for the holiday season, the passing loop at Llandrindod level crossing half-a-mile outside the station, will be moved into the station, where a disused second platform will be re-opened and equipped with a waiting shelter. This will not only ease the serving of Llandrindod Wells, a major tourist centre, by special excursion trains, but it will also avoid the present frustrating arrangement for passengers whereby southbound trains wait outside the station, but in view of it, when a northbound train is running late.

LEVEL CROSSINGS

Six level crossings operated by signalmen, crossing keepers or station staff will be automated or operated by train crews.

By October 1986 the level crossings at Llandrindod and Llandovery will be altered so that the barriers are lowered by train crews. The barriers will rise automatically after a train has passed.

Between July and October 1985 the level crossings at Ffairfach, Cilyrychen (between Ffairfach and Llandybie stations), Llandybie and Tirydail (at Ammanford station), will be converted to "open" crossings without barriers. Amber and flashing red lights will warn road users of the approach of trains, which will approach at reduced speed. There are already four level crossings of this type on the line. Later, the level crossing at Pantyffynnon may also be converted.

The alterations in level crossing control will add about eleven minutes to the present overall 3¾-hour journey time between Shrewsbury and Swansea, but this will be more than wiped out by the quicker running times of the new "Sprinter" diesel trains planned for the route from 1987.

Consultations by BR with staff representatives has yet to take place on certain aspects of the investment package, and these discussions will include the future of displaced staff.

Discussions will also be necessary with the Department of Transport. Their approval of certain details of the overall scheme, including necessary amendments to the Light Railway Order under which the Craven Arms-Pantyffynnon section of the Central Wales Line has been operated since 1972, is required, and the conversion of level crossings is subject to the issue of Statutory Orders by the Secretary of State for Transport.

BR Press Release re NSKT 18 April 1985.

3

Construction, Delays and Difficulties

The Llanelly Railway Company was first concerned with the extension of existing tram and rail transport within the town and to the docks. In 1833 it completed the first tram track of 1 mile 70 chains for horse drawn traffic from Gelly Gille Farm Mine to Machynis Pool. By June 1839, new track to take the first steam locomotives was laid as far as Pontarddulais.

The problems which were soon to beset the company (now the Llanelly Railway & Dock Company) were not concerned with physical construction but brought about by financial difficulties, over usage and insufficient maintenance of locomotives. Horse traction was re-introduced in the mid 1840s while the very necessary substantial overhauls were carried out. Attempts to sell the concern – mainly to the South Wales Railway Company – proving unsuccessful, the working of the line was contracted out to Ianson, Fossick & Hackworth who ran it until 1857.

Having struggled to its feet again at a time when the output of the South Wales iron industry reached its peak of 970,727 tons, the Llanelly Company, anxious to forge ahead to Llandeilo – a goal which it achieved the same year – replaced the existing track of 42 to 50lb per yard on that section with heavier rail of 70lb and installed semaphore signals at various junctions and stations.

Compared with the delays it had experienced in getting the line completed between Duffryn Lodge and Llandeilo, the 18 months hold up, ten years later, in the opening of the passenger route to Swansea Victoria in December 1867 might well seem, on the face of it, to have been a minor set back to a company which was used to being beset by problems. However, the financial implications were serious and complicated.

By the end of January 1865, all appeared to be set for the Swansea line to be completed. At a half yearly meeting, the directors reported that the first locomotive had been delivered on the 27th of that month and they anticipated that the line would soon be open, but in the ensuing six months little was done. Although it would appear that goods trains were running on the line by January of the following year, the terminus at Swansea had not been completed.

The delay was due to the contractors, the hitherto reliable Watson, Overend & Company who had run into difficulties. A merger with another company in 1865 to form the much underfunded 'Contract Corporation Co. Ltd' resulted in the company being wound up after just over a year. In May 1866, the city banking company, Overend, Gurney & Co. which financed them, crashed and the Llanelly Company found that the Contract Corporation Co. – which had taken over responsibility for purchasing land on their behalf – had not paid all the debts. This, added to the fact that the line was not completed, brought everything to a standstill for over a year.

If this were not enough, there was also the problem of locomotives which the Llanelly Company were hard pressed to find funds to purchase as these were originally to be supplied by the contractors. The LNWR, who were relying on the successful completion of the route to Swansea to link up with the Central Wales Extension and Vale of Towy Railways in order to establish a through route to the North, were understandably, more than ready to advance £40,000 to the Llanelly Company, but at a price – running powers over the whole of the latter's system.

This enabled work to go ahead and thus it was that the Swansea firm, Thomas, Watkin & Jenkins, completed the contract at commendable speed and the terminus at Swansea Low Level (Victoria) station opened within two months on 14 December 1867.

Although the *Cambrian Newspaper* devoted a great deal of space to the event there was, as the latter stated, little ceremony. The haste with which it was finally completed, the stress which preceded it and the drain on finances probably proved too much for the unfortunate Llanelly Company whose agreement to allow LNWR entire running rights could be seen to be the cause of its eventual disintegration.

An inspection in 1868 by G. P. Neele, the Superintendent of LNWR, resulted in a none-too-complimentary report that the line was out of date, badly maintained with crossing loops too short and some bridges built of wood to save cost and locomotives old and under maintained. Criticism was also levelled at the condition of the stations.

Swansea Victoria station in 1868 looking north eastwards to Kilvey Mill. The train in the left foreground is headed by Alice *and is on the Llanelly–Swansea service. This locomotive was originally an 0-4-0 built by Edward Bury in 1839 for the LNWR and acquired by the Llanelly company in 1847 and rebuilt as an 0-4-2 in 1859. The carriage carries roof boards which read 'Llanelly' and 'Swansea', a reminder that the line was at first a local system – the LRDC's intention to compete with the GWR by operating a service between Swansea and Llanelly. Wind Street Viaduct and station can just be seen in the background.*
(City of Swansea Archives)

In the Llanelly Railway (New Lines) Act 1 August 1861 granting permission to build the line, the Swansea and the Carmarthen Lines Undertakings were both designated as financially independent companies from the Llanelly Company and were responsible for finding the money to meet the requirements put forward in G. P. Neele's report.

Not suprisingly, in 1867, the Swansea Lines Undertaking went into receivership followed in 1871, by the Carmarthen Lines Undertaking. This state of affairs resulted in a bill on 16 June 1871 severing these two companies completely from their ties with the parent company and they thus became the Swansea & Carmarthen Railways Co.

The LNWR, who had backed the bill, re-inforced its hand by a working agreement with the new company, although it already had powers to run over the line. The Llanelly company made a vain attempt to terminate the latter in 1872, first by notification to the LNWR, then via the courts and finally, in desperation the matter was laid before the House of Lords but the appeal was overruled. The traffic on the route was considerable and the finances of the Llanelly company, with the LNWR reaping much of the profits, were severely affected.

Having acquired control of the main part of the Swansea section by 1871, the LNWR purchased it and the Llanmorlais branch in July 1873 for £310,000. By this time, the Llanelly company, reduced to running a small stretch, gave up the struggle and leased the remainder – which included the Pontarddulais–Llandeilo section, the running rights over which were vital to the LNWR – to the GWR.

Progress in the North, although less complex, was not altogether easy. The Knighton Railway Company, formed in 1858, having won an initial skirmish against a counter proposal from the Mid Wales Railway Company, appointed Brassey & Field as contractors to construct the line between Craven Arms and Stokesay and Knighton.

Already involved in the Shrewsbury & Hereford Railway Company, being contracted to the latter until July 1861, these two gentlemen proposed being also responsible for the working of the Knighton line from its opening until that date. (They in fact, worked it for a further year until July 1862.) Construction was delayed by several factors; a severe winter and a wet summer played some part and inability to obtain labour was another. Forecasts for opening by June 1860 were not realised.

The first 9-mile stretch – out of the total 12 from Craven Arms to Bucknell was not completed until October of that year. By the time the line reached Knighton in 1861, 'friendly co-operation and working' with the London & North Western Railway was agreed, and on 1 July 1862, it was run by the latter, as was the Shrewsbury and Hereford (from which it had spured at Craven Arms and Stokesay) but in the latter case, responsibility was shared with the Great Western Railway. Such off loading relieved the Knighton Railway of financial burdens involved in the running of the line which it had not foreseen at the outset.

The area covered by the Central Wales and Central Wales Extension railways respectively required considerable engineering expertise but the Knighton Railway engineer, Mr Henry Robertson, who was in charge of both projects, referring to the first 20 miles, expressed the view that there were 'no great difficulties' even though the work involved the erection of the Knucklas Viaduct (with 13 arches, each spanning 30ft, 75ft above ground at one point) and the 645-yard Llyncoch Tunnel three miles ahead at the line's summit of 980ft above sea level, after which there was a descent of 1 in 100 to Llangunllo station. The five years estimated for the actual construction did, however, prove to be over optimistic.

The engineer's report was read at a meeting in March 1860 and, in spite of bad weather, it was hoped to reach Penybont by August 1861. By the end of August 1860, two tunnel shafts had been sunk at Llyncoch and the earthworks at either end were nearly finished. However, a further report in the spring of 1861 advised that 2½ miles were completed in the direction of Penybont, a bridge over the River Teme and tracks laid as far as Knucklas Viaduct but progress on the Llyncoch Tunnel and earthworks to the summit were once more delayed by bad weather.

Originally, it had been intended to operate the line using tank engines only and turntables were not included in the specification. Later, Colonel Yolland, the Inspecting Officer for the Board of Trade, stipulated that engines must not be run bunker first on trains and instructed that turntables be installed at Knighton Railway's Craven Arms, at CWR's Builth Road Junction and at Llandrindod.

Messrs Hattersley and Morton were the contractors involved, the latter gentleman appearing to be mainly in charge of labour, the employment of which did not seem to have presented the problems of availability encountered in the early days of the Knighton Railway Company project but the inability to pay the wages, even before the viaduct was completed, began to be a real and very serious threat to progress.

At a Central Wales Company meeting on 31 August 1863, the engineer reported that work on the Knucklas Viaduct had been completed and permanent way laid as far as Llyncoch Tunnel, the inner faces of which were within ten yards of meeting and it was expected that September would see the track completed to a point seven miles from Knighton; approaches of Troedyrhiw cutting, just north of Llanbister Road, were well forward, being the only important earthworks still to be finished before reaching Penybont.

On 28 February 1865, it was reported that work on the stations was well ahead and that only the bridge over the River Ithon (at Crossgates) and two miles of permanent way needed to be finished to complete the route to Llandrindod. When the CWR finally arrived in Llandrindod in 1865 the Chairman of the Company, Sir Charles H. Rouse Broughton, spoke of the difficulties having been 'enormous', giving credit to those who had lent support not the least, the LNWR.

There now remained only the Central Wales Extension Railway track between Llandrindod and Llandovery to complete the through route from Shrewsbury to Llanelli and Swansea. Of all the examples of over optimism in the construction of the Central Wales Line, that of the CWER Company must have been the greatest in its expectancy of opening up a stretch of such difficult terrain within two years. (In a journal dated 6 March 1861, it was anticipated that a through line would be completed by 1862.)

Of the several independent sections in which the construction of this portion of the line was carried out, work was first begun on the most difficult – between Sugar Loaf and Llandovery, in November 1860. The summit of the line at the Sugar Loaf is 820ft above sea level, approached at a 1 in 80 gradient and descending at 1 in 70 through the tunnel and onwards towards Cynghordy at 1 in 60. The construction of the 1,000-yard tunnel involved dealing with an immense basin of water and dangerous rock. Some unsound sections previously constructed had to be replaced and lined.

There were also complications at the 283-yard long Cynghordy Viaduct (102ft at the highest of its 18 arches each of which has a 36ft 6in span) involving a change of contractors who removed some unsatisfactory foundations. The original estimate for building the viaduct was £15,610 11s 11d.

The additional work entailed meant that the financial and completion estimates were unrealistic. Extra time was needed for the last ten miles and this was obtained by a

Llwynjack Bridge spans the River Towy, 1932.
(Dorothy Bound)

The rebuilding of Glanrhyd Bridge in 1958. This was to collapse in flood conditions 30 years later with tragic consequences.
(Welsh Industrial & Maritime Museum)

Knucklas Viaduct in the 1920s.
(Courtesy Judith Dyke)

Sugar Loaf Tunnel, south west portal.
(HMRS/G. M. Perkins collection)

The north portal of Llangunllo Tunnel.
(HMRS/G. M. Perkins collection)

further Act in 1867. Mr William Clarke, inspector for the LNWR, reported on 19 February 1868 that 'the cost of the Sugar Loaf Tunnel to this date was considerably more than estimated by Mr Robertson, especially the northern end' (where some 62,000 cubic yards of earthworks had been removed). The report also mentioned that engineers working from Llanwrtyd and from Llandovery had nearly completed the permanent way but that there was still a one mile gap between Cynghordy Viaduct and the southern end of Sugar Loaf Tunnel. In accordance with Board of Trade instructions, a turntable was installed at each temporary terminus, being transferred from one section to another as work progressed.

The northern part of the CWER line opened as far as Builth Road in November 1866 where, near the ancient site of Cwrt Llechrhyd, it crossed above the Mid Wales Line (Moat Lane Junction to Brecon). First called Builth Road Junction, the CWER station was subsequently known as Builth Road High Level.

By March 1867, the line was completed to Garth where it was opened in very wintry conditions with snow drifts and hard frost. In spite of the bad spring weather, Garth to Llanwrtyd was opened in May 1867 although at this point it appears that only the running was satisfactory the travelling public complaining about the lack of shelters.

In June 1868, six years later than anticipated, the CWER line was finally completed to Llandovery. Among the party aboard the first through train on this momentous occasion, were CWER directors. LNWR officials and their Superintendent, G. P. Neele who, in the same year, was responsible for the very unflattering report on the Llanelly Railway's section of the line. Representatives of the latter were at Llandovery to welcome the train.

In his chronicles, G.P. Neele wrote:

> 'The opening to Llandovery was availed of to make some striking announcements of the saving of 55 miles between Manchester, Liverpool, Birmingham, etc. and Llanelly, Carmarthen and Swansea; which notices were probably not very acceptable to the Great Western authorities.'

Eventually, double track was laid on the Shrewsbury–Craven Arms and Stokesay–Knighton section, Llanbister Road to Penybont Junction, Penybont station to Llandrindod, Pantyffynnon to Llanelli and Pontarddulais to Swansea. It was single through Hendy Tunnel (between Pontarddulais and Llanelli).

Although the route covered by CWR and CWER was intended to be single track, the requisite land was bought and bridges so built to allow for doubling if necessary. In total, construction of the Central Wales Line took nearly 30 years.

4

Branch Lines

Brynamman Branch LRDC/GWR/BR

On 10 March 1840, the Llanelly company opened a line for freight from Pontarddulais, branching east at Pantyffynnon to Garnant (original station) and extending eastwards from Garnant Junction to Brynamman in 1842. Passenger services are thought to have operated from the commencement.

By the mid 1860s, the Midland Railway also had a branch to Brynamman. This ran from its Swansea St Thomas station (Colbren line) north-westwards where it joined – via a bridge under the main road – the 'Brynamman branch' from Pantyffynnon – by then owned by the GWR. The two companies had separate stations situated at either side of the bridge, in BR days that of the GWR being known as Brynamman West and the Midland Railway/LMS station as Brynamman East. For about a year after the Garnant-Brynamman section closed on 20 December 1963, some goods traffic from the latter was moved via the former Midland Railway's Gurnos Junction. (The Midland's section between Brynamman and Gurnos Junction closed on 28 September 1964.)

The first branch to Gwaun-cae-Gurwen, which ran south east from a junction between Glanamman and Garnant, was built by the Llanelly company and opened on 6 May 1841 for freight and mineral traffic but is thought to have conveyed passengers unofficially. The line ran through the

A view of the junction platform at Pantyffynnon with the 11.50am milk train ex Llangadog. On the right is the train from Brynamman West, May 1958.
(N. C. Simmons, Hugh Davies collection)

Pantyffynnon GWR station – Brynamman branch platform looking south.
(Bernard Matthews collection)

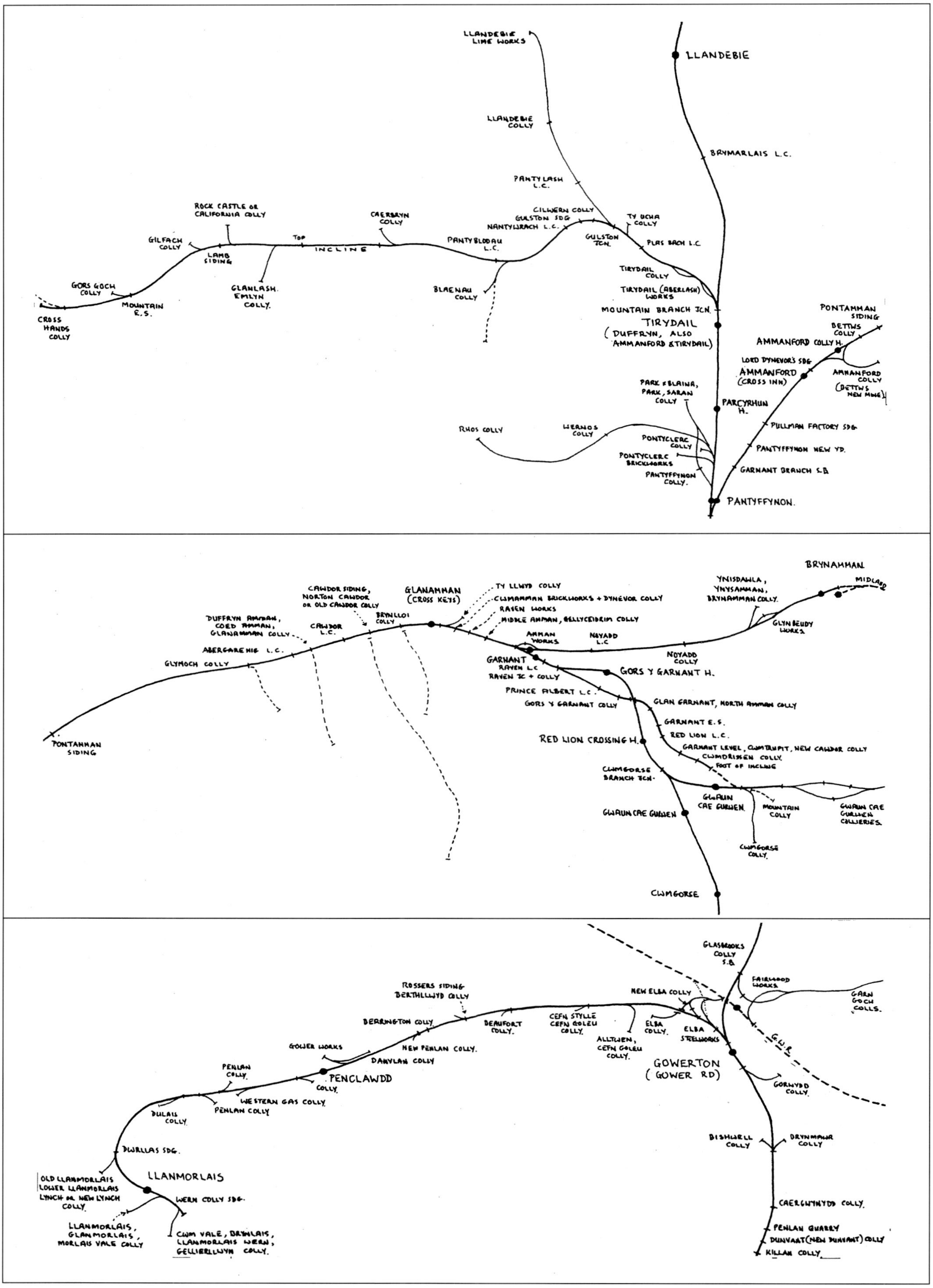

Branch line map. (R. A. Cooke)

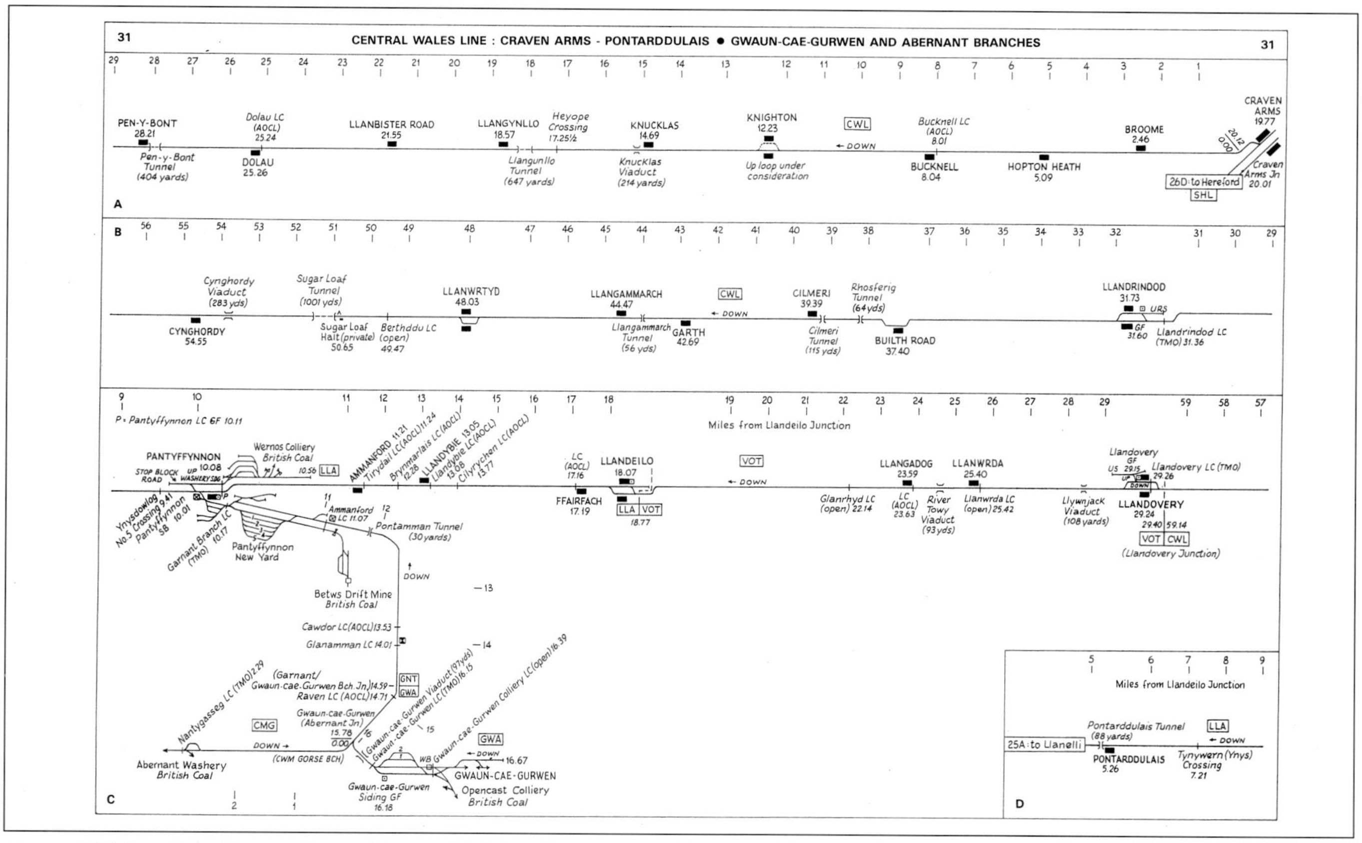

Central Wales Line Craven Arms–Pontarddulais. Gwaun–cae–Gurwen-Abernant branches track diagram. (Courtesy Quail Map Co.)

Pannier tank No. 7718 and a brake van at Garnant, looking east towards Raven Crossing, May 1958.
(Hugh Davies)

The viaducts at Gwaun-cae-Gurwen in the 1950s.
(N. C. Simmons, Hugh Davies collection)

The burnt out remains of Gwaun-cae-Gurwen station in September 1994. Accessible only by narrow lanes and paths, the fire brigade was unable to reach it in time.
(Rose Coleman)

Gwaun-cae-Gurwen looking west with an 0-6-0PT shunting over the level crossing.
(N. C. Simmons, Hugh Davies collection)

Glanamman station (originally Cross Keys), May 1958.
(N. C. Simmons, Hugh Davies collection)

Ammanford Colliery Halt, May 1958.
(N. C. Simmons, Hugh Davies collection)

The 12.15pm to Llandovery, ready to leave Brynamman West in May 1958.
(N. C. Simmons, Hugh Davies collection)

0-6-0PT No. 7718 and a brake van at Garnant, showing the station track layout, May 1958.
(N. C. Simmons, Hugh Davies collection)

Pantyffynnon station looking towards the Brynamman branch after track lifting.
(Courtesy John Lloyd)

valley to reach Gwaun-cae-Gurwen. The last incline, which was privately owned (originally by a Welshman, Charles Morgan, and after 1874 by Yorkshiremen who formed the Gwaun-cae-Gurwen Colliery Company) led to what was later known as the Old Pit and which was rope worked until 1886. An agreement on 3 February 1886 permitted the GCG company to work the last section of the line, repairs to be carried out by the GWR.

The GWR opened a new line to Gwaun-cae-Gurwen for goods on the 4 November 1907 and for passengers on 1 January 1908. This commenced at Raven Crossing, south east of Garnant, had a section at 1 in 40 for over a mile but avoided the incline at the end. When the new line to Gwaun-cae-Gurwen was constructed, part of the original track remained in use as far as Cawdor Colliery and became known as the Cawdor branch, eventually closing in 1951.

There was also a line southwards to Duke Colliery which was opened from Cwmgorse Junction (near Gwaun-cae-Gurwen Viaduct over the River Amman) on 11 September 1922 and this was extended to Abernant in 1944. There were two stations built on the latter, each with two platforms – one was called Gwaun-cae-Gurwen (the original station of that name, sited by the crossing, closed in 1926) and the other, Cwm Gorse, but neither was ever opened. They are still in existence although the former, ravaged by fire, is a mere shell.

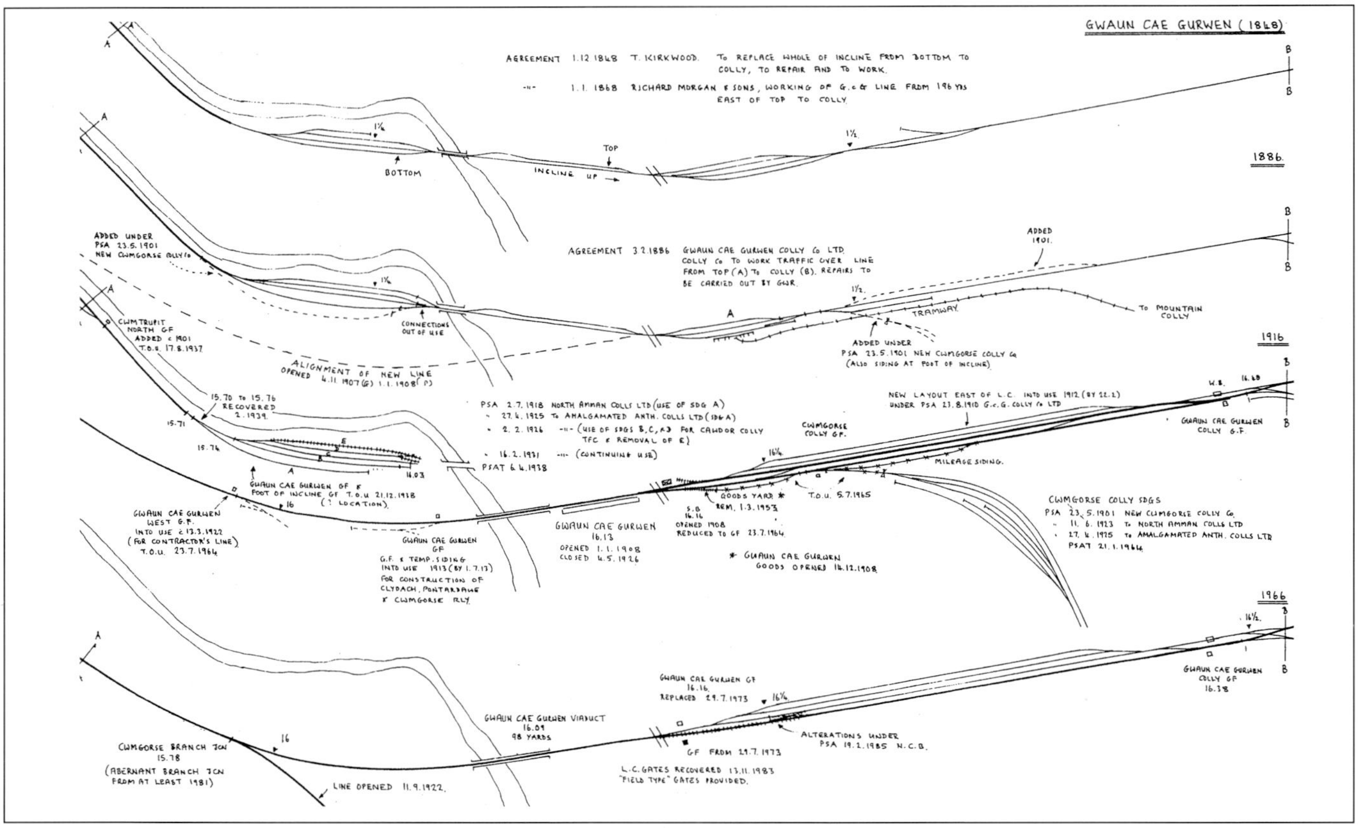

Gwaun-cae-Gurwen 1848-1966. (R. A. Cooke)

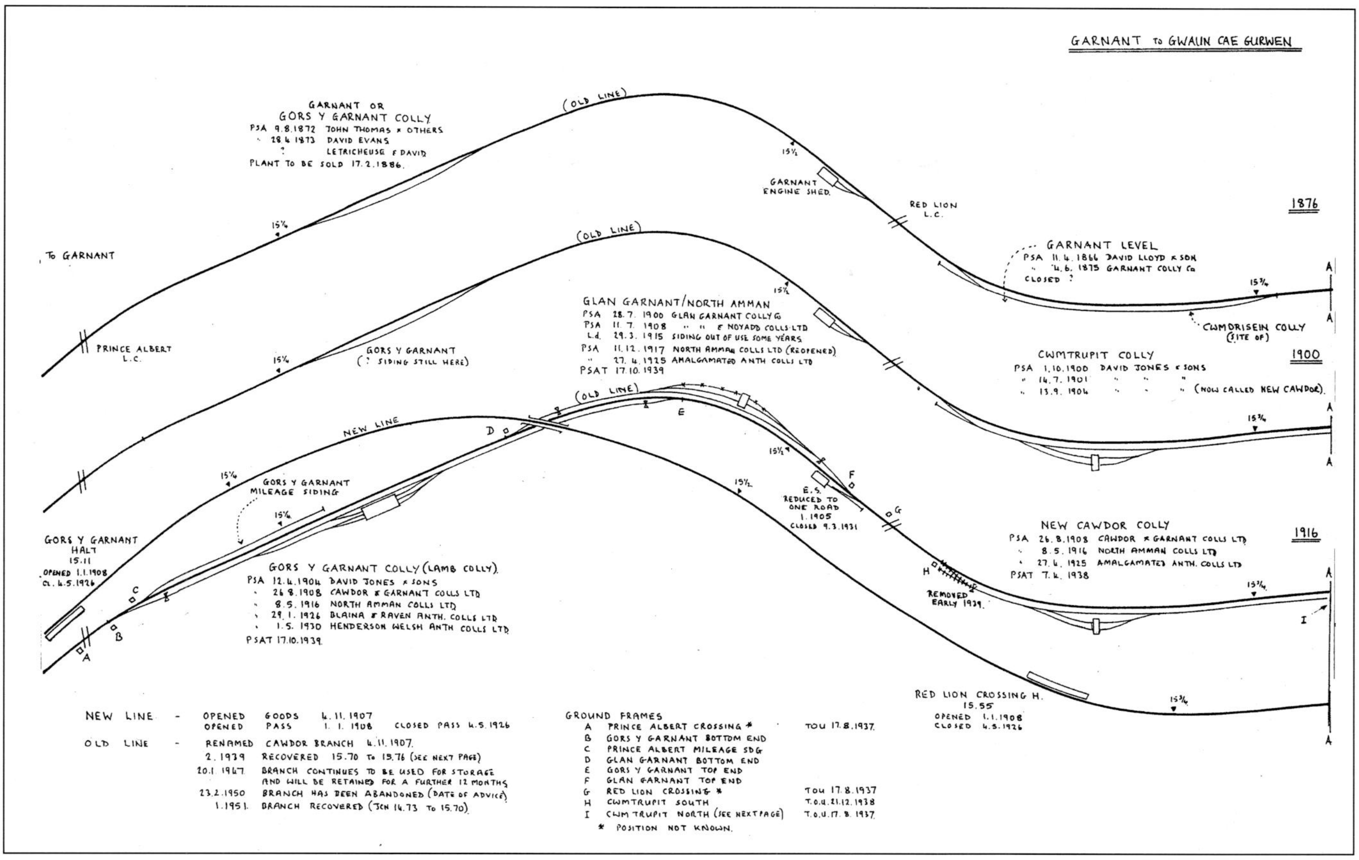

Garnant to Gwaun-cae-Gurwen 1876-1916. (R. A. Cooke)

In 1911, the GWR acquired powers to construct a line from Felin Fran (north east of Swansea) via Clydach and Trebanos, this to be extended along the Upper Clydach Valley northwards to Gwaun-cae-Gurwen. It reached Clydach in 1914, but was delayed by the First World War, eventually opening to Trebanos in 1923. However, no connection was ever made with Gwaun-cae-Gurwen as the remaining section was never built.

The LNWR had running powers over the original Brynamman and Gwaun-cae-Gurwen lines but did not exercise them.

Brynamman West. (Courtesy D. T. Davies)

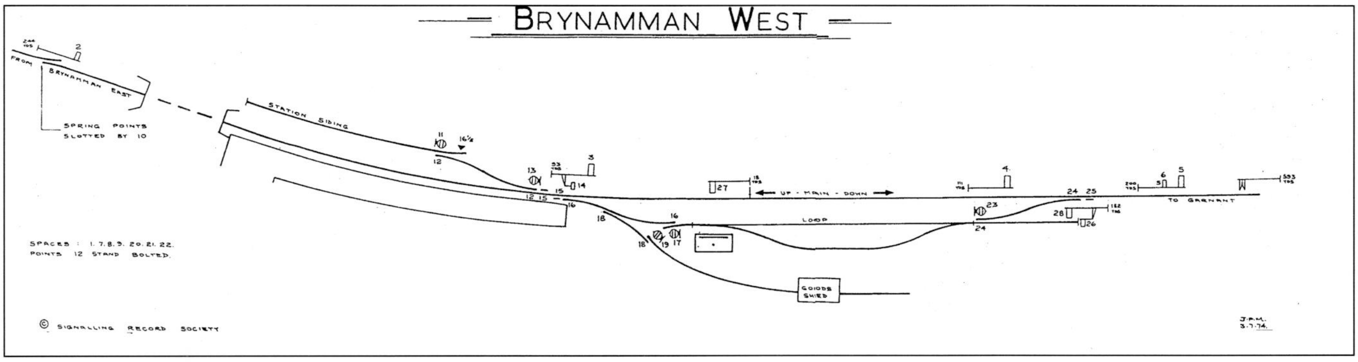

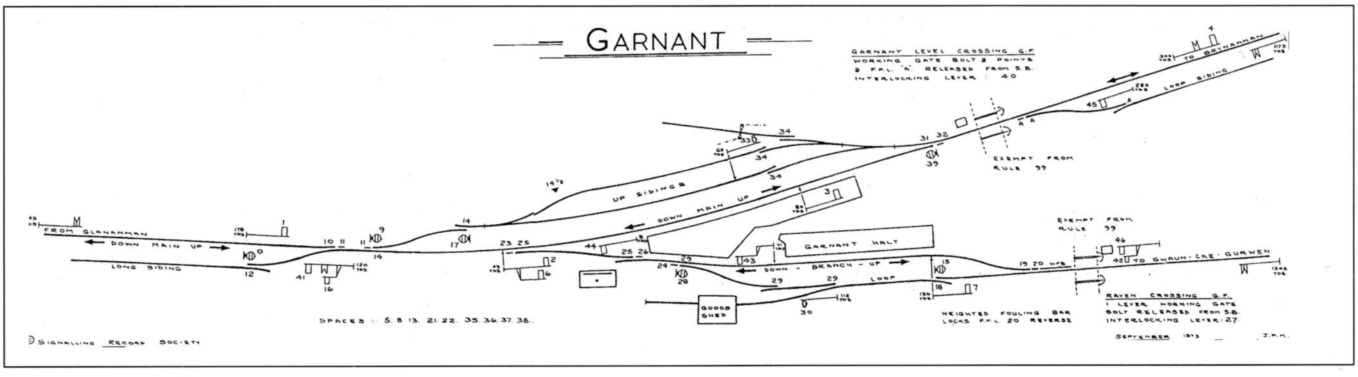

Garnant. (Courtesy D. T. Davies)

Stations on the Brynamman line

Cross Inn (Became Ammanford on 1 July 1883.) Opened 1840 to freight and passengers. Passenger traffic ceased on 18 August 1958.

Ammanford Colliery Halt Opened to freight 1 May 1905. Closed 18 August 1958.

Cross Keys (Became Glanamman on 1 December 1884.) Opened to freight 1840. Closed to passengers on 18 August 1958 and goods traffic ceased on 30 January 1965.

Cwmamman (First Garnant station.) Opened 1840. Goods depot closed on 18 August 1958 but the station was replaced by a new building slightly east of the orginal in 1907 when the GWR opened the new line to Gwaun-cae-Gurwen.

Brynamman (Became Brynamman West in January 1950 – Midland Railway Bryamman station had suffix 'East' added.) Opened June 1842 for freight and passengers. Closed to passengers on 18 August 1958 and to goods on 28 September 1964.

After the GWR opened the new line the stations to Gwaun-cae-Gurwen were:

Garnant Halt
Gors-y-Garnant Halt
Red Lion Crossing Halt
Gwaun-cae-Gurwen station

All the above were opened on 1 January 1908. Towards the end of the First World War they were closed from 2 April 1917 and reopened on 1 June 1920. Four years later, in 1926, they closed completely. A section of 6¾ miles between Pantyffynnon and Gwann-cae-Gurwen Colliery remains open for small amounts of freight.

Carmarthen Branch LRDC/Swansea & Carmarthen Railways/Central Wales & Carmarthen Junction Railway/LNWR/LMSR

The 13½-mile long Carmarthen branch was opened for freight by the Llanelly company, westwards from Llandilo Junction (Carmarthen Valley Junction) ½-mile south of Llandilo station, on 14 November 1864. Passenger services commenced on 1 June 1865. This involved an agreement with the Carmarthen & Cardigan Railway to run over its metals between Abergwili Junction and Carmarthen Town. Additional narrow gauge rail had been installed on the latter as far as its junction with the South Wales Railway.

The standard gauge Pembroke & Tenby Railway ran eastwards as far as Whitland from 1866 from which point the South Wales Railway operated broad gauge. In order to gain access to the Central Wales Line via Abergwili Junction the Pembroke & Tenby sought powers to construct a standard gauge line from Whitland on a different route looping northwards. However, this proved to be unnecessary as the GWR, having amalgamated with the South Wales Railway in 1863, converted the latter's 'up' line to Carmarthen to standard gauge, and a connection between the Carmarthen & Cardigan Railway (by then mixed gauge) and the Llanelly company's line was made via a short spur.

As explained in Chapter 3, 'Construction and Difficulties', the original Swansea and Carmarthen Lines Undertakings were financially independent of the Llanelly company and, having to bear the costs of updating requirements as outlined in 1868 by G. P. Neele (LNWR's

Llandeilo, 2 August 1962 with the Carmarthen branch on the right. (Courtesy John Horsley Denton)

Carmarthen new station – opened 1902, looking towards Llandeilo and Aberystwyth.
(HMRS/G. M. Perkins collection)

Superintendent of Line), out of its own funds, the impoverished Carmarthen Lines Undertaking went into receivership in February 1871.

Meanwhile, the situation of the Llanelly company, to whom fell the responsibility of providing locomotives, was not helped by the fact that one goods locomotive, 78 wagons and a van had to be returned to the Mid Wales Railway, the latter having been worked on the line by the then bankrupt contractors.

A clause in the Llanelly company's 1868 lease with the LNWR, in which the latter had, in addition to other sections, acquired running rights over the Carmarthen branch, was contested by the Llanelly company. The result was that in 1871 the House of Lords ruled that the Carmarthen branch – together with the section from Swansea Victoria to Pontarddulais – should constitute a separate company, even though there was a 12-mile distance between them (Pontarddulais to Llandilo Bridge) owned by the Llanelly company. The new company, which included the Llanmorlais branch, was known as the Swansea & Carmarthen Railways.

The LNWR obtained permission to work the Carmarthen branch from 1 July 1871 but as the newly formed Swansea & Carmarthen Railways possessed neither locomotives nor rolling stock, the Llanelly company worked local traffic until 1872/3 (and had, in fact, been using LNWR stock since December 1870). In the meantime, the LNWR had entered into an agreement to permit the working of its own trains over the line as from 1 February 1872 and Llanelly company trains ceased to appear.

After the LNWR had bought the Llanmorlais branch in 1873, the remaining section of the Swansea & Carmarthen was more suitably renamed the Central Wales & Carmarthen Junction Railway, until the LNWR finally acquired it outright on 1 July 1891.

There was a lot of jostling for power between the Llanelly company, which controlled the section from Llandeilo station to Llandeilo Junction, and the Central Wales & Carmarthen

Nantgaredig station in May 1958. (David Lawrence, Hugh Davies collection)

Llandilo station with Webb 2-4-2T No. 465 and the Carmarthen branch train in the bay. (HMRS/G. M. Perkins collection)

Junction Railway whose line to Carmarthen branched from the latter point, but the puppeteers were really the GWR and LNWR. The GWR, with its strong foothold in West Wales and, having changed to standard gauge in 1872, vied with the LNWR (Pembroke to Euston) by offering through coaches (Pembroke Dock to Paddington).

The pettiness of the disputes is illustrated by timetables in the early 1880s which stated that, 'Passengers will not be booked from Llandeilo to the Carmarthen line, or from Carmarthen, Abergwili, Nantgaredig, Llanarthy, Golden Grove or Llandeilo Bridge to Llandeilo'. Among the various agreements reached in 1889 – which included some pooling receipts – was one that stated that neither of the companies should acquire a sole interest in the Central Wales & Carmarthen Junction Railway. Why, in view of this, the LNWR did in fact do so in 1891, is not clear.

For a while, there were some through workings from Whitland by the GWR as a result of its connection with the Pembroke & Tenby Railway's interests. In contrast to its running and ownership, the line itself was peacefully situated and ran along the wide and picturesque Twyi Valley with very pleasant pastoral scenery. The River Twyi was traversed near Llanarthney by a 168ft lattice girder bridge, the River Cothi by one of 125ft span near Nantgaredig, and a third

[34 VICT.] *The Swansea and Carmarthen Railways Act*, 1871. [Ch. xlvi.]

CHAP. xlvi.

An Act to vest the Swansea and Carmarthen Lines Undertakings of the Llanelly Railway and Dock Company in a new Company, and to confer powers upon both the said Companies with reference to their respective undertakings; and for other purposes. [16th June 1871.] A.D. 1871.

WHEREAS by "The Llanelly Railway (New Lines) Act, 1861," (in this Act called "the Act of 1861,") the Llanelly Railway and Dock Company (in this Act called "the Llanelly Company") were authorised to make a railway from their railway in the parish of Llandilo Talibont to the lands of the Swansea Harbour Trustees in the parish of Swansea in the county of Glamorgan, with a branch therefrom in the parish of Loughor in the same county, which railway and branch were in the said Act referred to as "the Swansea lines," and to make another railway from their railway in the parish of Llandilofawr to the Carmarthen and Cardigan Railway in the parish of Saint Peter's in the county and borough of Carmarthen, which last-mentioned railway is in the said Act referred to as "the Carmarthen line," and by the same Act the whole undertaking of the Llanelly Company was divided into three separate undertakings, whereof the Swansea lines undertaking comprised the Swansea lines, and the lands, works, and property from time to time vested in the Llanelly Company by or under the Act for the purposes of the Swansea lines, and the Carmarthen line undertaking comprised the Carmarthen line, and the lands, works, and property from time to time vested in the Llanelly Company by or under the Act for the purposes of the Carmarthen line: 24 & 25 Vict. c. ccxvii.

And whereas by the Act of 1861 the Llanelly Company's capital was divided into three separate capitals, whereof the capital with respect to the Swansea lines undertaking, therein called "the

[*Local.–46.*] A 1

Extract from Act 16 June 1871. Powers granted to LRDC to build Carmarthen branch.

[36 & 37 VICT.] *The Swansea and Carmarthen and London and North-western Railway Act*, 1873. [Ch. cxciii.]

CHAPTER cxciii.

An Act for the transfer of the Swansea Lines Undertaking of the Swansea and Carmarthen Railways Company to the London and North-western Railway Company, and for authorising that Company to raise moneys; and for other purposes. [21st July 1873.] A.D. 1873.

WHEREAS by "The Swansea and Carmarthen Railways Act, 1871," the Swansea Lines undertaking and the Carmarthen Lines undertaking of the Llanelly Railway and Dock Company were vested in a company, by that Act incorporated under the name of "The Swansea and Carmarthen Railways Company" (in this Act called "the Company"): 34 & 35 Vict. c. xlvi.

And whereas the Company have agreed to sell, and the London and North-western Railway Company (in this Act called "the North-western Company") have agreed to purchase at or for the sum of three hundred and ten thousand pounds so much of the undertaking of the Company as it now exists as is situate between and inclusive of Pontardulais and Swansea, together with the Penclawdd branch and the Gower Road branch respectively, including all land and property belonging to the Company, and all their rights, powers, and privileges in and south of Pontardulais Station (which is in this Act referred to as the "Swansea Lines Undertaking"), and it is expedient that provision be made with respect to a transfer of the Swansea Lines undertaking of the Company to the London and North-western Company in pursuance of the said agreement:

And whereas it is expedient that the North-western Company be authorised and empowered to raise moneys for the purposes and in the manner by this Act authorised:

And whereas it is expedient that other provisions be made with respect to the Company and the North-western Company:

[*Local.–193.*] A 1

Extract from Act 21 July 1873. Transfer of Swansea & Carmarthen to LNWR.

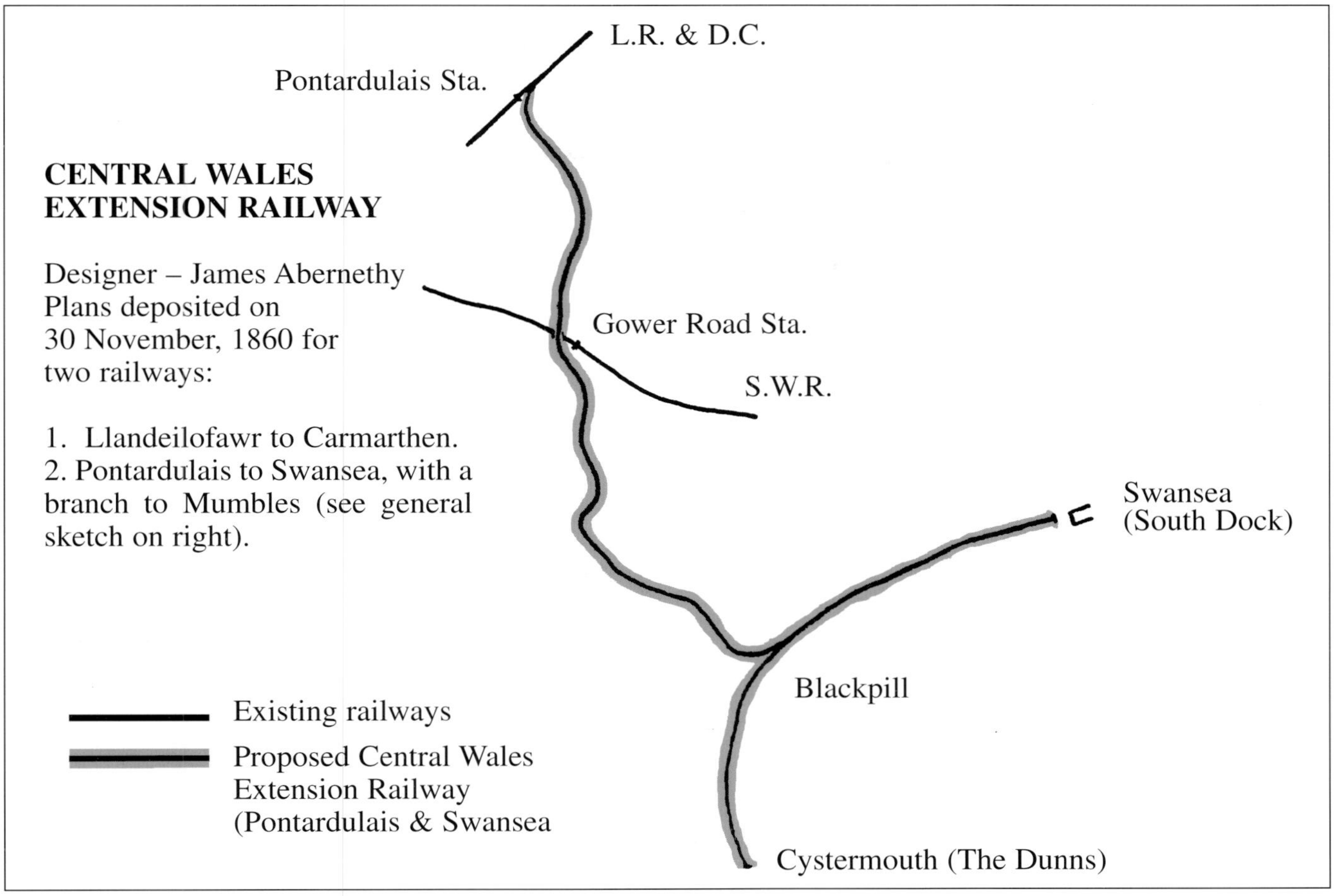

Map of proposed line Llandeilofawr-Carmarthen and Pontarddulais-Swansea. (Nigel Wassell)

bridge was built over the River Gwili west of Abergwili station. There were six viaducts and one 83yd tunnel, the latter situated between Nantgaredig and Abergwili.

Between Carmarthen Valley Junction and Abergwili Junction there were six stations:

Llandilo Bridge This was a block post but had no crossing loop. Passengers and freight. Closed 9 September 1963.

Golden Grove Crossing loop. Passengers and freight. Closed 9 September 1963.

Drysllwyn Passengers only until 13 October 1902 when freight traffic commenced. Became an unstaffed halt during the Second World War and staff rein stated at the end. It became unstaffed at certain times of the day from 4 June 1956 and closed 9 September 1963.

Llanarthney Crossing loop. Passenger and freight. Became an unstaffed halt 4 January 1954 and closed completely 1 June 1959.

Nantgaredig Crossing loop. Passenger and freight. Closed 9 September 1963.

(Whitemill Closed by Llanelly Railway Co. 1 November 1870.)

Abergwili Passenger and freight. Partially unstaffed from 4 June 1956. Closed 9 September 1963.

The LNWR station at Gowerton looking north. The Llanmorlais branch can be seen veering to the left and the main line to Shrewsbury to the right. A speed restriction of 20 mph was imposed as the junction was on a curve and no super elevation was possible. (Courtesy Michael Lewis)

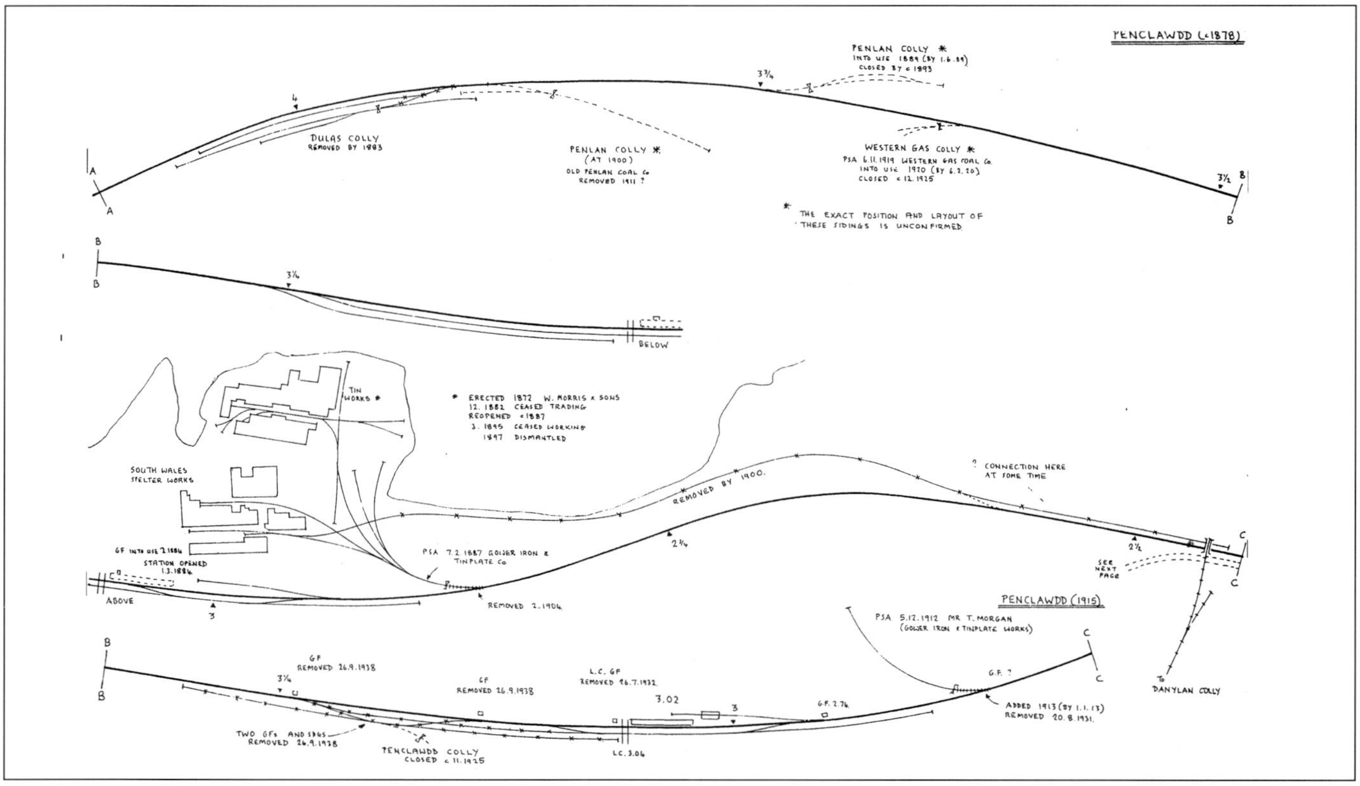

Penclawdd c1878-1915. (R. A. Cooke)

The stations were carefully constructed in local stone and all, with the exception of Llandilo Bridge, were acquired for private occupation after they closed, but that at Abergwili has since been demolished. The journey over this 13-mile single-track route took approximately three quarters of an hour.

Commenting upon the Carmarthen line in *Railway Magazine* of 1912, C. N. Ryan made the following rather sad assessment:

> 'It is at present very unimportant; the trains are very slow, and except on market days, passengers few and far between. However, a few years ago it came in quite useful as an alternative route to Swansea, when during a tremendous storm the Great Western main line was severely damaged by the sea between Ferryside and Kidwelly. The authorities then ran the heavy Fishguard express up to Llandilo and via Pontardulais to Swansea, where it got back on to Great Western Railway metals.'

In spite of being thus dismissed, the line continued for another 50 years and closed completely on 9 September 1963, it being estimated that this would save £21,000 per year.

The Gower

On the 30 November 1860, the Central Wales Extension Railway (with LNWR backing) deposited plans seeking permission to build a line from Pontarddulais to Blackpill, thence to run east to Swansea South Dock and west to Oystermouth, having traversed the South Wales Railway line east of Gower Road station. This was 'contemporaneous with the Llanelly Railway's successful bill which received the Royal Assent on 1 August 1861 but only the latter included provision for a branch into North Gower'.

Llanmorlais Branch LRDC/Swansea & Carmarthen Railways/LNWR/LMSR

This line ran westwards from a junction just north of Gowerton South (then Gower Road) station and was completed by the Llanelly company as far as Penclawdd in January 1866 when it opened for goods. It was originally intended to extend the line to Salthouse Pill where there was a shipping point. However, by the 1860s, the estuary was showing signs of silting up and coal could no longer be shipped out from the collieries. Passenger services to Penclawdd commenced on 14 December 1867 and the line was extended inland and southwards to Llanmorlais, this latter section being opened for freight and passengers in 1877. The distance from Gowerton to Llanmorlais was 4 miles 60 chains but the track extended to the 5-mile post.

After the House of Lords' ruling, which stipulated that the Llanmorlais line be part of the Swansea & Carmarthen Railways (see the **Carmarthen Branch**), the LNWR bought the Llanelly company's branch in 1873 for the sum of £310,000 and thus acquired its line into the Gower.

The Llanmorlais branch closed to passengers on 5 January 1931 and freight ceased on 2 September 1957. However, a section of the line was used by passengers during the Second World War, travelling to and from a new Royal Ordnance Department at Crofty. During this period, workers were conveyed in passenger carriages attached to the rear of goods trains.

The track – which remained in use for storage – was lifted in 1960.

The Gower Light Railway

The Central Wales Line would have had another connection with the Gower had the plans of H. F. Stephens (he became Lt Col. Stephens during the First World War) succeeded. This well-known railway entrepeneur envisaged the construction of a Light Railway across the peninsula in 1895.

This was to be narrow gauge and was intended to run over the Swansea & Mumbles Railway's standard gauge track, necessitating a third rail being laid, from Swansea (Rutland Street) through the Clyne Valley as far as Killay where it would have had a connection with the LNWR's section of

The 11.20am Gowerton South to Llanmorlais freight at Penclawdd, August 1957.
(Hugh Davies)

Llanmorlais station in August 1957.
(Hugh Davies)

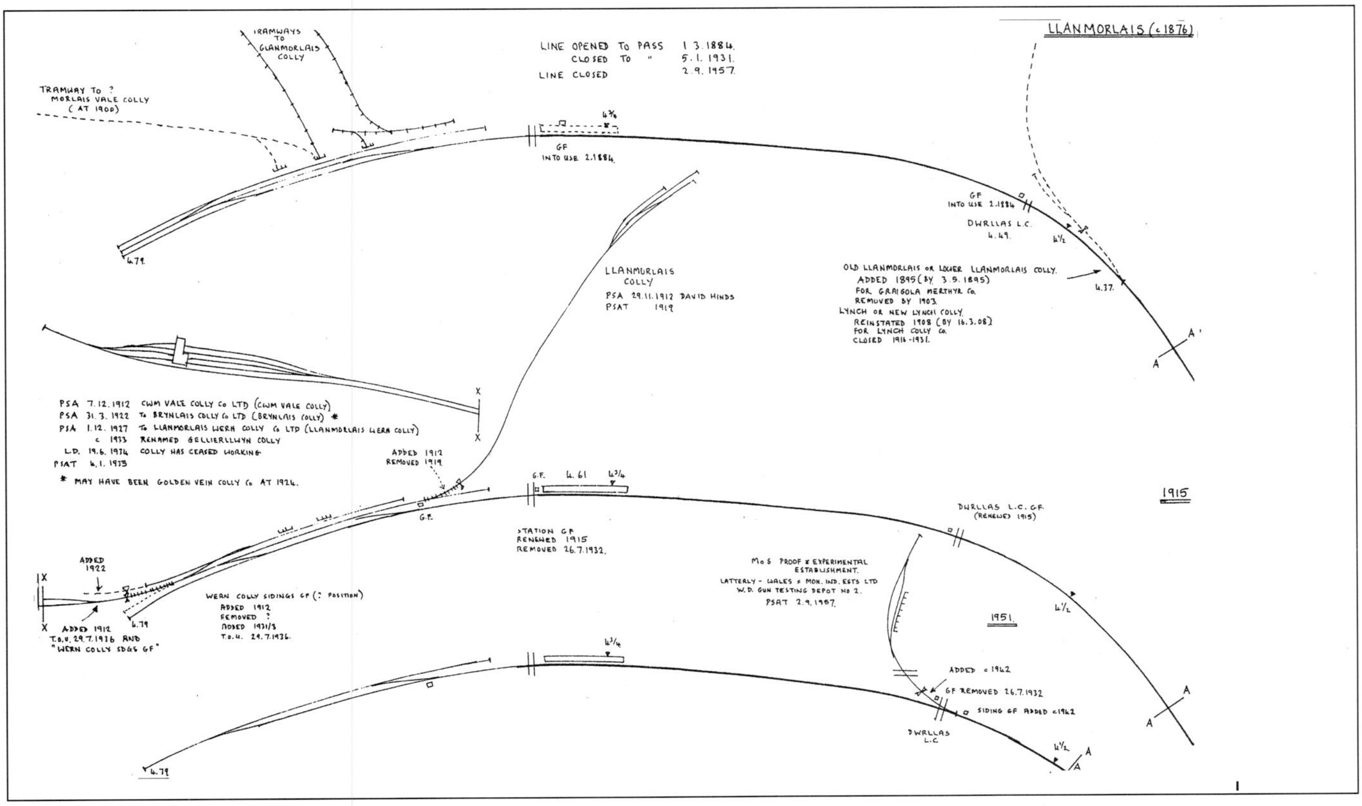

Llanmorlais c1876-1951. (R. A. Cooke)

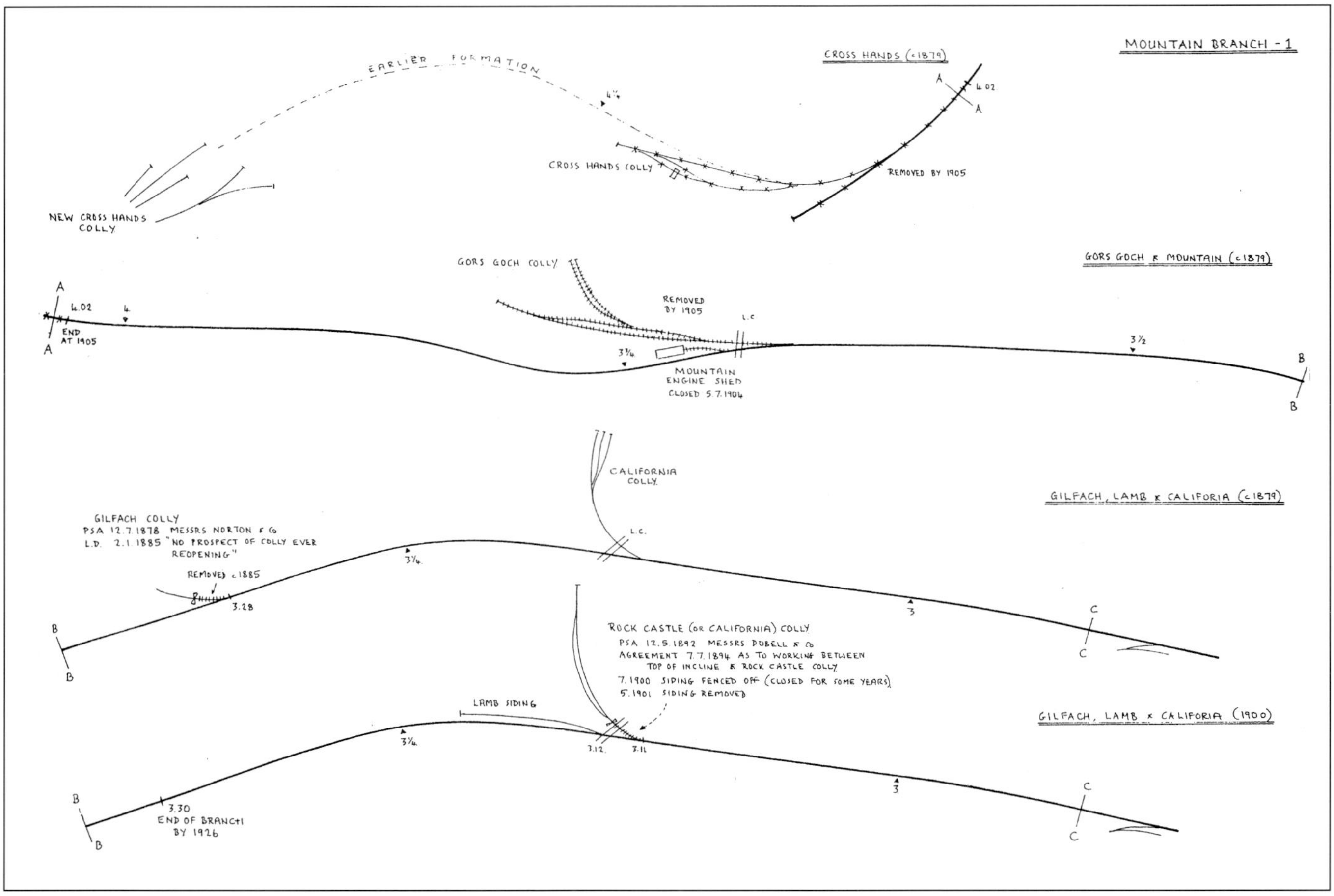

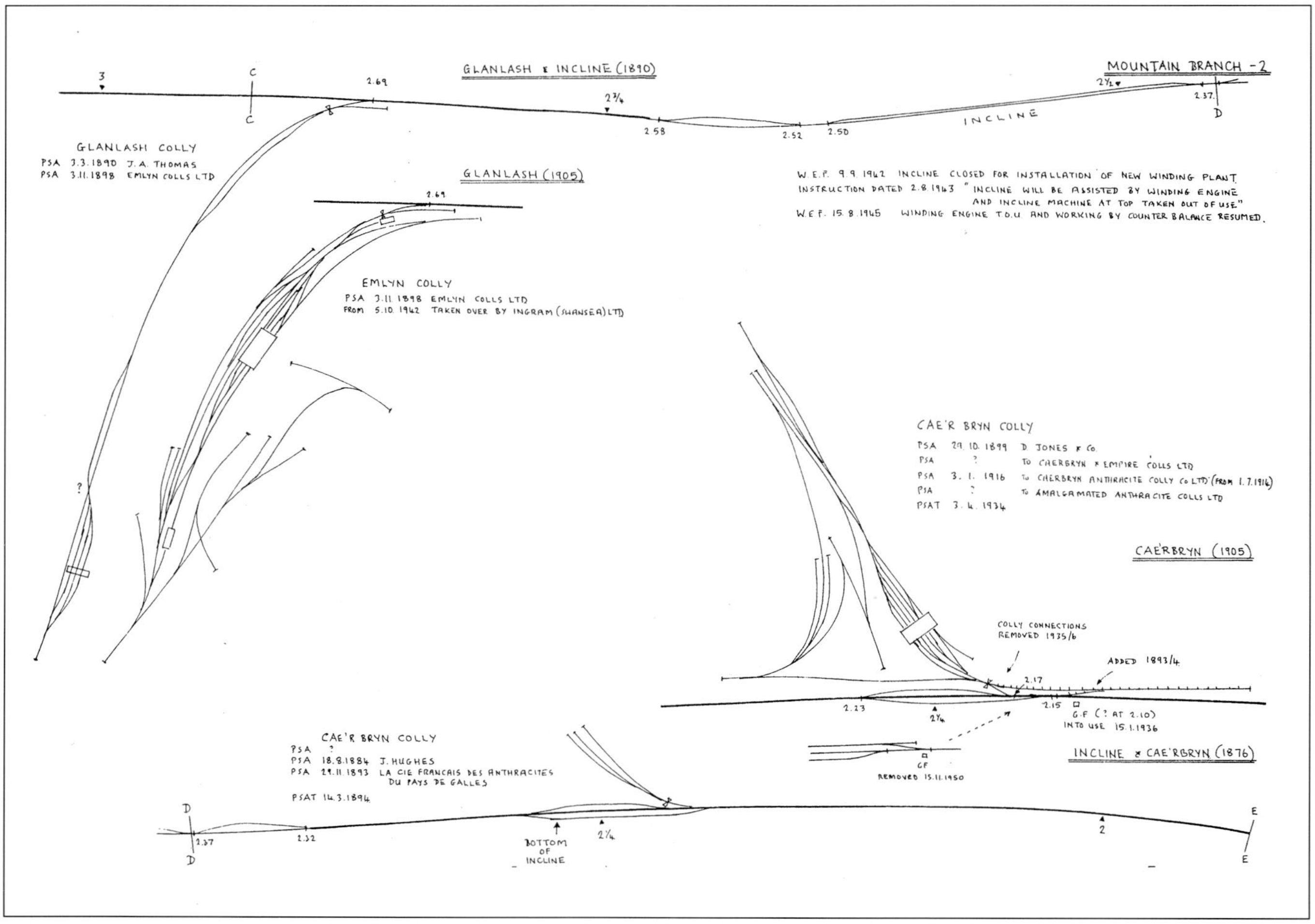

Mountain branch. (R. A. Cooke)

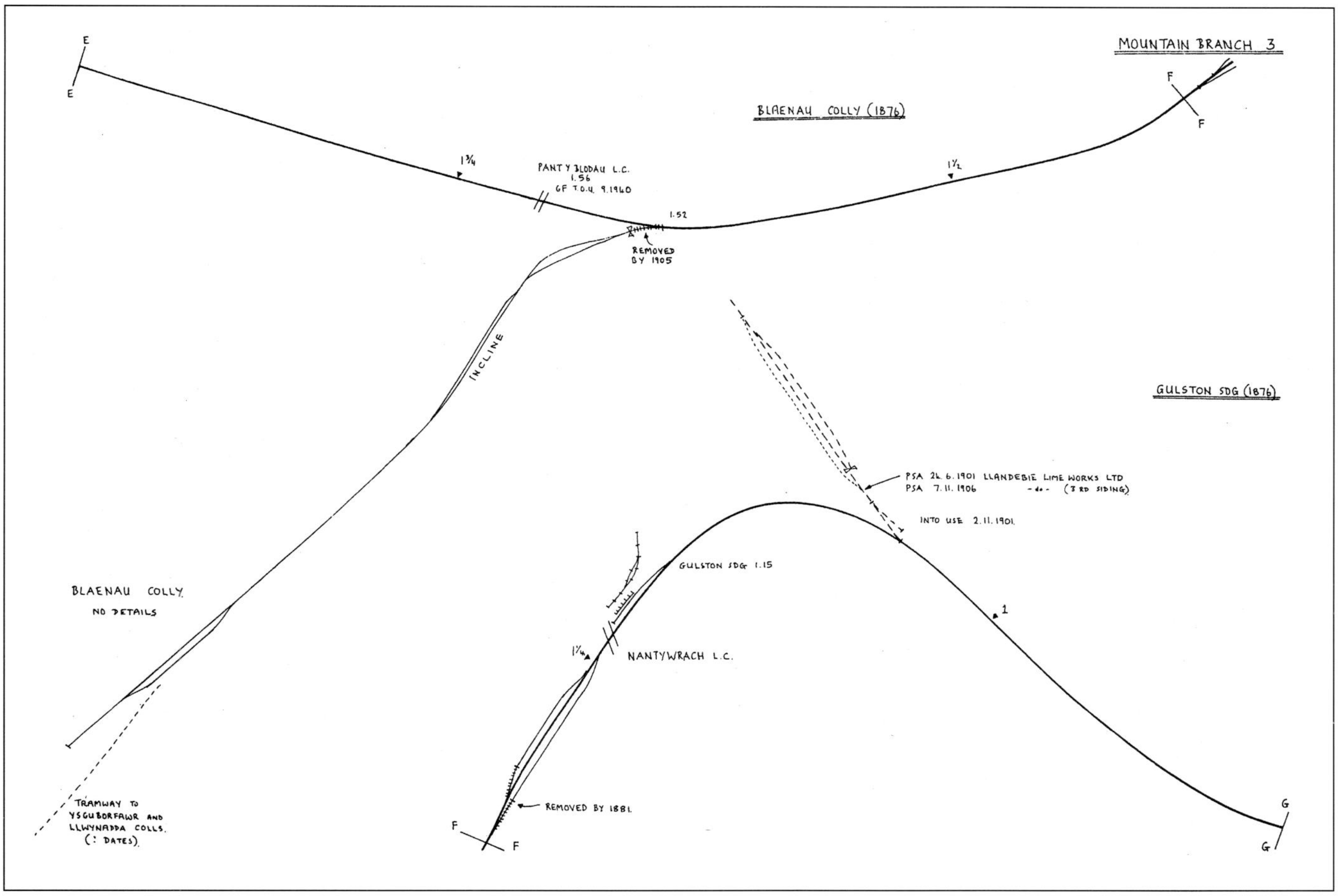
MOUNTAIN BRANCH 3
BLAENAU COLLY (1876)
GULSTON SDG (1876)
PANT Y BLODAU L.C.
1.56
GF T.O.U. 9.1960
1.52
REMOVED BY 1905
INCLINE
PSA 26.6.1901 LLANDEBIE LIME WORKS LTD
PSA 7.11.1906 -do- (3RD SIDING)
INTO USE 2.11.1901.
GULSTON SDG 1.15
NANTYWRACH L.C.
REMOVED BY 1881
BLAENAU COLLY
NO DETAILS
TRAMWAY TO YSGUBORFAWR AND LLWYNADDA COLLS. (? DATES)

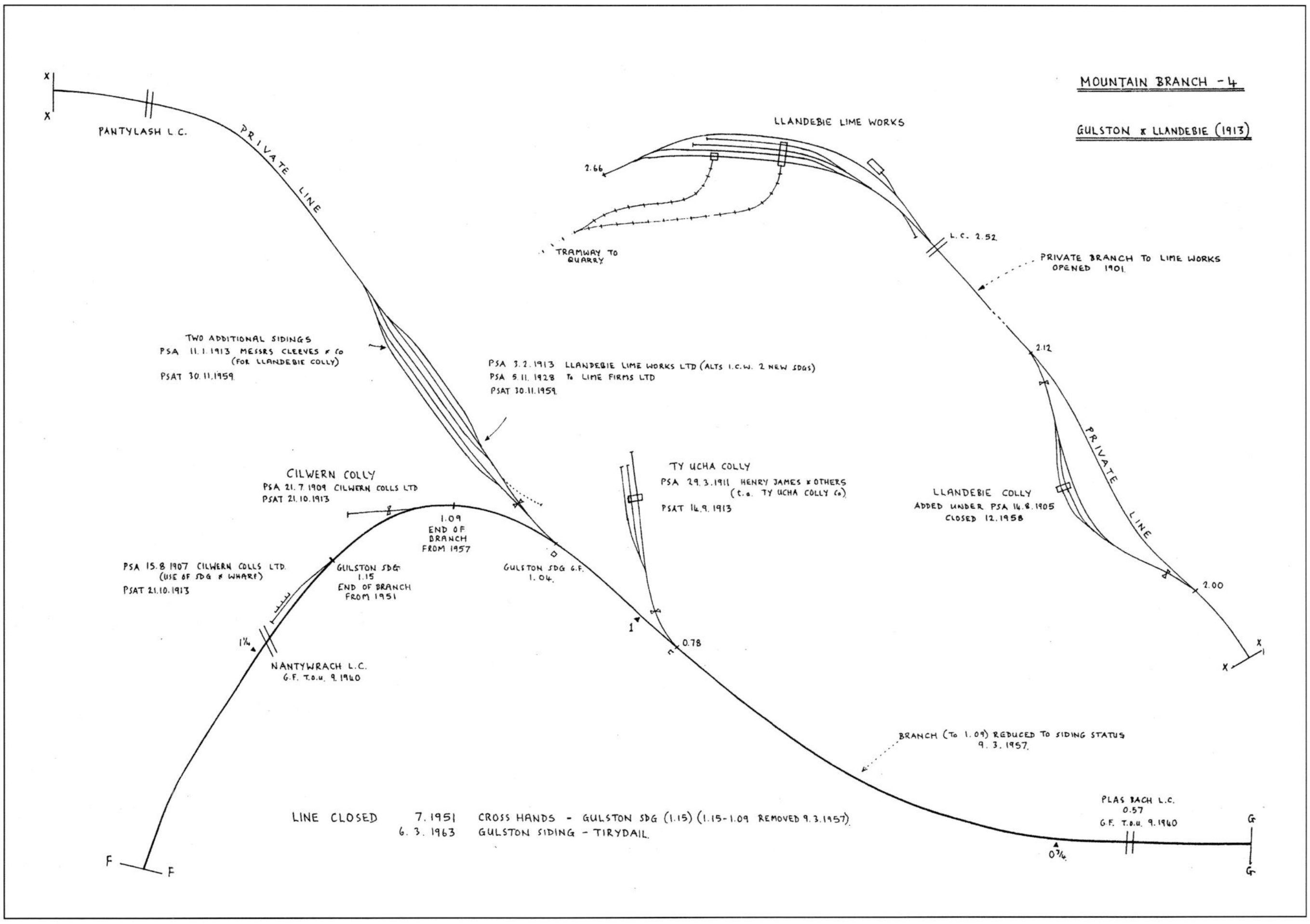
MOUNTAIN BRANCH - 4
GULSTON & LLANDEBIE (1913)
LLANDEBIE LIME WORKS
PANTYLASH L.C.
PRIVATE LINE
2.66
TRAMWAY TO QUARRY
L.C. 2.52
PRIVATE BRANCH TO LIME WORKS OPENED 1901
2.12
TWO ADDITIONAL SIDINGS
PSA 11.1.1913 MESSRS CLEEVES & CO (FOR LLANDEBIE COLLY)
PSAT 30.11.1959
PSA 3.2.1913 LLANDEBIE LIME WORKS LTD (ALTS L.C.W. 2 NEW SDGS)
PSA 5.11.1928 To LIME FIRMS LTD
PSAT 30.11.1959
CILWERN COLLY
PSA 21.7.1909 CILWERN COLLS LTD
PSAT 21.10.1913
TY UCHA COLLY
PSA 29.3.1911 HENRY JAMES & OTHERS (t.o. TY UCHA COLLY Co)
PSAT 16.9.1913
LLANDEBIE COLLY
ADDED UNDER PSA 16.8.1905
CLOSED 12.1958
1.09
END OF BRANCH FROM 1957
PSA 15.8.1907 CILWERN COLLS LTD. (USE OF SDG & WHARF)
PSAT 21.10.1913
GULSTON SDG 1.15 END OF BRANCH FROM 1951
GULSTON SDG G.F. 1.04
2.00
0.78
NANTYWRACH L.C.
G.F. T.O.U. 9.1960
BRANCH (To 1.09) REDUCED TO SIDING STATUS 9.3.1957.
LINE CLOSED 7.1951 CROSS HANDS - GULSTON SDG (1.15) (1.15-1.09 REMOVED 9.3.1957).
6.3.1963 GULSTON SIDING - TIRYDAIL.
PLAS BACH L.C.
0.57
G.F. T.O.U. 9.1960

Mountain branch – continued. (R. A. Cooke)

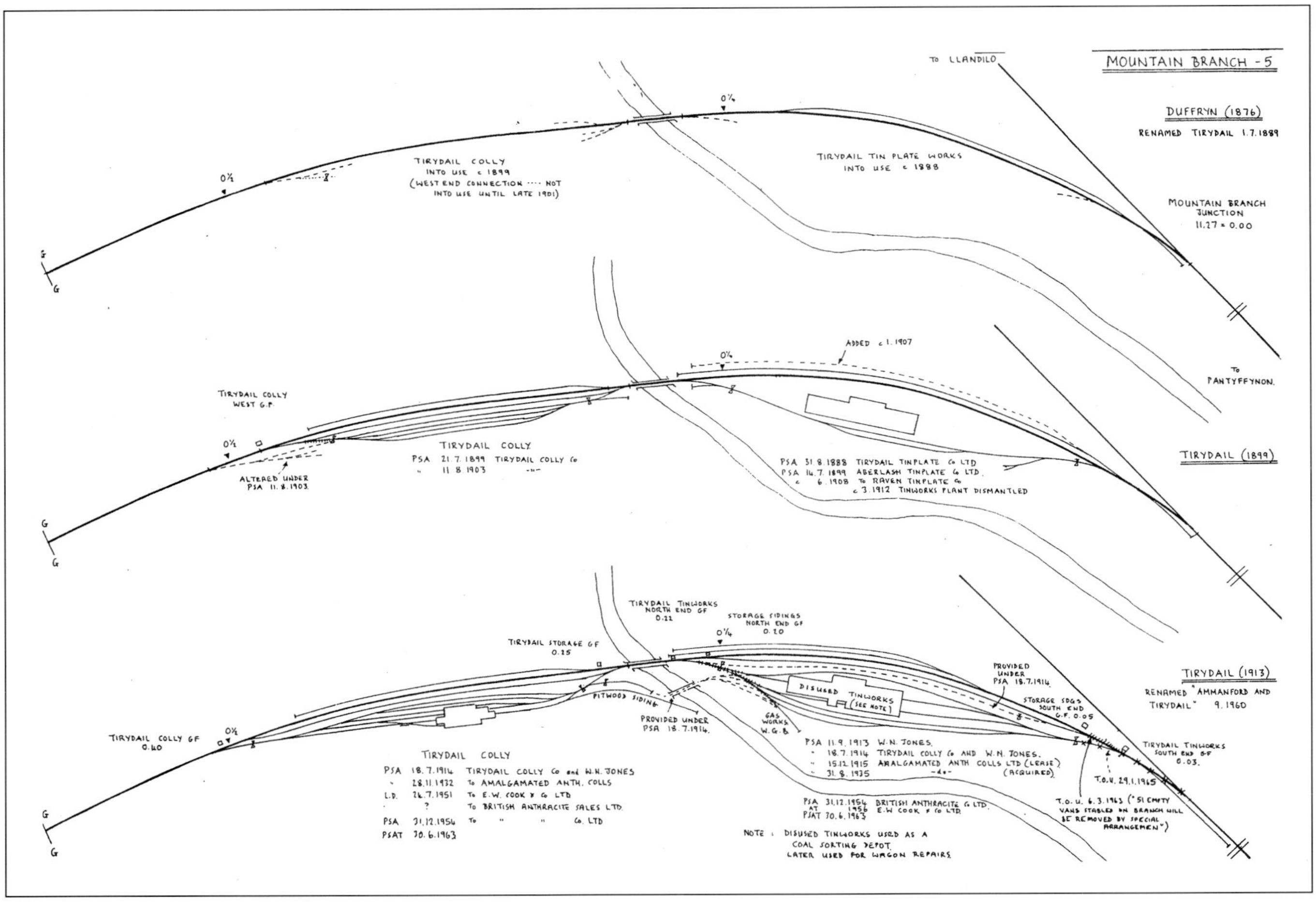

Mountain branch – continued. (R. A. Cooke)

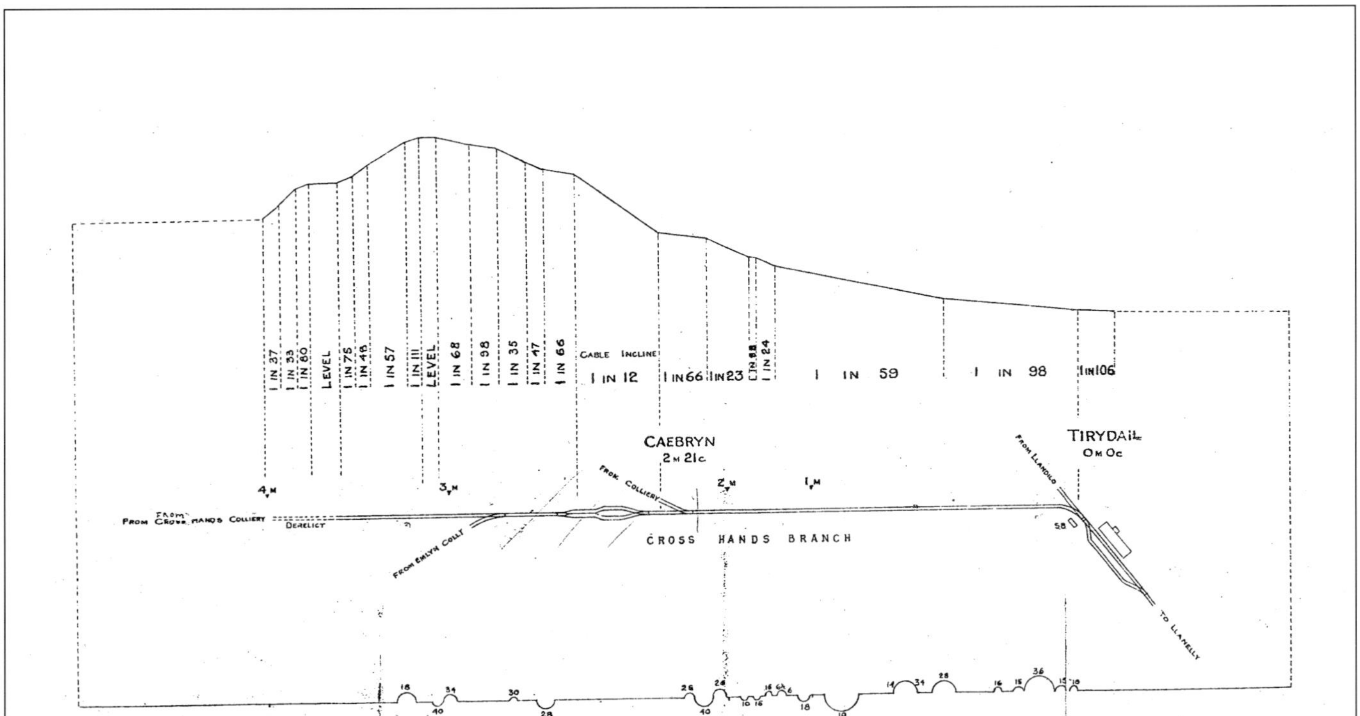

Gradient – Cross Hands branch.

the Central Wales Line from Pontarddulais to Swansea Victoria. From Killay, the branch would have continued via Three Crosses, Cilibion, Frog Moor, Knelston, Port Eynon and – originally – on to Worm's Head. The following year, the plan was altered and the whole line was to be standard gauge running only as far as Port Eynon. Approval was received in 1898 and again in 1902 but construction was unable to proceed due to lack of financial support.

A third attempt in 1912 nearly succeeded, surveys having been carried out and contracts allocated, but the commencement of the First World War put paid to the scheme and, although after the cessation of hostilities, efforts to renew it continued until 1924, the 'Swansea & Worm's Head Railway' was not to be.

Mountain Branch LRDC/GWR

On 6 May 1841, the Llanelly company opened a four-mile line westward from a junction north of Duffryn (later Tirydail and then Ammanford and Tirydail, and now Ammanford) over Mynydd Mawr to Cross Hands. It was known as the Mountain branch and for good reason.

At least two long inclines were rope worked. The one at Cross Hands had a gradient of 1 in 12 for 24 chains and there was a private branch (although worked by Llanelly company men) at Blaenau, 46 chains beyond Gulston Junction, which is also thought to have been rope worked.

Speed limits on the Mountain branch did not exceed 15mph and locomotives hauled out towards Tirydail and banked empty on the return. The LNWR originally had running powers to Cross Hands but these were not exercised and in 1889 the branch was taken over by the GWR when it bought out the Llanelly company.

Llandybie Lime Works branch – not to be confused with the Limestone branch from the CWL proper near Cilyrychen – ran north-westwards from Gulston Junction.

There was also a line which ran to Cross Hands from Llanelly via Cynheidre and Tumble, owned by the Llanelly & Mynydd Mawr Railway (formerly the Carmarthenshire Railway) and according to D. S. M. Barrie in *A Regional History of Railways of Great Britain Volume 12*, the Mountain branch and GWR were 'mutually accessible at their far extremities, through colliery sidings'. This probably refers to the usage, by collieries opened subsequent to the closure of the Cross Hands end of the line, of a stretch of abandoned track still then existing, to convey coal via the Llanelly & Mynydd Mawr Railway.

By the commencement of the Second World War, five paths in each direction per day were provided for coal trains on the Mountain branch. November 1, 1950 saw the closure of the public goods depot at Cross Hands and the line between Cross Hands and Gulston Sidings closed in July of the following year but the Gulston Sidings to Tirydail section remained open until 6 March 1963.

Limestone Branches

These were opened in the late 1870s from the Central Wales Line south of Cilyrychen Crossing, eastwards to Pistill (or Pystill) Works and westwards to Pentregwenlais and were privately owned. Pentregwenlais had its own engine, a saddle tank *G. S. Gulston* named after the Gulston family of Llandybie who owned much of the land, including the Cylyrychen Quarries. The 'Limestone train' ran empty from Pantyffynnon to the quarry every day and returned down the line transporting lime to Port Talbot.

Pistill closed in 1953 but Pentregwenlais remained in operation until 1969. The Cilyrychen site is now owned by Alfred McAlpine & Co. and a diesel oil tank stands on top of the impressive old kilns which can be seen from the Central Wales Line. Although sealed up, they are interesting and easily accessible.

5

Freight

At the southern end of the line, the Llanelly Railroad & Dock Company was the first to achieve its goal of transporting freight. The benefits to be derived from gaining rail access to Llandilo had been recognised well before 1835, this being the year in which the LRDC applied for permission to build the line. At this time, the LRDC was already transporting coal from a mine at Gelly Gille Farm to the docks via what was later to be known as the Dafen branch. The route to Gelly Gille – which was horse-drawn – opened in 1833 and was approximately two miles in length.

In 1839, it was reported that anthracite consumption in Llandilo and nearby area was 750 tons daily which, at that time, was conveyed by road – a situation which was changed when the line opened from Duffryn to Llandilo in 1857.

The interest of the Llanelly company lay in transportation between the Llandovery area and southwards to the docks from which its company could ship cargo to Europe and to other parts of the world. This region was rich in anthracite, bituminous coal, iron ore, lead, slate, copper and limestone and from Llanelly New Dock there were direct lines to tinplateworks, brickworks, foundries, chemical works and copper works. There was also a connection with the South Wales Railway (later GWR) Llanelly to Paddington line at Llandilo Crossing (now Llandeilo Junction), which the Llanelly company's line traversed en route to Llandilo.

From 1840 onwards, branch lines feeding the CWL spread over the mining areas in the south to such an extent that by 1871, collieries and other works served by the Llanelly company alone amounted to approximately one hundred with nearly 200 wagons belonging to its subsidiary wagon company working traffic on its lines.

The opening of the section to Cwmamman (later known as Garnant), eastwards from Pantyffynnon in 1840 and its subsequent extensions to Brynamman and Gwaun-cae-Gurwen, meant that a very considerable quantity of Amman Valley anthracite could be conveyed to Llanelly docks by rail. In 1922 the line from Gwaun-cae-Gurwen (known as GCG) was extended to Duke Colliery. Much later, by the 1960s there was considerable working from the National Coal Board Abernant Colliery on this branch where a sinking to a depth of nearly 2,700ft was completed in 1958.

The Llanelly company opened a line westwards from Gower Road and a freight service to Penclawdd commenced in 1857. This extended to Llanmorlais in 1867 and served various collieries, copper and tin works including the large Elba Steel Works.

With the opening of the Carmarthen branch in 1864, goods and mineral traffic from the Llanelly company's line reached West Wales. At first, access was only to Pembroke Dock due to the remaining West Wales lines being broad gauge. By 1870 conversion of one line (Pembroke & Tenby Railway) to 'narrow' gauge had been undertaken to allow through services to and from the Central Wales Line.

By the 1870s the GWR had opened a line westwards from a junction north of Duffryn Lodge (Tirydail) to Cross Hands Colliery. This branch included tortuous rope-hauled lines with some sections 1 in 12 and was the aptly named 'Mountain Branch'.

Limestone branches

There was substantial mining development and steel and tin plate works in the Grovesend and Gorseinon area, south of Pontarddulais on the Llanelly company's section to Swansea Victoria, which was taken over by LNWR in 1873. These included Mardy Tin Plate works, Bryngwyn Steelworks and Grovesend and Bryn Lliw collieries. The freight on the Central Wales Line was mostly industrial but agricultural traffic was also carried, particularly from the Vale of Towy northwards. There were milk sidings at Llangadog and Ffairfach and many stations had cattle pens. Timber was transported from Bucknell.

In the early days, drovers who had already made an arduous journey over rough terrain were able to make for the railheads which meant a considerable decrease in costs for the dealers, reducing expenses in drovers wages, lodgings, refreshments, feeding and shoeing of livestock and payment of tolls. Local farmers also benefited from lime deliveries (although those living near quarries used to carry it in their

A farm removal at Llanrwda on 2 October 1934.
(Welsh Industrial & Maritime Museum)

Knucklas station in the 1920s. The station master, right, poses with some men in front of poultry crates.

(Courtesy Judith Dyke)

own horses and carts) but these declined after a while when use of artificial fertilizers was found to be cheaper.

Fish trains from Swansea South Dock made their way northwards picking up extra freight from the Carmarthen branch – including additional fish vans from Milford Haven – and a 'Beer train' ran down the line overnight from Burton-on-Trent to Swansea, where barrels and crates were stored under the brick arches of the viaduct behind Victoria station. Meat was conveyed to London and fruit to Liverpool and other cities. A warehouse for Fyffe's Bananas was situated next to Swansea Victoria station.

In the early days there were great hopes of rich pickings from freight traffic. An opinion expressed in an article in the *Illustrated London News* in 1865 was that if Milford Haven became a major port for American trade 'a large amount of traffic would be obtained'. The main objective of the LNWR, however, was through access to Swansea. Interest was not solely in export: the transport of minerals from South Wales to the North of England had been a major factor in the considerable and successful initiative of the LNWR in taking control of the line. There was intense rivalry with the GWR which had a route northwards via Cardiff and with the Midland Railway via Brecon and Hereford.

Before the Second World War 6,000 tons of anthracite per week were conveyed from South Wales to the North of England while scrap metal went in the opposite direction to the South Wales steelworks. For some time, the movement of coal for home consumption and for export was immense.

In the early 1920s, from the GWR territory of the Amman Valley, the total weight of goods and mineral traffic – of which the latter formed the largest proportion – amounted to about two million tons per year. Some 20 years later, by the commencement of the Second World War, although coal traffic from Garnant, Brynamman and Gwaun-cae-Gurwen had risen in the interim, the overall annual total of goods and mineral traffic from other sources had fallen by nearly a million tons. However, there were still a number of heavy freights on the CWL in 1950. Classes for long distance goods were usually D (fully vacuum fitted express freight), E (express freight – partly vacuum fitted) and H (unfitted freight).

A class E freight left Swansea Eastern Depot for Shrewsbury (Crewe Bank) at 12.30am, a class H at 1.30am and a class D at 2.40am, both for Shrewsbury (Coton Hill). Llandeilo Junction despatched a class D for Stafford at 4.30am arriving early afternoon and at 8.40am a through freight left Swansea Eastern Docks for Harlescot Sidings (Shrewsbury).

There was a 5.15pm 'parcels' from Pontarddulais to Crewe, followed by the 'Fish train' which departed from Swansea Dock at 4.45pm picking up extra fish vans from Milford Haven at Llandeilo Junction and following the 'York Mail' northwards.

A class D to Shrewsbury (Coton Hill) was despatched from Swansea Eastern Depot at 6.45pm, the empty 'Beer Train' stock departed for Burton-on-Trent at 8.45pm and a class E freight left Llandeilo Junction for Crewe at 8pm being scheduled to follow the 'Beer train' empties. A class H and a class D to Shrewsbury departed Swansea at 9.45m (for Coleham) and 11.20pm for Coton Hill.

In the 'down' direction, the 'Beer train' left Burton-on-Trent for Swansea Victoria at 9.15pm preceding the 'York Mail' as far as Llandovery where it was shunted to allow the latter to pass. There followed a class E 'Liverpool Goods' which departed at 1.45am but did not arrive in Swansea until the afternoon. A class D freight departed Shrewsbury (Coleham) at 9.20am and picked up freight from Llandovery onwards including some from a class H which had run down from Craven Arms to Llandovery.

The next freight from Coleham Yard was a class H at 1.35pm and this was followed by the 3.15pm which arrived at Llandeilo Junction at 10.10pm. An overnight class D for Swansea left Coleham at 5.55pm, and a class E departed at 7.40pm.

With the approach of the 1960s, in accordance with national policy regarding freight movement on certain routes, the downward trend began.

Freight traffic on the Llanmorlais line, which had become intermittent but had been re-introduced to serve private sidings to Crofty Royal Ordnance Depot during the war, had already ceased in 1952.

The Mountain branch closed in 1963, and in the spring of that year the marshalling yard at Pontarddulais was taken out of use and Central Wales Line freight was sent through to Llandilo Junction. Coal trains from Abernant went to Pantyffynnon marshalling yard and thence to Margam Yard and Swansea and Barry Docks. Complete closure of the Llandeilo to Carmarthen branch followed on 9 September 1963 and freight traffic ceased between Garnant and Brynamman in December of that year.

On 10 August 1964, in order to reduce running costs and as an alternative to complete closure which had been

(Dorothy Bound)

A goods train at Llandovery yard, looking north in the early 1930s.

narrowly escaped (the passenger services between Swansea Victoria and Pontarddulais had ceased on 13 June 1964), most CWL freight north of Llandovery was withdrawn, much of it redirected via Hereford and Cardiff – a route which could take heavier trains on easier gradients. As a consequence, the signalling system on the Central Wales Line was simplified on 10 August 1964.

However, some local freight services continued to operate. Bucknell remained open for some time, served from Craven Arms, Knighton did not close to local freight until 1 March 1965 and Llandrindod, which was served by Pantyffynnon – as was Llandovery and Llandeilo – remained open to freight until May 1967.

The branch line to Pistyll Limestone Works was removed on 24 May 1953 and by 1969, the Pentregwenlais Limestone branch had closed. After freight from Swansea Victoria ceased in October 1964 the track was singled from Pontarddulais to Gorseinon. The line from Pontarddulais was closed on 22 September 1974 but a new chord line from Grovesend Colliery Loop Junction was reinstated enabling coal traffic to continue.

This served Brynlliw Colliery (which had closed in 1927 but was reopened by the National Coal Board in 1961), and Gorseinon. Production at Brynlliw ceased on 21 July 1983 and

Llandeilo Junction hump yard, looking towards Llanelli on 22 August 1922.
(Welsh Industrial & Maritime Museum)

A southbound goods train banked and piloted ready for the climb to the summit crosses Knucklas Viaduct.
(HMRS/G. M. Perkins collection)

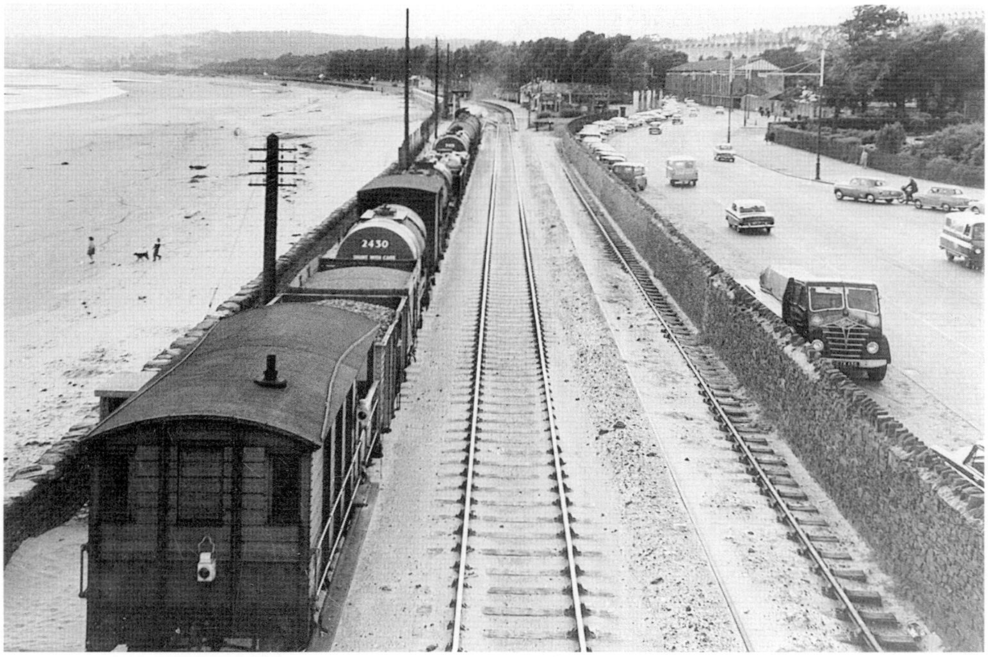

A pre June 1964 northbound goods train on the ex LNWR section, approaching Swansea Bay station, looking south west from Slip Bridge. Since 1960 cars had been parked to the right of wall on the former Mumbles Railway trackbed.
(City of Swansea Archives)

'Warship' No. D602 Bulldog *heads a southbound freight train through Llandrindod in the mid-1960s.*
(Roy Palmer)

The viaduct at Gwaun-cae-Gurwen in September 1994. This was the last section of the Brynamman branch to remain open.
(Rose Coleman)

A 1994 view of the track from Gwaun-cae-Gurwen level crossing, looking towards the mine.
(Rose Coleman)

the last train from Gorseinon Coal Depot left on 25 May 1984. The line from Brynlliw to Gorseinon was severed on 17 December 1984 but gradual clearance of coal from Brynlliw continued via Grovesend Colliery Loop Junction until 1988.

By 1981, the only freight traffic ran south of Llandovery, consisting mainly of incoming coal deliveries and agricultural feed. At this time 35,000 tons of coal per week were still being transported – some, until 1991, from the NCB drift mine at Bettws via Gwaun-cae-Gurwen washeries – for home and overseas markets.

The line to Wernos washery, north of Pantyffynnon, finally succumbed on 23 September 1988. Bettws coal also went up the branch and through the Abernant washery. There now remains only a 6¾-mile section running off the old Brynamman branch to Gwaun-cae-Gurwen Colliery (owned by Powell Duffryn) and this produces very little traffic.

The present position can be summarised as follows:

The line north of Craven Arms is open for both passenger and freight but none of the latter runs via the Central Wales Line.

There is no freight between Craven Arms and Pantyffynnon.

Gwaun-Cae-Gurwen to Pantyffynnon and Hendy Junction to Grovesend Colliery Loop Junction and thence to Port Talbot is freight only, as is Morlais Junction to Grovesend Colliery Loop Junction (although passenger excursions are sometimes operated over the Swansea District Line).

Pantyffynnon to Llanelli is used by both passenger and freight trains.

No freight is carried between Llandeilo Junction and Swansea except on some occasions when the Swansea District Line is closed. However, late Spring 1996 saw a temporary return of freight to the CWL when the main South Wales line closed for repairs to a road bridge. The 1996/97 HOWLTA newsletter mentions a new design of wagon, more adaptable to the current market, and the proposal to use all available lines for freight, 'including the Heart of Wales'.

6

Stations

Swansea Victoria to Builth Road

Swansea Victoria (Llanelly Railway Co./LNWR/LMSR/ BR (WR))

This was opened by the Llanelly company for freight in January 1866 and commencement of passenger services followed on 14 December 1867. By the next year, the first locomotive shed was in operation (this would appear to have been on the site opposite the gas works upon which the later shed was built – (an OS map indicates a turntable, building and sidings on this location in 1878). Paxton Street shed (although it did not officially bear this name until after Nationalisation in 1948) opened on 6 January 1882. By the end of the 19th century there was a large carriage shed and a goods yard which could take over a hundred wagons.

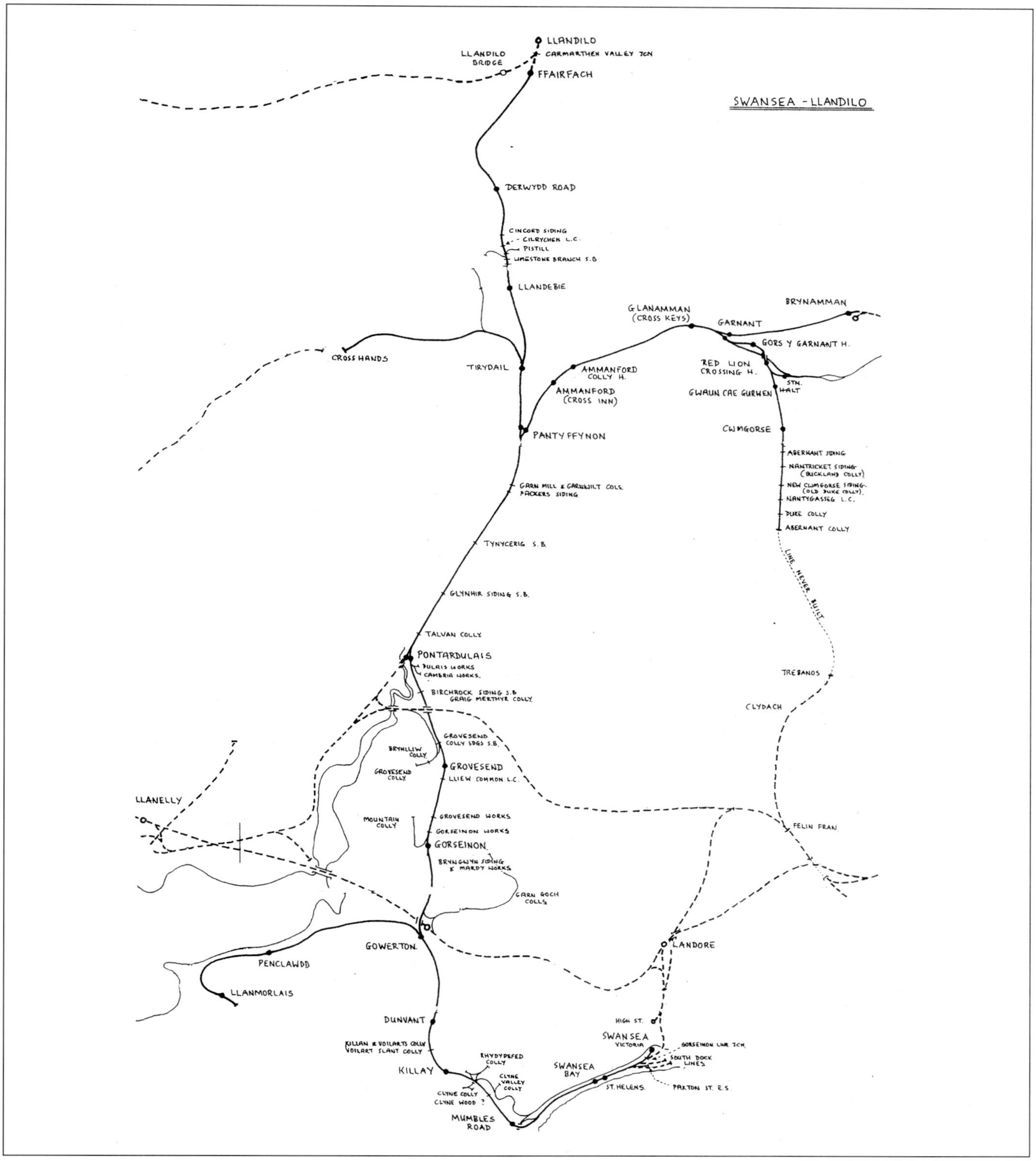

The line from Llandilo to Swansea Victoria. (R. A. Cooke)

Pre Second World War view of Swansea Victoria station from the forecourt.
(HMRS/G. M. Perkins collection)

Swansea Victoria in 1965 with post war damaged roof.
(Courtesy Colin Pritchard)

Swansea Victoria station with glass removed from the canopy in the early 1960s.
(Courtesy Michael Lewis)

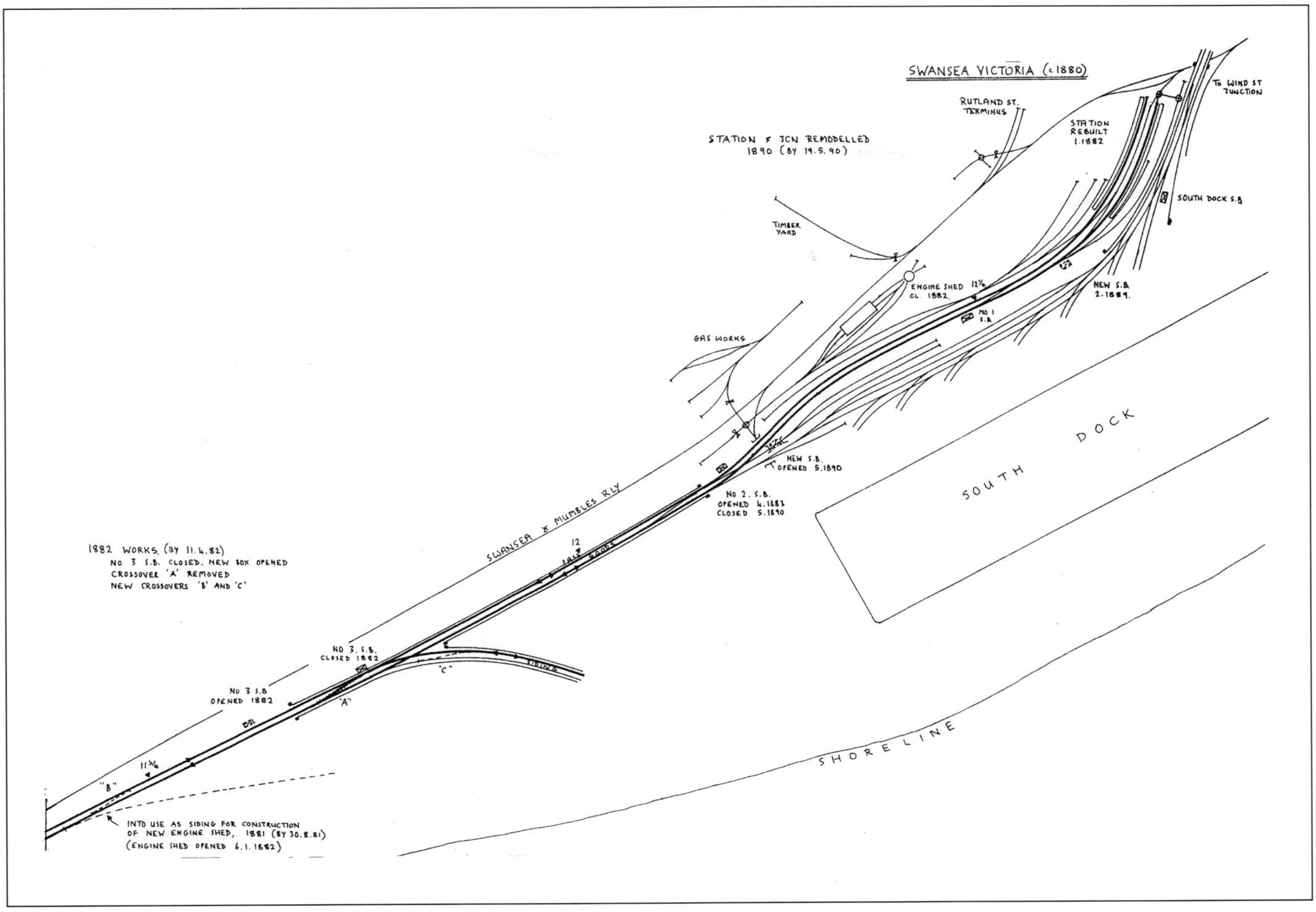

Swansea Victoria c1880. (R. A. Cooke)

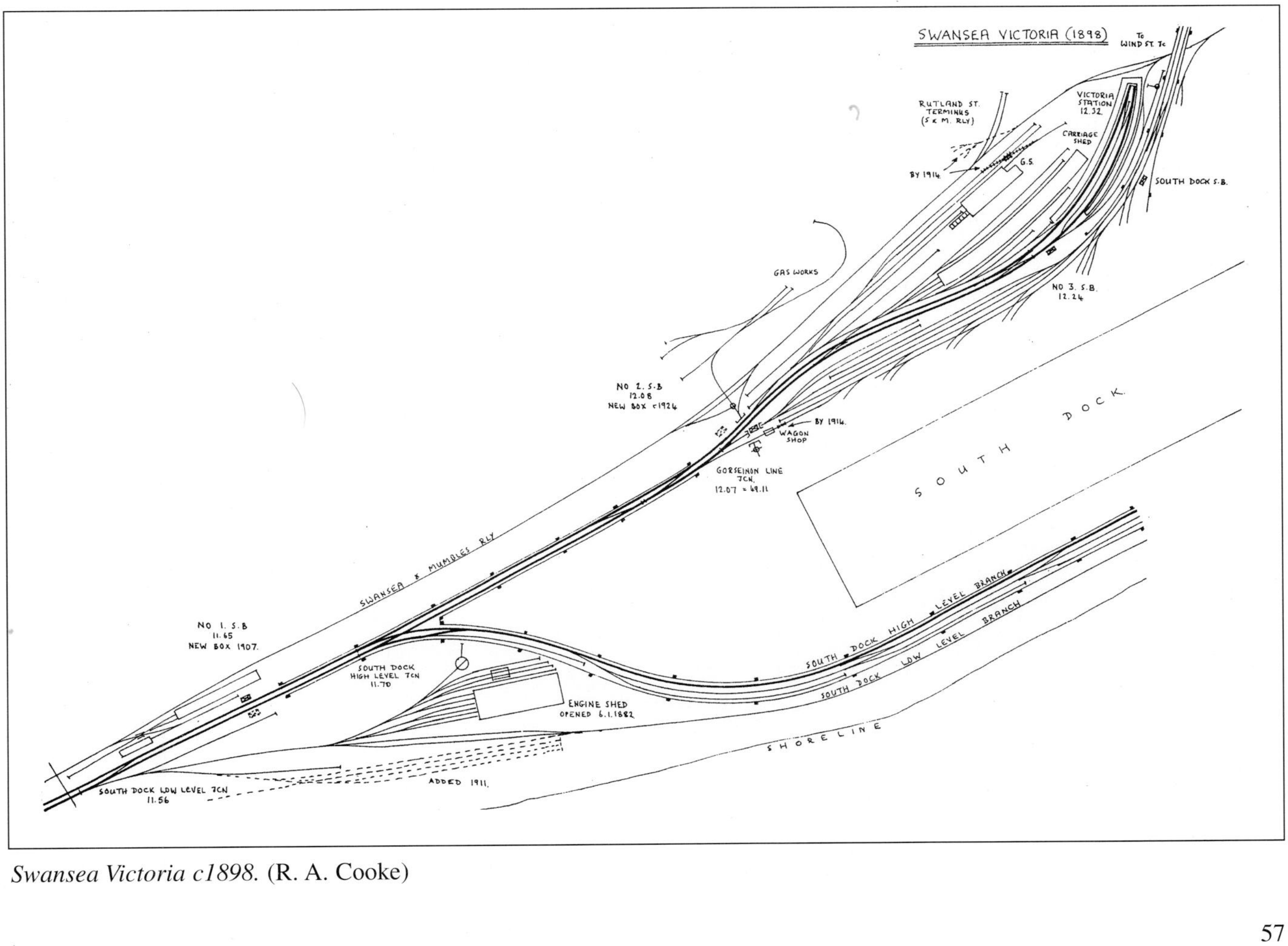

Swansea Victoria c1898. (R. A. Cooke)

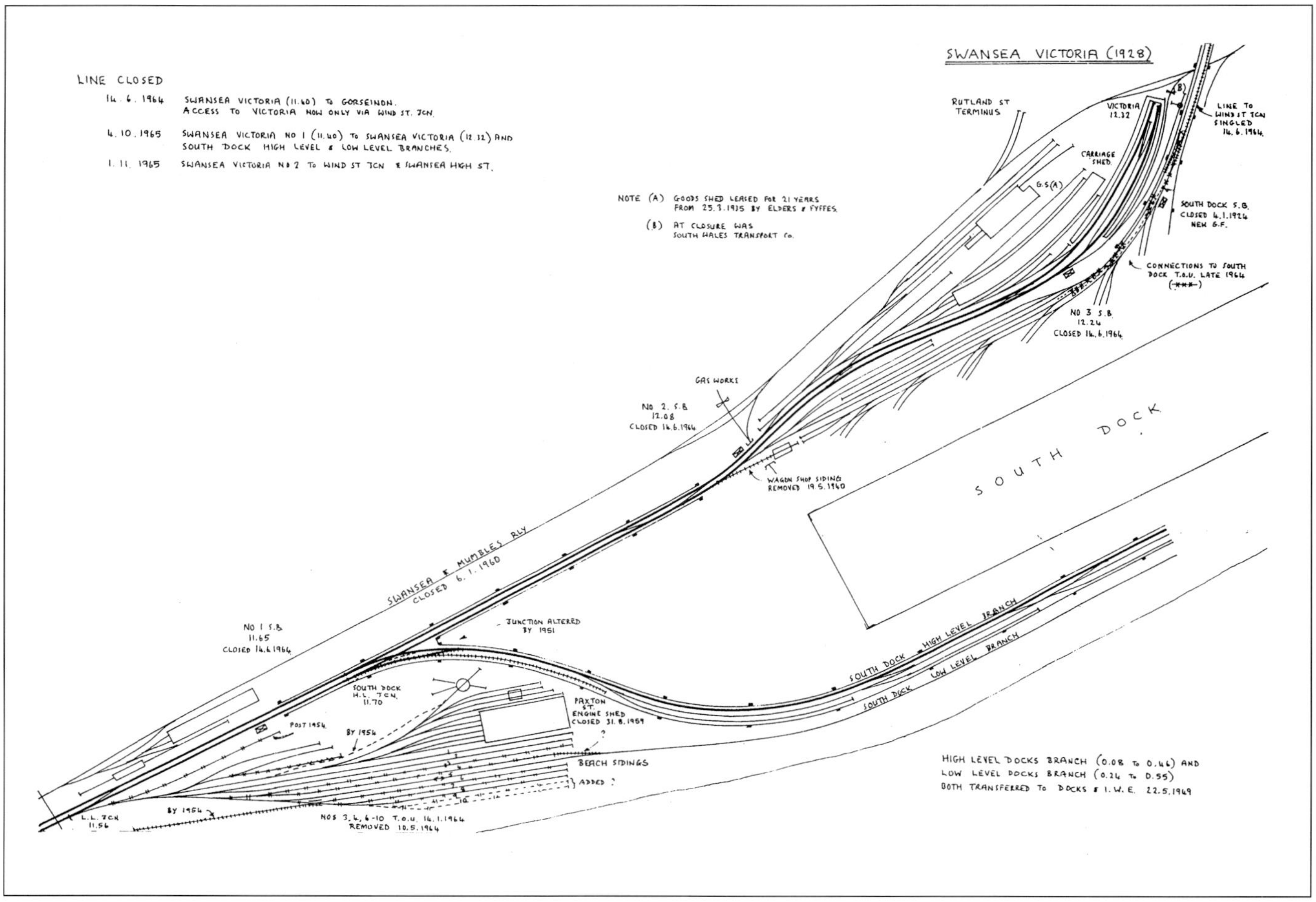

Swansea Victoria 1928. (R. A. Cooke)

The station was provisionally named Low Level Station and then Victoria Street by the Llanelly company but appeared in the 1875 copy of *Bradshaw* as Swansea Victoria, although the *Cambrian Newspaper* referred to it simply as Victoria for a number of years.

It was constructed in record time by Thomas, Watkins & Jenkins as the original contractors, Watson, Overend & Co. had failed to build it due to financial complications. Thus, tenders were invited by the Llanelly Railway Co. on 11 October 1867 'for the completion of Swansea Low Level Station. Plans and specifications will be ready for inspection on or after Tuesday 15th next'. That any sort of building should be completed in under two months was an achievement.

During 1881, with the LNWR in control, the main buildings of wooden construction, were rebuilt and 1882 saw Swansea Victoria with an overall glass roof supported by iron columns. There were two platforms with room for seven coaches apiece and a road between to facilitate removal of engines from terminating services.

Paxton Street shed closed on 31 August 1959 while passenger services continued until 13 June 1964. When crowds assembled to see the last 'York Mail' pull out, a somewhat bitter admonition was chalked up. 'Did you use this line? No?

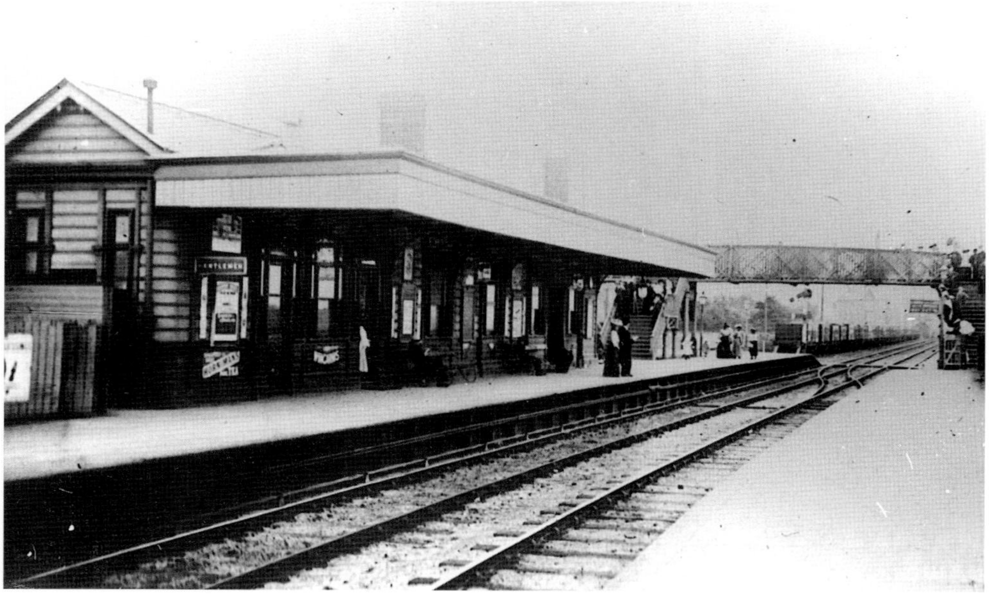

Swansea Bay station looking towards Swansea Victoria in the early part of the 20th century. (Bernard Matthews collection)

Swansea Bay very much out of use, 1965. (Courtesy Colin Pritchard)

Why come now then? It's too late'. The station was closed to freight on 4 October 1965, the goods yard having been served until then from the High Street station via the high level line.

Second World War air raids caused a lot of damage in Swansea and Victoria station received its share. No efforts were made to replace its shattered glass canopy and it presented a forlorn sight in an area which, at that time, was no longer blessed with shopping facilities. In the end Swansea Victoria was demolished in 1966 and a leisure centre built upon the site. A small amphitheatre is set in the former high level track embankment.

It does not take too much detective ability, when wandering around the present Swansea Marina and westwards towards the sites of Killay and Dunvant stations, to discover clues of the former rail route.

Swansea Bay Dunvant Valley Railway (Llanelly Railway Co./LNWR/LMSR/BR (WR))
This line was built by the Llanelly company but was known as the Dunvant Valley Railway due to the fact that the latter had originally planned to construct it. Swansea Bay opened 1 January 1878 as a passenger station and was constructed

Swansea Bay station forecourt 18 August 1959, showing the proximity of the route to that of the Mumbles Railway, the track of which can be seen on the right. (Welsh Industrial & Maritime Museum)

mainly of wood, was situated just east of what until then had been St Helens sidings and served the community of that name. On 30 May 1892, the LNWR opened Swansea Bay to goods traffic and the station was moved westwards, with two platforms with the doubling of the line. The new station was opened to passengers on 2 June 1892. Passenger traffic ceased on 15 June 1964 and freight on 4 October 1965.

Mumbles Road Dunvant Valley Railway (Llanelly Railway Co./LNWR/LMSR/BR (WR))
Situated just west of a connection of the line with the Swansea & Mumbles Railway, the station was put to extensive use for goods traffic by the LNWR in the late 1890s. Originally single-track, the line was doubled from 29 May 1892. Goods traffic ceased 12 October 1959 and the station closed to passengers on 15 June 1964.

Killay Dunvant Valley Railway (Llanelly Railway Co./LNWR/LMSR/BR (WR))
Opened 14 December 1867, the line was doubled to Gowerton from 13 February 1876 and to Swansea in 1892. Killay served the Clyne Valley Brickworks, the siding for which was situated south of the station off the 'down' line. The station closed on 15 June 1964.

Dunvant Dunvant Valley Railway (Llanelly Railway Co./LNWR/LMSR/BR (WR))
Opened 14 December 1867 and situated south east of Dunvant Colliery, this station had private sidings at the north end. (The first shipment from Dunvant Colliery was on 9 November 1865 but this was conveyed over the Swansea extension.) Like its neighbours, Dunvant closed on 15 June 1964.

Killay station looking south. The signal box was replaced by a ground frame in 1938.
(Bernard Matthews collection)

Killay station building stands dejected and unused in 1965.
(Courtesy Colin Pritchard)

Dunvant station, looking north.
(Bernard Matthews collection)

Gowerton (LMS) station in the 1920s. The train is a Swansea to Pontarddulais local hauled by an LNWR coal tank.
(Nigel Wassell collection)

Gowerton South station.
(Courtesy Dorothy Bound)

Gowerton South Dunvant Valley Railway (Llanelly Railway Co./LNWR/LMSR/BR (WR))
Opened in 1866 for goods and on 14 December 1867 for passengers. Originally known as Gower Road until 8 June 1886 when it was renamed Gowerton. This was also the name of a station on the Swansea–Llanelli route and on 1 January 1950, it became Gowerton South to distinguish it from the ex-GWR station, both then being controlled by British Railways (WR).

There was a branch line to Penclawdd (copper works) and Llanmorlais as well as access to various collieries and to the Elba Steel Works. Slightly to the east the line crossed the GWR Swansea–Llanelli route. Passenger traffic on the Llanmorlais branch finished in 1931. 'Down' sidings ceased to be used 13 May 1956 and the station closed on 15 June 1964.

(The temporary closure of Cockett Tunnel in 1899 had necessitated a connection into Gowerton in July of that year. This was taken out of use in 1903.)

Gorseinon (Llanelly Railway Co./LNWR/LMSR/BR (WR))
Opened 14 November 1867 and originally named Pontardulais South. The line was doubled to Gowerton from 11 February 1894, served Mountain Colliery and local steel and tin plate works including Bryngwyn, Mardy and Grovesend. Passenger traffic ceased on 15 June 1964 when this was re-routed via Llanelli and the line to Swansea Victoria was closed. The track to Pontarddulais was singled 14 June 1964 and remained open for freight until 1974 although the line to Bryngwyn and Mardy works was closed in 1966.

Ex LNWR 0-8-0 No. 49146 at Gorseinon, 24 March 1957.
(Courtesy Michael Lewis)

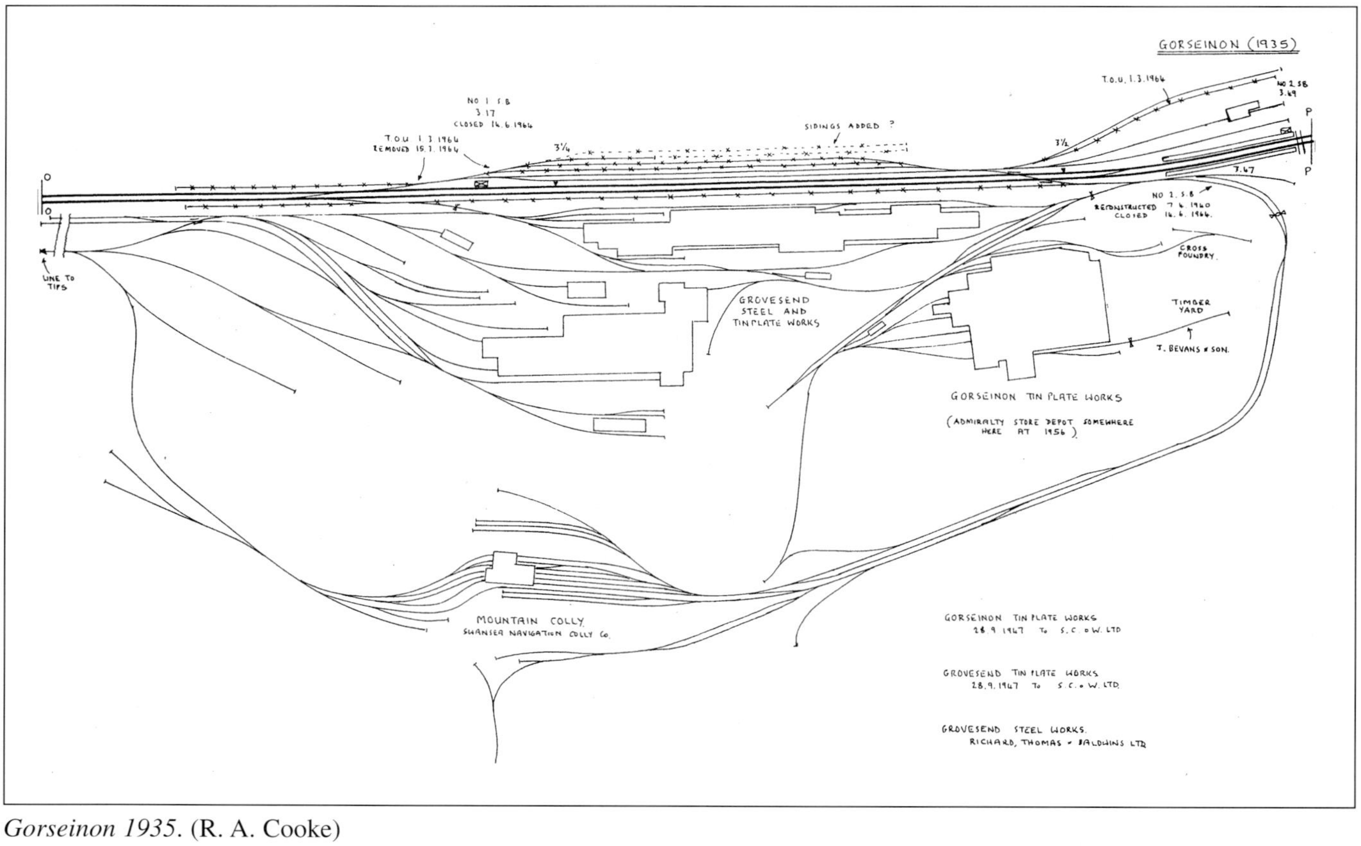

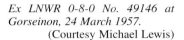

Gorseinon 1935. (R. A. Cooke)

Gorseinon station crossing in the early 20th century.
(Courtesy Michael Lewis)

Grovesend (LNWR/LMSR/BR (WR))
Opened 1 January 1910. Passenger traffic ceased 6 June 1932. The singled track to Pontarddulais closed in 1974 when a chord line was opened from the colliery loop.

Pontardulais (Pontarddulais from 12 May 1980) (Llanelly Railway Co./GWR/BR (WR))
Opened 1 June 1839 with track doubled to Pantyffynnon 25 September 1893 and to Gorseinon 28 May 1893. It was once a busy junction with sidings serving tinplate works and a small marshalling yard, south of which, the LNWR which had running rights over GWR metals – parted company with the latter to run south for twelve miles to Swansea Victoria while GWR services headed south-westwards towards Llanelli. The station had a footbridge which spanned four platforms. These formed a V, two on the east side used by GWR and those on the west by LNWR.

Of its three signal boxes, two were owned by the GWR and the the third by LNWR. The marshalling yard was taken out of use in 1963 and the line was singled in the direction of Pantyffynnon in 1964, closing to freight a year afterwards, the station being down graded to a halt. Some 20 years later, a potential traveller enquired as to its whereabouts only to be wrongly informed by someone in the locality that the line had closed 'years ago': a sad indication of the status of this once busy place. In 1985, a Manpower Services Commission project set about improving the appearance of the one platform left in use (the original Llanelli 'down') planting

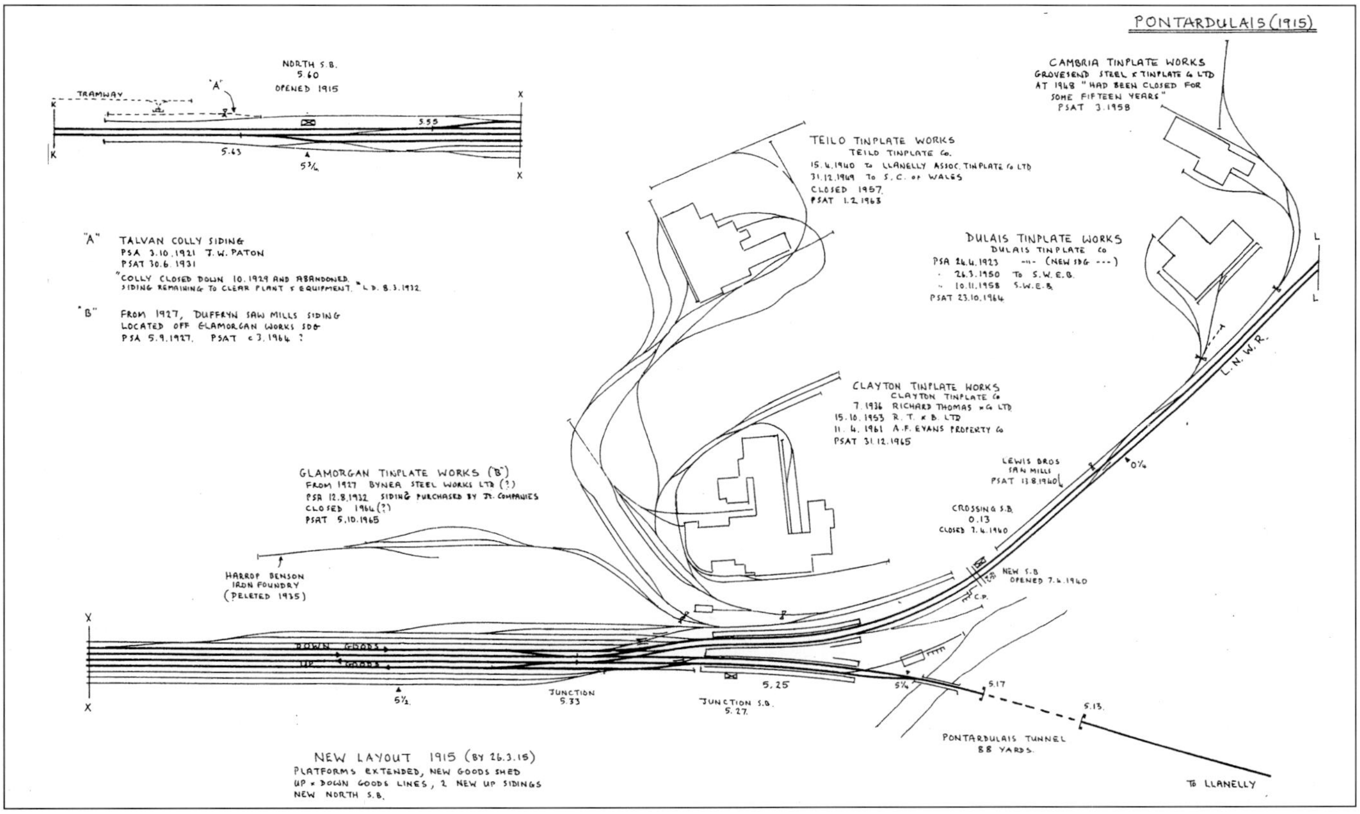

Pontardulais 1915. (R. A. Cooke)

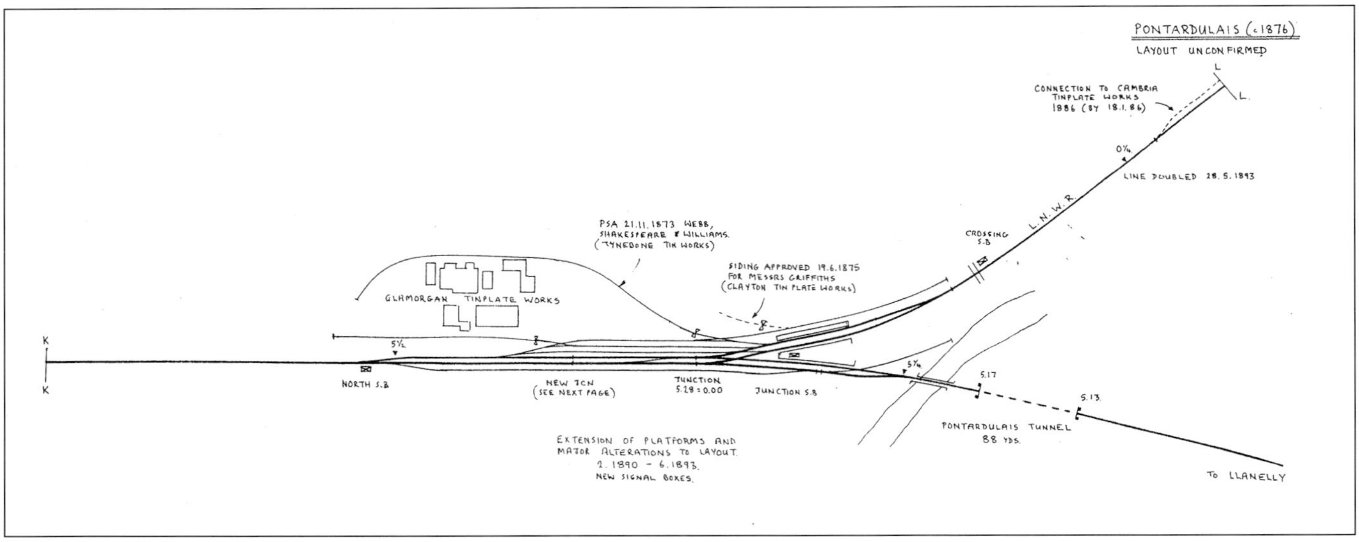

Pontardulais c1876. (R. A. Cooke)

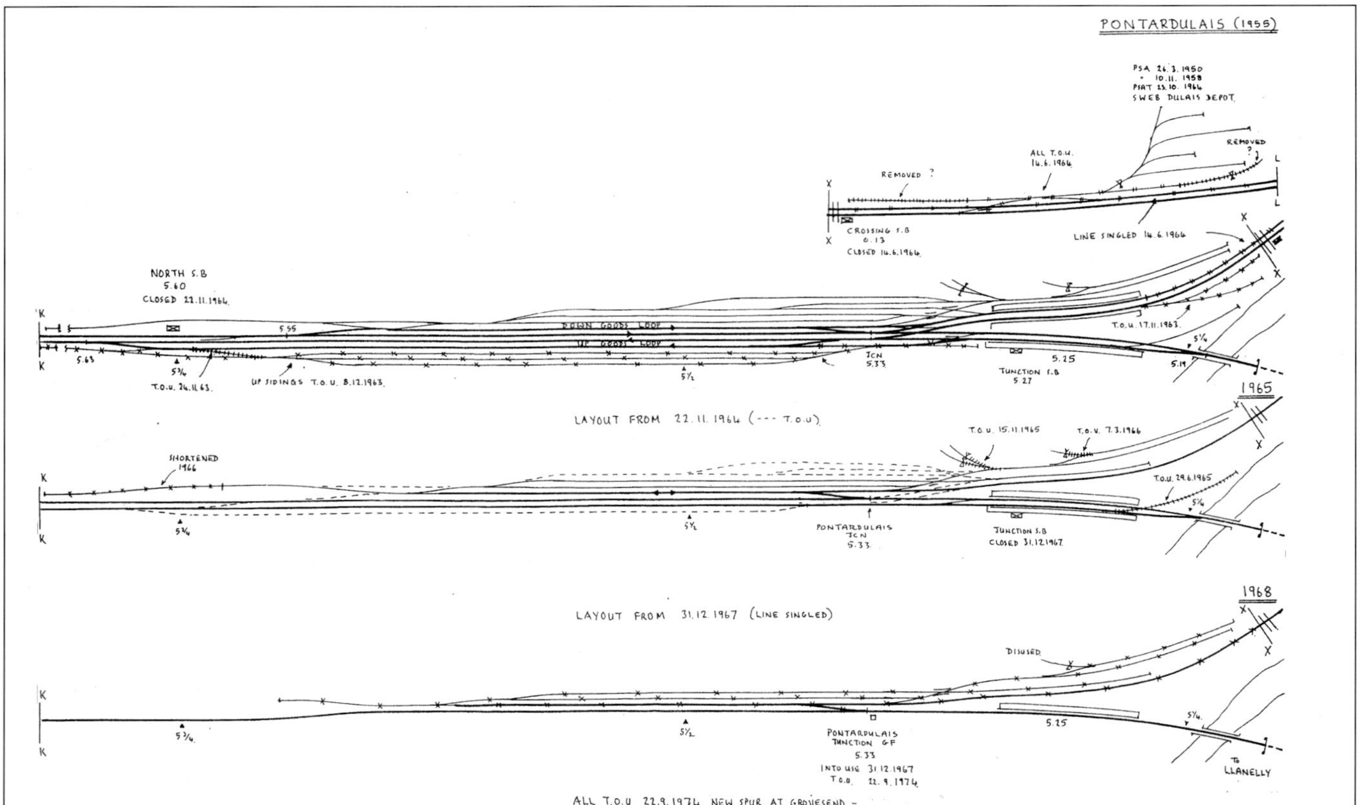

Pontardulais 1955. (R. A. Cooke)

Pontardulais station, pre 1964, looking south.
(Bernard Matthews collection)

Pontardulais station, looking north. The noticeboard once bore the lettering 'Pontardulais Junction. Change for Shrewsbury and the North', but this was removed when the Swansea Victoria line closed in 1964.
(Bernard Matthews collection)

In contrast to its bustling past, it is hard to believe that this is the same station. Although still in use, Pontardulais (looking north) has a sad, deserted air in 1994.
(Rose Coleman)

trees and flowers but the rest was left to sink into greater neglect.

The station is subject to vandalism and in 1989, in a desperate attempt to get something done about its appearance, the then Area Manager of BR, Simon Lane, offered a £ for £ arrangement to local authorities and firms who might be prepared to contribute funds towards improvement of the station approaches.

In 1991 a Station Survey reported that Pontarddulais was a 'lighted station with a waiting area' but the halt has a dejected air and its shelter is a target for graffiti. Railtrack announced an allocation of £9,717 to upgrade the station in 1997. It is now a 'request only' stop.

Pantyfynnon (Pantyffynnon) (Llanelly Railway Co./GWR/ BR (WR))
Opened 10 March 1840, this was an important junction which had a branch to Brynamman (carrying passengers until 1958) and to Garnant from beyond which ran a line to Gwaun-cae-Gurwen, passengers being carried to the latter until 1926. There were lines to several collieries and a motive power depot. With the opening of these lines anthracite could then be transported by rail direct to the docks.

The 1931 GWR engine shed, with a 15-engine allocation, originally opened due to the closure of Garnant Depot, was closed in September 1964. (LNWR/LMS sheds were at Swansea Victoria and Llandovery.) General freight ceased in 1965 with the line being singled from 31 December 1967. However, even in the late 1980s there remained a lot of activity on the former Brynamman branch where the Abernant and Gwaun-cae-Gurwen collieries still functioned, as did the Wernos washery which was situated on the 'up' side of the main line towards Tirydail, but this closed in 1988. Sidings are still in use and station buildings on the 'down' platform are used as offices and as a 'signing on' point for freight train crews.

One of Pantyffynnon's claims to fame is that its manned GWR signal box is the only one on the line south of Craven Arms. Although no longer the hive of activity as in the old

Pantyffynnon 1969, with the footbridge no longer in existence, looking north.
(Roy Palmer)

Pantffynnon GWR station, looking north in busier times during the BR period.
(Bernard Matthews collection)

Pantyffynnon station – now with only the 'down' platform in use – bathed in autumn sunshine, 1994.
(Rose Coleman)

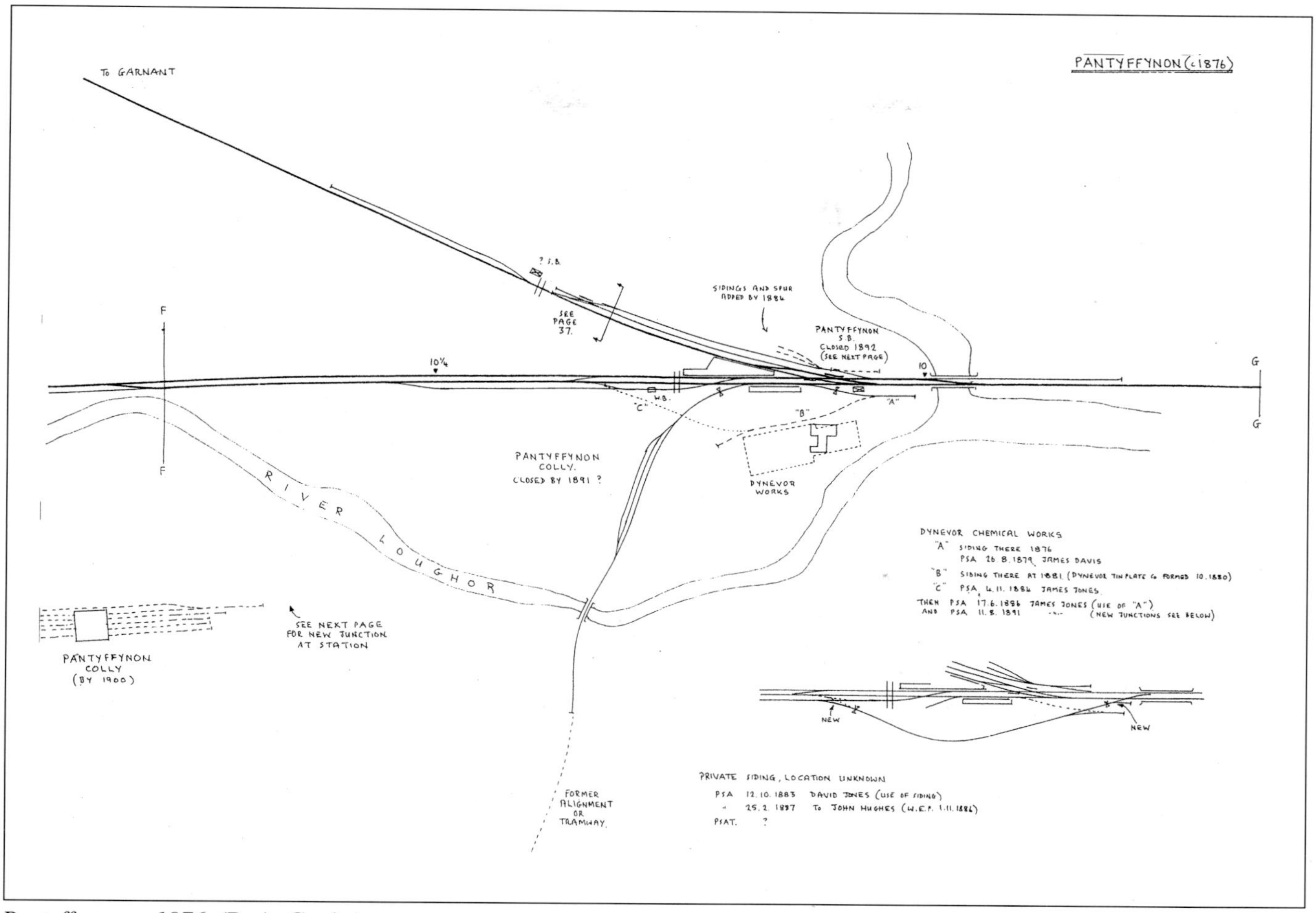

Pantyffynnon c1876. (R. A. Cooke)

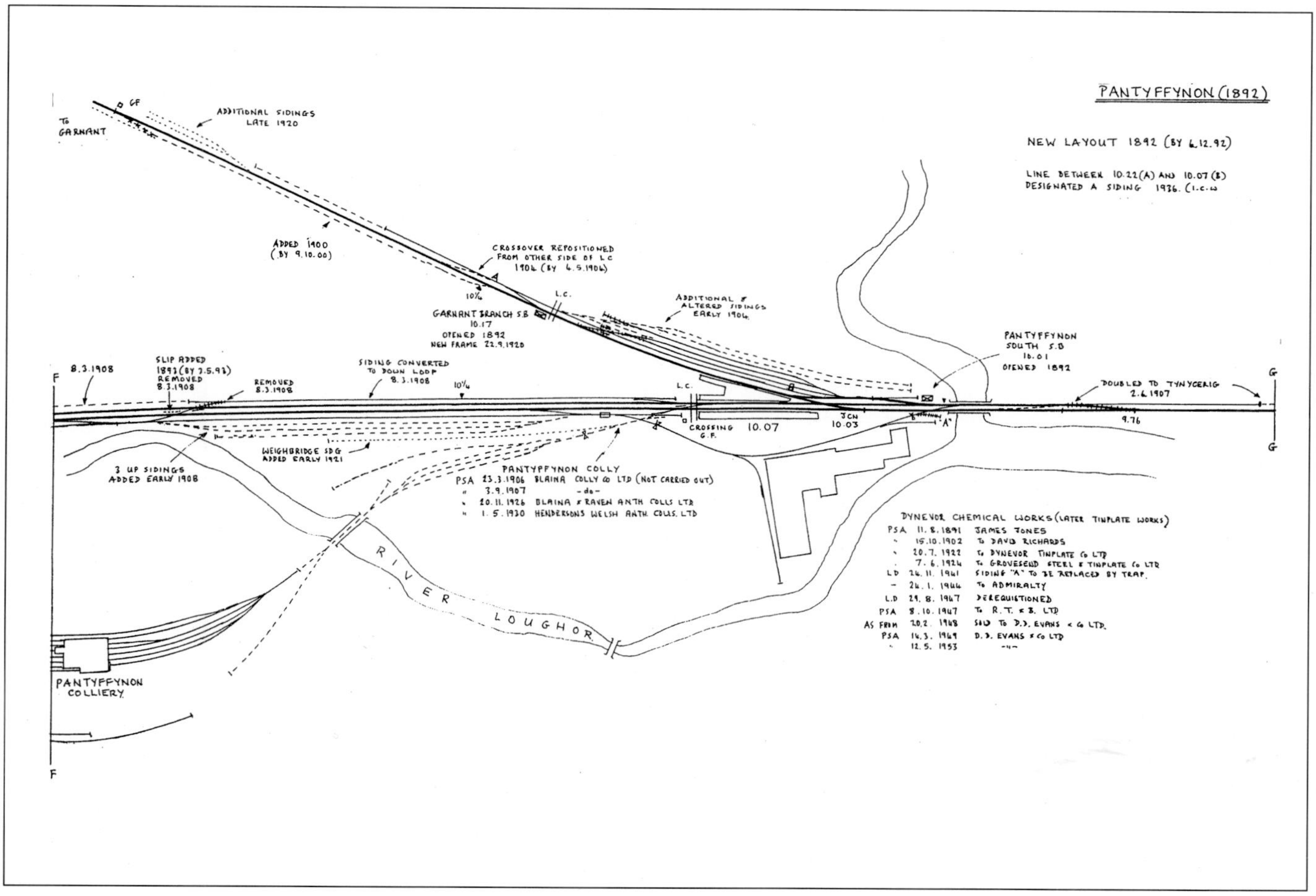

Pantyffynnon 1892. (R. A. Cooke)

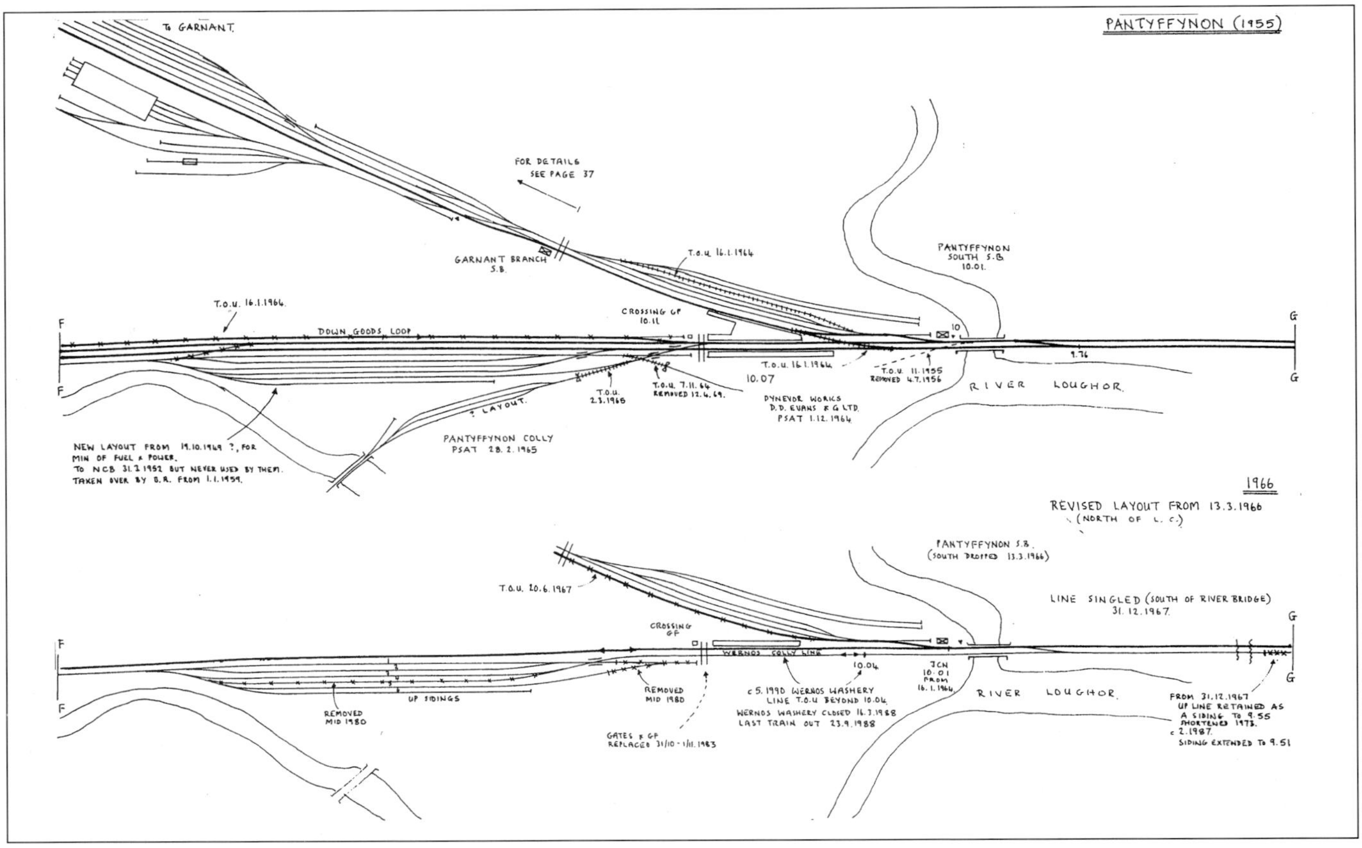

Pantyffynnon 1955. (R. A. Cooke)

days, this box, with its delightful view over the river, is still a busy place, receiving 'phone calls for the release of tokens on the 79-mile section northwards as well as acting as a fringe box for the main Port Talbot Power Box. Some semaphore signals remain in use in the station area.

On 19 August 1992 a plaque was unveiled to commemorate the centenary of the box. In the same year Pantyffynnon also received a 'Best staff maintained station' award and the BEM was awarded to one of the long serving signalmen (see Chapter 13 Workforce).

Although the line is singled and the 'up' platform no longer in use, the latter is very well kept by the staff. In 1993, the station won first prize in the 'Staff maintained' category of the South Wales and West Railflora 93 competition and this was followed by a commendation in 1994 in the Wales in Bloom competition. Railtrack announced an allocation of £24,487 to upgrade the station in 1997.

Parcyrhun Halt (GWR/BR (WR))
Opened 4 May 1936 on single track, and closed 13 June 1955. This was the last halt to be opened on the Central Wales line.

Ammanford and Tirydail (Rhydaman/Ammanford) (Llanelly Railway Co./GWR/BR (WR))

Ammanford station 1994, complete with preserved narrow gauge wagon on the platform. (Rose Coleman)

Llandybie halt – adopted by the local county primary school as indicated on the bilingual plaque.
(Courtesy John Horsley Denton)

Opened 6 May 1841 as Duffryn or Duffryn Lodge, it was known as Tirydail in 1889 and, when the original Ammanford station on the Brynamman branch line closed in 1960, it became Ammanford and Tirydail. The present station, an unstaffed halt since 1965, bears the name Rhydaman/Ammanford. Ammanford closed to freight on 2 November 1964. In GWR times, it was used by their traffic exclusively until 1939.

The Llanelly company's line ended here until 24 January 1857 when, after a ten-year delay, it finally opened to Llandeilo. It was from the Duffryn main line signal box that the Mountain branch, which had gradients of 1 in 12 on some rope-worked sections, was controlled. Duffryn had a goods yard and a passing loop (although passenger trains could not pass there) but once the Mountain branch closed in 1964, the goods yard followed suit and the signal box was reduced to a crossing box. Later, still bravely bearing the name Tirydail, this was demolished. Several accidents have occurred on the automatic crossing which replaced it, caused by motorists not heeding the warning signals. The station buildings suffered the same fate as the signal box but the present halt has a shelter and efforts are made to keep the appearance of the platform pleasing, the local Ladies Circle providing floral displays. It is now a 'request only' stop.

Ironically, the original Ammanford station on the old Brynamman branch, still intact after 30 years of closure, with a greatly threatened freight line, presented a more solid image in 1991 than its successor.

Llandebie (Llandybie) (Llanelly Ralway Co./GWR/BR (WR))
Opened 1 January 1857, Llandebie served a lime wharf, a colliery and the Cilyrychen quarries. Its loop was lengthened in 1906 but passenger trains could not pass. Prior to Nationalisation, use was restricted to GWR trains. Once very busy with a staff of over 20 during the Second World War period, Llandybie became an unstaffed halt 6 September 1965 having closed to freight in May of that year. The signal box was removed to Bronwydd Arms on the Gwili Railway.

An arson attack upon its stone buildings in 1985 caused considerable damage but some repairs to the roof were carried out by British Rail to retain the salvaged section as a waiting room. In the same year, an effort to boost the

Ffairfach halt and level crossing, November 1994.
(Rose Coleman)

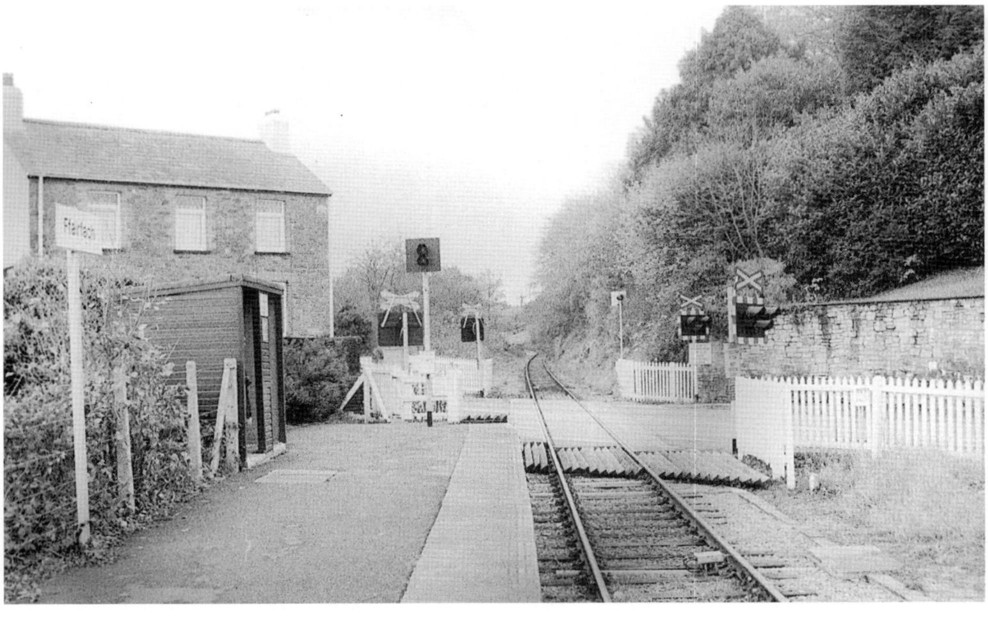

station's image was made by the local Women's Institute who provided some floral decorations and there was a well-maintained brick-built shelter. The platform was shortened on 22 November 1982.

Like many unmanned halts, Llandybie has received its share of vandalism but in 1989 it was adopted by the local primary school who effected a complete transformation, resulting in a new fence, fresh paint (the original chocolate brown and cream GWR colours were used), a bench erected and flower beds planted and tended. Their efforts were rewarded when, in November 1991, they received a Rail Flora award in the Special floral display section. Railtrack announced an allocation of £11,200 to upgrade the station in 1997. It is now a 'request only' stop.

Derwydd Road (Llanelly Railway Co./GWR/BR (WR))
Opened 1 January 1857 to serve a limestone area. Passenger traffic ceased 3 May 1954 and the station building became privately owned. The loop (the only one on the Llandeilo-Pantyffynnon section where passenger trains could pass) was removed in 1965 and the signal box was taken out of use on 13 March 1966, the station closing to freight the following day. A goods loop which was situated behind the 'up' platform was taken out of use 16 December 1963.

Ffairfach (Llanelly Railway Co./GWR/BR (WR))
Opened 1 January 1857 as single line, there were sidings to the gas works and, in 1935, beyond the crossing, there were milk sidings to a creamery (the latter resulting in Sunday working for some years), both being removed 1 December 1963.

An unstaffed halt from 1 May 1961, Ffairfach retains its original peaceful image with the standard basic shelter and one platform, even though it is jammed in close to the A483, the crossing traversing the latter now being automatic. It is now a 'request only' stop. Park and ride facilities became available (on the 'up' side) in 1997.

Llandilo (Llandeilo) (Vale of Towy-Llanelly Railway Co./GWR/LNWR/BR (WR))
Opened 1 January 1857, this was once a large and important station, the largest between Swansea and Craven Arms. Being the junction of LNWR's (originally Llanelly Company's) line to Carmarthen, it had to be enlarged after the opening of that branch in 1865.

This was the northern tip of the former Llanelly Railway Company's section, taken over by GWR, the point from

Llandeilo station in 1900. (Welsh Industrial & Maritime Museum)

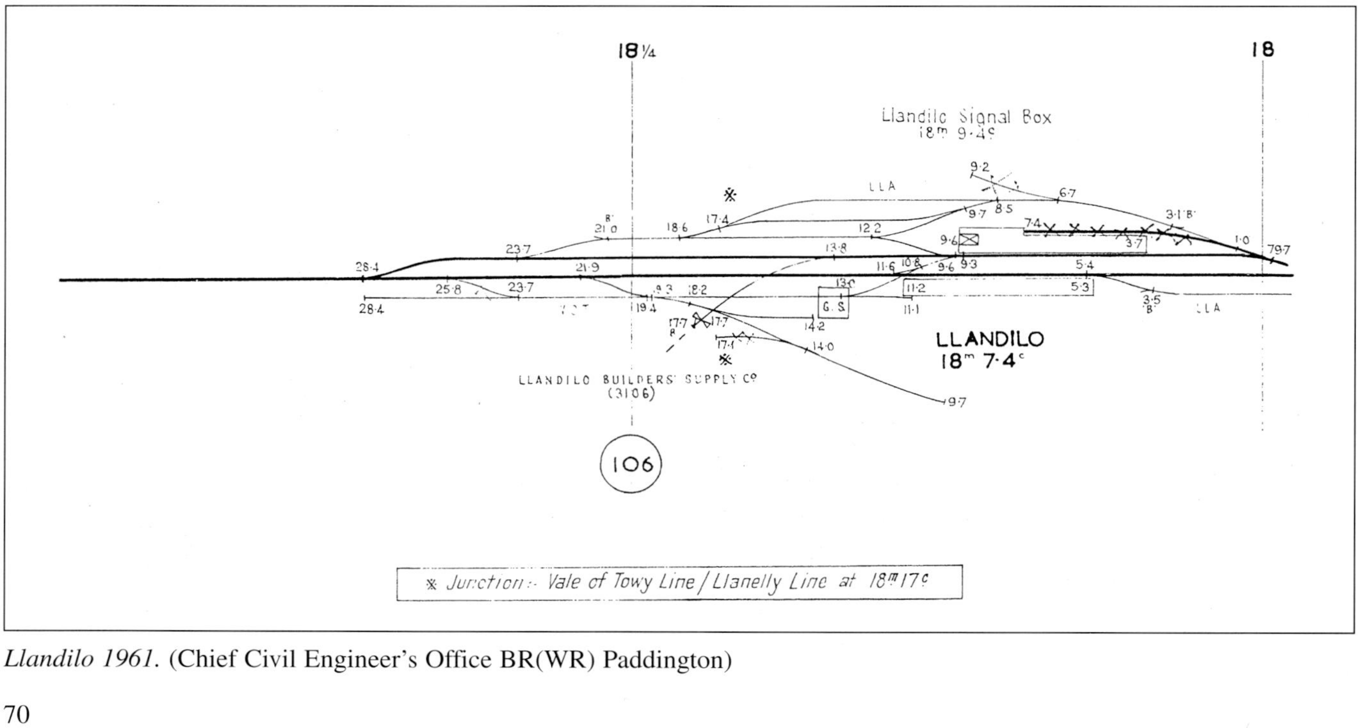

Llandilo 1961. (Chief Civil Engineer's Office BR(WR) Paddington)

The 14.17 ex Swansea ('Sprinter' No. 153303) approaches Llandeilo in November 1994.
(Rose Coleman)

A 'behind the scenes' view of Llandeilo station buildings in 1994.
(Rose Coleman)

which the 'Premier Line' had to abandon its 'joint running' status and take second place in running over GWR metals southwards, ignoring intermediate stations, as far as Pontarddulais in order to gain access to Swansea Victoria.

There were sidings at the northern end on both 'up' and 'down' sides and, in its heyday. Llandeilo had a turntable, 60ft goods shed, a cattle dock, coal yard, goods loops and a passenger bay. The Carmarthen trains ran into a bay on the 'down' side.

Originally, Llandeilo had staggered platforms and the GWR carried out considerable re-building work which included extending the 'up' platform. By 1988, just one refuge siding on the 'up' side remained and, although in that year part of 'up' side building's glass canopied roof was still intact, the station was still manned and operating the Red Star parcels service and other facilities, but its refreshment room and bar had closed necessitating a steep climb to the town for any thirsty travellers.

In the 1970s, an urn from the refreshment room was taken on to the train to serve tea to the passengers – an echo of past concern for the comfort of the travelling public when the LNWR advertised the availability of 'footwarmers' at Llandeilo.

Nevertheless, pride in the station continued and from 1990 it was entered for the Wales in Bloom competition and won a local award for its floral display the following year.

Llandeilo became an unstaffed station in 1992 but still retains its passing loop for passenger trains, being one of the points from which drivers have to 'phone Pantyffynnon to gain permission to enter the next token section. The appearance of the station had deteriorated considerably by the winter of 1995 as it was known that the buildings were due for demolition because of a road improvement scheme. This took place in 1996 and a new shelter was installed.

Talley Road (Vale of Towy-Llanelly Railway Co./GWR-LNWR/BR (WR))

Opened 1858, it became an unstaffed halt in 1941 and

SERIOUS RAILWAY ACCIDENT.

Considerable alarm was created along the Llanelly railway on Saturday night, by a report of a serious accident said to have occurred near Llandilo. The report, unhappily, was soon confirmed. It appears that as the 5.10 p.m. train from Llandovery was proceeding past a small station called Glanrhyd to Llandilo, one of the wheels of the engine broke. The train being at its usual speed, the engine at once shied off the line, into a dyke on the side of the railway, drawing the tender after it, which alighted on the top of the engine. Had it not been for the protection afforded by the guard of the engine, under which the driver and stoker stood, they must inevitably have been smashed to pieces. Fortunately, however, the guard was sufficiently strong to bear the weight of the tender. The third-class carriage next to the tender was smashed to pieces. There were about twenty-five passengers in this carriage, and it was a miracle how any escaped uninjured. From twelve to fifteen were more or less injured, seven very severely. Several of the injured were at once conveyed to a farm house near, where medical men from Llandilo were soon in attendance. The Carmarthen train which was at Llandilo waiting the arrival of this down trains steamed up to the scene of the accident as soon at it was known, and took away the passengers that were uninjured. We are sorry to learn that amongst the injured are Mr. D. Harries, one o, the Techon Colliery Co., and Mr. Frederick Lloyd, Bookseller, Llanelly.

Glanrhyd accident. Llanelly Guardian *5 November 1868.*

closed to passenger traffic 4 April 1955 but retained sidings for storage for a few years. Until 1939, it was only used by the GWR.

Glanrhyd (Vale of Towy-Llanelly Railway Co./GWR-LNWR/BR (WR))
Opened 1 April 1858 for local use, became an unstaffed halt in 1938 and closed 7 March 1955, but the station building survives as a private dwelling, the door of which fronts the platform.

Prior to 1939, only GWR traffic called here. A tragic accident caused Glanrhyd to hit the headlines in 1987 when, on 19 October, in severe flood conditions, the bridge (rebuilt in 1958) over the River Tywi collapsed just as the 05.20 from Swansea was crossing it. The first carriage of the dmu fell into the river, resulting in the immediate deaths of three passengers and the driver, John Churchill. Later, the Permanent Way Section Supervisor from Llanwrtyd Wells, Mr Jim Campbell, who was not involved in the accident in any way became ill at the scene of it, and died on his way home. A new bridge, built by Lanarkshire Welding Company at a cost of £800,000 and which had been assembled off site, was lowered into position in October 1988.

Some 120 years previously, in November 1868, Glanrhyd station had been the site of an accident and although there were no fatalities, several serious injuries resulted. Another incident took place on 7 March 1959 in which the driver of a car was killed when the vehicle was driven over the line and was hit by the 'up' 'York Mail'.

Llangadock (Llangadog) (Vale of Towy-Llanelly Railway Co./GWR-LNWR/BR (WR))
Opened 1 April 1858, Llangadock (it became Llangadog on 15 May 1958) had a passing loop by 1880. The station buildings were of stone construction.

Llangadog had 'staggered platforms' which were uncommon in Mid Wales. Later, there was a private siding to a creamery at the southern end of the 'up' line. The siding did not close until 23 September 1966 but the loop was taken out of use in 1965 when general freight ceased.

There had once been a plan for a goods loop at Llangadog but this did not materialise. Equipment was delivered, including points motors and these were left on the site to deteriorate until they had only scrap value, finally being disposed of in the 1960s.

Llangadog was closed for twelve months (October 1987-88) pending replacement of the Glanrhyd Bridge during which time it fell into a state of neglect, probably because of suspicions that it would remain closed for good. Local efforts, however, soon remedied this state of affairs once the station, an unstaffed halt since 1965, was re-opened.

Track has been taken up on the 'down' side and shelter and information boards erected on the 'up' platform. Railtrack announced an allocation of £11,426 to upgrade the

Llangadog station with crossing gates closed, during BR period. (Bernard Matthews collection)

station in 1997. Now a 'request only' stop.

Llanwrda (Vale of Towy-Llanelly Railway Co./GWR-LNWR/BR (WR))
Opened 1 April 1858. Like Llangadog, it had a passing loop in 1880.

Llanwrda, originally known as Lampeter Road, was an important agricultural rail centre with cattle pens on the western side of the station. Between the wars, a considerable amount of livestock was moved here – one record for 1923 mentions over 10,000 tons of goods but freight traffic ceased on 6 March 1965, the loop was removed in September of that year and Llanwrda became an unstaffed halt.

It was the first station to be 'adopted' by a Community Council and others who were interested in its upkeep. Like its neighbour, Llangadog, it was unused between October 1987 and 1988 and suffered similarly but concern for its well being was revived, in the form of the local Women's Institute who tended the 'up' platform.

In 1993, with work having been carried out by two or three residents in the locality, it was commended in the Wales in Bloom station competition and in 1994 won second prize in catagory 18. Railtrack announced an allocation of £16,800 to upgrade the station in 1997. Now a 'request only' stop.

Llandovery (Vale of Towy-Llanelly Railway Co./GWR-LNWR/LMS/BR (WR))
The Vale of Towy Company opened Llandovery from the south on 1 April 1858. By 1 June 1868, when the whole line was completed, the LNWR was involved through its interest in the Central Wales Extension Railway bringing in the line from the north. An official opening of the Central Wales Extension Railway to the public took place on 8 October

Llandovery station looking north.
(Bernard Matthews collection)

A scene from a past age – Llandovery station looking south.
(HMRS/G.M. Perkins collection)

A car hurries over Llandovery crossing a few minutes before the arrival of the 'down' train in October 1994.
(Rose Coleman)

Llandovery marshalling yard and main line looking north in the 1930s.
(Dorothy Bound)

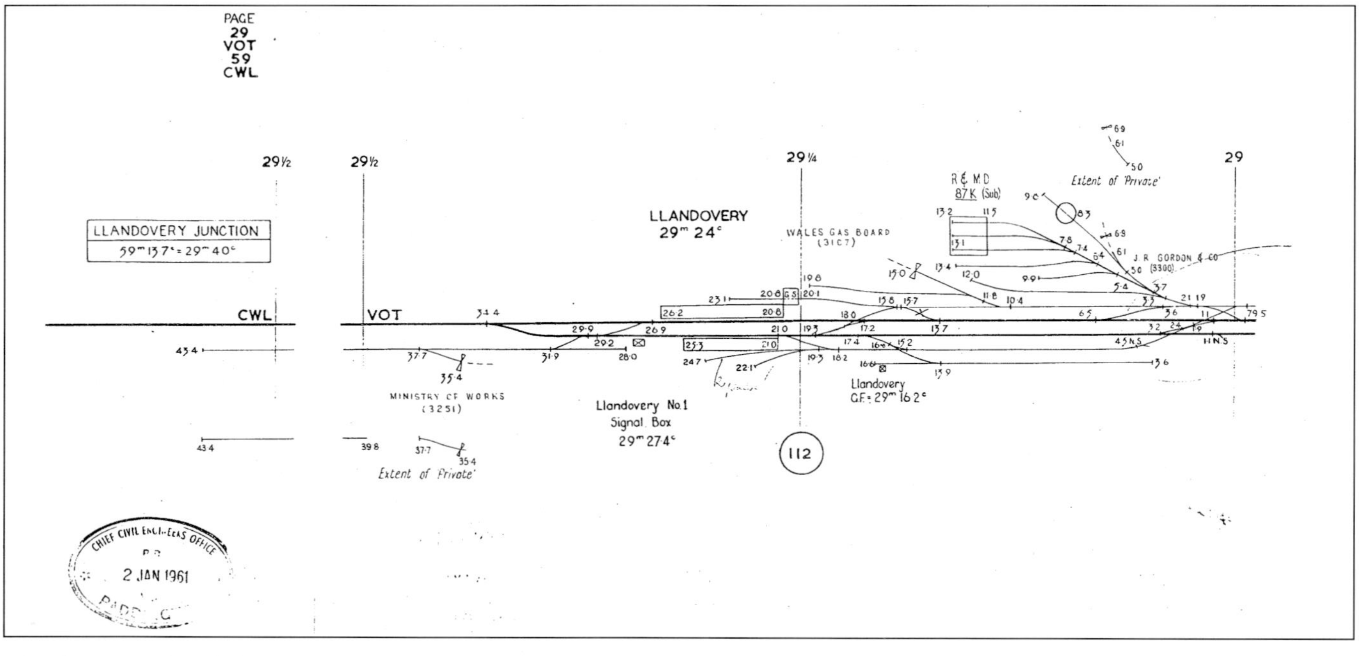

Llandovery 1961. (Chief Civil Engineer's Office BR(WR) Paddington)

1868 with traditional celebrations including parades, bands and bonfires.

This was an important and busy station although in the early 1900s, the community itself numbered under 2,000. In 1884, double track was laid between Nos 1 and 2 signal boxes. There were locomotive sheds belonging to both companies, the LNWR having the larger, built in 1901 to replace a temporary 1868 structure and housing eight engines with four roads and a 42ft turntable. Banking engines had always to be on hand for the steep gradient to the Sugar Loaf summit to the north. This shed was situated on the 'down' side where there was also a sizeable goods shed with a single through road and extensive station buildings with a glass canopy, plus a number of sidings on both sides.

The small GWR shed built in 1868 (one road – two-locomotive capacity) on the 'up' side did not survive that of the LNWR/LMS, closing in 1935, the latter continuing in use until the withdrawal of steam traffic from the line in 1964 when it closed on 10 August. When through freight ceased and the locomotive depot closed, 44 men became unemployed. Many of the train crews, particularly the 'Shrewsbury men' changed at Llandovery, leaving the alien route to Swansea to be worked by the locals.

The station retains its passing loop which was extended with the introduction of the NSKT (no signalman key token) system in 1986 at which time just two sidings remained on the 'up' side. Later, the signal box went to the Gwili Railway while the original level crossing gates have gone to the National Railway Museum at York and in 1992, this once important rail centre joined the ranks of the many unstaffed stations on the Central Wales Line. The former goods yard is now rented by a coal merchant in 1994. Railtrack announced an allocation of £19,330 to upgrade the station in 1997.

A pre 1929 view of Cynghordy station – looking north.
(Bernard Matthews collection)

Cynghordy station shelter in September 1994 – its boarded up appearance gives no hint that it is over a century old but its origins are made known, if you know where to look.
(Rose Coleman)

Sugar Loaf Summit Platform shortly after completion, c1910.
(HMRS/G. M. Perkins collection)

Sugar Loaf platforms, looking south with part of the access steps visible, 19 May 1986.
(Courtesy John Horsley Denton)

Cynghordy (LNWR/LMSR/BR (WR))
Opened 28 July 1899 by the LNWR whose new building in 1875 replaced that erected by the Central Wales Extension Railway in 1867, when the viaduct to the north (now a listed structure of architectural and historical interest) was completed. The LNWR had no passing loop between Sugar Loaf Summit and Llandovery and its traffic was restricted as a consequence. The LMS rectified this on 28 July 1929 by constructing a passing loop at Cynghordy.

There had been a small goods yard on the 'down' side but this was taken up on 11 May 1964 and the station, already partially unstaffed on 16 February 1959, closed to freight on 28 September 1964 on which date it became an unstaffed halt. The line was singled in 1965. The wooden passenger shelter, although hardly a thing of beauty, survived until 1995, still bearing the date 1892 on the Llandovery side of the structure. Railtrack anounced an allocation of £16,876 to upgrade the station in 1997. Cynghordy is now a 'request only' stop.

Sugar Loaf (LNWR/LMSR/BR (WR))
This was originally opened as Sugar Loaf Siding in 1899 by the LNWR. There was a passing loop, two platforms and 'up' and 'down' sidings. The halt was for use only by staff, dwellings for some of whom, including two signalmen and a ganger were built on the 'up' side but have long since been demolished. Children were conveyed to and from school at Llanwrtyd on morning and afternoon 'locals' and the wives of staff could also travel to the Friday market at Llandovery.

The line approaches from Cynghordy on a 1 in 60 gradient for four miles: this section, with its breathtaking views, is a delight for passengers but was a challenge for steam locomotives and the 1,000-yard tunnel just before the summit provided unpleasant conditions for the crews of 'up' trains. The descent northwards is at 1 in 80 over three miles. All freight traffic halted at the summit and was not permitted to proceed until checked by the guard and the handbrakes secured.

The passing loop was extended 165yd southwards by the LMS in 1943 during the period of the Second World War and the catchpoints at the northern end resited. Lie-bys were also constructed. These sidings were taken out of use in June 1965 but the connections were left to serve as runaway catchpoints.

'Sprinter' No. 153305 forms the Swansea bound 13.20 at Llanwrtyd in November 1994.
(Rose Coleman)

A picnic area is seen in preparation behind Llanwrtyd station buildings in Autumn 1994.
(Rose Coleman)

Having closed in 1965 and used on four Saturdays in 1984 in connection with organised rambles from Llanwrtyd, this isolated halt was re-opened on 21.6.1987 – this time for the use of passengers on the summer Sunday Recreation Rambler services which had been introduced that year – although the halt did not appear in the timetables until 1992.

The tiny platform on the 'down' side also still exists but is much overgrown.

Llanwrtyd (Llanwrtyd Wells) (CWER/LNWR/LMSR/BR (WR))
Opened 6 May 1867. Although the official ceremony did not take place until that date, (when the station master was the LNWR's Mr Bayldon), the station building bears the date 1865. There was a run round loop by 1868 and a small goods yard was situated on the 'up' side. This spa town was well known for its sulphur spring which attracted many visitors, particularly from South Wales and at the end of 1883 the station was named Llanwrtyd Wells.

The GWR and LNWR used to hold the Railwayman's Show at Llanwrtyd. Based at the Abernant Hotel, adjacent to the station, this was a social gathering for all grades of both companies and was an important event.

Freight traffic ceased on 7 June 1965. The NSKT system reached Llanwrtyd Wells in July 1986 when semaphore signals were removed, as was the signal box and the station became unstaffed by autumn of that year.

The station retains a passing loop and both platforms; the footbridge is no longer there nor are the buildings on the 'down' side which has a modern wooden shelter. Those on the 'up' side – which also still house a passenger waiting room – were 'listed' by CADW, the organisation formed to care for Welsh buildings of historic interest, and a project to convert them into rural workshops commenced in April 1988.

The recipient of several awards for its appearance in the past, the station is still well kept – these days by the efforts of the Town Council and local organisations and individuals. 1994 saw the laying out of a very pleasant and well planted

The once-busy Llangamarch presents the quiet picture of many CWL halts today, with freshly painted white gate and single platform.

(Rose Coleman)

picnic area behind the station buildings, and plans made to tarmac the frontage to facilitate access for the disabled. This community project provides a useful facility to be enjoyed both by travellers and local inhabitants. Railtrack announced an allocation of £28,407 to upgrade the station in 1997.

Llangammarch (Llangammarch Wells) (CWER/LNWR/LMSR/BR (WR))
Opened 8 May 1867 with one platform on the 'up' side behind which there was a small goods yard. 'Wells' was added to the station name in June 1883. It closed to freight and became an unstaffed halt on 28 September 1964 but floral displays still present a pleasing appearance and there is a modern wooden shelter replacing the red brick station building. Railtrack announced an allocation of £13,400 to upgrade the station in 1997. It is now a 'request only' stop.

Garth (CWER/LNWR/LMSR/BR (WR))
Opened 11 March 1867. The station master, the LNWR's Mr Morton, arrived in extremely wintry conditions and the station was opened during a snowstorm. There was a small goods yard on the 'up' side. A loop was opened in 1868 and taken out of use in 1965.

During the Second World War, in 1943 lie-bys were constructed at Garth. It became an unstaffed halt on 28 September 1964 and goods traffic ceased 28 September 1966. It now has one neat platform on the 'up' side with a modern shelter and is a 'request only' stop. Railtrack announced an allocation of £17,935 to upgrade the station in 1997.

Cilmery (Cilmeri) (CWER/LNWR/LMSR/BR (WR))
Originally known as Cefn-y-Bedd this was opened 11 March 1867 with a single platform and small goods yard on the 'up' side. It became an unstaffed halt 31 August 1938 and freight traffic ceased 3 August 1959. Local individuals and organisations have been responsible for its upkeep. It is now a 'request only' stop.

Builth Junction (Builth Road High Level/Builth Road)

The well-kept halt at Garth in late 1994.

(Rose Coleman)

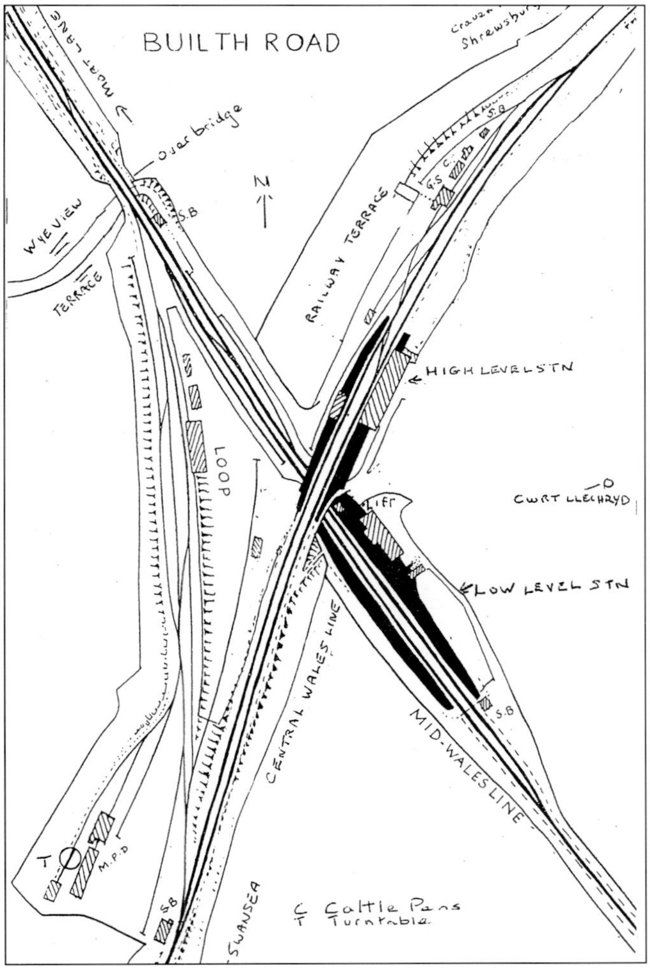

Builth Road High and Low Level station diagram.

(CWER/LNWR/LMSR/BR (WR))
Opened 1 November 1866 with a passing loop constructed in 1868. This was the point were the Central Wales Railway crossed the route of the Mid Wales Railway/Cambrian Railways/GWR (Brecon to Moat Lane Junction) line which opened in the early 1860s and ran beneath using Builth Road Low Level station (formerly known as Llechryd).

The LNWR had a goods yard and passenger bay at the northern end of the 'up' side with a single-road engine shed and a 40ft turntable at the southern end. There was a workshop and permanent way depot. Locomotives were housed for shunting and for banking to Howey or double headed to Llangunllo. (The Cambrian line had its own MPD at Builth Wells, 1½ miles to the south east.)

There was a connection, (with a small goods yard and an LNWR MPD and Permanent way depot) between the two lines south west of the Builth Road stations, opened for use by passenger trains in 1883, but advantage was not taken of this spur on a regular basis. It was used to work a Royal train in 1904 and for some Barry–Llandrindod Wells trains in the 1930s and occasionally for goods trains.

A wooden construction housed a water lift for parcels and luggage between the High and Low level stations and a refreshment room and bar were situated on the 'down' platform of the latter. Passengers gained access via ramp and steps.

By 1892 two rows of terrace houses had been built for railway workers. Permanent way staff, shunters, signalmen, etc., occupied Wye View Terrace, close to the Cambrian Line with access via a bridge, now dismantled, while station staff lived in Railway Terrace built alongside the Central Wales Line. These houses still remain, those of the latter being of typical LNWR design.

Builth Road station looking south in 1994. The buildings are now used for private flats.

(Rose Coleman)

Fowler Class 4 2-6-4T No. 42385 takes water at Builth Road High Level, while working a Swansea Victoria–Shrewsbury train.
(David Lawrence)

The connecting track at Builth High and Low Levels in pre-Grouping days.
(HMRS/G. M. Perkins collection)

Builth Road and Railway Terrace looking north in November 1994 with the old goods shed, right, on the former 'up' side. The cottages were built for the railway workforce but are now privately owned.
(Rose Coleman)

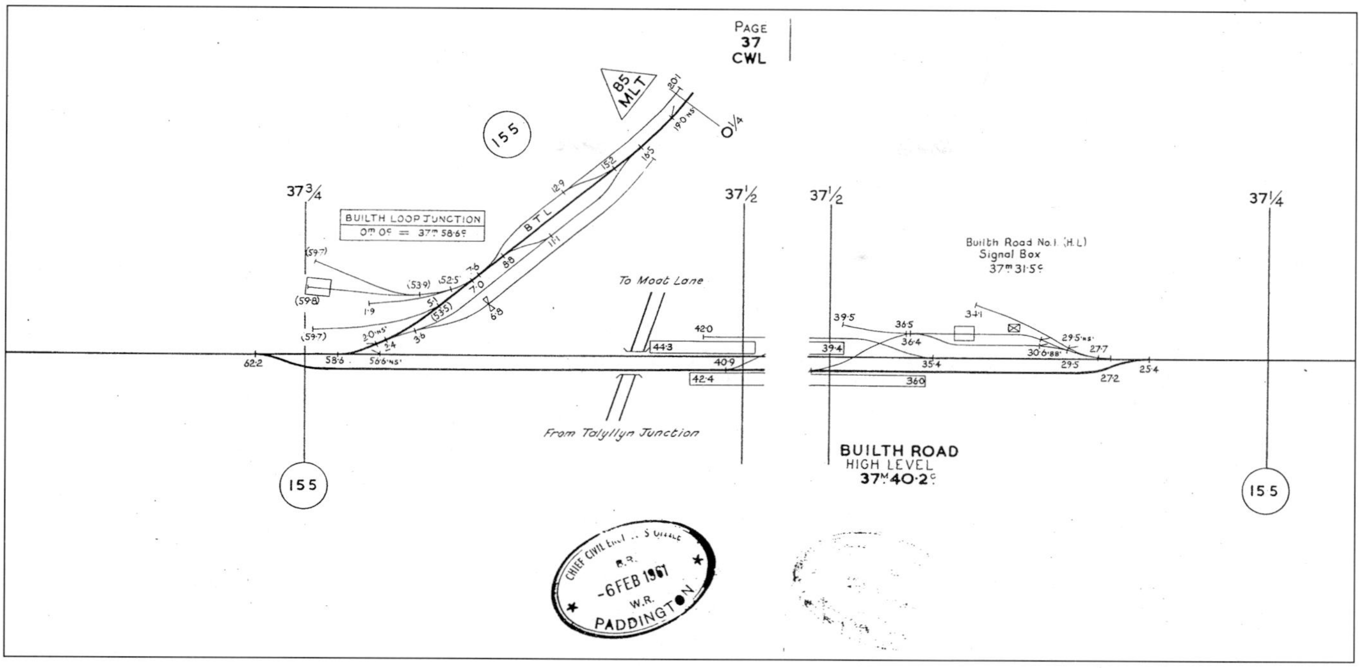

Builth Road 1961. (Chief Civil Engineer's Office BR(WR) Paddington)

A 1994 view from the bridge at Builth Road under which the Mid Wales Line ran. The Cambrian Arms, on the left, was once the refreshment room for both high and low level stations.
(Rose Coleman)

In the early 1900s, the 'up' platform of Builth Road High Level was used as a bay during summer months from which trains departed to and from Llandrindod to enable holiday makers from the latter to visit Builth for a few hours, via the Low Level station.

The Cambrian Line closed 31 December 1962 and after 1968, the 'Top Station' as it was often referred to was no longer known as High Level but connecting track to the 'Bottom Line' was not lifted for some time.

Builth Road became an unstaffed halt on 6 September 1965 and the passing loop was taken out of use, freight traffic having ceased in April of that year.

The former refreshment room is now the Cambrian Arms, standing on the site of the 'down' platform of the former Low Level while the 'down' side station building on the High Level, now simply Builth Road, has been converted into flats. The former locomotive and permanent way depots are now used by a commercial concern.

Only the 'down' platform remains and trains stop by request. Nevertheless, Builth Road still retains much of the atmosphere of a once self contained railway community. Railtrack announced an allocation of £5,600 to upgrade the station in 1997.

Llandrindod to Shrewsbury

Llandrindod (Llandrindod Wells) (CWR/LNWR/LMSR/ BR (WR))

Opened to passenger and freight 10 October 1865 and, for some time, known to locals as Llanerch Halt, after a nearby inn, although appearing in 1867 as Llandrindod in the LNWR timetable.

The station had a goods yard on the 'down' side and double track running northwards to Penybont station. With the popularity of Mid Wales spa towns at the end of the 19th and beginning of the 20th centuries when 100,000 passengers a year was the average, there were many hotels, and plenty of porters to handle luggage. The suffix 'Wells' was used at the station at the end of 1883. According to C. N. Ryan, writing

Passengers awaiting the arrival of the 12.51 'up' at Llandrindod in 1994.

(Rose Coleman)

in *Railway Magazine* in 1912, this was then 'the most valuable station to the LNWR on the line. All through the summer, crowds of people arrive and leave on every train and a very large proportion as first class passengers'.

Several lines ran into the goods yard and there was stabling for horses.

Until the late 1930s, a timber bridge traversed the roadway from the local quarry over which hoppers worked on a pulley system, carrying stone direct into wagons on the line.

During the Second World War, rail passengers included Army personnel for whom the town was a training base for OCTU (Officer Cadet Training Unit) and hundreds of evacuees from the Bootle area of Liverpool.

After the retreat from Dunkirk, some wounded came by rail direct from the landing beaches to Highland Moors on the outskirts of the town and various hotels used as convalescent homes. Under the Lease Lend arrangement with the USA, all kinds of new agricultural machinery came up the line for distribution.

On 23 October 1952, Queen Elizabeth II stepped on to Welsh ground for the first time as sovereign when she arrived by Royal train at Llandrindod Wells en route to open the Claerwen Dam, some 15 miles away. A commemorative slab is situated on the 'down' platform to mark the spot.

An employee in one of the offices in the 1950s describes the station yard as still being a busy place with three coal merchants, two oil depots and a GPO storage area. The place was full of 'Pigeons, porters and permanent way staff'. In 1952, the prize for best section of line was won by supervisor Ray Davies with his team of 36 gangers.

By the mid 1950s however, the amount of traffic had decreased considerably, the double line section was altered to commence ¾ mile in the Shrewsbury direction north of the crossing (No. 1 box) and the 'up' platform was taken out of use, (its buildings used for permanent way department offices when the depot at Builth Road closed), and the

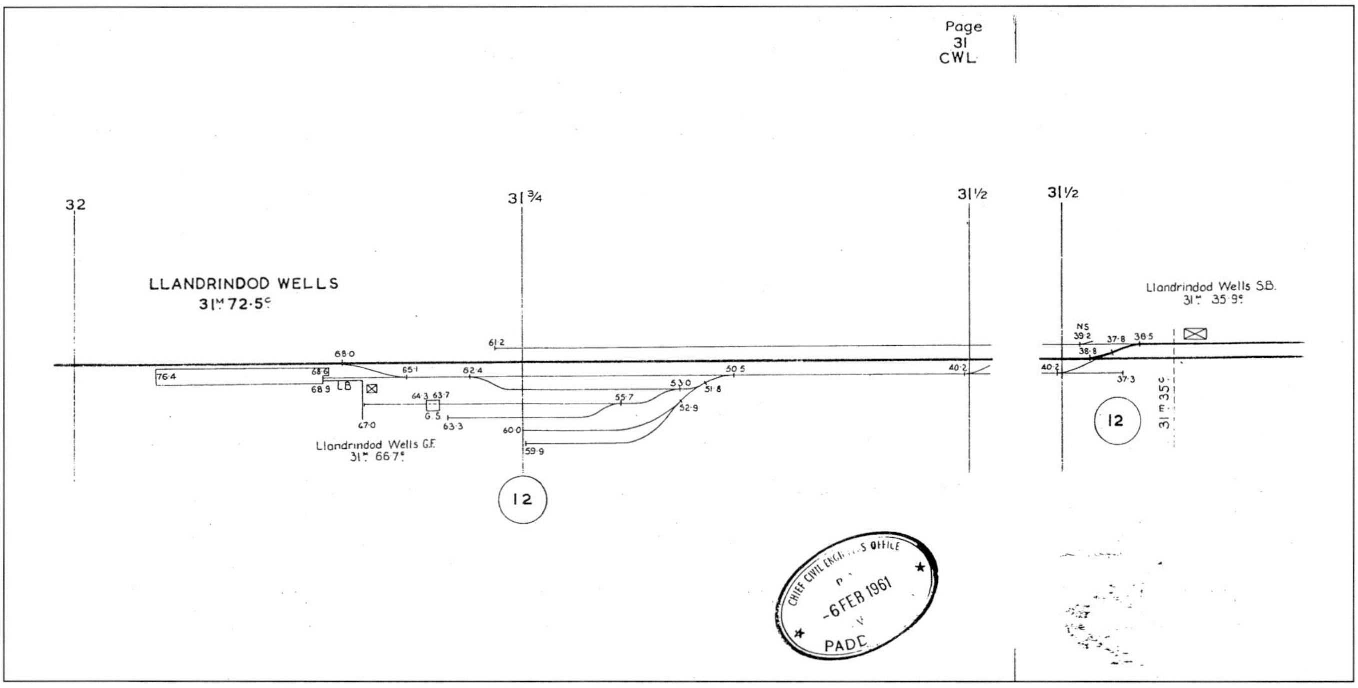

Llandrindod 1961. (Chief Civil Engineer's Office BR(WR) Paddington)

A *'19th century porter' struggles with a cabin trunk during Llandrindod's Victorian Festival in 1988.*

(The late Alan H. Martin)

'down' platform No. 2 signal box closed. Closure of the goods yard followed in May 1967 when local freight traffic ceased. With the singling of the line to Penybont in 1964, a passing loop was created at the crossing.

In 1969 Llandrindod became an unstaffed halt but staff were re-instated in 1971 when the booking office re-opened. The loop was moved to the station in early March 1986 and was officially in use from 2 June 1986. With the loop at the station, both platforms were again in use and station staff were heard enjoying directing passengers to 'Platform 2', although this resurrected 'up' platform had to wait until 1988 before it received new lighting.

By October 1986, the 'up' side of the old loop was removed as were the semaphore signals but the century-old LNWR signal box received a preservation order and was eventually moved, in 1989, to the 'down' platform south of the station building and is open to the public at limited times. The level crossing barriers north of the station are operated by train crews.

At the beginning of the 1980s, an annual Victorian Festival brought the town's heritage to the notice of tourists and local authorities alike.

The Post Office which had, by some means, managed to remove a precious Victorian post box from Machynlleth (some 50 miles away) erected this on the 'up' platform and in 1990, the cast iron canopy which had been dismantled at the Powys County Council offices when these were demolished, was renovated and erected on the 'down' platform buildings in an effort to return the station to its former glory. The cost, £33,000, was shared by various bodies including the local councils and Mid Wales Development and a ceremony to celebrate what was referred to as 're-Victorianisation' took place on 25 August 1990 during that year's Victorian Festival: a commemorative plaque is situated on the 'down' platform building.

In April 1992, a high-roofed supermarket lorry ran right through the wooden canopy on the road side of the station buildings housing the booking office. Fortunately, as this was early in the morning, there were no personnel injuries. This is more than could be said for the station front

Penybont station, signal box and goods yard viewed from the north in the mid 1960s.

(David Lawrence)

The Chipman weed killing train as it approaches Penybont station in April 1989.
(Roy Palmer)

Penybont Halt, although overgrown, still reveals its old flower pots bearing the words 'Safety', 'Speed', 'Comfort' and 'Efficiency' in December 1994.
(Rose Coleman)

from which the whole canopy was torn down.

With Llandovery and Llandeilo unstaffed in 1992, Llandrindod Wells became the only staffed station between Pantyffynnon and Shrewsbury. The workforce of two was reduced to one in 1994 and is responsible for almost everything, including the pleasing appearance of the station. At the end of 1993, the barrow crossing at the north end of the platforms was removed.

Penybont (CWR/LNWR/LMSR/BR (WR))
Opened 10 October 1864 (originally named Crossgates and was a temporary terminus) Penybont had a wagon lay-by on the 'up' side and a goods yard and shed on the 'down'.

The station, which once had a workforce of about a dozen on 24-hour duties, became unstaffed on 6 September 1965. The track was singled 21 June 1964 and freight traffic ceased 24 May 1965. Once possessing one of the best florally decorated gardens, adorned with minute sea shells, Penybont deteriorated considerably and wore a somewhat neglected look in the 1990s until the local Women's Institute made attempts to improve it.

On the 'up' platform, which remains in use, there are four concrete flower containers in the former gardens which bear the words *Safety*, *Speed*, *Comfort* and *Efficiency* – an echo of its LNWR past. On the slab set between them can be read the well-known verse:

The kiss of the sun for a pardon
The song of the birds for mirth
One is nearer God's heart in a garden
Than anywhere else on earth

Penybont Junction, north of the station, was simply the point where the line became single to pass through Penybont Tunnel. It was not a junction in the conventional sense although, had past projects proceeded, it might have become so. The Mid Wales Railway obtained authorisation in June 1865 to build a line from Rhayader to join the Central Wales at Penybont and in 1874 authorisation was granted to the Worcester & Aberystwyth Junction Railway to extend a line from New Radnor to Rhayader, but neither scheme came to fruition.

Penybont is now a 'request only' stop.

Dolau (CWR/LNWR/LMSR/BR (WR))
Opened 10 October 1864 with a temporary station building on the 'up' side to which LNWR later made improvements, Dolau had a small goods and coal yard on the 'down' side. The track was singled 21 June 1964. Freight traffic ceased the following day and Dolau became an unstaffed halt 6 September 1965, the signal box ceasing to be a block post in the same year but for a while was used for crossing duties.

The 'up' line is in use from Penybont Junction to Llanbister Road but it was slewed to the 'down' side through Dolau due to the state of a bridge north of the station being weak and it was decided to swing the line over rather than carry out repairs.

By 1983, the station had a very neglected appearance which prompted local volunteers, under a newly formed Dolau Station Action Group, to begin improvements. The transformation has been such that this little halt has become a showpiece and it is almost a certainty that, in any competition with the appropriate category, an

The prize-winning Dolau halt in 1994.
(Rose Coleman)

award will be won by Dolau. These have included Customer Care, Wales in Bloom, Community interest in unstaffed Stations, Rail Flora and BR National Award for unstaffed Stations as well as a prize in the Anglo-Irish Best Station Award.

By the beginning of the 1990s, the front wall of the platform was in need of attention and during May and June 1991, refurbishment was carried out by British Rail and the height of the platform raised 6-8in.

A new shelter was also provided and this has seating, an information rack, local literature, photographs and even poetry – a poem by Thomas Corbet, a 19th century Llanfihangel Rhydithon postman:

They started from Knucklas
O'er a viaduct grand
Where the scenes of the Teme
Are at your command
In the month of October in
The year sixty four
An engine they started which
N'er ran before.

Floral decorations on the platform, an old platelayers' trolley brought from Penybont and restored, a Victorian type lamp and a clock are some of the features which make the halt so attractive. The disused 'up' platform is also tended. To complete the railway scene, a local enthusiast has one of the ex Llandrindod Wells semaphore signals working in his garden close by the track and uses it to indicate whether or not he is at home to callers. (Another one ended up in East Anglia.) Dolau is now a 'request only' stop.

Llanbister Road (CWR/LNWR/LMSR/BR (WR))
Opened to goods and passengers on 10 October 1864 with double track being provided to Penybont Junction on 10 May 1871. A second platform had been built by 1876 and Llanbister Road had a goods yard and shed on the 'down' side beyond the station in the Shrewsbury direction. A garden furniture centre now occupies the site.

The line was singled 21 June 1964, the 'down' platform which had had the original stations buildings (now restored and privately occupied) taken out of use and freight traffic ceased a week later when the station became an unstaffed halt on 28 June 1964 and is now a request stop.

The informative interior of Dolau station shelter in 1994.
(Rose Coleman)

Llanbister Road looking south, Autumn 1994.
(Rose Coleman)

Dolau Station Action Group set about effecting some improvements to the state of its neighbour in the late 1980s. In 1990, a small local group began undertaking maintenance and provided the halt with a seat. There is no village community close to the station which is 848ft above sea level and is situated in one of the isolated scenic parts of the line. Its nearest village is Llangunllo which is served by its own station, the village of Llanbister being five miles away. Railtrack allocated £11,200 to upgrade the station in 1997.

Llangunllo (Llangynllo) (CWR/LNWR/LMSR/BR (WR)) Opened 10 October 1864 with a welcome by local church musicians playing harps, violins and flutes. It had a passing loop and siding with the signal box built above the waiting

Staff pose for a photograph at Llangunllo station in the 1920s.
(Courtesy Judith Dyke)

'Sprinter' No. 153355 calls at Llangunllo in October 1994.
(Rose Coleman)

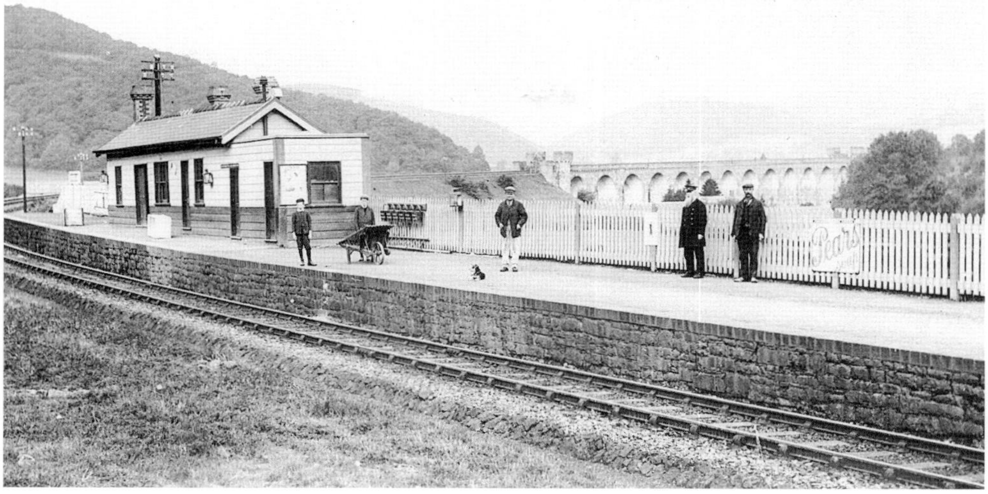

Knucklas station c1914. Second from the right is Station Master Evan Jones.
(Courtesy A Thomas)

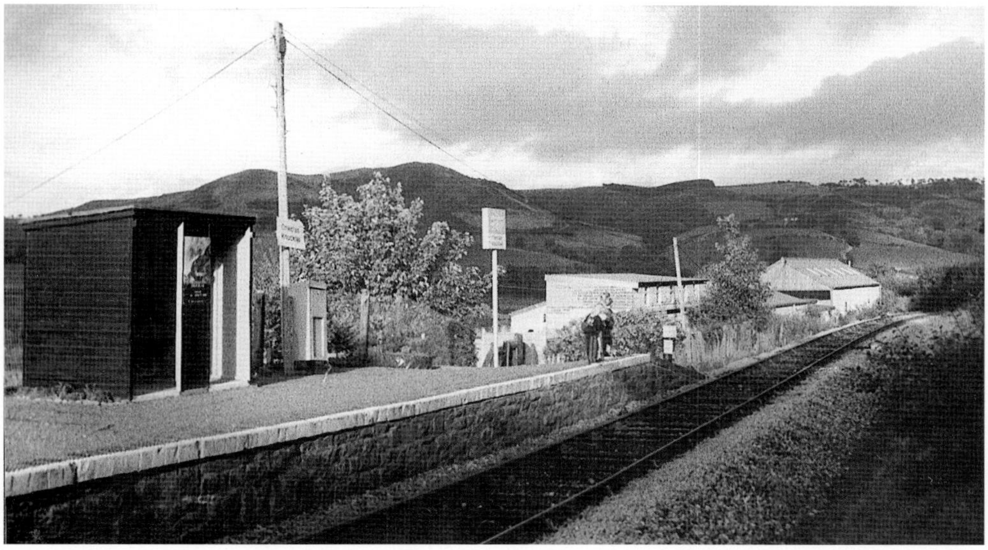

Knucklas station looking north in 1994.
(Rose Coleman)

room. This is the closest station/halt to the summit of the line (980ft above sea level). Freight traffic ceased 20 April 1964 and the passing loop was taken out.

Only the 'up' platform is now in use. Llangynllo became an unstaffed halt 6 September 1965 and it is now a 'request only' stop.

Flowers and small trees were planted in the early part of 1990 but as with many remote halts on the line, maintaining appearance is a problem. There is a basic shelter and platform lighting was installed in 1992. Railtrack allocated £16,800 to upgrade the station in 1997.

Knucklas (Cnwclas/Knucklas) (CWR/LNWR/LMSR/BR (WR))
Opened 10 October 1864, mineral traffic commenced between Knucklas and Knighton in 1861 and passengers were conveyed from 1862. There was a single platform and goods yard on the 'up' side, the LNWR replacing its original insubstantial shelter with a brick and timber structure. In its heyday, with an agricultural traffic depot, the station was a focal point for deliveries to the farming communities of the Teme Valley. A steam crane was used to load timber.

Freight traffic ceased 21 November 1957 and the goods yard closed in October of that year, Knucklas having become an unstaffed halt on 1 February 1956. By the spring of 1969, only the chimney breasts of the old station building were left.

Knucklas Viaduct is situated just over 200 yards away in the Swansea direction. Like that at Cynghordy, it is a listed structure.

Once a frequent winner in competitions for its station gardens and floral displays, the condition of the halt has varied over the last decade having been unaccountably prone to vandalism in the 1980-90s. The platform was resurfaced in 1990 and the shelter repainted. Flower beds have been planted in containers made from old sleepers and in tractor tyres and a volunteer working group is now responsible for the halt's pleasing appearance. In 1993 and 1994, it was commended in the Wales in Bloom station awards. Railtrack allocated £11,200 to upgrade the station in 1997.

It is now a 'request only' stop.

Knighton (Trefyclawdd/Knighton) (Knighton Railway/ CWR/LNWR/LMSR/BR (WR))
Opened 6 March 1861. A single-road locomotive shed was opened on the 'up' side in 1870 (mainly to house engines for banking to Llangunllo Summit) and the track to Craven Arms was doubled a year later. Knighton depot was a small sub shed of Shrewsbury. There was a goods yard on the 'down' side and a lay-by capable of taking 45 wagons. The locomotive shed closed 1 January 1962, Knighton becoming an unstaffed halt on 28 September 1964 and freight traffic ceased 1 March 1965.

Tracks were lifted on the 'up' side on which the buildings were also demolished but the substantial grey stone

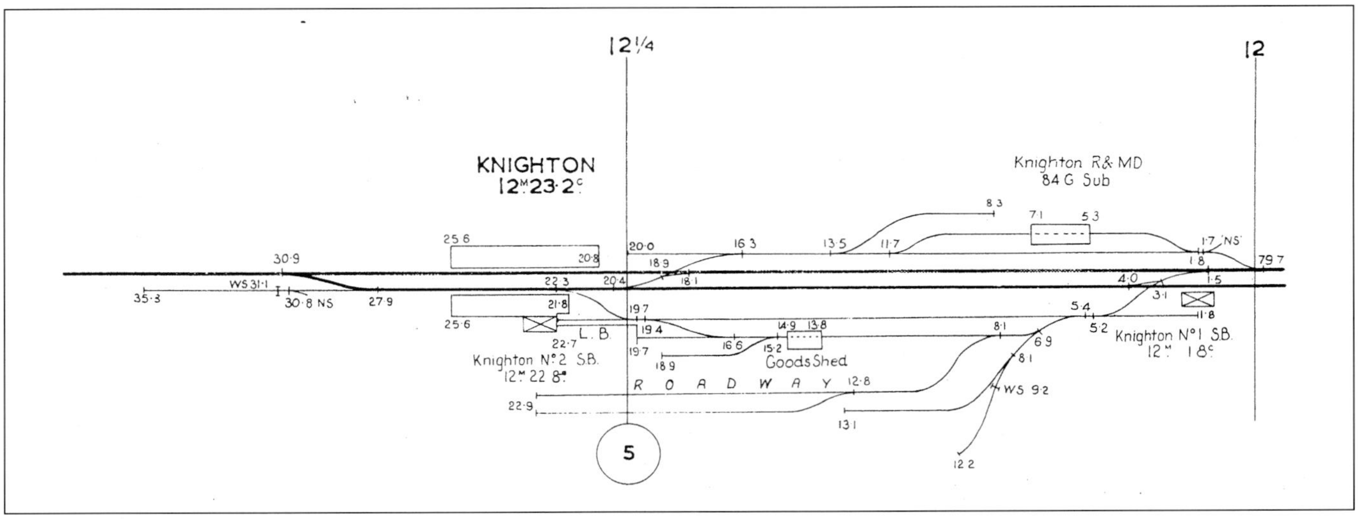

Knighton 1961. (Chief Civil Engineer's Office BR(WR) Paddington)

Knighton station in LNWR days. The signal box was supplied by Saxby & Farmer.
(HMRS/G. M. Perkins collection)

buildings on the 'down' side remain intact. In the late 1980s, it was decided to re-lay the loop, at a cost of £240,000, part of which was covered by a grant from the Wales Tourist Board – the first of its kind for this type of project – thus relieving the line of some of the problems of what had been a 31-mile stretch of single track between Craven Arms and Llandrindod Wells. The work commenced in February 1990 and was completed that summer. This required restoration of the 'up' platform and the provision of a footbridge. In LMS days. Knighton station was the recipient of that company's

Bucknell station with staff and passengers posing for an official photograph on the 'down' platform, alongside a passenger train. The station building is now a private dwelling.
(Bernard Matthews collection)

Bucknell station, 19 May 1986.
(Courtesy John Horsley Denton)

'Silver Spade' First Class Award for several years and finally earned the right to keep it. It was housed in a glass case in the waiting room but is now in private hands.

Alas, by 1990 the platforms, once well known for their floral displays, had fallen into neglect. With the re-instatement of a loop, the 'up' platform was resurfaced and plans made by the Town Council to provide seating and new shelters. By 1993, there was lighting on both sides and the platforms had been tidied.

The station, the Welsh name of which was wrongly spelled by British Rail for some time as Trefydo instead of Trefyclo or Trefyclawdd (meaning 'the town on the dyke') is actually in England while the town which it serves, is in Wales. Railtrack allocated £14,119 to upgrade the station in 1997.

Bucknell (Knighton Railway/CWR/LNWR/LMSR/BR (WR))
Opened 1 October 1860 for goods and for passengers 6 March 1861 with double track from 1871. The 'down' side had a goods shed and yard – although these were not completed in time for its opening – and gabled neo gothic station buildings. The latter are now in private occupation but there is still a shelter on the 'down' side, the track having been singled 28 September 1964.

The station became an unstaffed halt on 6 September 1965 and trains now stop only on request.

Freight traffic ceased 28 June 1965 and the large LNWR signal box was then reduced to ground-frame status, remaining in use to operate the crossing gates until Bucknell was designated as an 'open' crossing in the 1980s. Bucknell station, which is in England, is now cared for by the local Women's Institute and both platforms are well decorated. In 1993 and 1994 it was commended in the Wales in Bloom stations competition.

From this point, the line proceeds north eastwards into Shropshire. Railtrack allocated £17,026 to upgrade the station in 1997.

Hopton Heath (Knighton Railway/CWR/LNWR/LMSR/BR (WR))
Opened 1 October 1860 with single track which was doubled in 1871.

The goods yard on the 'down' side and signal box on the

Hopton Heath on 6 March 1966 with the line singled but the station building is still impressive in the gloom.
(Roy Palmer)

Broome station. An LNWR DX class 0-6-0 locomotive heads a passenger train.
(Bernard Matthews collection)

Broome station showing the station building and the signal box during BR days.
(David Lawrence)

'up' side were situated at the southern end, the latter being replaced by a modern box in 1945.

The attractive red brick buildings on the neat 'down' platform side are now privately owned. The line was singled again 28 September 1964 and Hopton Heath became an unstaffed halt. Freight traffic ceased 1 March 1965. Trains now stop only on request.

Broome (Knighton Railway/CWR/LNWR/LMSR/BR (WR))
Opened 1 October 1860. It had a single road goods shed and a small goods yard on the 'up' side. The line was doubled in 1871. Freight traffic ceased 1 March 1964 and Broome became an unstaffed halt 28 September 1964 by which time the line had been singled again. The signal box which, since Nationalisation, had frequently been 'switched out', closed 21 April 1965. An engineering company took over the goods shed and the 'down' platform and buildings have been demolished. However, the 'up' platform which is the one in use, has an informative shelter display. Railtrack allocated £11,501 to upgrade the station in 1997. Trains now stop only on request.

Craven Arms (Craven Arms and Stokesay) (Shrewsbury & Hereford Railway–Knighton Railway/West Midland Railway/LNWR-GWR/LMSR/BR (WR))
Opened by the Shrewsbury & Hereford Railway to passengers 20 April 1852 and for goods the following July, it took its later name – the 'Stokesay' was added in 1879 – from a local inn (which was situated in the Lordship of the Manor of the Earls of Craven) and from the parish of Stokesay in which the station stood.

Originally single track from Shrewsbury, the line was doubled to Craven Arms in 1862. The Knighton Railway Company opened the line for freight to Bucknell (the first

Craven Arms 1876/7. Passengers and station staff outside the refreshment room. An LNWR 2-4-0 is probably running on the Knighton line. Note the low-level platform.

(Bernard Matthews collection)

Craven Arms and Stokesay station with LNWR and GWR signs in the BR period.

(Bernard Matthews collection)

Craven Arms station in December 1994.

(Rose Coleman)

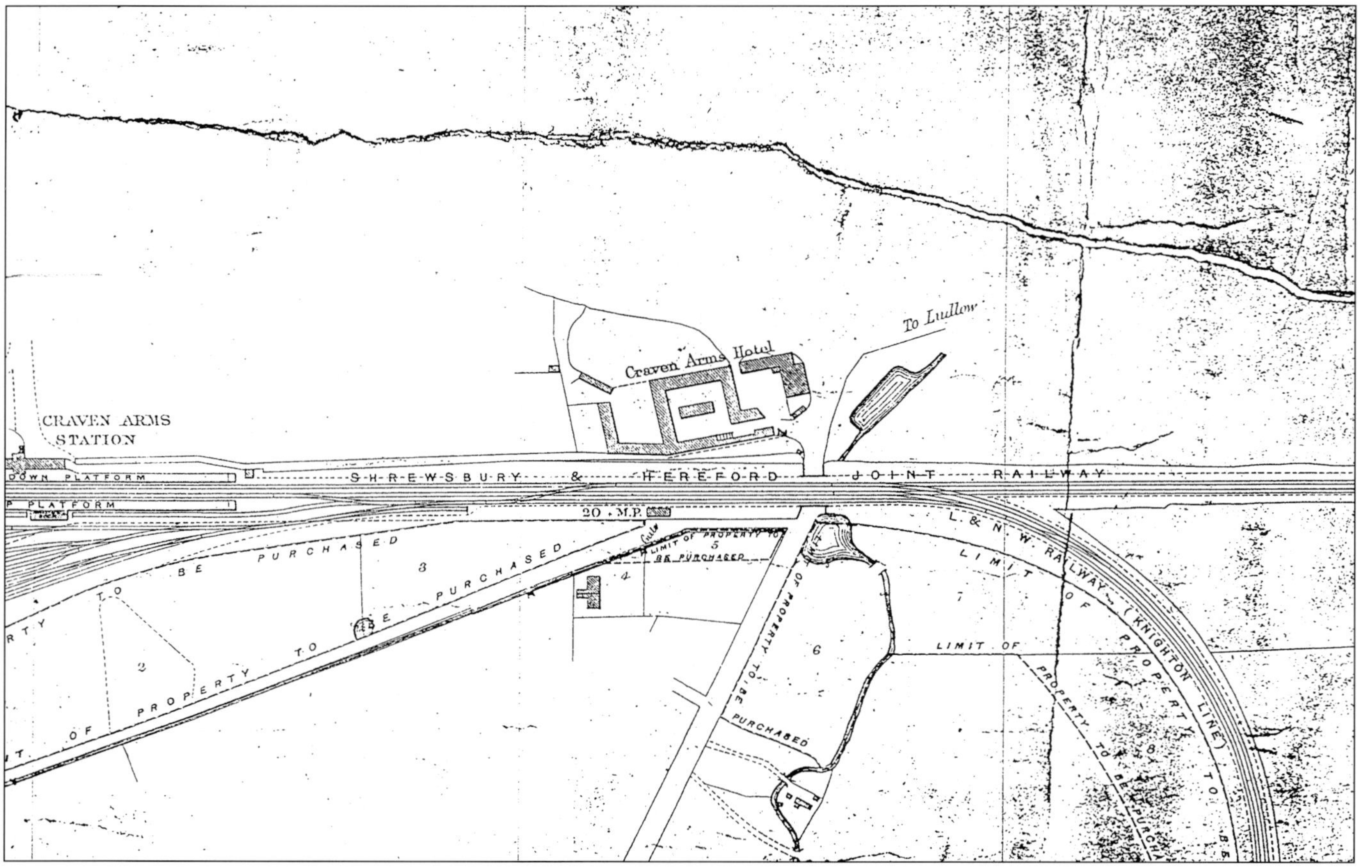

LNWR plan of additional land – proposed purchase 1877 at Craven Arms. (John Horsley Denton)

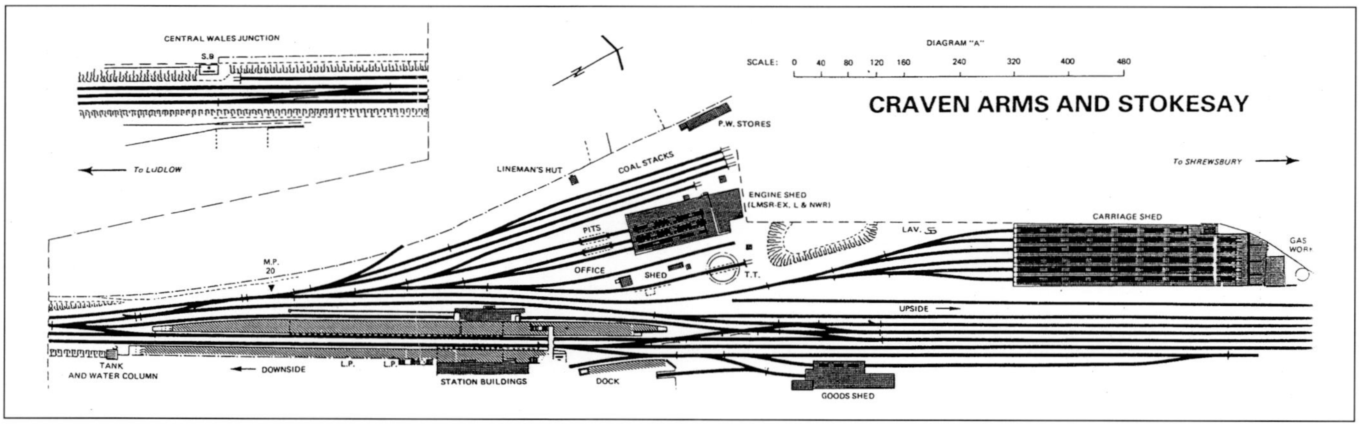

Craven Arms c1947.

stage on the route to Knighton) in October 1860 at the Central Wales Junction to the south of the station, after which point it curved 90° westwards and in 1861 a turntable for the Knighton Railway was installed. Passenger services commenced 6 March 1861 and the line to Knighton was doubled in 1871.

Once a very busy junction the station, which was joint GWR/LNWR consisted of substantial stone buildings and was situated on both sides. Terrace houses were constructed for the railway staff. Platform canopies were built after 1857 as a result of complaints from local inhabitants about the inadequacies of passenger facilities at the station and in 1908 a footbridge was constructed.

Craven Arms and Stokesay had branches to Bishops Castle and to Wellington via Much Wenlock. The four-road locomotive shed was constructed of stone and there was a large goods yard and a quantity of private sidings.

Plans dated 1877 show that the LNWR intended to acquire a considerable amount of land on the 'up' side but for whatever purpose this was intended, the purchase did not take place.

The immediate population was very small but many country roads met in the vicinity. In the mid 1850s, bark went to clog making and tanning industries and there were storage sheds for guano fertiliser. By the early 1900s, a livestock market was held opposite the Craven Arms Hotel necessitating additional cattle pens and sidings at the station which also served an extensive sheep farming area – in 1925 nearly 20,000 sheep were transported. Special trains were provided for market traffic to Knighton and Llandrindod Wells.

There is little or nothing left from the former bustling days. The locomotive shed closed 22 May 1965 and the line was singled to Knighton in the same year.

During the Second World War a long train was 'hidden away' in one of the sheds at Craven Arms. The 'top secret' accommodation was said to be held for members of the government in case of emergency.

The Central Wales junction box closed in 1965.

Church Stretton station's ancient plaque showing height above sea level (613ft), and other data, January 1995.
(Rose Coleman)

Southbound trains for the Central Wales Line cross to the 'up' track at the station and, until June 1986 when the points became operated from the signal box north of the station, the guard had to set and re-set these himself at the ground frame at the very far end of the 'up' platform.

Through freight on the CWL ceased in 1964 and local freight was withdrawn 22 May 1965 after which the MPD closed. Western Region freight traffic ceased 6 May 1968 and the 'up' line station buildings were demolished in 1969, those on the 'down' side soon following. For a while, very inadequate facilities were offered to waiting passengers but substantial brick shelters have since been erected – one with a telephone attached.

In 1992, a new footbridge was built a short distance down the platforms to the south of the position of the old one. The station is now unstaffed but the signal box, complete with semaphore signals is still in operation. At this point the last single-line token is relinquished and the line continues as double track northwards to Shrewsbury.

Wistanstow Halt (Shrewsbury & Hereford/Joint GWR/LNWR/LMSR)
Opened 1850s and closed 11 June 1956.

Marsh Brook (Shrewsbury & Hereford/Joint GWR/LNWR/LMSR)
Opened 1850s. Closed to passengers 9 June 1958 and to goods 2 December 1963.

The attractive station building is privately owned and the signal box at the level crossing was still in operation in 1994.

Little Stretton Halt (Shrewsbury & Hereford/Joint GWR/LNWR/LMSR)
Opened 1850s and closed in 1950s.

Church Stretton (Shrewsbury & Hereford/GWR-West Midland Railway-LNWR/GWR-LMSR/GWR-BR (WR)-BR (LMR))
First opened 21 January 1852 by Shrewsbury & Hereford Railway. A second station was opened 23 May 1914 a few yards south of the previous one. There were goods shed sidings accommodating 19 wagons and sidings north and south of the goods shed able to take nearly 50 more.

Cattle pens held 15 wagons and an 'up' refuge siding could take 47 wagons. A further 14 could be accommodated between this and the second junction with the main line. In addition, 60 wagons could be held in the 'down' refuge siding. The latter was converted into a running loop in September 1941 to assist with extra traffic during the Second World War.

Goods traffic ceased 19 September 1966 and this once busy place became unstaffed 3 July 1967. It is well maintained with shelters and an informative plaque giving details of altitude and position, situated on the 'up' platform: 'Height above sea level 613ft. Latitude 52° 32'. Longitude 2° 48'. Real noon 11 minutes 12 seconds later than Greenwich'. The latter being a reminder of the days when Greenwich Mean Time was still a thing of the future.

The original station buildings are still in existence beyond and the signal box now operates for repair work only.

All Stretton (Shrewsbury & Hereford/Joint GWR/LNWR/LMSR)
Opened 1850s. The station was closed 4 Januay 1943 and re-opened 6 May 1946, closing finally on 9 June 1958.

Leebotwood (Shrewsbury & Hereford/Joint GWR/LNWR/LMSR)
Opened 1850s, became unstaffed 2 July 1936 and closed 9 June 1958.

Dorrington (Shrewsbury & Hereford/Joint GWR/LNWR/LMSR)
Opened early 1850s. Closed to passengers 9 June1958 and for goods 15 March 1965 (except for some private sidings), although *official* closing date was 3 June 1965. The signal box was still in operation at the level crossing in 1994.

Condover (Shrewsbury & Hereford/Joint GWR/LNWR/LMSR)
Opened 1850s. Closed to passengers 9 June 1958 and for goods 7 October 1963.
At date of closure, it was functioning only as a coal depot.

Shrewsbury (Shrewsbury & Hereford/GWR-West Midland Railway-LNWR/GWR-GWR/LMSR – BR (WR) – BR (LMR))
This had become a well-established rail centre serving the Midlands by the 1840s. A number of companies had interests here and the station was a joint venture completed by 1849. The Shrewsbury & Hereford Railway was the first company to have its own locomotive shed. This was situated at Coleham, south of the station on the east side of the River Severn and closed in June 1970. The line to Craven Arms and Hereford was opened from Shrewsbury in 1852 and was doubled by 1862.

Shrewsbury station exterior – Shrewsbury & Herereford Railway/GWR/LNWR. (Bernard Matthews collection)

The station building was originally two stories high with a central clock, the ground floor having all the passenger services while the upper housed staff offices. There was a wrought iron roof and two platforms. The building now consists of three stories, the below ground area having been excavated to form the present ground floor.

By the turn of the century, a large island platform had been added and the platforms numbered 1 to 10. Restructuring has since taken place and in 1961 the station was rebuilt by BR and the footbridge removed.

The station buildings at Shrewsbury (referred to as 'Salop' by railwaymen) were nearly demolished in 1967 but, saved by public outcry, were restored in 1985 and the offices, which had been transferred to Chester Street, about 200 yards away, returned. Passenger facilities were upgraded and there is now a ticket office and travel centre on the ground floor, the buffet remaining at platform level.

In 1991, plans were made to replace all the Shrewsbury area signal boxes with the installation of an up-to-date system. The imposing Severn Bridge Junction box, British Rail's largest remaining manual lever box, situated within a triangle of track, has become a listed building and still functions.

Originally, Central Wales Line trains used Platforms 1 and 2 but there are now no platforms bearing these numbers. Through trains pull in at numbers 4 and 7 and the Central Wales Line, with no through service to Crewe, terminates at 5 or 6. Platform 3 is rarely used for passenger traffic.

Swansea-Llanelli-Pontarddulais

Swansea High Street (South Wales Railway/GWR/BR (WR))

Opened 18 June 1850 by the South Wales Railway, approaching Swansea from the east, this was originally a wooden building with two platforms which accommodated the 6-700 people who attended the opening ceremony. Some additions were made in 1879.

The South Wales Railway was absorbed by the GWR in 1863 and the original broad gauge track was converted to standard gauge in 1872. The station, which was also the terminus of GWR's West Wales system, was rebuilt in the 1930s with impressive canopies over the platforms. It was

Platform 3 at Shrewsbury. This is rarely used. (Bernard Matthews collection)

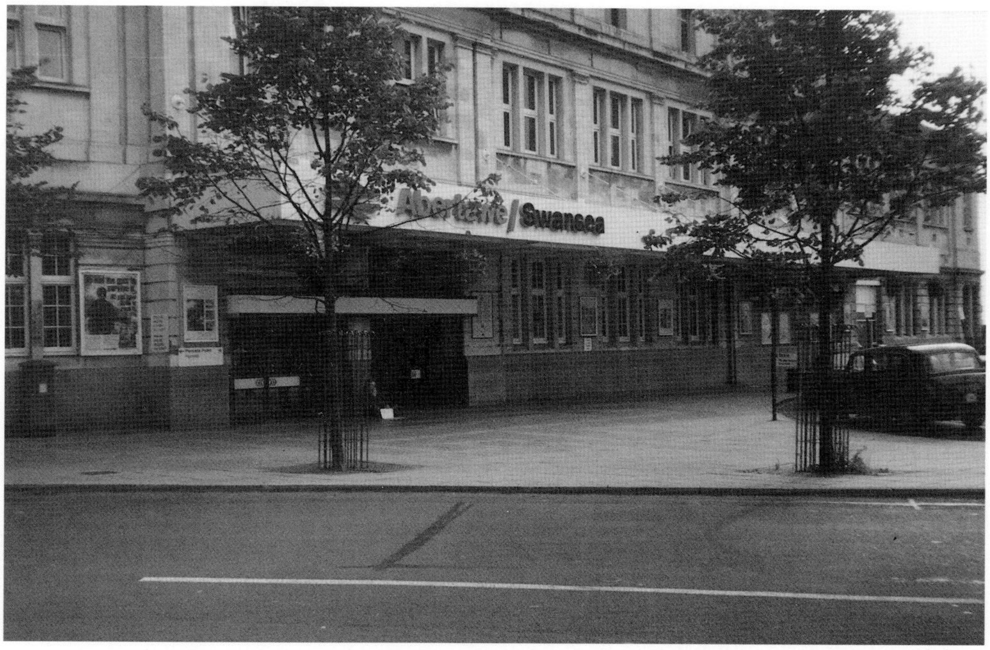

Swansea High Street station exterior in 1994.
(Author)

modernised by British Rail in the 1980s, and providing good facilities for passengers, the new concourse and travel centre were officially opened by broadcaster and author, the late Wynford Vaughan Thomas, on 15 September 1984.

Swansea High Street has four platforms and in 1994 was the only Central Wales Line terminus with InterCity services direct to and from London: this facility having been withdrawn from Shrewsbury. It did not become the terminus for Central Wales Line until 1970. (When Swansea Victoria closed in June 1964, trains commenced running only as far as Llanelli over the old GWR route.)

InterCity motive power servicing is dealt with at Landore diesel depot, situated about a mile to the north east, in the triangle formed by the South Wales and West Wales route and the connecting line between them which avoids Swansea station. The steam shed here closed in June 1961.

Cockett (GWR)
Opened June 1871. This was approached by a 1 in 50 gradient in each direction. It was closed to passenger traffic on 15 June 1964 but the platforms have not been removed.

On 19 June 1899, due to mining operations taking place beneath, the roof of the 789-yard Cockett Tunnel, situated between the station and Landore depot, collapsed. As a consequence, GWR trains were diverted for a considerable period, running via North Dock Junction (north of High Street station) over the LNWR's Swansea line.

Gower Road (Gowerton/Gowerton North) (Tre-Gwyr/Gowerton) (South Wales Railway/GWR/BR (WR))
Opened 1 August 1854, it was known as Gower Road until 1 July 1886, Gowerton until January 1950, and Gowerton North until 6 May 1968 when it once more became Gowerton.

Originally double track with platforms 576ft in length, Gowerton was situated in close proximity to the LNWR station of the same name with the sidings of which it had complicated connections. The total capacity of these was over 300 wagons.

Goods traffic ceased 7 June 1965 except for some private sidings and the signal box closed in May 1969. The station became an unstaffed halt 28 September 1964. The shelter was repainted in 1980 when the Royal National Eisteddfod of Wales was held in the area, at which time two platforms were in use. Only the 'down' platform now remains.

Loughor (Llwchwr) (GWR)
Opened 11 October 1852. It closed to passenger and goods traffic 4 April 1960, although some private sidings, (including new ones opened after the closure of the station), existed for some time.

Llanelly (Llanelli) (South Wales Railway/GWR/BR (WR))
Opened 1852. Access for Llanelly Rail & Dock Co. opened 1 June 1853 from its own platform, the latter being standard gauge system while the South Wales Railway used broad gauge. No connection was therefore possible although

A GWR 517 class 0-4-2T at Llanelly GWR station.
(Bernard Matthews collection)

Llanelli station looking towards the level crossing in the 1990s.
(Roy Palmer)

Llanelly Goods Yard, 22 September 1927. In the early 1980s, the Area Manager's office was in part of the Llanelly goods shed.
(Welsh Industrial & Maritime Museum)

Llanelli station, May 1992.
(Roy Palmer)

A 3-car diesel multiple unit approaches a deserted Llangennech in September 1970. (Roy Palmer)

movement of coal from one to the other was effected by means of elementary machinery which swung the load from one track to the other.

Until this time, the southern passenger terminus for the Llanelly RDC had been at Llanelly Dock, (some 3/4 mile from the Town station) and this closed 1 September 1879.

There was considerable freight traffic requiring many sidings. The large motive power depot was a double roundhouse, the shed allocation being approximately 60 locomotives and in BR days, was the last steam shed in South Wales, finally closing to steam 4 October 1965. Between 1964 (when Swansea Victoria closed) and 1970, Llanelli was the southern terminus of the Central Wales Line, trains originally departing from a bay, the indicating sign for which only appeared in 1968 (after it had been taken out of use!). After 1970, the trains were timetabled as 'through' to Swansea and reversed out of Llanelli station to continue to High Street station. The station was refurbished in the 1980s and has an up to date booking hall, waiting area, limited private refreshment facilities on the town side together with adequate parking space and work during 1995/96 created a pleasant forecourt.

In 1966, the town council requested that the station signs bear the Welsh name Llanelli. Later this became the first station on the line to have its name displayed in bilingual Welsh/English. The station is still busy, being on the main line from Swansea to West Wales.

Bynea (Bynie/Bynea) (Llanelly RDC/GWR (LNWR/LMSR Running Powers)/BR (WR))
Opened c1850s. Formerly, Bynea had a brick-built station, booking office and waiting rooms on the 'up' platform. There were private sidings to Bynea Steel Works and Yspitty Tin Works and from a junction situated south west of the station there was access both to Llanelly Town station (permitted by the South Wales Railway in 1853) and to Llanelly Docks, the latter remaining until after the GWR took over the Llanelly Railway & Dock Co.

Goods traffic ceased 12 July 1965 at which time Bynea had the doubtful claim to fame in the shape of being a site where steam locomotives from all over Britain were cut up for scrap.

It is now reduced to an unstaffed halt with basic shelters of steel and glass on both platforms, all the original buildings having been demolished. There are car parking facilities on the 'down' side but the 'up' platform is accessible only by a gravel path. Bilingual signs were erected in 1991 and it is now a request stop. Railtrack allocated £11,425 to upgrade the station in 1997.

Llangennech (Llanelly RDC/GWR (LNWR/LMSR Running Powers/BR (WR))
Opened c1850s. The Llanelly company half-yearly report, 30 April 1852 records that the cost of buildings at Llangennech was £393.

There was a goods loop (Llangennech Siding) on the 'up' side to the south of the station with a junction for the ordnance depot.

Goods traffic ceased 12 July 1965. In an attractive situation but exposed to the elements, Llangennech was for some time without any form of shelter. It now has steel framed glass shelters on both platforms and a notice board with local information. Trains stop on request. Railtrack allocated £19,587 to upgrade the station in 1997.

7

Motive Power

Originally, horse-drawn trains covered the routes of the Llanelly Railroad & Dock Company (first operated in 1833 between the Gelly Gille Farm coal mine and the docks – a distance of two miles). The company acquired locomotives *Victoria* and *Albert* in 1839. These, designed and made by T. Hackworth & Co., weighed 14 tons when in operational order and were 0-6-0 tender engines with 4ft driving wheels, a horizontal boiler separating the driver and the fireman.

The Fossick & Hackworth *Princess Royal*, another 0-6-0 of the same type and weight was sent by boat from Liverpool via Bristol in 1842. As Hackworth & Company were based in County Durham, obtaining spares was complicated.

The next year, *Prince of Wales* – an 0-6-0 with outside cylinders – which had been under construction for some three years or more (begun after the acquisition of *Victoria* and *Albert*) and was the product of the Llanelly company's own designers, was put into operation. By this time, Waddle and Margrave were in charge of the locomotives.

It was a period of trial and error and the horses were always on standby to resume their duties. This they were in fact called upon to do after about twelve months when *Victoria* and *Albert* were taken out of service for extensive repairs and the overworked (and, one suspects, not entirely successful) *Prince of Wales* required a thorough overhaul and some reconstruction, not to return until 1847.

It was at this time that Grylls & Co. took over and *Princess Alice*, a Bury 0-4-0 tender was bought from the LNWR. By 1850, Ianson, Fossick & Hackworth were in control, Grylls & Co. having gone bankrupt. Mr Joseph Hepburn, the Llanelly company's Locomotive Superintendent, purchased *Prince Alfred* in 1853 (when *Prince of Wales* had yet again been taken off for modification), and *Princess Helena* in 1855, both identical to *Princess Alice* and bought from the LNWR. The fate of these 'personalities' can be traced to the end of the century and a little beyond.

The first to go – rather too literally – was *Victoria* which blew up outside Pantyffynnon station early in 1858.

0-6-0PT No. 1652 shunting above Swansea Victoria station on 28 July 1957. The line that runs behind the platform connected with the Mumbles Railway.
(Hugh Davies)

(Norman Simmons)

Swansea Paxton Street shed on 18 May 1958.

'Black 5' No. 45298 with the 12 noon ex Salop at Swansea Victoria, 29 June 1962.
(Courtesy Colin Pritchard)

(*Princess*) *Royal* was retired in rather less spectacular fashion in the same year, eventually ending up plying a section of the line to Cross Hands, having been hired out to the Mynydd Mawr Colliery Company in 1859.

In 1859 (*Princess*) *Alice* was rebuilt as an 0-4-2 and her partner, (*Prince*) *Alfred* was similarly converted in 1863. (*Princess*) *Helena* – all the Royal titles had been dropped – was taken out of service in 1870. No one wanted *Albert* in case it had similar suicidal tendencies to that of its partner, and it was 'swapped' for a mineral wagon in 1861. (*Prince of*) *Wales* was sold in 1872 for £250. The company was evidently not superstitious as *Victoria* and *Albert* rose from the ashes in 1859 when the two 0-4-2 locomotives which had come to Llanelly from Beyer Peacock & Co. in Manchester in 1847, were so named.

There followed 0-6-0s, mainly for transport of coal, an 0-4-2 passenger locomotive, (*Beatrice*) from Fossick & Hackworth, 2-4-0 saddle tanks from Hopkins, Gilkes and, in 1865, the Llanelly company constructed its own 0-6-0 named *Alexandria*.

One cannot but feel that these 'Llanelly engines', although only working the extreme southern end, deserve a special mention because they are a fair representation of the locomotive power at the beginning of the development of the Central Wales Line.

By the time the Great Western Railway had a larger say in the affairs of the Llanelly Rail & Dock Company, most of the existing engines had to be taken out of service due to lack of standardisation. Attempts were made in 1868 to solve this problem when 0-6-0s with inside cylinders were ordered from Beyer Peacock. However, although various efforts of conversion were put in hand, the state of the stock at the time of the 'take over' by GWR was such that only *Napoleon III* survived after 1886 – complete with new GWR fittings and boiler – to continue service on the main route until 1906 although some others (re-numbered GWR 894-914) were retained for a time.

Meanwhile, in the north, the Knighton Railway Company, having completed its proposed section of the line below Craven Arms in 1861, took delivery of its own locomotive, an 0-4-2 saddle tank (weighing 22½ tons when in operational order) from Beyer Peacock & Co. Within two years, this prize possession was leased to the LNWR who had had a working agreement with the company since May 1861 and who finally purchased *Knighton* and then disposed of it to a coal company after 1865.

LMS 'Black 5' No. 45406 about to leave Mumbles Road station.
(The late V. Amundson, courtesy M. Amundsen)

An ex LNWR Webb Class 2F 0-6-0 'Cauliflower' heading towards Swansea passing the foreshore of Swansea Bay.
(The late V. Amundson, courtesy M. Amundsen)

The view towards Swansea Bay station in the 1950s.
(The late V. Amundson, courtesy M. Amundsen)

BR Class 5MT 4-6-0 No. 73021 passing Swansea Bay foreshore en route to Mumbles Road station in the early 1960s.
(The late V. Amundson, courtesy M. Amundsen)

A GWR 0-6-0 pannier tank running along the Swansea Bay foreshore. Before Nationalisation these trains were hauled exclusively by ex LNWR Webb 0-6-2Ts. This is probably the 1pm Saturdays only Pontarddulais to Swansea.
(The late V. Amundson, courtesy M. Amundsen)

Pannier tank No. 9678 on the ex LNWR Swansea Bay section, heading north eastwards towards Singleton Park and University from Blackpill Burrows with a civil engineer's inspection saloon, probably after closure. (City of Swansea Archives)

Peckett 0-4-0ST No. 2140, built at Bristol in 1955 for Grovesend Steel Works, Gorseinon. Photographed on 20 October 1956.
(Courtesy Michael Lewis)

Class 7F 0-8-0 No. 49376 of 87K on a ballast train at Gowerton South, 27 May 1956.
(Courtesy Michael Lewis)

A 'pickup' goods at Tirydail in the early 1960s.
(Courtesy John Lloyd)

Llandovery shed in LMS days.
(Bernard Matthews collection)

Fowler 2-6-4T No. 2307 approaching Llanwrtyd from the north.
(The late V. Amundson, courtesy M. Amundsen)

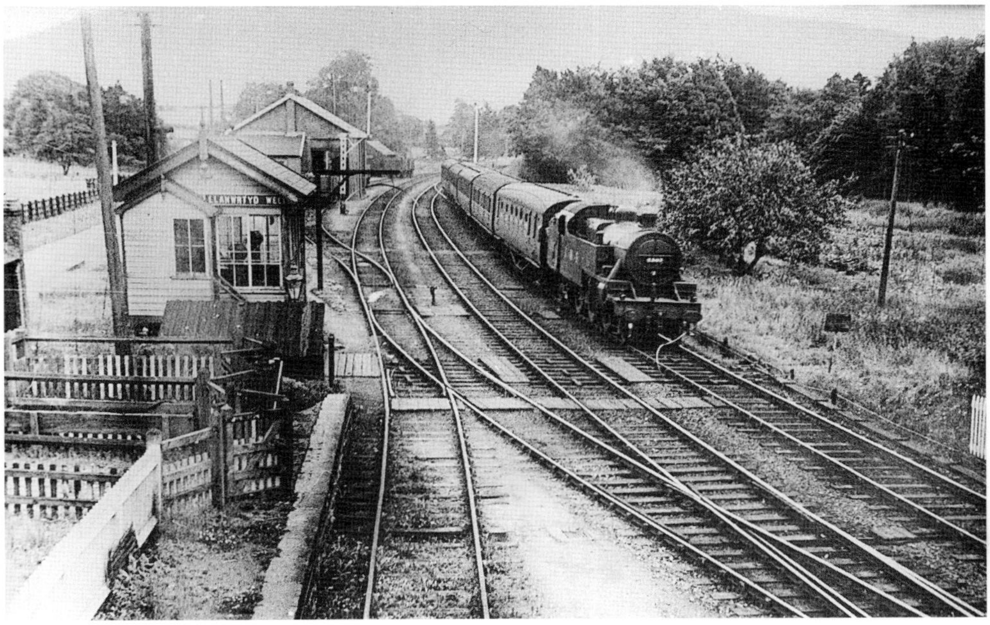

A LNWR 4-6-0 on a northbound fish train viewed from the signal box at Llandovery. The Webb 4-cylinder compound 4-6-0 goods were introduced 1903-5. Built to replace the 0-6-0 'Cauliflowers', they were considered to be poor engines by the workforce, slow, sluggish and unreliable and were nicknamed 'Bill Baileys' after the popular song, 'Bill Bailey – won't you please come home?'. This is thought to be No. 1407 built in 1904. They were all scrapped by 1920. Llandovery was used by the GWR and LNWR as is illustrated by the GWR loco shed on the right but the water column and signals are of LNWR design. When the GWR shed closed in 1935, all engines then used the LNWR depot. The group posed for the camera includes the station master and other station staff.
(HMRS/G. M. Perkins collection)

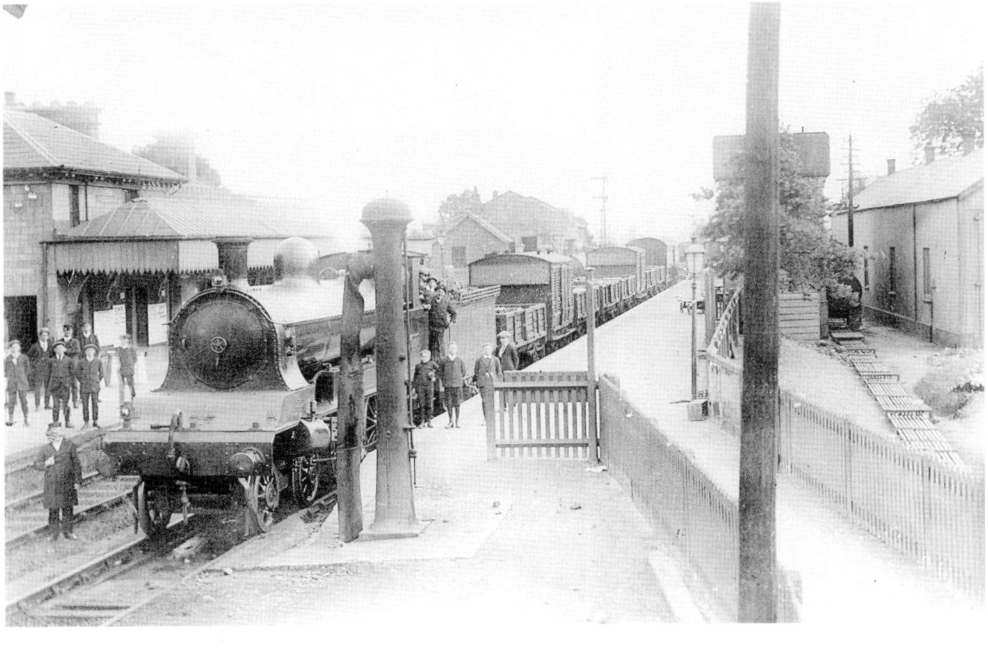

LMS 4-6-0 No. 5011 at Builth Road High Level. This was one of the first batch of Crewe-built Class 5s of 1935. (Courtesy Noel Trigg)

BR Standard 4-6-0 No. 73034 and three other locomotives, including 8F class 2-8-0 No. 48470 at Llandovery LMS shed. (Nigel Wassell collection)

Ex LNWR 0-8-0 goods No. 9031 departing from Llandovery in the 1930s. (Dorothy Bound)

Sidings and locomotive shed at Llandovery in 1932. (Dorothy Bound)

By 1862, when the LNWR and GWR shared running powers of the line existing between Shrewsbury and Knighton, traffic on this stretch consisted of Crewe built 2-2-2 and 2-4-0 tender engines. Ramsbottom 'standardisation' was underway and DX 0-6-0 (full weight when in operational order – 27 tons) were in use.

Often double headed, 2-2-0s were used for passenger traffic.

By the time the whole line was opened in 1868, passenger traffic was hauled by Webb 'Precedent' class 2-4-0s – they were 'unchokeable' locomotives capable of 80mph in suitable circumstances. These replaced most of the 2-2-2 tender engines. Old Crewe built 2-4-0s were in charge of some of the heavy freight, supported by 'Newton' 2-4-0s on the long haul down the total stretch of the line.

Many Ramsbottom 0-4-0s and 0-6-0 saddle tanks made an appearance in 1870, the LNWR and GWR having joint ownership of the Shrewsbury to Craven Arms section.

The gradual disappearance of many of the old Crewe 2-4-0s occurred in 1909 when Bowen Cooke, then Locomotive Superintendent of the LNWR, replaced them with 0-6-2 (coal tanks), Webb 2-4-2Ts and Bowen Cooke 4-6-2 tanks. These were ideal for South Wales terrain. The coupled wheels took a great deal of their weight which assisted adhesion and the flexibility of the trailing wheels was useful in negotiating the bends. Use of Webb 2-4-2s continued almost until Nationalisation in 1948.

The latter engines covered much of the work where speed was a factor in spite of the fact that the 2-4-2Ts and 0-6-2Ts 'ran hot' – an opinion expressed by the Swansea fitters – and had to be replaced on occasion, by 19in 4-6-0 goods.

The Webb 4-cylinder compound 4-6-0 goods sometimes made an appearance. This type was much prone to failure and was nicknamed 'Bill Bailey' from the popular song in the early thirties, 'Bill Bailey, won't you please come home'.

It was a busy time for tank engines on the line and the 'coal tanks' in particular were well employed operating passenger traffic well into the 1950s. Webb 1400 class compound 4-6-0s were on the line in 1910. These, from a batch of 30 built at the end of the 'Webb period', were for experimental purposes only. In 1910, some of the powerful Bowen Cooke 4-6-2T locomotives were in use.

C. N. Ryan, writing in *Railway Magazine* the following year, on the appearance of the 'Precursors' in 1911, commented:

> 'Last summer witnessed the introduction of a few large and powerful tank engines of the 'Precursor' type on this branch, and it is no exaggeration to say that they 'played' with the trains. For years the hauling had been done by old fashioned tank engines of the type that vanished a few years ago from the London and Watford trains. Compared with them superheater engines 'romp' along, and are always able to make up time, if only given a chance. Further accelerations will do much to develop the traffic to this charming country.'

G1 class 0-8-0s were brought in from Crewe. They were known as 'Super Ds' or 'Wheezeboxes' and together with Bowen Cooke 0-8-2 and 0-6-2 tanks, were mainly responsible for the coal traffic. The 0-8-2Ts were also used for Sugar Loaf banking. Llandovery sub shed mainly housed banking locomotives. Records show the allocation in 1917 as being two 5ft 6in 2-4-2Ts, two 18in 0-6-0 goods and two 17in 0-6-0 goods.

No 0-8-2T is mentioned but one, (No. 563) is listed on Swansea (shed No. 33) which may have worked from Llandovery. In the north, Knighton (sub shed of Shrewsbury) usually housed DX 0-6-0s as bankers to Llangunllo gradient.

Two years after the formation of the London Midland & Scottish Railway in 1923, the G2 – also an 0-8-0 but with greater boiler pressure than the Bowen Cooke Gl – joined the latter in hauling heavy freight and excursions. At the southern end, the formation of the LMS with Fowler as Chief Mechanical Engineer, meant that Paxton Street began housing 1F and 3F 0-6-0 tanks, followed by 2-6-4Ts (also Fowlers) to replace those designed by the LNWR. The Webb 'Cauliflower' 0-6-0 was popular for light goods and, in the 1930s, the Fowler 'Jinty' 0-6-0T was also in operation.

The Fowler 2-6-4Ts worked on the line for over 30 years being moved to Landore when Paxton Street closed in 1959 and eventually replaced by BR Standard Class 4 2-6-4Ts in 1962.

Paxton Street shed (LNWR shed code 33, LMS 4B and BR(WR) (84G) had opened on 6 January 1882 and closed on

LNWR No. 2667 at Knighton. This was one of the first batch of Bowen Cooke 4-6-2Ts built in 1911. It was renumbered LMS 6952 in 1928 and withdrawn in 1937.
(HMRS/G. M. Perkins collection)

LNWR 0-6-0 No. 1373 at Knighton. This DX Goods was built in 1865, rebuilt as a Special DX with vacuum brake in 1894, and withdrawn in 1906.
(HMRS/G. M. Perkins collection)

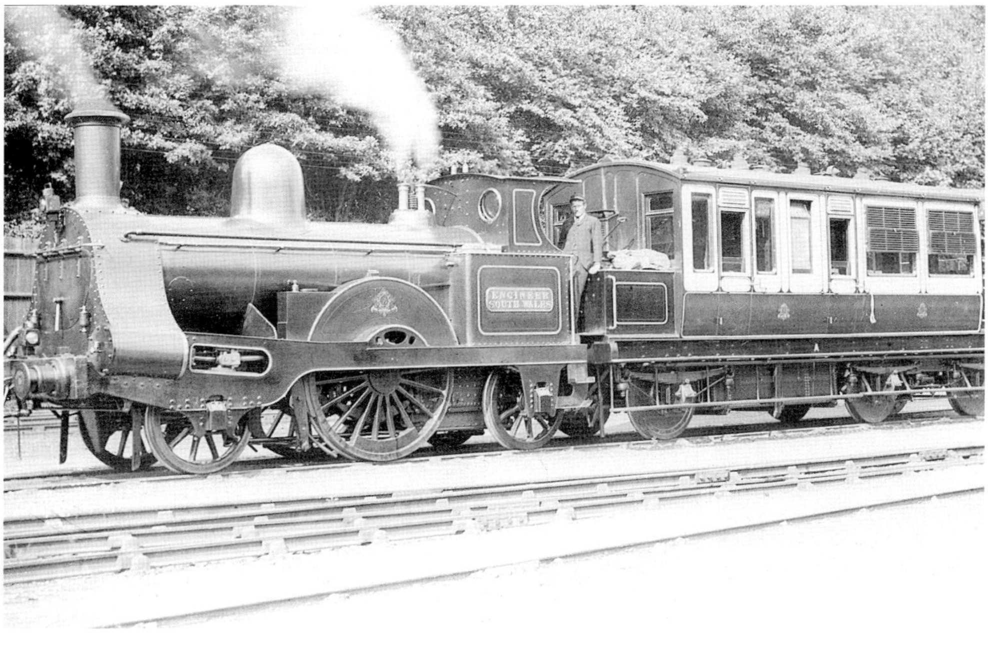

LNWR 2-2-2T Engineer South Wales *and inspection saloon at Knighton c1905. Built at Crewe in 1857 as No. 110* Canning *it was rebuilt in 1875 and transferred to the Engineer's Dept. It was* Engineer Westford *in 1891,* Engineer Lancaster *in 1894 and became* Engineer South Wales *in 1903. It was scrapped in 1911. (As* Engineer South Wales, *it replaced an engine of the same class which was scrapped in 1903.) The LNWR District Engineer's Office was at Abergavenny.*
(HMRS/G. M. Perkins collection)

An LNWR 2-4-2T heads a southbound passenger train at Llangunllo in the early part of the century.
(HMRS/G. M. Perkins collection)

A Bowen Cooke 4-6-2T double heading a 'Cauliflower' 0-6-0, hauling mostly LNWR stock leaves Knucklas for Llangunllo c1910.
(HMRS/G. M. Parkins collection)

A watering point situated in a remote location on the Llangunllo–Knucklas section, between the north portal of the tunnel and Heyope Crossing, c1910. The tank and pipe were painted dark grey and the woodwork tarred.
(HMRS/G. M. Perkins collection)

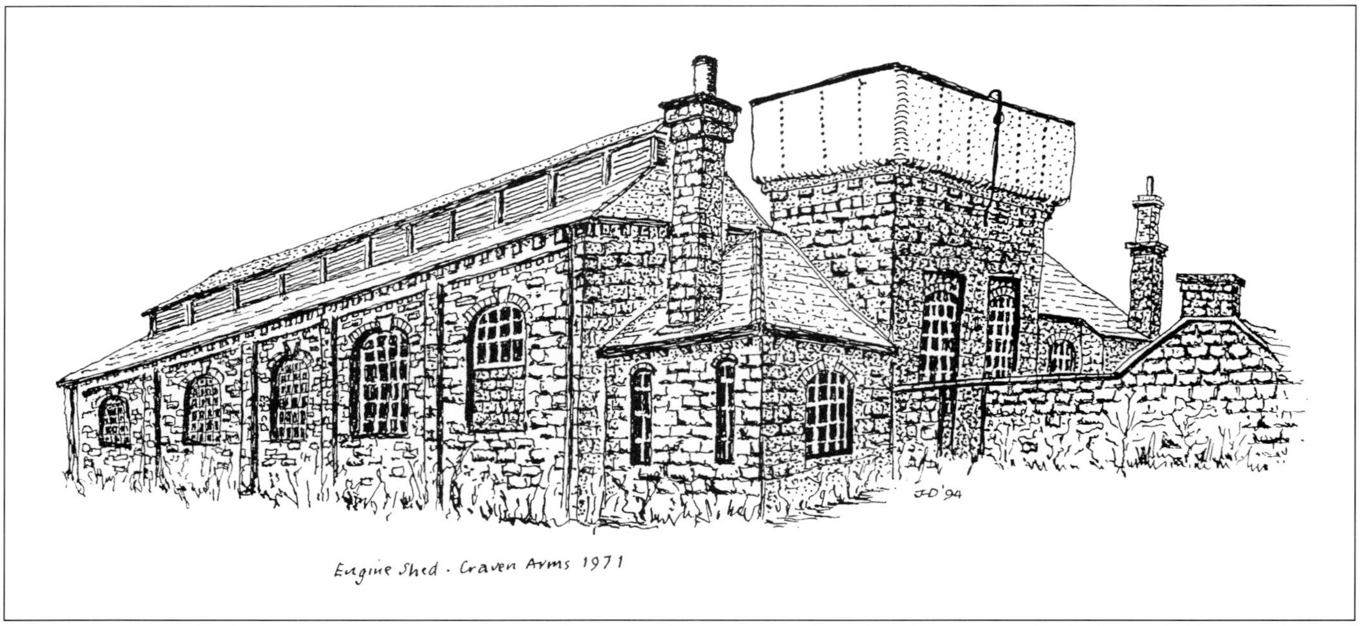

A sketch of Craven Arms shed by John Horsely Denton.

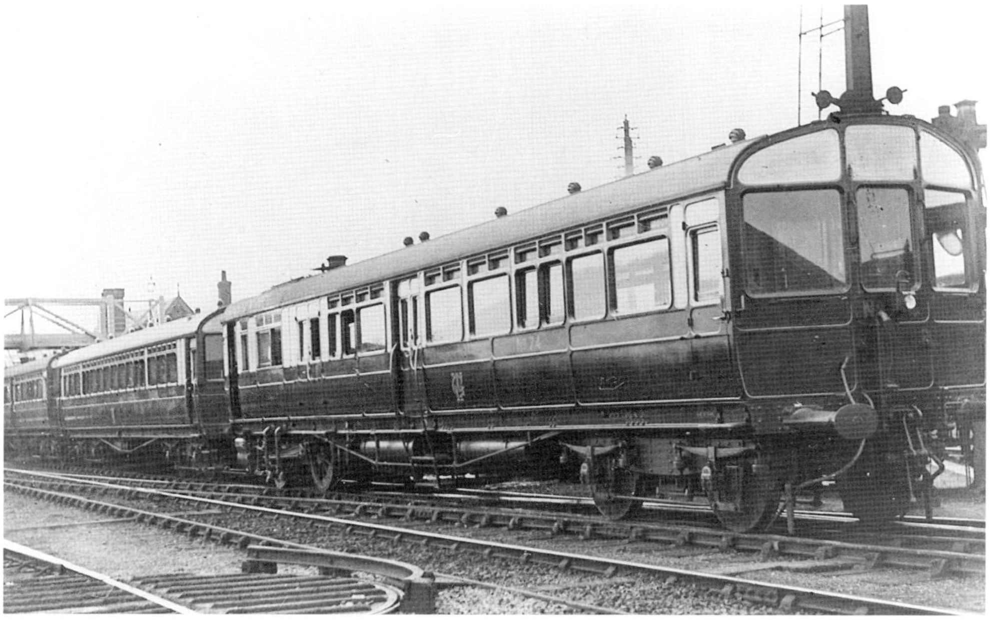

Steam rail motor No. 77 with a trailer and another steam rail motor at Craven Arms c1905.
(HMRS/G. M. Perkins collection)

Another view of steam rail motor No. 77 at Craven Arms, together with an 0-4-2T and LNWR goods stock.
(HMRS/G. M. Perkins collection)

BR Standard Class 4 4-6-0 No. 75006 arrives at Craven Arms in 1956.
(P. Gardner courtesy Nigel Wassell)

31 August 1959 but remained open for watering and turning engines until 1964. Landore closed to steam June 1961 when some engines transferred to Neath.

When Stanier took over as CME, the well-known 'Black 5s' were introduced on the line, hauling heavy passenger stock (up to 230 tons was allowed), from 1936 and the following year saw the appearance of 8F 2-8-0s hauling freight. (The Stanier 'Black 5s' were replaced by BR Standard Class 5s during 1969/61 but reappeared in 1963 to replace in their turn, the BR Standard Class 4s which were needed elsewhere.)

With Nationalisation in 1948, the coal tanks and older Fowler 'Jinties' working local passenger routes, were phased out and replaced by Stanier Class 2 2-6-2Ts and former GWR pannier tanks. Within ten years the bulk of the southern local passenger services was hauled by the latter. Attempts to use the larger GWR engines on locals on the northern section of the line caused problems due to lack of cylinder clearance.

By 1958, the Bowen Cooke 0-8-2 tank engine and the G2 0-8-0s had both been withdrawn.

After the closure of Paxton Street shed in August 1959, Landore duly received the Fowler 2-6-4Ts, probably without much enthusiasm as due to their age and condition, maintenance was a problem. Most of the ex GWR panniers went to Swansea East Dock as did the 8Fs and BR Standard Class 4-6-0s, although quite a number of the latter were later sent to Llanelli motive power depot.

Locomotives travelled over the Wind Street Viaduct to reach Landore and Swansea East Dock. After this was declared unsafe in 1963 and was subject to loco axle weight restriction by the civil engineer, this could only be used by tank engines.

Landore had to wait three years to be completely rid of the Fowler 2-6-4Ts. They had been replaced by Fairburn Class 4 2-6-4 tanks after the closure of Paxton Street but only on a temporary basis. A trial of the Standard Class 3 2-6-2 tank engines found them to have inadequate fuel capacity for the gradients involved. However, in 1962 BR Standard Class 4 2-6-4Ts arrived, having been sent from London, Tilbury & Southend system (then newly electrified).

From March 1962, ex LMS 'Jubilee' class 4-6-0s were operated from Shrewsbury shed sharing the working with BR Standard Class 5 4-6-0s and Class 4 2-6-4Ts. Class 8F 2-8-0s hauled heavy freight until the closure of Swansea (Victoria) line, after which nine of these were sent to Llanelli MPD for storage and some went to the Somerset & Dorset line, as did a few BR Standard Class 4 4-6-0s.

As the steam period drew to a close, ex GWR 5600,

LNWR 2-4-0 No. 307 Victor *at Shrewsbury.*
(Bernard Matthews collection)

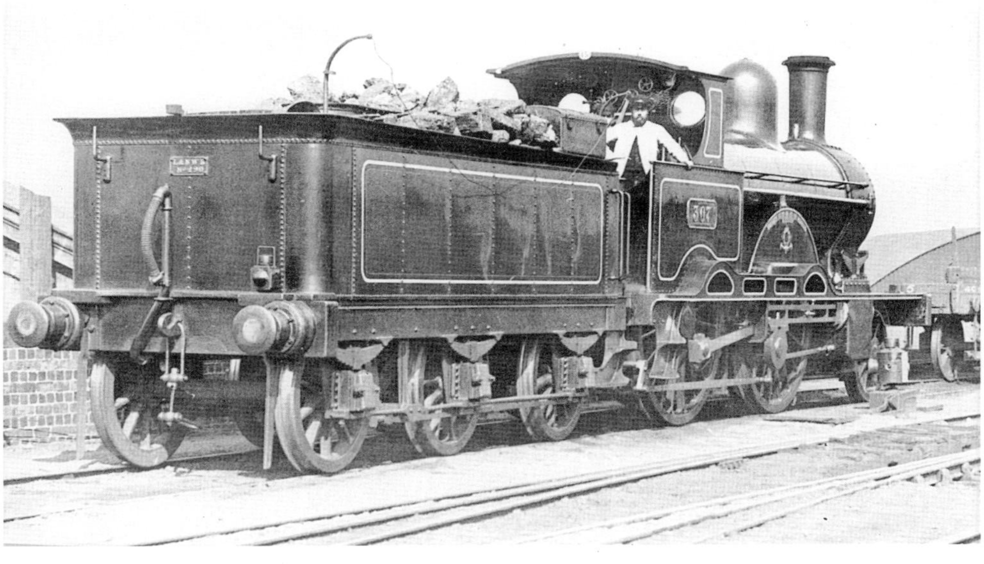

Shrewsbury shed in 1932.
(Bernard Matthews collection)

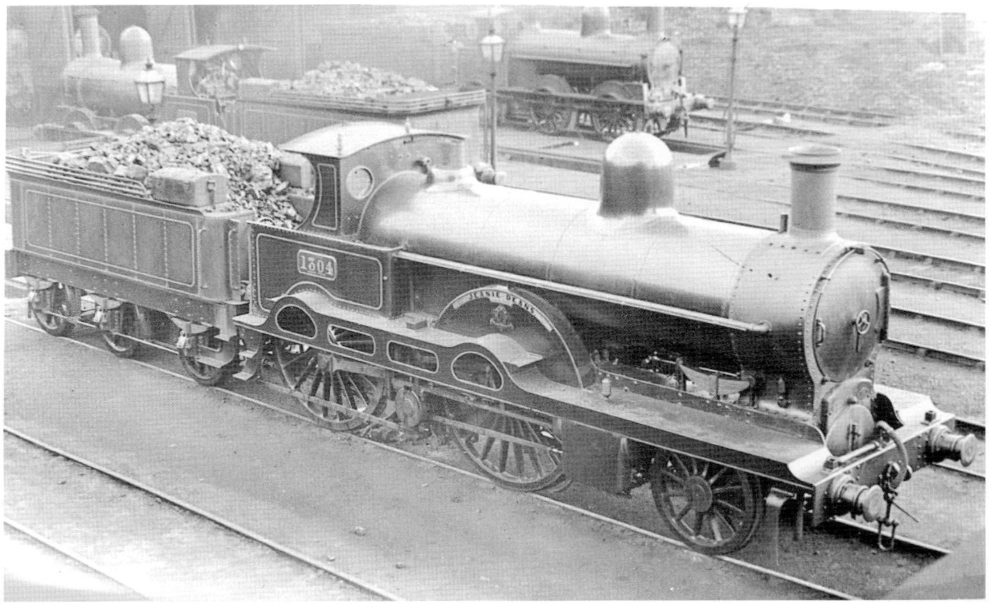

LNWR No. 1304 Jeanie Deans *at Shrewsbury shed. A 'Teutonic' class 2-2-2-0, built in 1890 and scrapped in 1906.*
(Bernard Matthews collection)

LNWR Class A compound 0-8-0 No. 1843 built 1898. Rebuilt as Class D 'simple' in 1908, renumbered LMS 9048 in 1927, rebuilt to Class G1 in 1933 and G2A in 1939. Withdrawn as BR No. 49048 in 1959 at Shrewsbury.
(Bernard Matthews collection)

Webb 0-6-0ST No. 7342 at Shrewsbury 18 January 1933. Built in 1876 as LNWR No. 2232, renumbered 3194 in 1894, 1732 in 1907, fitted with cab and heating apparatus by 1912, renumbered 3653 in 1919, became LMS No. 7342 in 1927 and scrapped in 1933.
(Bernard Matthews collection)

Webb 0-6-0ST No. 27384 at Shrewsbury. Built 1878 as LNWR No. 2306, renumbered 3049 in 1895, fitted with cab in 1913, renumbered LMS 7384 in 1926 and 27384 in 1934. It was scrapped in 1940.
(Bernard Matthews collection)

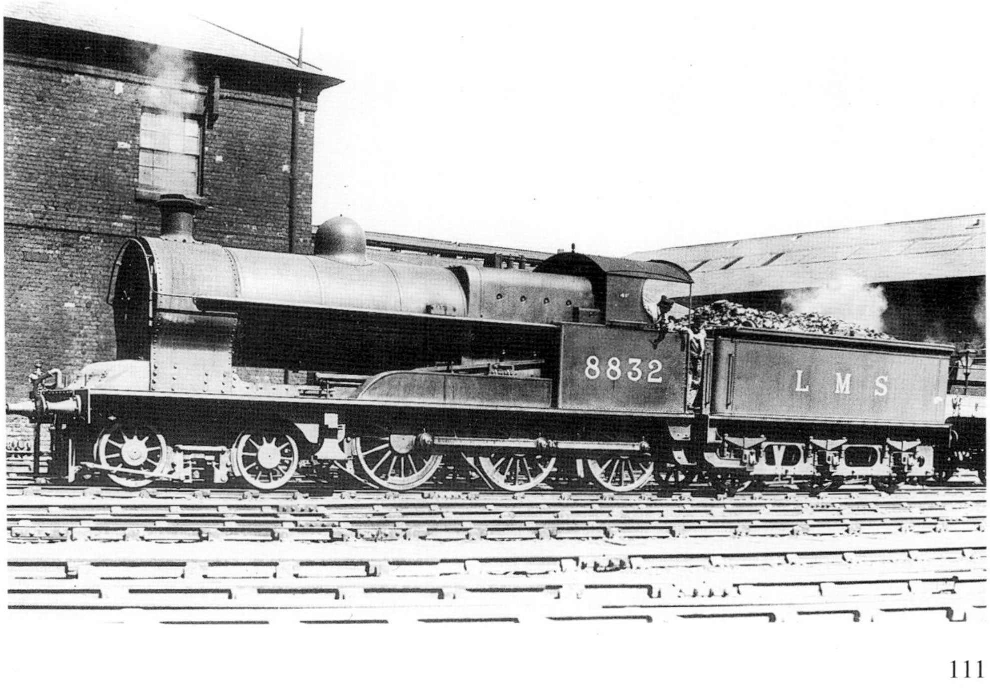

LMS No. 8832, a 4-6-0 Whale 19in Goods at Shrewsbury 30 June 1928. Built in 1908 as LNWR No. 2619 and withdrawn in 1936.
(Bernard Matthews collection)

A ballast train hauled by a Class 37 at Llandrindod.
(Courtesy Tony Williams)

0-6-2Ts and 5700 pannier tanks worked on shunting and trip freight and ex GWR 7200 2-8-2 tanks hauled coal out of Pantyffynnon.

Diesels

The first trial of diesel mutliple units on the line took place in 1959 and there were workings between Pontarddulais and Llanelli – replacing some of the 0-6-0 pannier tanks – prior to 1964.

On 2 April 1964, a 3-car Swindon unit worked a pilot service between Llanelli and Shrewsbury. These cross country sets were the main units (later in 2-car form) on passenger services until Metro-Cammell units from Bristol made their appearance on the line in 1982.

There were occasional workings by locomotives such as Class 37s. During one of the hottest summers (1976) they were seen in action when dmus suffered from boiling radiators.

In the south, English Electric Type 3 diesel locomotives and some Brush Type 4s were mainly in charge of coal and what was left of the freight traffic. In 1967 'Warship' No. D602 *Bulldog*, sent to Canton (Cardiff) from Plymouth to support the above, ran a trial on 22 August up to Llandrindod to check clearance but was found to be unsuitable.

In 1972, the line operated under a Light Railway Order which, among other stipulations, meant the imposition of a 20-ton axle load limit. Between Pantyffynnon and Craven Arms, the maximum speed limit for dmus – but only on certain sections – was 60mph. With restrictions applying at the many crossings and other specified parts of the route, this could hardly be said to be the norm. Locomotive-hauled stock was restricted to an upper limit of 30mph but was later increased to 45mph.

The maximum speed for diesel units between Llanelli and Llandeilo Junction is 75mph and this also applies on some sections between Craven Arms and Shrewsbury. Between Pantyffynnon and Craven Arms speed restrictions of 45/60mph apply.

From the mid 1970s, excursions were hauled by Class 37

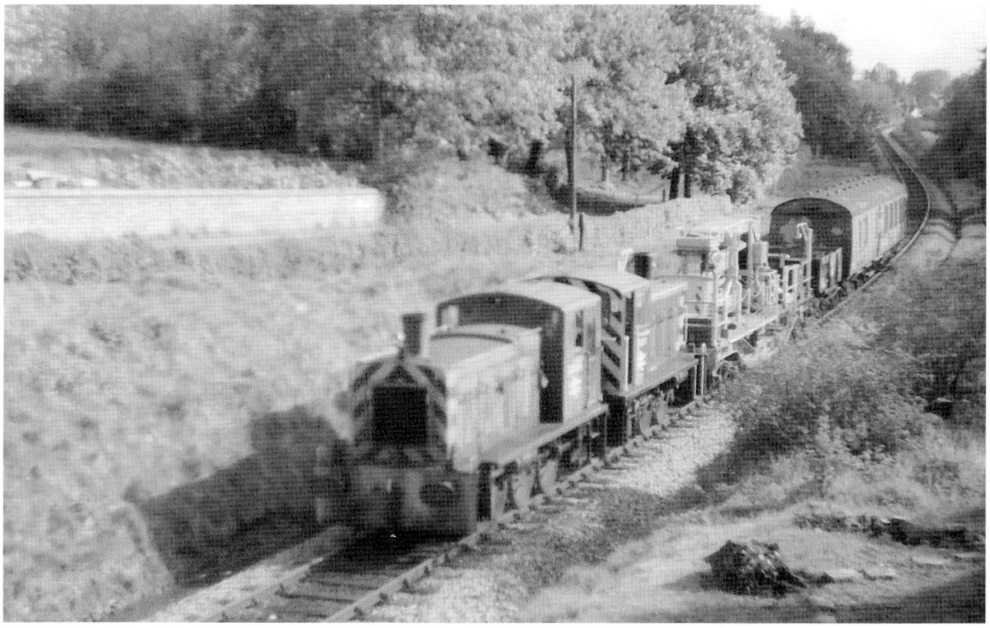

Two Class 03 0-6-0 diesels work the line in May 1981 after the ban on large locomotives was imposed at the beginning of that year.
(Roy Palmer)

and 47 diesel locomotives and were joined by Classes 33 and 40 in the 1980s. Portable headlamps appeared in 1979, being a long-awaited and rather obvious solution to the problems of running excursions more economically. Up until this time, any such trains coming from the north had to be hauled by one of the few spotlight-fitted Class 37s sent specially from Pantyffynnon to Craven Arms with the resultant cost to the organisers.

In 1981, due to cut backs, renewal of CWL track was deferred and as a consequence, an almost total ban of loco-hauled traffic was imposed and the thrice weekly freight train, which ran up the line to Llandovery, was hauled by a Class 03 diesel.

The ban was lifted in 1983 and on 17 June 1987 Class 37 No. 37431 was named *Sir Powys/County of Powys* by County Councillor Mrs R. M. Thomas, Chairman of Powys County Council on the 'up' platform at Llandrindod.

DMU Roster Summer 1986 (Supplied by BR to HOWLTA – Heart of Wales Line Travellers Association.)

First Duty (2 x 2-car unit)

04.00	Shrewsbury	to Llanelli	Empty stock to Pembrey to form
08.22	Pembrey	to Swansea	Empty to Landore depot for fuel and inspection.
	train divides here and part forms		
11.54	Swansea	to Shrewsbury	
16.25	Shrewsbury	to Cardiff	Empty to Canton for washing and fuel
23.00	Cardiff	to Hereford	Goes on to perform set 2's duties

Second Duty

06.20	Shrewsbury	to Swansea	Empty to Landore for fuel washing and inspection
14.10	Swansea	to Milford Haven	
16.18	Milford Haven	to Swansea	
18.52	Swansea	to Shrewsbury	Empty to Abbey Foregate to form 1st unit duties as above

Third Duty

	split of 1st unit duty – runs to Swansea in same timings then divides to form		
09.38	Swansea	to Shrewsbury	
15.55	Shrewsbury	to Swansea	Empty to Landore for fuel, washing and inspection
23.45	Swansea	to Carmarthen	Empty stock
	then forms 6th unit roster		

Fourth Duty

05.20	Swansea	to Shrewsbury	
10.48	Shrewsbury	to Swansea	
15.02	Swansea	to Llanelli	Coupled to another unit –
15.25	Llanelli	to Shrewsbury	through CWL train
19.55	Shrewsbury	to Chester	Empty for fuel and inspection
22.15	Chester	to Shrewsbury	
	then forms with another 2-car set to form 1st unit duties		

Fifth Duty

04.40	Swansea	to Pembroke Dock	
07.05	Pembroke Dock	to Whitland	
08.15	Whitland	to Milford Haven	
09.26	Milford Haven	to Carmarthen	
10.40	Carmarthen	to Swansea	Coupled to 6th unit
13.55	Swansea	to Cardiff	Empty stock
15.40	Cardiff	to Shrewsbury	Coupled to another unit
18.37	Shrewsbury	to Swansea	
	then forms 4th unit's roster		

Sixth Duty (Saturdays only)

05.30	Carmarthen	to Swansea	
06.50	Swansea	to Whitland	Empty stock
08.15	Whitland	to Milford Haven	
		Coupled to 5th unit	
09.36	Milford Haven	to Carmarthen	
10.40	Carmarthen	to Swansea	Detatched from 5th unit
11.38	Swansea	to Canton	Empty stock for washing
15.40	Cardiff	to Shrewsbury	
18.37	Shrewsbury	to Swansea	
	then forms 5th unit's duties		

Seventh Duty (Sundays only)

13.15	Shrewsbury	to Llandrindod	
16.15	Llandrindod	to Shrewsbury	
18.20	Shrewsbury	to Chester	Empty stock – fuel and inspection
20.22	Chester	to Abbey Foregate	
	then forms 1st unit's duties		

The start of the great dmu race! Trains pass, north of Llandrindod crossing.
(Courtesy Tony Williams)

A dmu with first class accommodation approaches Llandrindod crossing from the north.
(Tony Williams)

A 2-car dmu forms the 15.43 ex Salop and waits at Llandrindod crossing on 3 September 1982.
(Tony Williams)

The prototype Class 140 on trial at Llandrindod in 1992.
(Roy Palmer)

Single-unit 'Sprinter' No. 153377 halts on time at 13.34 – Cynghordy, Autumn 1994.
(Rose Coleman)

The Saga of the Sprinters 'This year, next year, sometime??'

By 1986/87 the very old Metro-Cammell units and the Gloucester Cross Country sets were giving cause for complaint, being often in bad condition. One test of stamina for the travelling public was to complete a journey on the whole length of the line with toilets out of order and locked. Another was to take the 'down' train to Swansea on a bitterly cold January day when there was no heating at all. On this latter occasion, conditions on the return journey were also very trying as the last 'up' train, a 3-car dmu, with one faulty engine, barely managed to climb the Sugar Loaf at just over 10mph to Llanwrtyd Wells. There, the extremely cold passengers changed over to the comparative luxury of a warm – if shaky – 3-car Gloucester set, originally intended for the 'down' journey, the former occupants of which had to transfer to the ailing set to continue the easier run south.

February 19, 1987 saw the 09.38 from Swansea cancelled due to dmu failure. Some 'Sprinters' had put in brief appearances. There was a 2-car unit, No. 150134, on the northern end of the line on Sunday, 7 September 1986 and two 2-car 'Sprinter' sets in service for Royal Welsh Show in July 1987. However, anyone who thought these were the shape of things to come in the near future was disappointed – their introduction was postponed until 1988.

One of the local football leagues changed its name from 'Central Wales' to the 'Sprinter League'. As the editorial in one of HOWLTA (Heart of Wales Line Travellers' Association) newsletters said, 'All we need now are the 'Sprinters'.

By autumn 1987, the carrot continued to extend even further in front of the donkey's nose with the news that introduction of the 'Sprinter' service would not be until 1989 with the donkey, in the form of the ancient dmus still struggling to cover the track.

The following extract from a letter in 1987 from BR in answer to complaints passed on by HOWLTA illustrates the difficulties under which the line was operating.

> '. . . Ideally, we would also have strengthened the 07.16 Swansea but you will appreciate that our resources are not unlimited and the situation is particularly critical on Summer Saturdays. You will also know that we have lost one of our units following the Llandrindod collision.'

The Chipman weed killing train waits in Llandrindod siding on 26 April 1989. This is worked by a pair of Hunslet-Barclay owned Class 20 locomotives, in this case they are Nos 20904 Janis *and 20901* Nancy, at the rear.
(Roy Palmer)

Ballast being laid at Llandrindod in 1990.
(Roy Palmer)

Staff pose on the 'up' platform at Knighton on 10 June 1990 following arrival of the first dmu on the newly installed loop.
(Tony Williams)

Class 155 'Sprinter' No. 155321 on trial, Sunday, 16 April 1989, checking platform clearances on the Southern section of the line to Llandrindod.

(Roy Palmer)

The collision referred to took place on 8 August 1987 when the 11.55 Crewe to Tenby train ran into a tractor which had been left across the line – fortunately there were no serious injuries.

The tragic accident at Glanrhyd Bridge meant a revised schedule at the end of November 1987 which resulted in a 'Sprinter' set working one of the timings between Shrewsbury and Llandovery and back. Occasionally, a 'Sprinter' made an appearance as a substitute for a failure. However, they were only 'visiting'. It was not much comfort to learn that these elusive sets had proved so successful in other areas that more had to be diverted elsewhere to cover increased passenger needs. The Central Wales Line, being last in the pecking order, saw no reason to hope for their full introduction until 1990.

With the line still split in two, pending the repairs at Glanrhyd, the northern section was provided with stock which, to quote an editorial in HOWLTA newsletter, ranged from the 'mediocre to the diabolical'.

Meanwhile Landore depot busied itself with carrying out engine servicing on the existing dmus together with general refurbishments, the latter with some first class results, in preparation for yet another winter. The stock on the southern section compared very favourably with that at the northern end, although the former was not entirely successful and the service was maintained with difficulty, many of the units being in too old a state to cope with the demands of the line.

A visitor had previously described his pleasure in travelling in a vintage dmu, 'belching fumes and swaying alarmingly, even at low speeds'. Such behaviour tends only to endear itself to the enthusiast! Landore were doing their best but with restricted finances, the progress was slow. By March 1989, it became clear that yet another postponement for the introduction of the 'Sprinter' service was to occur. It was now not expected until 1991. However, hope, as they say 'springs eternal' and considerable optimism was engendered by the proposal to split the 2-car Class 155 'Sprinters', in use on other routes, into singles in the summer of 1990. These units (as Class 153s) would then, in the opinion of British Rail, be appropriate for use on the CWL.

Many, however, experiencing the improvement in the 30-year old dmus, lovingly refurbished and still battling on, were beginning to question the practicality of a single unit 'Sprinter'. The number of cycles, pushchairs, backpacks and all the general luggage of local community and tourist traffic – to say nothing of the buffet trolley would be difficult to fit in to the limited space available. Also, a single-engine unit failing on the single track would cause problems. But their introduction was not imminent, one reason being that the delivery to BR of the Class 158 'Super Sprinters', the use of which would have released the lesser units for lines like the CWL, had been delayed by at least a year. Thus 'early 1991' was not to be.

The next forecast – the delay this time being put down to production and driver training problems – was 'early 1992' with the possibility of a full service by the summer. Meanwhile, the 35-year old dmus soldiered on.

It was hoped that by the beginning ot 1992, BR would be able to test out the 153 'Sprinters' in the Cardiff area where any teething problems could more easily be righted than when in service on the CWL. There would be room for two bicycles (pre-booked) and one wheelchair. Finally, on 17 February 1992, the first 'Sprinter', No. 153304, worked the 06.44 Swansea–Shrewsbury service with a promise of full introduction by May of that year. Opinion was divided on its merits. One of the disadvantages of the single unit Class 153s was that they offered less visibility, an important factor on such a scenic line. Others were as had been anticipated – the lack of luggage space and the potential failure of single-engined units.

The latter fears soon proved to be justified with units stranded on some of the long single-track sections. This unfortunately, was not an infrequent occurrence, sometimes due to the new acquisitions not being very reliable and on other occasions, through simple inefficiencies like failure to check that they were topped up with radiator coolant. They were, and are, often inadequate for the passenger loadings, particularly on the northern part of the line and during holiday periods.

Old Class 108 dmus still appeared, together with some incredibly unsuitable Cardiff Valley sets without toilet facilities. (Maintenance had by then been transferred from Landore to Cardiff). In 1992 passengers had to put up with many failures, some acute enough to require bus services being put on to cover them.

Another problem was that single-unit 'Sprinters' in fact provided room for only *one* bicycle, not a fact

Two CWL 'Sprinters' at Swansea High Street, 27 May 1992.
(John Horsley Denton)

likely to endear them to those who used the area for that sort of holiday, nor indeed to those who promoted tourism.

At a meeting of the Central Wales Forum on 23 May 1992 attended by representatives from Dyfed, Powys, Shropshire and West Glamorgan County Councils, Mid Wales Tourism Council, Transport User's Committee of Wales, Sports Council of Wales, Heart of Wales Line Travellers' Association and BR (Regional Railways) the latter undertook to look into this problem and that of overcrowding on certain services.

Little success has so far resulted; 2-car units do run from time to time but their appearance is spasmodic, and often seems completely unrelated to passenger needs. The carriage of bicycles is still limited to one, which must be pre-booked with an overall £3 charge – irrespective of distance – not a very good bargain for some locals wishing to travel a couple of stations up the line.

The estimated cost of one solution to the problem – entailing replacing four seats with a tip-up type to make space available for two bicycles – was quoted as £5,000 at a meeting of the Central Wales Forum in 1994. Mike Wilson, Development Officer for the line, said that as there was no dedicated rolling stock, 18 carriages would need to be so modified.

On Sunday, 16 May 1993, in celebration of the 125th anniversary of the opening of the line, the first of three steam excursions appeared with Class 4MT 2-6-4 tank locomotive No. 80079 working from Shrewsbury to Carmarthen. This was followed on Sunday, 23 May by another 'down' train, the trip originating in Coventry and hauled from Shrewsbury to Carmarthen by LMS 4-6-0 'Black 5' No 44767 *George Stephenson*. In both cases, the return journey was undertaken by a Class 37 diesel, that on 23 May using the Cardiff–Hereford route.

Sunday, 6 June saw both steam locomotives double heading an excursion up the Central Wales Line from Carmarthen to Shrewsbury. All three trains carried a buffet car and the two latter served a three-course meal. During their sojourn in the south, the steam locomotives were not idle but were used to run excursions down the West Wales routes over the May Bank Holiday weekend. Central Wales Line stock is serviced at Cardiff or Crewe as Landore (Swansea) is an InterCity depot.

The Hertfordshire Rail Tours' 'Sugar Loafer' excursion from Paddington at Llandrindod on 19 November 1994. Comprising InterCity stock it is seen here hauled by Class 33 No. 33109 Captain Bill Smith RNR.
(Rose Coleman)

Locomotive Summary

Southern Section

Introduced on line		*Withdrawn*
June 1839	Llanelli to Pontarddulais LRDC (colleries etc) Opened	
1839 LRDC	*Victoria* 0-6-0 T. Hackworth	1858
1839	*Albert* T. Hackworth	1859
1841	Pontarddulais to Duffryn Lodge (later Tir/Amman) Opened	
1842	*Princess Royal* 0-6-0 tender engine Fossick & Hackworth	1858
1843	*Prince of Wales* 0-6-0 tender engine Llanelly Rly Co. (renamed *Wales* in 1856)	(sold) 1871
	Llanelly Rly Co.'s locomotives worked by Waddle & Margrave	
1847	Llanelly Rly Co.'s locomotives worked by Grylls & Co.	
1847	*Princess Alice* 0-4-0 tender engine Bury. Converted to 0-4-2 in 1859.	* 1877
1848	Grylls & Co. went bankrupt	
1850	Dawson, Fossick & Hackworth worked locos	
1851	Shrewsbury to CravenArms/Stokesay Opened (South Hereford Railway)	
1853	*Prince Alfred* 0-4-0 tender engine bought by Joseph Hepburn then Locomotive Superintendent of the line. Converted 0-4-2 in 1863 renamed *Alfred*	* 1877
1855	*Princess Helena* 0-4-0	1870
1857	Duffryn to Llandeilo Opened, first to freight then passenger	
1857	*Victoria* (the 2nd) 0-4-2 tender engine Beyer Peacock & Co.	*1883
1857	*Albert* (the 2nd) 0-4-2 tender engine Beyer Peacock & Co.	*1874
1858	Llandeilo to Llandovery Opened VOT leased to LRDC	
1858	*Towy* (small engine purchased from contractors)	1876
1858	*Arthur* 0-6-0 Fossick & Hackworth	*1876
1858	*Leo* 0-6-0 Fossick & Hackworth converted to 0-8-0T 1871	*1877
1859	*Alice* 0-4-2 (formerly *Princess Alice* 0-4-0) rebuilt	1877
1860	*Louisa* 0-6-0 Fossick & Hackworth (mainly coal) (for sale 1871/72)	*1876
1860	*Beatrice* 0-4-2 Fossick & Hackworth (passenger)	*1882
1863	*Alfred* 0-4-2 (formerly *Prince Alfred* 0-4-0) rebuilt	1877
1865 LRDC	*Victor* 0-6-0 Fossick & Hackworth (mainly coal) – sold to Carmarthen & Cardigan Railway 1871 – worked until 1881 preserved at Swindon but broken up in 1889	
1865	*Loughor* 2-4-0 saddle tank Hopkins, Gilkes & Co.	*1886
1865	*Amman* 2-4-0 saddle tank Hopkins, Gilkes & Co. converted to a tender engine from 1871	*1886
1865	*Alexandria* 0-6-0 Llanelly Railway Company	*1881
1866	Goods Swansea to Pontarddulais Opened LRDC	
1867	Passenger Swansea to Pontarddulais Opened LRDC	
1866	*Edinburgh* 0-6-0 Fossick & Blair	*1881
1866	*Ernest* 0-6-0 Fossick & Blair	1881
1868 LRDC	*Napoleon III* 2-4-0 James Kitson (passenger)	1906
1868	*Dunvant* 'Standard' 0-6-0 Beyer Peacock & Co.	1877
1868	*Towy* (the 2nd) 'Standard' 0-6-0 Beyer Peacock & Co.	*1886
1870	*Grongar* 0-6-0 Beyer Peacock & Co.	*1886
1870	*Teilo* 0-6-0 Beyer Peacock & Co.	*1880
1870 LRDC	*Stradey* 0-6-0 Beyer Peacock & Co.	*1879
1870	*Drysllwyn* 0-6-0 Beyer Peacock & Co. Renamed *Royal* by 1873	*1877
1871	*Leo* 0-8-0T (converted from 0-6-0)	1877
1871	*Amman* 2-4-0 (originally 2-4-0 saddle tank)	1884
1873	*Wales* (the 2nd) 0-6-0 Llanelly Company	*1880
1873	GWR took over what was left of the Llanelly company's operating area	

* Locomotives transferred to GWR stock

Northern Section

Introduced on line		*Withdrawn*
1860	Craven Arms to Bucknell Opened Knighton Railway	
1861	Knighton Railway Co.	
	Knighton 0-4-2 saddle tank No. 230 Beyer Peacock & Co. operated only on Northern section Out of service after 1865	
1861	Bucknell to Knighton Opened Knighton Railway	
	LNWR had working agreement with Knighton Railway	
1862	LNWR/GWR joint lease of Shrewsbury–Craven Arms (Hereford)	
1865	Knighton to Llandrindod Opened CWR	
1868	CWER Section completed – whole line opened	
1870	LNWR/GWR joint ownership of Shrewsbury-Craven Arms (Hereford)	
1873	LNWR controlled 80% of line with running rights over GWR territory in south	
	LNWR locomotives working through services and local services north of Llandovery	
1868	2-2-2 tender engines built at Crewe (mainly passenger) (eventually replaced by Webb 2-4-0 'Precedent' class)	
	2-4-0 old Crewe types with 6ft driving wheels (heavy freight) (Out of service by 1909)	
	2-4-0 'Newton' with 6ft $7\frac{1}{2}$in driving wheels	
	After Ramsbottom standardisation began 1858	
1870/80	DX 0-6-0 goods (and often for banking Llangunllo gradient)	
	0-4-0s Ramsbottom	
	0-6-0s tank engines	
	2-4-0 'Precursors' (Webb) operating from Craven Arms	
1881-96	0-6-2Ts (Webb) coal tanks 'Gadgets' (still operating 1933)	
After 82	2-4-0 'Precedent' class (Webb)	
1890-97	2-4-2Ts Webb replaced some 2-4-0s	
1902	2-2-2-0s Webb Compound (Northern end of line)	
	2-2-2s GWR	
	2-4-0s GWR	
1906	'Precursor' tanks (Whale)	
From 1910	4-6-2 tank engines (Bowen Cooke) Arrival on CWR 1911/1912	
to 1916	4-6-0 goods (Whale) often to subsitute 4-6-2 tanks	
	4-4-0s GWR (replaced by GWR 4-6-0s after 1918)	
	4-6-2s operated on local passenger services until LMS era	
	Some replaced by Fowler 2-6-4 tank engines in 1928 and all replaced by BR Standard Class 4 2-6-4Ts by 1962	
	4-6-0 freight 'Bill Bailey' (Webb 4-cylinder compound)	
1910	Webb 1400 class compound 4-6-0s	
1911	Superheater 'Precursors'	
	4-6-2T (Bowen Cooke)	
1912	0-8-2 tank engines (Bowen Cooke).	
	4-6-0 'Prince of Wales' class	
	0-6-2 tank engines (Bowen Cooke) (0-8-2Ts withdrawn about 1955)	
	G1 0-8-0s (Super Ds) transferred from Crewe for heavy freight	
1918	4-6-0s GWR replaced 4-4-0s	
1922	4-6-0 'Experiment' taking Shrewsbury to Swansea Victoria passenger train (not frequent)	
1923	LMS formed. Only Pontarddulais–Llandeilo remained under the control of GWR	
	LMS took over LNWR running powers Pontarddulais–Llanelli and gained full ownership of Craven Arms–Llandovery and Pontarddulais–Swansea sections	
1925	LMS G2 0-8-0s – mostly for heavy freight	
	LMS G2s and Bowen Cooke Gls also used for excursions	
	LMS G2 0-8-0s withdrawn April 1958	
1925	'Vale of Towy' 3F and 1F 0-6-0 side tank engines (Derby)	

1928	Fowler 2-6-4 tank engines sent to Paxton Street (replacing some LNWR 4-6-2Ts)
1920/30	Webb 'Cauliflower' 0-6-0s (lighter minerals and goods) (still operating 1947)
1930	LMS Fowler 'Jinty'
1934	GWR 'Dean Goods' 0-6-0 No. 2382 – freight
1930s	LNWR 0-8-4T working as a banker.
	LMS Stanier 'Black 5' 4-6-0s (officially 5P/5F class) introduced – heavy passenger traffic. Working from Shrewsbury.
	'Prince of Wales' 4-6-0s
	Horwich 'Crab' 2-6-0s
	Whale 4-6-0 goods
	Stanier 3in 2-6-2Ts
	Beames 7ft 0-8-4Ts
	Stanier 6P5F 2-6-0s
	0-6-0 3F (branched off at Gowerton) Llanmorlais branch freight train (Cockles from Penclawd)
1937	8F 2-8-0 heavy freight locomotives – still operating in 1964 (eventually sent to Swansea East Dock then to Llanelli mpd)
1938	Midland Compound 4-4-0 appeared twice
1939	GWR 5700 0-6-0 pannier tanks
1947	WD 2-8-0s short period – then removed as unsuitable for line and reluctance of staff to man them (Replaced by Stanier 2-8-0s)
1947	Stanier 8F 2-8-0s
	Webb 2-4-2Ts still working
	Webb 0-6-2Ts
	Webb 0-6-0s
	Beames 0-8-4Ts
	Johnson 0-6-0Ts
	Fowler 2-4-2Ts

1948 (1 January) Nationalisation (British Railways)

	Stanier Class 2 2-6-2Ts and ex GWR pannier tanks on local passenger services (replaced some 'Jinties' and remaining coal tanks) Sent to Swansea Dock 1959
1948	Shrewsbury shed allocation also includes ex LMS Fowler 2-6-2Ts Johnson 2F 0-6-0 No. 58211 at Pontarddulais in August – probably substituting for a failed 'Black 5'
23.10.1952	Two 'Castle' class (GWR) 4-6-0s (first appearance on line) (Nos 7030 *Cranbrook Castle* and 7036 *Taunton Castle*) hauling Royal train (preceded by No. 6971 *Athelhampton Hall* for checking line clearance and for shunting at Llandrindod) (GWR 4-6-0s did not normally work the line – the clearance between Pantyffynnon and Llandovery thought to be the reason.)
1953	BR Standard Class 4 4-6-0 for short period
1953	Some 5600 0-6-2Ts Llandovery–Llandeilo
	Mostly 5700 0-6-0 pannier tanks Llandovery–Llandeilo
	5700 Llanelli–Llandrindod on summer Saturdays
6. 8.1955	Ex LMS Stanier 2-8-0 No. 48309 on Royal train Builth Road–Llandovery/Llandeilo
8.1955	Stanier Class 3 2-6-2T
1955	Ex GWR pannier tanks used on local, Southern section passenger services
c1955	Bowen Cooke 0-8-2 tanks withdrawn
Mid 1950s	Webb 0-6-2T on Pontarddulais–Swansea route.
	Midland 3F at Craven Arms for banking
	2251 class 0-6-0 at Builth Road – banking
	Johnson 2F 0-6-0s at Knighton – banking
4.1958	G2 0-8-0s withdrawn
18. 2.1959	Hughes-Fowler 'Crab' 2-6-0 hauled fish train ex Swansea
8.1959	Paxton Street shed closed
	Fowler 2-6-4 tanks sent to Landore
	Most ex GWR pannier tanks sent to Swansea East Dock
	Ex LMS8Fs sent to Swansea East Dock
1959	First trial run of dmu
1960/61	Three Fairburn Class 4 2-6-4 tanks temporarily at Landore to replace Fowler 2-6-4 tanks
	Standard Class 3 2-6-2 tank engines at Landore for trials
1960/61	Standard Class 5s worked line, gradually replacing Stanier Black 5s (See 1936)
1961	Ex GWR 2251 class 0-6-0 piloted Standard class engine to Shrewsbury on Rugby excursion to Edinburgh
1962	Ex LMS 'Jubilee' class 4-6-0s (still operating 1963/64)
	2251 class 0-6-0s replaced 2Fs as Knighton banking.
	BR Standard Class 4 2-6-4Ts to Landore. These replaced Fowler 2-6-4Ts and substitutes. (See 1928 and 1960)
15. 6.1962	0-6-0PT No. 8785 still in service (goods) Pontarddulais–Hendy Junction area
1963	Stanier 'Black 5s' reappeared, mainly replacing some BR Standard Class 4s required elsewhere.
8.1963g	Lancashire & Yorkshire B7 class 0-4-0ST parked at Knighton – thought to be en route for scrapyard but moved to Keighly & Worth Valley Railway, Yorkshire
1963/64	'Jubilees' still operating
	Standard Class 5 4-6-0s and Class 4 2-6-4 tanks.
	8Fs still operating on heavy freight. Eventually sent to Swansea East Docks, then to Llanelli MPD after 1964
1963	Some dmus on Llanelli–Pontarddulais stretch – Gloucester Cross Country sets
1963	Class 120 Cross Country dmus – withdrawn by May 1986 (some replaced by Metro-Cammell's, 1984)
4.1964	3-car Swindon dmu – pilot service Llanelli and Shrewsbury
13.6.1964	6.25pm Swansea to York mail Class 5 4-6-0 No. 45406 (Last 'down' 'York Mail' was hauled by No. 45272)
	Last steam-hauled regular passenger service on the line (Some continued for a while on Saturdays during summer season eg a Stanier 2-8-0 (normally used for freight) and BR Standard 2-6-4Ts.
13. 6.1964	Passenger service from Swansea Victoria closed
10. 8.1964	End of steam-hauled long distance freight from Llandovery to north
10. 8.1964	Llandovery (Sugar Loaf banking) engines sent to Southern Region MPD
1964	Late Summer
	Swindon Cross Country sets operating Shrewsbury–Llanelli passenger service
	Swindon Cross Country 2 and 3-car sets used on line until 1982
	Trial run with 1963 Swindon Inter-city 3-car units
10.1964	Freight from Swansea Victoria discontinued although line north of Gorseinon remained open for coal traffic.
1964	English Electric Type 3 diesel-electric locomotives plus Brush Type 4s – freight and mineral
1. 5.1965	8F No. 48732 hauled last 'official' steam *local* freight from Pantyffynnon to Craven Arms
1966	Headlamps fitted to illuminate ungated crossings and unlit platforms
1967	'Warship' class No. D602 *Bulldog* for a limited period.
4. 9.1968	2-car Swindon towing corridor coach
	Late 1960s 'Hymek' Type 3 permanent way work north end of line
1971/72	'Western' Class 52 diesel tested north of Llandovery 1972
	Introduction of Light Railway Order between Pantyffynnon and Craven Arms. (One section imposed a 20-ton axle load limit)
25.10.1975	Class 47 (No. 47252) diesel piloted by Class 37 (No. 37177) Llanelli–Blackpool excursion

The prototype Class 140 dmu on trials at Hopton Heath in May 1992.

(Roy Palmer)

6.1976	Class 37s temporarily hauling passenger services (dmus overheating due to severe summer drought conditions)
4.1977	Class 40 diesel (No. 40l74) hauled failed dmu south to Llandrindod
1979	Introduction of portable headlamps
20/21.12.1980)	No. 40030 hauled last heavy passenger train Leeds–Llandrindod excursion
1.1981	Almost total ban on locomotives due to condition of track but occasional Class 37s on permament way work. Also, Class 03-worked freight Llandeilo–Llandovery three times per week.
1981	Class 37 and Class 08 worked freight from Pantyffynnon
30. 6.1881	Class l40 dmu demonstration run Carmarthen–Cynghordy–Carmarthen
5. 7.1981	Class 03 shunting engines Nos 03145 and 03151 Llanelli–Craven Arms and back to unload ballast.
7.1l.1981	Three-coach Western Region Class l20 diesel set Midland Region 3-coach set-first visit to line – no spotlight
4. 1.1982	Experimental 2-car Class l40 dmu in use. Withdrawn few weeks later – track circuit and gearbox problems
5.1982	Metro-Cammell units introduced
6.1982	Class 140 dmu returned to service after modifications
1983	Ban on locomotive hauled trains lifted
1. 6.1983	No. 37300 hauled first heavy passenger train after lifting of weight restriction
1984	Class 25-hauled excursion train
18. 4.1985	No. 37180 *Sir Dyfed/County of Dyfed* and Newport inspection saloon ran over line
19. 4.1985	Two Class 33s (first time on line) hauled 'VSOE'
7-22.9.1985	No. 37306 GWR 150th Anniversary Exhibition Train at Llandrindod Llandovery, Llanelli and Swansea
21. 9.1985	Class 25s (Nos 25175 and 25034) Special Manchester–Landore Open Day
1986	Class 119 dmu suburban sets Class 101 Metro-Cammell dmus Class 120 Windsor Cross Country sets
24. 5.1986	Two engines on Class 101 set failed at Shrewsbury. (Towed to Llanelli by No. 25265)
6.1986	2-car dmu (failed at Knighton) pushed by Class 25 No. 25266
7. 9.1986	2-car 'Sprinter' No.l50034 first time on Northern end of line
1986/87	Ancient Metro-Cammell and Gloucester Cross Country units giving considerable cause for complaint
1986/87	Regular 'Sprinter' service postponed until 1988
11-12.1986	Class 37s hauling failed sets

1987 Spring	Some Cardiff Valley sets in use the whole length of line Some 2-car Metro-Cammell sets introduced (originally 3-car sets with centre car removed) Maintenance for some undertaken at Landore (Swansea) thus not only some numbers changed but also prefix altered 'C' to 'S'.
3.1987	'Bubble car' track recording saloons, based at Reading travelled the line
1987 Early Summer	DMUs (sent from other areas covered by 'Sprinters') Classes l0l, l08, l16, l17, 118, 119. Mostly 2-car with exception of Cardiff Valley sets. Some improvement in condition of cleanliness
17. 6.1987	No. 37431 named *Sir Powys/County of Powys*
2. 7.1987	Two Class 20s haul excursion from Leicester
21-23.7.1987	Royal Welsh Show Week two 2-car 'Sprinter' sets Nos 150261 and 150265 (first *up* line) between Swansea and Builth Road (Llandrindod Wells sidings used, as none at Builth Road)
26. 7.1987	3-car suburban dmu from Tyseley – excursion Wellington to Tenby
15. 8.1987	Three 2-car 'Sprinters' Nos 150261, 150265 and 150263 Return charter Salop–Port Talbot (Shrewsbury Flower Show) (First *down* line)
1987 Autumn	Introduction of regular 'Sprinter' service postponed until 1989
30. 9.1987	Class 37 No. 37431 *Sir Powys/County of Powys* used on a 4-coach track recording train
11.1987	During emergency following Glanrhyd Bridge disaster, trains south of Llandeilo serviced Landore or Canton, north of Llandovery by Chester. Class l22 'Bubble car' and Class l14 unit in emergency service
1988 Spring	Units S807 (294) S994 and S946 re-allocated, carrying 'CH' and Chester's famous 'Eastgate' logo. Worked Northern section 'Sprinter' Class l50 units also worked Northern section but replaced by Tyseley Surburban sets on Saturdays
1988 Summer	Landore existing dmus for use on CWL fitted with replacement engines and had general refurbishment Northern section. Units from Chester and Tyseley poor quality including one Class l04
9.1988	Class l08 dmu (Landore) Llandeilo–Swansea route. lst class refurbishment inside and out
10.1988	Sundays – 'Bubble car' unit No. Tl34 (from Tyseley) 'down' line from Shrewsbury – drivers re-familiarising

A Class 122 'Bubble Car' and a Class 114 dmu (from Chester and Birmingham) at Llandrindod in November 1987. During the emergency services put into operation after the collapse of the Glanrhyd Bridge in October 1987, various unusual combinations appeared on the Northern section of the line.

(Roy Palmer)

	with whole route prior to re-opening of Glanrhyd Bridge
26.10.1988	Ballast train hauled by No. 37146
30.10.1988	Light engine No. 37212 testing bridge
	Whole line re-opened with 2-car Class 101 dmu No.C985 up the line. Sprinters' withdrawn from Northern section
1.11.1988	2-car 'Sprinter' track recording unit on line
1988/89 Winter	
	Many units performing inadequately. Most reported in poor mechanical condition
25.2.1989	InterCity Class 47 (No. 47612) hauled 10-coach excursion – first through train after re-opening of line
16.4.1989	Class 155 'Sprinter' on section south of Llandrindod checking platform clearances
4.11.1989	Class 37 hauling three Mark 3 coaches (incl. one 1st class corridor coach) Swansea–Crewe–Swansea service to replace dmus needed on Valley service for 'All Blacks' rugby fans
11.1989	Class 47 No. 47705 hauled inspection train with four coaches over whole line
	Class 37 No. 37264 with engineers' coach travelled the line
1989/90	Class 108 dmus still in use
20. 1.1990	Class 37 hauling three InterCity coaches incl. one 1st class to service passenger traffic to Cardiff (Rugby match)
1990 Spring	Proposals to divide 2-car Class 155 'Sprinter' units in use on other lines to singles for use on Central Wales Line
	Refurbishment to many old dmus complete and satisfactory
9.1990	Class 31 hauled failed Class 108 dmu Crewe–Swansea.
20.11.1990	Failed Class 108 Swansea–Crewe (hauled by Class 31)
21.12.1990	Class 31 hauled 07.25 Crewe–Swansea as far as Llandrindod – set of five coaches with Network SouthEast, livery almost concealed by grime
1.1991	Class 31 carried out same run (NSE coaches)
	Class 37 No. 37428 *David Lloyd George* also hauled three NSE coaches
1991	Three Cardiff (Canton) dmus, Nos 50666, 50712 and 56293 fitted with headlamps to work line
28. 7.1991	Two dmu failures (hauled by Class 37 No. 37418 *Pectinidae*
17. 2.1992	First 'Sprinter' in operation as regular daily service train (No. 153304) as 06.44 Swansea to Shrewsbury
	Many old class 108 dmus still in use
16. 5.1992	Class 37 hauls 2-car Valley set.
16. 4.1992	No.47974 hauled 5-coach inspection special on the 'up' line (livery – blue, orange and dark grey)
	No. 47971 hauled the return journey south
5.1992	Two Class 20s 'top and tail' weed killer train

On 4 November 1989 Class 37 No. 37426 Y Lein Fach/Vale of Rheidol *replaced the usual dmu on the 09.48 Swansea–Crewe – seen here at Llanwrtyd.*

(Roy Palmer)

1992 Early Summer	
	Old Class 108 dmus still operating
	Some Cardiff Valley sets
	2-car 'Sprinter' units Classes 150/1, 150/2 and 153
10.5.1992	Responsibility for Regional Railways stock at Landore ceased
	Class 108 dmus transferred to Cardiff
	Replaced by Class 153s based at Cardiff
23.1.1993	No. 50007 *Sir Edward Elgar*' (first Class 50 to visit the line)
16.5.1993	First of three steam excursions for 125th anniversary of line
	Class 4MT 2-6-4 tank No. 80079 Shrewsbury–Carmarthen
	Return journey, Class 37 diesel (No. 37414)
23. 5.1993	LMS 4-6-0 'Black 5' No. 44767 *George Stephenson* worked Shrewsbury–Carmarthen (Coventry to Carmarthen excursion) Return journey diesel'hauled
6.6. 1993	Double-headed BR 2-6-4T No. 80079 and LMS 4-6-0 No. 44767 hauled 'Central Wales Anniversary Ltd,' excursion Carmarthen–Shrewsbury (nine coaches)
29.1.1994	High Speed Train (InterCity 125) ran over line.
19.11.1994	No. 33109 *Captain Bill Smith RNR* hauled 'The Sugar Loafer' excursion – round trip Paddington (seven InterCity coaches)

Locomotive Allocations

Shed 33 Swansea October 1911

4-6-0	19in Goods	2592
0-8-0	D	2526
0-8-0	G	1190
0-8-0	G1	2174, 2386
0-6-0	18in	39, 74, 87, 164, 195, 319, 420, 1298, 1716, 2305, 2321, 2330
0-6-0	DX	3094, 3117, 3128, 3400
4-6-2T		91, 1183, 2667, 2669
2-4-2T	5ft 6in	204. 465, 1374

Shed 30 Shrewsbury and Sub Sheds (Part allocation)
Craven Arms, Knighton and Builth Road

4-4-0	'Jubilee'	1906 *Robin Hood*, 1928 *Glatton*
4-4-0	'Alfred the Great	1956 *Invincalde*, 1959 *Revenge*, 1963 *Bodicea*, 1965 *Charles H. Mason*, 1970 *Good Hope*, 1972 *Hindustan*
2-4-0	6ft 'Jumbos'	401 *Zeno*, 628 *Tartarus*, 885 *Vampire*
4-6-0	19in Goods	1350, 2508, 2593
2-4-2T	5ft 6in	187, 199, 402
4-6-2T		217, 375, 1366

Shed 33 Swansea October 1917

4-6-0	19in Goods	393, 1421
0-6-0	18in	177, 245. 1719, 2312
0-6-0	DX	3306, 3410, 3445, 3499
0-6-0	17in Coal	3354
4-6-2T		376, 716, 962, 2669
0-6-2T	Coal	183, 296, 373, 436, 493, 629, 747, 991, 1079
0-6-0ST	Special	1453, 3182
0-8-2T		563

Sub Shed Llandovery

0-6-0	18in	128, 676
0-6-0	17in Coal	1085, 3117
2-4-2T	5ft 6in	1145, 1758

Shed 30 Shrewsbury and Sub Sheds October 1917
(Craven Arms, Knighton and Builth Road)
(Not all the following would have worked on the CWL.)

2-4-0	6ft 6in 'Precedent'	696 *Director*, 919 *Nasmyth*, 1194 *Miranda*, 1212 *Pioneer*, 2178 *Pluck*
2-4-0	6ft 'Samson'	35 *Talisman*, 733 *Chimera*, 758 *Hardman*, 792 *Theoram*, 793 *Martin*
4-6-0	19in	285, 992, 1058, 1607, 1795, 2209
0-8-0	C	1861
0-8-0	D	1819, 1827, 1880, 2540, 2548
0-6-0	18in	79, 458, 1007
0-6-0	DX	3005, 3040, 3275, 3482
0-6-0	17in Coal	1313, 2437
4-6-2T		704, 858, 1021, 1728, 2668
2-4-2T	5ft 6in	1157
0-6-2T	Coal	119, 292, 2459
0-6-0ST	Special	751, 1107, 1546, 3161, 3351
2-4-0T	'Chopper'	1000

The following were 'on shed' at Shrewsbury but not recorded as working on the CWL

4-6-0	'Experiment'	893, 1621, 1689
4-4-0	'George V'	2279
4-4-0	'Precursor'	366, 419
4-4-0	'Alfred the Great'	1949, 1950, 1952, 1965, 1966, 1970, 1972
4-4-0	'Jubilee'	1933 *Barfleur*
0-4-0T		3033, 3103, 3245

(Above courtesy of D. Whitworth, L&NWR Society, Sandy Croall, Hywel Rees and N. Wassell.)

8

Signalling

Much of the CWL has always been single line. However, the section between Swansea Victoria and Pantyffynnon was doubled by 1893 and those from Llandrindod to Penybont station, Penybont Junction (north of Penybont Tunnel) to Llanbister Road and Knighton to Craven Arms were doubled by the 1870s. Double line between Craven Arms and Shrewsbury had already been completed by 23 June 1862. Swansea High Street to Pantyffynnon via Llanelli was double track except for the section from Hendy Junction to Pontarddulais station.

Double track remains on the Northern section between Craven Arms and Shrewsbury and in the south between Morlais Junction and Llanelli, thence from Llanelli via Llandeilo Junction to Duffryn West, followed by single track through Gowerton as far as Cockett West where it is once more double to Swansea Loop West, single again to Swansea Loop East and double into Swansea High Street.

Single lines were originally worked by staff and ticket. This required the driver to collect a wooden or metal 'staff' from the signalman at the commencement of each section of the line or, if the next train was to travel in the same direction, to be shown the staff and then receive a written 'ticket' as authorisation. The last train through in that direction carried the staff, enabling the signalman at the other end to hand this, or a ticket, to the driver of the next train in the opposite direction. In the case of a double headed train, (if another train was to follow with the staff) both drivers had a ticket, otherwise the staff was given to the leading driver.

This system was replaced by electric token/staff working probably towards the end of the 19th century. In this method, a token or staff could only be released singly through interlocked electrically controlled instruments. The signalman could only obtain the release of the staff to enter the block section after that from the preceding train had been inserted in the instrument at the other end of the section.

Tokens, being smaller than staffs, were handed over in a leather pouch to which was attached a metal loop and the exchange, if effected while the train was in motion, required some skill on the part of the crew to whom it was a matter of pride to be able to carry this out with precision.

From 1873, railway companies were required to make annual reports in connection with use of 'Lock and Block' (interlocking block signalling) but there were no powers to compel its installation and it was not until the Regulation of Railways Act of 1889 that the Board of Trade was able to insist on the introduction of this system, together with continuous brakes, on passenger lines. This resulted in a great deal of activity on the signalling front.

In an article on the Anglesey Central Railway (LNWR Amlwch branch), Mike Christensen comments on the Webb-Thompson electric train staff.

> 'The invention of the Electric Train Tablet system in 1878, and the parallel Electric Train Staff system in 1888, revolutionised the working of single lines, to the extent that thereafter very few single lines were doubled. Both of these systems improved safety and, more importantly from the operational point of view, considerably increased the flexibility of working to the point of increasing line capacity.
>
> No longer would there be delays to traffic because the train staff was at the wrong end of the section when out-of-course working was required. The Electric Train Staff system was devised by A. M. Thompson, the LNWR's Signal Superintendent, in conjunction with the Chief Mechanical Engineer, F. W. Webb. Patented early in 1889 (Patent 1263, applied for on 23rd January 1889), the system was tried out on the Bedford to Cambridge line in 1888/9. Having proved itself, the system was rapidly extended (from late 1890) to other single line sections of the LNWR.'

On the ex GWR section boxes of the Central Wales Line, the electric token system, was in force between Pantyffynnon North and Llandeilo South.

Methods of Working from LNWR Working Timetables of 1909 and 1920

Section	Line	Method of working
Craven Arms – Knighton No. 2	D	LNW Absolute Block
Knighton No. 2 – Llanbister Road	S	LNW Electric Staff
Llanbister Road – Penybont Jcn	D	LNW Absolute Block
Penybont Jcn – Penybont Stn	S	LNW Electric Staff
Penybont Stn – Llandrindod No. 2	D	LNW Absolute Block
Llandrindod No. 2 – Builth Road No. 1	S	LNW Electric Staff
Builth Road No. 1 – Builth Road No. 2	D	LNW Absolute Block
Builth Road No. 2 – Llandovery North	S	LNW Electric Staff
Llandovery North – Llandovery South	D	GWR Disc Block
Llandovery South – Llandilo North	S	LNW Electric Staff
Llandilo North – Llandilo South	D	LNW Absolute Block
Llandilo South – Pantyffynnon North	S	GWR Electric Staff
Pantffynnon North – Pontarddulais Stn	D	GWR Disc Block
Pontarddulais Crossing – Swansea Vic.	D	LNW Absolute Block

In the mid 1960s, in order to cut costs, the wooden staff and card ticket system was re-introduced between Pantyffynnon and Craven Arms but Hendy Junction to Pantyffynnon South continued to be controlled by electric token.

By 1964 the following block sections were in operation south of Craven Arms:

Swansea No. 3 – Swansea No. 2 – Swansea No. 1 – Swansea Bay No. 2 – Swansea Bay No. 1 – Mumbles Road – Dunvant – Gowerton South No. 2 (Elba Steelworks became Gowerton No. 1 after 1926 and the original No. 1 became No. 2 box) – Glasbrook Sidings – Gorseinon No.2 – Gorseinon No.1 – Grovesend Colliery Sidings – Pontarddulais Crossing – Pontarddulais Junction Stn.

Llandilo Jcn East – Genwen Jcn – Bynea – Llangennech Siding – Llangennech Stn – Morlais Jcn – Hendy Jcn – Pontarddulais Jcn Stn.

Pontarddulais Junction Stn – Pontarddulais Junction North – Glynhir Siding – Pantyffynnon South – Pantyffynnon North – Tirydail – Llandebie – Cilyrychen Crossing – Derwydd Road – Ffairfach – Llandeilo (replacing Carmarthen Valley Jcn – Llandilo South – Llandilo North in 1955) – Llangadog – Llanwrda – Llandovery No. 2 – Llandovery No.1 – Cynghordy – Sugar Loaf – Llanwrtyd Wells – Garth – Builth Road No. 2 – Builth Road No. 1 – Howey – Llandrindod Wells No. 2 – Llandrindod Wells No. 1 – Penybont Stn – Penybont Jcn – Dolau – Llanbister Road – Llangunllo – Knighton No. 2 – Knighton No. 1 – Bucknell – Hopton Heath – Broome – Craven Arms Junction.

Due to the cut backs in 1964, sections of line were singled, loops taken out of use and signal boxes closed. The route to Swansea Victoria was terminated.

Sugar Loaf Summit looking north. The signal box closed on 12 October 1965.
(HMRS/G. M. Perkins collection)

Llangunllo Tunnel, south portal, showing the distant signal for Llangunllo station.
(HMRS/G. M. Perkins collection)

The crew of the 12.33 'up' train receive the token at Llandrindod in June 1985.
(Courtesy Tony Williams)

An 'up' dmu slows to receive the token at Llandrindod level crossing, 1969.
(Roy Palmer)

The staff and ticket system was then in force on the remaining five sections of single track – Pantyffynnon South to Llandeilo, Llandeilo to Llandovery, Llandovery to Llanwrtyd, Llanwrtyd to Llandrindod Crossing (the former No. 1 box) and finally the lengthy stretch between Llandrindod and Craven Arms Crossing (formerly known as 'Long Lane Crossing').

The 30 miles 999 yards of the latter section was then the longest single-line block section operating on British Railways. In 1960, it had been proposed to install a Centralised Traffic Control Scheme based at a new Llandrindod Wells box. This was to cost £676,000 and would have operated the complete section between Llandovery and Craven Arms which was to be continuously track circuited, eliminating 21 signal boxes and introducing automatic level crossings. However, the British Transport Commission's approval was subsequently overturned and the project did not proceed. As this development would have reduced signalling costs and increased long distance freight capacity, it is difficult to comprehend why, having instigated the idea, the authorities abandoned it. Long distance freight was diverted via Hereford which route, although longer, has easier terrain and can take longer trains without double heading but presumably this option had already been considered before the Centralised Traffic Control Scheme was mooted.

The decision to operate the line under a Light Railway Order in 1972, which was estimated to reduce annual losses by approximately £150,000, meant that many crossings were designated as 'open', that is, without gates or barriers; eventually these were Tirydail, Brynmarlais, Llandybie, Cilyrychen, Glanrhyd, Llangadog, Llanwrda, Berthddu, Dolau, Heyope and Bucknell – although some retained gates for several years after the LRO was made. Thus even in 1981, Pantyffynnon, Tirydail (Ammanford), Llandybie, Cilyrychen, Ffairfach, Llangadog, Llandovery, Llandrindod

The driver of No. 55500, Class 140 Prototype 2-car diesel multiple unit, relinquished the wooden staff at Llandrindod in July 1982. This unit was tested between Swansea and Shrewsbury but proved unsatisfactory.
(Courtesy Tony Williams)

Station Master Lewis and Signalman C. Cann at Gorseinon No. 2 signal box, 20 October 1956.
(Courtesy Michael Lewis)

Wells, Dolau and Bucknell still enjoyed the luxury of resident crossing keepers or a signalman. (However, by 1994 this applied only to Pantyffynnon level crossing.)

Glanrhyd, Llanwrda, Berthddu and Heyope were left with only warning boards, the remainder being operated by the AOCL system (Automatic Open Crossing Locally Monitored), under which train drivers receive confirmation of the functioning of the road traffic lights as they approach fully automated crossings.

By 1992, the situation at Cilyrychen Crossing, designated as 'open' in 1986, had been re-assessed as a result of the Stott Enquiry and automatic half barriers installed. Subsequently local pressure and a risk analysis by management led to half barriers being introduced at Tirydail, but without change in operating arrangements at the crossing.

Some crossings, such as Cilyrychen, function automatically in at least one direction or, in the case of, for example, Llandovery and Llandrindod Wells, are operated by the train crew in both directions.

The introduction of the present NSKT (No Signalman Key Token) system at a cost of £473,000 was met by British Rail, Mid Wales Development, various local authorities and the Wales Tourist Board, and began in February 1986 being completed by the end of that year. Under this system the introduction of hydro-pneumatic, self-acting points enables trains to be routed in the appropriate direction without manual assistance. 'Draw ahead' indicators at the side of the track display the setting of points, retro-reflective signal distant boards replaced existing fixed distant signals, and 'Start of Section' and 'End of Section' notices were placed at each crossing loop.

Now the driver is responsible for obtaining clearance to proceed at the commencement of every section by telephoning Pantyffynnon box (via BT telephone lines) from which the supervising signalman gives permission for the 'no signalman' token to be withdrawn and the driver then removes this from the instrument in the token hut on the platform. The release of the token key is safeguarded by electric interlocking at the next block post. The setting of the points is also subject to an electronic detection system. Token released two-lever ground-frames give access to the sidings at Llandovery and Llandrindod.

Multiple aspect electric signalling from the 'panel' box at Port Talbot, for which Pantyffynnon acts as a fringe box,

Craven Arms with a wooden 'Mink' and an iron 'Mink' with a GWR 0-6-0 standard goods, with the signal box beyond.
(HMRS/G. M. Perkins collection)

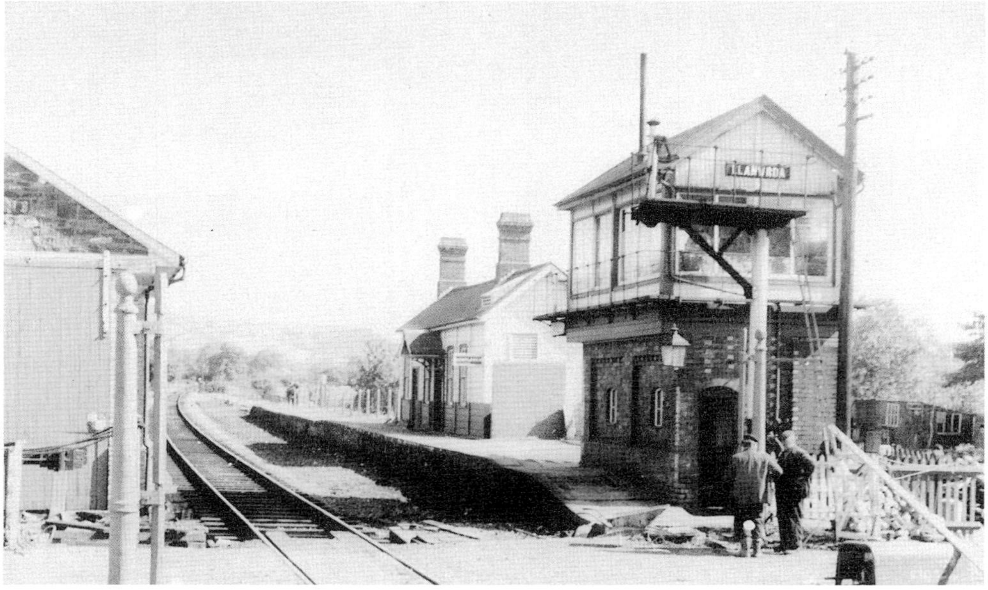

Llanwrda station and signal box.
(Nigel Wassell collection)

Pontardulais Crossing signal box in 1965.
(Courtesy Colin Pritchard)

Llandovery loop and signal box in 1932.
(Dorothy Bound)

Interior of Pantyffynnon box bathed in sunlight, September 1994.
(Rose Coleman)

controls trains on the Pantyffynnon–Swansea section of the line.

At some officially classified 'request' halts, the train has to stop, whether or not passengers wish to join or leave it, to enable the guard to gain access to the plunger housed in the white box on the platform in order to operate the flashing lights at the crossing. This occurs if the trains halts at a platform just prior to traversing a crossing. As a safeguard for motorists who may become impatient while the train is stationary for a few minutes, the crew must activate the level crossing traffic lights. If the train approaches the crossing prior to entering the platform, the sequence is activated automatically. 'Up' trains are required to stop for this purpose at Tirydail (Ammanford), Llandybie, Llangadog, Dolau and Bucknell. On the 'down' journey, Ffairfach is subject to a similar procedure.

At the northern end of the line, prior to 1965, traffic was controlled from Craven Arms Junction signal box, and after 1965, from a ground-frame situated near the site of this signal box at the southern end of the 'up' platform. It was then necessary for guards on Central Wales 'down' trains to set the points themselves, wait for the train to run past them and then re-set the route: an unenviable task on a cold winter's night.

However, from the end of June 1986, the points and signals giving access to the Central Wales Line at the junction were operated from the signal box at Craven Arms Crossing to the north of the station and the ground frame was abolished.

In 1990, at the extreme northern end of the line at Shrewsbury, a scheme for signalling rationalisation was proposed involving a single power box to replace the existing boxes but this was deferred due to lack of funds.

As a result, BR's largest surviving manual signal box, Severn Bridge Junction – which is situated in the centre of a triangle of track south of Shrewsbury station – still survives and is a listed building.

Since 1991, Regional Railways have been endeavouring to negotiate the closure of some of the many private level crossings on the Central Wales Line itself and were looking to reduce these by 112. There had been some concern on the grounds of safety but priority of funding did not cover

The impressive Severn Bridge Junction signal box at Shrewsbury is now protected by a preservation order.

(Roy Palmer)

suggested solutions involving telephone systems or warning lights and the Department of Transport, (with the introduction of a lower speed limit to increase the 'sighting time' – but with the penalty of a slower timetable) considered the crossings safe.

The Llandrindod loop which had been created at the level crossing 36 chains (1½ miles) north of the station when the line northwards was singled in 1964 was moved to the station site on 2 June 1986 and Knighton loop was laid in the summer of 1990.

Thus there are five passing loops on the Central Wales Line between Pantyffynnon and Craven Arms, at Llandeilo, Llandovery, Llanwrtyd, Llandrindod and Knighton. Pantyffynnon does not have a passing loop on the CWL but retains the last manual signal box on the line and the only one south of Craven Arms to control semaphore signals. The GWR box at Pantyffynnon was built in 1892 and still has its original 48-lever frame. A plaque commemorating its centenary was unveiled on 19 August 1992 in the presence of the signalmen. In 1995 Pantyffynnon won the Railtrack Great Western award for the best maintained signal box.

Llandrindod Wells No. 1 box at the level crossing had a preservation order placed on it and in 1989 was moved to the south end of the 'down' platform and opened as a museum, approximately on the site of the original No. 2 box.

Llanwrtyd box was sold and one of its former occupants, signalman John Price, actually passed it while motoring back from work at Llandovery, when it was being conveyed on a transporter en route to its new home at Porthyrhyd. Cilyrychen, Llandybie and Llandovery No. 1 boxes went to the Gwili Railway, parts of the latter being incorporated in Bronwydd Arms station building and that from Llandybie being re-erected there. Cilyrychen box is stored at Cynwyl Elfed station and Ffairfach box, which was first purchased by the Vale of Neath Railway Society, was also moved to the Gwili Railway in the spring of 1984 and has seen use as a mess hut at Bronwydd Arms. Ammanford box still bore the name Tirydail when it was demolished. Dorrington and Marsh Brook boxes remain open to operate level crossings.

Sleepers being unloaded south of the station during construction of the Knighton loop in 1989.

(Roy Palmer)

A crew change when the Llandrindod loop was situated north of the crossing.
(Courtesy Tony Williams)

A 2-car dmu heading 'up' line, approaches the newly installed Knighton loop in June 1990.
(Courtesy Tony Williams)

A 3-car dmu waits on the 'down' side at Llandrindod crossing. After the line was singled and before the loop was moved to the station, trains crossed here – a situation which was very frustrating for passengers if the one from the opposite direction was delayed.
(Courtesy Tony Williams)

Pantyffynnon signal box, September 1994.
(Rose Coleman)

The plaque commemorating the centenary of Pantyffynnon signal box.
(Rose Coleman)

Llandrindod signal box interior.
(Courtesy Tony Williams)

Llandrindod Wells No. 1 signal box, north of the crossing. It is now preserved as a museum on the 'down' platform.
(Courtesy Tony Williams)

Marsh Brook Crossing, still controlled by the signal box, December 1994. (Rose Coleman)

Dorrington signal box, which currently controls the level crossing. The proposed construction of a bypass alongside the track could well necessitate the replacement of this box with one on the 'up' side, but whether all the levers would be re-installed is doubtful. Depicted in January 1995. (Rose Coleman)

The Supervising Signalman watches over operations at Dorrington box in January 1995. (Rose Coleman)

SHREWSBURY AND HEREFORD JOINT LINE.

SIGNALLING ON THE DOUBLE ROAD.

On a Stopping Train, or one travelling slowly, passing an Intermediate Station, the **Danger Signal** will be shown for **Five Minutes**, to stop the Engine of any following Train, when the **Caution Signal** will be turned on for **Five Minutes** more, to complete the Ten Minutes' precautionary signal.

On an Express Train or Single Engine passing, the **Caution Signal** only need be shown for **Five Minutes.**

The **Danger Signal** will be shown while a Train is stopping at a Station, and for **Five Minutes** after its departure, when the **Caution Signal** will be turned on for **Five Minutes** more.

DOWN TRAINS are to be signalled by Telegraph the moment they leave the Stations; from Salop to Stretton; Stretton to Craven Arms; Craven Arms to Ludlow; Ludlow to Leominster; Leominster to Dinmore; and *vice versa.*

CHURCH STRETTON INCLINES.

All Goods, Cattle, and Mineral Trains must stop at Church Stretton, both Up and Down, to examine the loading of Wagons, particularly of Timber and Iron Rails; and the Enginemen must instruct the Guard to pin down such a number of breaks as will give him control over the Train while descending the Inclines. The speed under no consideration is to exceed FIFTEEN MILES per hour.

Telegraphing Trains from Marsh Brook to Craven Arms.

Enginemen and others are particularly instructed to note, that when "Line clear" is given from Marsh Brook to Craven Arms, it only extends to the Signalman at the Bishops Castle Junction and from thence to the Signalman at the North end of the Station at Craven Arms; and Enginemen must be prepared to stop when approaching these points.

To Enginemen and Guards.

NOTE.—**The Block between Dorrington and Craven Arms,** and intermediate Stations, is not in use on **Sundays,** between the hours of 7.0 a.m. and 7.0 p.m.

Great Caution must be observed by Enginemen running between Coleham and Shrewsbury Junction. Every Engineman must have his Engine and Train under his *immediate* control.

BY ORDER.

July 1st, 1866

Signalling of Shrewsbury–Hereford Joint Line, July 1866.

LIST OF SIGNAL BOXES—continued.

Distance Box to Box. M.	C.	NAME OF BOX.	TIMES DURING WHICH BOXES ARE OPEN. Week Days. Opened. Mondays.	Other Days.	Closed at	Sundays. Opened at	Closed at	Whether provided with Switch.
		SWANSEA (Victoria) AND CRAVEN ARMS (Central Wales Junction Exclusive).						
—	—	Swansea 3	6. 0 a.m.	6. 0 a.m.	10.20 p.m. or last Train.	—	—	No.
—	16	" 2	6. 0 a.m.	—	—	—	After last train Sunday morning.	Yes.
—	22½	" 1	6. 0 a.m.	—	—	—		Yes.
—	31	Swansea Bay 2	6. 0 a.m.	—	—	—		No.
—	17½	Swansea Bay 1	10.50 a.m.	10.50 a.m.	12.50 p.m.	—	—	Yes.
1	34¾	Mumbles Road	6. 0 a.m.	6. 0 a.m.	5.30 p.m.	—	—	Yes.
3	15¾	Dunvant	6.30 a.m.	6.30 a.m.	10. 0 p.m.	—	—	Yes.
1	43¼	Gowerton No. 2	6. 0 a.m.	—	—	—	After last train Sunday morning.	No.
—	19½	Glasbrooks Sidings	As required.	As required.	—	—	—	Yes.
1	14¼	Gorseinon No. 2	6. 0 a.m.	—	—	—	After last train Sunday morning.	No.
—	32½	Gorseinon No. 1	7.15 a.m.	7.15 a.m.	10.5 p.m. (SX) 9.20 p.m. (SO)	—	—	Yes.
1	24¼	Grovesend	As required.	As required.	—	—	—	Yes.
1	10¼	Birch Rock Siding	As required.	As required.	—	—	—	Yes.
—	49½	Pontardulais	6. 0 a.m.	—	—	—	After last train Sunday morning.	No.
—	43§	Pontardulais Junction Station	5.30 a.m.	—	—	—	After last Freight train Sunday morning.	No.
			—	—	—	9.30 a.m.	B	
			—	—	—	2.45 p.m.	C	
—	32¾	Pontardulais Junction North	5.45 a.m.	—	—	—	4. 0 a.m. N	Yes.
—	41½	Glynhir Siding	As required.	As required.		—	—	Yes.
3	60½	Pantyffynnon South	5.40 a.m.	—	—	—	After last Freight train Sunday morning.	Yes.
						9.35 a.m.	B	
						2.40 p.m.	C	
—	37	Pantyffynnon North	5.50 a.m.	—	—	—	After last Freight train Sunday morning.	No.
						9.45 a.m.	B	
						2.35 p.m.	C	
—	66	Tirydail	5.50 a.m.	—	—	—	After last Freight train Sunday morning.	No.
						9.45 a.m.	B	
						2.35 p.m.	C	
1	64¼	Llandebie	5.55 a.m.	—	—	—	After last Freight train Sunday morning.	No.
						9.50 a.m.	B	
						2.30 p.m.	C	
—	67¾	Cilyrychen Crossing	5.55 a.m.	—	—	—	After last Freight train Sunday morning.	No.
						9.50 a.m.	B	
						2.30 p.m.	C	
—	47¾	Derwydd Road	6. 0 a.m.	5.15 a.m.	7.55 p.m.	—	—	Yes.
2	52	Ffairfach	6. 0 a.m.	—	—	—	After last train.	No.
						9.55 a.m.	C	
—	28	Carmarthen Valley Junction	6.10 a.m.	—	—	—		No.
—	40¾	Llandilo South	6.10 a.m.	—	—	—	After last train.	No.
—	15¼	Llandilo North	6. 0 a.m.	—	—	—		No.
5	42½	Llangadock	5.55 a.m.	—	—	—		No.
1	62	Llanwrda	5.45 a.m.	—	—	—		No.
3	33½	Llandovery South	5.15 a.m.	—	—	—		No.
—	28	Llandovery North	5.15 a.m.	—	—	—		No.
4	55½	Cynghordy	5. 5 a.m.	—	—	—	After last train Sunday morning.	No.
3	63¾	Sugar Loaf Summit	4.50 a.m.	—	—	—		No.
2	70½	Llanwrtyd Wells	4.35 a.m.	—	—	—		No.
5	2¼	Garth	4.20 a.m.	—	—	—		No.
5	14½	Builth Road No. 2	3.50 a.m.	—	—	—		No.
—	28	Builth Road No. 1	3.50 a.m.	—	—	—		No.
2	57	Howey	3.45 a.m.	—	—	—		No.

§—Distance from Pontardulais Level Crossing 11 chains.
B—Close after clearing of 9.30 a.m. Empty Milk Tanks, Llanelly to Ffairfach.
C—Close after clearing of 5.30 p.m. Milk, Ffairfach to Llanelly.
N—Or after last train performing work has left.

LIST OF SIGNAL BOXES—continued.

Distance Box to Box. M.	C.	NAME OF BOX.	TIMES DURING WHICH BOXES ARE OPEN. Week Days. Opened. Mondays.	Other Days.	Closed at	Sundays. Opened at	Closed at	Whether Provided with Switch.
		SWANSEA (Victoria) AND CRAVEN ARMS (Central Wales Jct. Exclusive)—Continued.						
2	61½	Llandrindod No. 2	3.35 a.m.	—	—	—	After last train Sunday morning.	No.
—	37	Llandrindod No. 1	3.35 a.m.	—	—	—		No.
3	12½	Penybont	3.25 a.m.	—	—	—		No.
—	46½	Penybont Junction	3.25 a.m.	—	—	—		No.
2	33¾	Dolau	9. 0 a.m.	9. 0 a.m.	4.20 p.m.	—	—	Yes.
3	52¼	Llanbister Road	3.20 a.m.	—	—	—	After last train Sunday morning.	No.
2	73	Llangunllo	2.45 a.m.	—	—	—		No.
6	36	Knighton No. 2	2. 5 a.m.	—	—	—		No.
—	21	Knighton No. 1	As required.	As required.		—	—	Yes.
4	1	Bucknell	1.50 a.m.			—	After last train Sunday morning.	No.
2	66½	Hopton Heath	As required.	As required.		—	—	Yes.
2	45½	Broome	7.30 a.m.	7.30 a.m.	2.50 p.m.	—	—	Yes.
		GOWERTON AND LLANMORLAIS.						
—	18¾*	Gowerton No. 1	As required.	As required.		—	—	No.
		PANTYFFYNNON AND BRYNAMMAN.						
—	16	Pantyffynnon (Garnant Branch)	5.0 a.m.	—	—	—	After last Freight train Sunday morning.	No.
—	69½	Ammanford Station	6. 0 a.m.	6. 0 a.m.	After last train.	—	—	No.
—	27	Ammanford Colliery Siding	6. 5 a.m.	6. 5 a.m.		—	—	No.
2	47½	Glanamman	6.10 a.m.	6.10 a.m.		—	—	No.
—	60½	Garnant	6.15 a.m.	6.15 a.m.		—	—	No
1	53½	Brynamman	6.30 a.m.	6.30 a.m.		—	—	No.
		GARNANT AND GWAUN-CAE-GURWEN.						
1	34¾	Gwaun-cae-Gurwen	7. 0 a.m.	7.0 a.m.	After last train.	—	—	No.
		BURRY PORT AND CWMMAWR.						
—	—	Dock Junction	5.30 a.m.	5.30 a.m.	After last train.	—	—	No.
4	56	Kidwelly Junction	5.40 a.m.	5.40 a.m.	After last train.	—	—	No.
2	73	Pontyates	5.50 a.m.	5.50 a.m.		—	—	No.
3	28½	Pontyberem	6.10 a.m.	6.10 a.m.		—	—	No.
1	40½	Cwmmawr	6.25 a.m.	6.25 a.m.		—	—	No.
		LANDO R.O.F. BRANCH.						
—	49	Lando R.O.F. Ground Frame	—	As required.		—	—	—
		CARMARTHEN AND ABERYSTWYTH.						
—	29† 25‡	Carmarthen Station	—	Continuously.		—	—	No.
—	26½	Carmarthen Crossing	4.40 a.m.	—	—	— 3. 0 p.m.	7.35 a.m. V 8.15 p.m. K	No.
—	34¾	Carmarthen Goods Yard	4.50 a.m.	4.50 a.m.	After last train.	3.15 p.m.	After Clearing of 5. 0 p.m. Pont-Llanio.	No.
—	71¾	Abergwili Junction	4.50 a.m.	4.50 a.m.		3.15 p.m.		No.
5	2½	Conwil	4.50 a.m.	4.50 a.m.		3.15 p.m.		No.
3	9	Llanpumpsaint	5.10 a.m.	5.10 a.m.		3.25 p.m.		No.
5	1	Pencader	5.25 a.m.	5.25 a.m.		3.35 p.m.		No.
2	6½	Bryn Teify	6.30 a.m.	6.30 a.m.		3.40 p.m.		No.
1	63¼	Maesycrugiau	6.30 a.m.	6.30 a.m.		3.40 p.m.		No.
3	69¼	Llanybyther	6.30 a.m.	6.30 a.m.		3.40 p.m.		No.
5	6½	Lampeter	7. 0 a.m.	7. 0 a.m.		4. 0 p.m.		No.
2	25	Derry Ormond	7. 0 a.m.	7. 0 a.m.		4. 0 p.m.		No.
5	2½	Pont-Llanio	7. 0 a.m.	7. 0 a.m.		4.15 p.m.		No.
2	43	Tregaron	7. 0 a.m.	7. 0 a.m.		—	—	No.
4	77	Strata Florida	6.55 a.m.	6.55 a.m.		—	—	No.
4	78¾	Trawscoed	6.45 a.m.	6.45 a.m.		—	—	No.
3	7	Llanilar	6.40 a.m.	6.40 a.m.		—	—	No.
5	68	Aberystwyth	6. 0 a.m.	6. 0 a.m.		—	—	No.
		CARMARTHEN VALLEY JCT. AND ABERGWILI JCT. BRANCH.						
—	4¼	Llandilo Bridge	7.10 a.m.	7.10 a.m.	After last train.	—	—	—
2	11¼	Golden Grove	7. 0 a.m.	7. 0 a.m.		—	—	—
5	29¼	Nantgaredig	6.55 a.m.	6.55 a.m.		—	—	—
4	2	Abergwili Junction	4.50 a.m.	4.50 a.m.	After last train.	3.15 p.m.	After clearing of 5 .0 p.m. Pont Llanio.	No.
		PENCADER AND NEWCASTLE EMLYN.						
3	42¼	Llandyssul	6. 0 a.m.	6. 0 a.m.	After last train.	—	—	No.
4	2	Henllan	7.20 a.m.	7.20 a.m.		—	—	No.
2	69	Newcastle Emlyn	7.20 a.m.	7.20 a.m.		—	—	No.
		LAMPETER AND ABERAYRON.						
7	24	Felin Fach	6.50 a.m.	6.50 a.m.	After last train.	Closed.		No.
6	14	Aberayron	6.30 a.m.	6.30 a.m.		Closed.		No.

* Distance from Gowerton No. 2.
†—Distance from Myrtle Hill Junction.
‡—Distance from Carmarthen Bridge.
K—After clearing of 6.30 p.m. Neyland to Paddington
V—Or after clearing of 6.10 a.m Fishguard Harbour to Paddington.

Signal boxes, Swansea Victoria–Craven Arms, 1949/50.

No. 10 149

SWANSEA (Victoria) and CRAVEN ARMS.

Single Line worked by Electric Train Staff between Knighton No. 2 and Llanbister Road ; Penybont Junction and Penybont Station ; Llandrindod Wells No. 2 and Builth Road No. 1 ; Builth Road No. 2 and Llandovery North ; Llandovery South and Llandilo North ; Llandilo South and Pantyffynnon North.

The Line is double between Craven Arms and Knighton No. 2 ; Llanbister Road and Penybont Junction ; Penybont Station and Llandrindod Wells No. 2 ; Builth Road No. 1 and Builth Road No. 2 ; the North and South Boxes at Llandovery ; the North and South Boxes at Llandilo and between Pantyffynnon North Box and Swansea (Victoria), and is worked under the regulations for Train Signalling on Double Lines.

Line.	SECTIONS.	Crossing Stations.
Craven Arms and Swansea (Victoria)	Knighton No. 2 and Llangunllo	Knighton No. 2.
	Llangunllo and Llanbister Road	Llangunllo.
	Penybont Junction and Penybont Station	Penybont Junction.
	Llandrindod Wells No. 2 and Howey	Llandrindod Wells No. 2.
	Howey and Builth Road No. 1	Howey.
	Builth Road No. 2 and Garth	Builth Road.
	Garth and Llanwrtyd Wells	Garth.
	Llanwrtyd Wells and Sugar Loaf	Llanwrtyd Wells.
	Sugar Loaf and Cynghordy	Sugar Loaf.
	Cynghordy and Llandovery North	Cynghordy (except two passenger trains booked to call at Cynghordy).
	Llandovery South and Llanwrda	Llandovery.
	Llanwrda and Llangadock	Llanwrda.
	Llangadock and Llandilo North Box	Llangadock.
	Llandilo South Box and Carmarthen Valley Junction ..	Llandilo
	Carmarthen Valley Junction and Ffairfach	—
	Ffairfach and Derwydd Road	Derwydd Road.
	Derwydd Road and Cilyrychen Crossing	Cilyrychen Crossing. a
	Cilyrychen Crossing and Llandebie	Llandebie. a
	Llandebie and Tirydail	Tirydail. a
	Tirydail and Pantyffynnon North Box	Pantyffynnon.

a—Two Passenger trains must not cross at these places, but a Passenger Train and a Freight train may do so ; the Freight train must be admitted into the Loop so that the Passenger train can run over the Main Line.

BRYNAMMAN, GWAUN-CAE-GURWEN AND CAWDOR BRANCHES.

Single Lines, worked between Pantyffynnon South and Brynamman by Electric Train Staff, between Garnant and Gwaun-cae-Gurwen by Electric Train Staff and between Raven Junction and foot of Incline by Ordinary Train Staff (round, colour yellow).

Gwaun-cae-Gurwen and Duke Colliery wooden train staff, round, coloured black, only one engine in steam or two or more coupled together allowed in section Goods Line only.

Line.	SECTIONS.	Crossing Stations.
Brynamman Branch ..	Pantyffynnon South Box and Pantyffynnon (Garnant Branch) Box.	—
	Pantyffynnon (Garnant Branch) Box and Ammanford.	a Pantyffynnon East. (Garnant Branch).
	Ammanford and Ammanford Colliery Siding.	a Ammanford Colliery Siding.
	Ammanford Colliery Siding and Glanamman.	a Glanamman.
	Glanamman and Garnant.	a Garnant.
	Garnant and Brynamman.	a Brynamman.
G.C.G. Branch	Garnant and G.C.G.	a Garnant & G.C.G.
Cawdor Branch	Raven Junction and Foot of Incline.	—

a—Two Passenger trains must not cross at these places, but a Passenger train and a Freight train may do so ; the Freight train must be admitted into the Loop so that the Passenger train can run over the Main Line.

Swansea Victoria–Craven Arms. Brynamman-Gwaun-cae-Gurwen and Cawdor, 1949/50.

For the use of the Company's Employees only. BR 30176/6 (Block Reg 6)

Great Western Railway.

Alterations and Additions to the Book of Regulations for Train Signalling on Double and Single Lines.

To come into operation on 12th April, 1943.

REGULATIONS FOR TRAIN SIGNALLING ON DOUBLE LINES BY THE ABSOLUTE BLOCK SYSTEM.

REGULATION 19.—TRAIN PASSED WITHOUT TAIL LAMP.—page 16.

Clause (f) to be amplified to read :—

(f) Should a freight train pass without a tail lamp and also without side lamps, the Signalman must assume that the train has become divided and carry out Regulation 20. He must, in addition, send the "TRAIN PASSED WITHOUT TAIL LAMP" signal (4—5) to the Box in rear. If, however, there is a rising gradient in the section from the Box in rear the Signalman must carry out the provisions of Regulation 22, in which case the "TRAIN PASSED WITHOUT TAIL LAMP" signal (4—5) must not be sent.

(B.R.6 4/43.O.M. 12024.)

REGULATION 25.—FAILURE OF INSTRUMENTS, BELLS, OR GONGS.—page 22.

The words "if practicable" to be added after the words "the Signalman must" in the second paragraph of Clause (e).

(B.R.6 4/43. R.C.H.Min. 7670.)

REGULATIONS FOR TRAIN SIGNALLING ON SINGLE LINES BY THE ELECTRIC TOKEN BLOCK SYSTEM.

The following to be inserted on page 32 :—

Instructions for Operating Intermediate Token Instruments.

(1) To place token in instrument.

Press token forward into aperture in the centre of the instrument as if using an ordinary key in a lock (the key end of the token must engage on the centre pin of the instrument) then turn the token left to right as far as possible, withdraw token from centre pin and lower same into either of the columns of the magazine. Advise appropriate Signalman by means of telephone provided that token has been placed in the instrument.

When the token has been replaced in the instrument the Signalmen must immediately withdraw tokens in accordance with Regulation 27 (Testing Instruments) of the Electric Train Token Regulations, and the shunter or other person responsible for operating the intermediate token instrument must remain there until the test has been made and the Signalman has informed him that everything is again in order.

(2) To obtain token from instrument.

After obtaining the authority of the appropriate Signalman by means of the telephone provided to withdraw a token, lift it from the column of the magazine to the centre opening of the instrument, press the token forward as if using an ordinary key in a lock (the key end of the token must engage on the centre pin of the instrument), then turn the token right to left as far as possible. Wait until the needles in both the indicators are deflected (this takes place when both Signalmen hold down on their respective token ringing keys and afterwards continue to turn the token from right to left until the token is free when it can be withdrawn from the instrument. Advise Signalman by means of the telephone provided that the token has been obtained from the instrument.

(B.R.6. 4/43. L.49736/99.)

REGULATIONS FOR TRAIN SIGNALLING ON SINGLE LINES BY THE TRAIN STAFF OR TRAIN STAFF AND TICKET BLOCK SYSTEM.

REGULATION 25.—FAILURE OF BLOCK INSTRUMENTS, BELLS, OR GONGS.—page 74.

The words "if practicable" to be added after the words "the Signalman must" in the second paragraph of Clause (e).

(B.R.6. 4/43. R.C.H.Min. 7670.)

2

REGULATIONS FOR SIGNALLING TRAINS AND ENGINES BY PERMISSIVE BLOCK SYSTEM OVER GOODS RUNNING LOOP LINES.—page 88.

Clause 8 (b) to be amended to read :—

(b) As soon as a train has passed on to the loop line and inside the catch or siding points the Guard must advise the Signalman by the quickest means, either by telephone or by the exhibition of a hand signal by day or a green light by night or during fog or falling snow to indicate that the train is in clear. The Guard must continue to exhibit the hand signal until it is acknowledged by the Signalman, who will, at night or during fog or falling snow, exhibit a white light held steadily.

(B.R.6. 4/43. O.M.12091.)

Clause 19 (c) to be amended to read :—

(c) When the shunted train is removed at the signal box in the rear, the Signalman must give the "Train Withdrawn" signal, 7 beats (5—2) to the signal box in advance and this must be acknowledged, and if the section is clear, the block indicator placed in the normal position, but should the section be still occupied in advance of such train the Signalman in advance must reply to the 5—2 signal by one beat on the bell and both Signalmen must move the tell-tale discs on their block instruments back one number.

(B.R.6. 4/43. O.M.12024.)

The following additional note to be inserted as a separate note preceding the existing note at the end of Section VII on page 88 of the Book of Regulations for Train Signalling on Double or Single Lines :

NOTE.—The above regulations are to be regarded as also applying to loops and goods lines controlled by one signal box insofar as they are applicable.

(B.R.6. 4/43. O.M. 12091.)

April, 1943.

JAMES MILNE,
General Manager.

Each member of the Staff receiving a copy of this circular is required to read carefully and note the contents, and, if supplied with a copy of the Book of Regulations for Train Signalling on Double and Single Lines, to alter or cancel in ink the present instructions on the subject appearing therein, afterwards pasting the amendments in the proper places in the book.

Station and Depot Masters are responsible for seeing that copies of the Book of Regulations for Train Signalling on Double and Single Lines supplied to Signal Boxes, etc., under their supervision are corrected in accordance with this circular.

(This form must be detached and forwarded to the Head of Department.)

................................19......

....Station.

RECEIVED copy of Circular (B.R.6.) dated April, 1943, containing alterations and additions to the Book of Regulations for Train Signalling on Double and Single Lines.

....

Pages 1 and 2 GWR Alterations and Additions to the Book of Regulations for Train Signalling on Double and Single Lines, 12 April 1943.

7

WORKING OF FIXED SIGNALS.—page 37.

The second sentence of clause (b) to be amplified to include reference to Regulation 25.

(B.R.7. 11/47. O.M. 12248.)

REGULATION 18A—LAST TRAIN SIGNALLED INCORRECTLY DESCRIBED.—page 49.

The following to be inserted as Regulation 18A on page 49 :

18A. Last Train Signalled Incorrectly Described. (5–3.) Should a Signalman in forwarding the "Is Line Clear?" signal for a train, incorrectly describe the train, and wish to alter it after such signal has been acknowledged by the Signalman in advance, he must give the "Last Train Signalled Incorrectly Described" signal to the token station in advance, and after this signal has been acknowledged, he must forward the correct "Is Line Clear?" signal. The Token must not be restored to the instrument. An entry must be made in the train register book recording the fact of the train being re-described.

(B.R.7. 11/47. Op. Supts. Min. 69.)

REGULATION 20.—TRAIN DIVIDED.—page 49.

The word "likely" to be substituted for "about" in the second line of clause (a).

(B.R.7. 11/47. O.M. 12148.)

REGULATION 25.—FAILURE OF TOKEN APPARATUS.—page 52.

The following amendments to be made :

Clause (e)—The words "or gongs" to be deleted from the eighth line.

(B.R.7. 11/47. O.M. 12044.)

Clause (g) (i)—The first paragraph to be amended to read :

(i) No train must be allowed to pass on to or foul the section under the Pilotman's control without the Pilotman being present. The Pilotman must inform the Driver and rear Guard of each train, also the Driver of an engine assisting in rear, if any, of the failure, and when practicable accompany every train. He must also instruct the Driver, or Drivers, TO PASS AT DANGER THE SIGNAL CONTROLLING THE ENTRANCE INTO THE SECTION AHEAD IN ACCORDANCE WITH RULE 38, CLAUSE (b) AND to proceed cautiously through the section. When an engine supplied specially for the use of the Pilotman is coupled to a train it must be attached to the front unless it is necessary for such engine to be used for ASSISTING purposes where the use of ASSISTANT engines is authorised. If the Pilotman travels on a train with two or more engines he must ride upon the rearmost engine. If the Pilotman travels on an electric train, rail motor, auto train, OR STREAMLINE RAIL CAR, he must ride with the Driver.

(B.R.7. 11/47. O.M. 12248.)

Clause (g) (ii)—The words "or gongs" to be deleted from the first, third and fourth lines of this clause.

(B.R.7. 11/47. O.M. 12044.)

The last paragraph to be deleted and the following substituted :

THE SIGNAL CONTROLLING THE ENTRANCE TO THE SECTION AHEAD MUST BE MAINTAINED AT DANGER IN ACCORDANCE WITH RULE 38 CLAUSE (b) AND the Pilotman must obtain the permission of the Signalman before allowing a train to enter the section.

(B.R.7. 11/47. O.M. 12248.)

Clause (g) (iii)—The words "or gongs" to be deleted from the first line.

(B.R.7. 11/47. O.M. 12044.)

The following to be inserted as clause (k) :

(k) WHEN A TOKEN FAILURE OCCURS IN A SECTION IN WHICH AN INTERMEDIATE TOKEN INSTRUMENT IS PROVIDED AT A SIDING OR LOOP, THE PILOTMAN, WHO WILL BE APPOINTED IN ACCORDANCE WITH THIS REGULATION, WILL, IF NECESSARY, APPLY TO THE LINEMAN FOR A TOKEN TO ENABLE WORK TO BE CARRIED OUT AT THE SIDING OR LOOP. IN SUCH CIRCUMSTANCES THE PILOTMAN MUST, WHILE A TRAIN IS WORKING AT THE SIDING OR LOOP, REMAIN WITH SUCH TRAIN UNLESS IT IS NECESSARY FOR HIM TO PROCEED TO THE TOKEN STATION IN ADVANCE OR RETURN TO THE TOKEN STATION IN REAR TO ENABLE OTHER TRAINS TO BE PASSED OVER THE SINGLE LINE, IN WHICH CASE HE MUST SATISFY HIMSELF THAT THE TRAIN IS CLEAR OF THE SINGLE LINE, AND THAT THE POINTS ARE SECURED TO PREVENT THE SINGLE LINE BEING FOULED. HE MUST KEEP THE TOKEN IN HIS POSSESSION UNTIL THE TRAIN AT THE INTERMEDIATE SIDING OR LOOP HAS BEEN WITHDRAWN OR THE FAILURE RECTIFIED. THE TIME THE TOKEN IS WITHDRAWN AND RETURNED MUST BE ENTERED IN THE TRAIN REGISTER BOOK, AND THE ENTRIES INITIALLED BY THE SIGNALMAN AND PILOTMAN.

8

Regulation 25.—Failure of Token Apparatus.—page 52—continued.

SHOULD, HOWEVER, A TOKEN FAILURE OCCUR WHEN A TRAIN IS AT SUCH SIDING OR LOOP THE PILOTMAN HAVING ACCOMPANIED A TRAIN TO THE POINT WHERE THE INTERMEDIATE TOKEN INSTRUMENT IS SITUATED MAY INSTRUCT THE DRIVER OF THE TRAIN ON WHICH HE HAS TRAVELLED TO PROCEED TO THE TOKEN STATION IN ADVANCE, WHILE HE REMAINS AT THE SIDING TO DEAL WITH THE TRAIN AT THE SIDING OR LOOP. IF THE PILOTMAN IS NOT IN POSSESSION OF THE TOKEN, THE SERVICES OF THE LINEMAN MUST BE OBTAINED TO RELEASE THE TOKEN FROM THE INTERMEDIATE TOKEN INSTRUMENT AND ON COMPLETION OF THE WORK AT THE SIDING THE PILOTMAN MUST RETURN THE TOKEN TO THE LINEMAN WHO WILL RESTORE IT TO THE INTERMEDIATE TOKEN INSTRUMENT UNLESS THE FAILURE HAS IN THE MEANTIME BEEN RECTIFIED, IN WHICH CASE THE TOKEN WILL BE TAKEN BY THE PILOTMAN TO THE TOKEN STATION TO WHICH HE IS PROCEEDING, IN ORDER THAT WORKING BY PILOTMAN MAY BE CANCELLED IN ACCORDANCE WITH THE REGULATIONS.

The existing clauses (k) and (l) to be relettered (l) and (m) respectively.

(B.R.7. 11/47. O.M. 12299.)

Relettered Clause (l)—The words "or gongs" to be deleted from the second and fourth lines of the second paragraph.

(B.R.7. 11/47. O.M. 12044.)

REGULATIONS FOR TRAIN SIGNALLING ON SINGLE LINES BY THE TRAIN STAFF OR TRAIN STAFF AND TICKET BLOCK SYSTEM.

BELL SIGNALS.—page 61.

The following additional entry to be inserted :

See Reg.		Beats on Bell.	How to be given.
18A.	Last train signalled incorrectly described.	8	5 pause 3

(B.R.7. 11/47. Op. Supts. Min. 69.)

REGULATION 18A—LAST TRAIN SIGNALLED INCORRECTLY DESCRIBED—page 70.

The following to be inserted as Regulation 18A on page 70 :

18A. Last Train Signalled Incorrectly Described. (5–3.) Should a Signalman in forwarding the "Is Line Clear?" signal for a train, incorrectly describe the train, and wish to alter it after such signal has been acknowledged by the Signalman in advance, he must give the "Last Train Signalled Incorrectly Described" signal to the signal box in advance, and after this signal has been acknowledged, he must forward the correct "Is Line Clear?" signal. The position of the Block Indicator must not be altered. An entry must be made in the train register book recording the fact of the train being re-described.

(B.R.7. 11/47. R.C.H. Op. Supts. 69.)

REGULATION 20.—TRAIN DIVIDED.—page 70.

The word "likely" to be substituted for "about" in the second line of clause (a).

(B.R.7. 11/47. O.M. 12148.)

REGULATION 25.—FAILURE OF INSTRUMENTS, BELLS OR GONGS.—page 72.

The following to be substituted for the existing regulation :

25. Failure of Instruments and/or Bells. In the event of any failure of the Block Instruments and/or Bells so that the necessary signals cannot be forwarded and received in the ordinary way, the following instructions must be observed :

(a) (i) A train must not in any circumstances be allowed to pass a signal box into that section of the line where the failure exists (whether the failure has occurred to the Instrument for one or both directions) without having previously been brought to a stand and the Driver and Rear Guard, also the Driver of an engine assisting in the rear, if any, advised of the failure. The Signalman must, before handing the train staff or ticket to the Driver, or Drivers, INSTRUCT THEM TO PASS AT DANGER THE SIGNAL CONTROLLING THE ENTRANCE INTO THE SECTION AHEAD IN ACCORDANCE WITH RULE 38, CLAUSE (b) AND to proceed cautiously through the section.

9

Regulation 25.—Failure of Instruments, Bells or Gongs.—page 72—continued.

When a Driver has been stopped at a Signal Box and advised by the Signalman of the failure of instruments and/or bells or of a track circuit controlling the Block Instruments, the Driver must draw his train forward and bring it again to a stand with the Brake Van near to the Signal Box to enable the Signalman to verbally inform the Guard in rear and Driver of an engine assisting in the rear, if any, of the failure. After the train has thus been brought to a stand for the Signalman to communicate with the Guard and Driver of an engine assisting in rear, the Driver must not start again until he receives a green hand signal from the Signalman.

(ii) The Signalman at whose box the Block Instruments and/or bells have failed must advise the Signalman at the box at the other end of the section of the failure by speaking instrument. When speaking instruments are not available TRAINS MUST BE DEALT WITH IN ACCORDANCE WITH CLAUSE (a) (iv) OF THIS REGULATION.

(iii) When the Bells only, or Bells and Block Instruments have failed and a speaking instrument is available WITH THE SIGNAL BOX IN ADVANCE, the Signalman must, unless instructions to the contrary are given, send the necessary Bell signals as messages on the speaking instrument, for example :

Is Line Clear for * ....
Line is Clear for * ....
SECTION CLEAR BUT STATION OR JUNCTION BLOCKED FOR * ....
* Train entering Section
* Train out of Section
AND ANY OTHER BLOCK SIGNALS.

*—*Description of Train to be given.*

A Signalman forwarding signals as above described must satisfy himself that he is speaking to the Signalman who should receive the communication.

When the Bells only have failed, the Block Instruments must be worked in conjunction with the speaking instruments. When the block instruments only have failed TRAINS MUST BE SIGNALLED ON THE SPEAKING INSTRUMENTS AS DESCRIBED ABOVE AND the bell signals must ALSO be given in accordance with the Regulations.

A train must not be allowed to enter the section until the "Is Line Clear?" signal has been accepted by the Signalman in advance.

Time Interval Working.

(iv) When the speaking instruments are not available TIME INTERVAL WORKING MUST BE PUT INTO OPERATION. THE DRIVER OF THE FIRST TRAIN THAT IS BEING CAUTIONED MUST BE HANDED A COPY OF FORM 4981, PROPERLY FILLED UP AND SIGNED AND BE INSTRUCTED TO STOP AT THE SIGNAL BOX TO WHICH IT IS ADDRESSED AND HAND THE FORM TO THE SIGNALMAN THERE.

A train must not be allowed to follow another train until the time usually taken by the preceding train to clear the section, after allowing for the train having been stopped, has elapsed, but in no case with a less interval than three minutes. When a tunnel intervenes in a Block Section, an interval of not less than ten minutes must be allowed between two trains, unless the Signalman can satisfy himself that the tunnel is clear.

(v) In the event of a failure as described in paragraph (iii) the Driver of the first train travelling on an adjoining line must be advised of the circumstances, and instructed to proceed cautiously through the section.

In cases where trains on one line have to be worked in accordance with paragraph (iv), all trains on the next adjoining line or lines must be stopped and the Driver of each train instructed to proceed cautiously. Trains on the next adjoining line need not, however, be stopped and cautioned on this account when the failure occurs on a line not worked in accordance with the Block Regulations.

(vi) When trains are being signalled in accordance with paragraph (iii), all signals sent on the Bell or speaking instruments must, unless instructions to the contrary are given, be recorded, whether the ordinary block signals are usually recorded or not, and when trains are being worked in accordance with paragraph (iv) the departure time of each train must be recorded.

(b) Steps must be taken immediately to have the apparatus put into working order, and when the failure has been remedied and the apparatus is again in working order, OR SHOULD SPEAKING COMMUNICATION ONLY BE RESTORED, the Driver of the next train allowed to proceed through the section must be cautioned and supplied with a notice on FORM 4810 intimating that the train carrying this notice will be the last train to work on the TIME INTERVAL SYSTEM through the section, and he must also be instructed to stop at the next signal box and hand this notice to the Signalman. The Signalman receiving this notice must then give the "Train Out of Section" signal in accordance with Regulation 10 and the ordinary method of signalling OR WORKING IN ACCORDANCE WITH CLAUSE (a) (iii) will be resumed. WHEN THE BLOCK APPARATUS AND BELLS ARE RESTORED THEY MUST BE TESTED IN ACCORDANCE WITH REGULATION 27.

Pages 7, 8 & 9 GWR Alterations and Additions to the Book of Regulations for Train Signalling on Double and Single Lines, 1947.

In 1994 the complement of signalling staff was:
Pantyffynnon
3 Signalmen (2 regular, 1 relief)
3 Crossing keepers (2 regular, 1 relief)
3 Signal and Telecommunications staff.

Craven Arms
3 Signalmen
Marsh Brook
3 Signalmen
Dorrington
2 Signalmen (closed nights)
Sutton Bridge Junction
2 Signalmen, 1 Signalwoman
Severn Bridge Junction
3 Signalmen
Total 23.

Branch Lines

Brynamman Branch (Gwaun-cae-Gurwen and Abernant)
The line from Pantyffynnon South box which was opened in 1840, was single throughout and was worked by staff and ticket until the 1890s after which the electric train staff system was introduced.

When the new line to Gwaun-cae-Gurwen, built by the GWR, opened in 1907, the Garnant box was re-sited and ground-frames were installed. That at Raven Crossing was renewed in 1964 and by 1985 AOCL was in operation at this point. There were two ground frames west of Gwaun-cae-Gurwen level crossing and one at the colliery. The crossing signal box was reduced to a ground frame in 1964.

On the Abernant branch which opened in 1922, ground-frames were installed at Nantricket (by 1926) and at Cwmgorse North, Cwmgorse South, Abernant North and Abernant South by the 1940s. The line to Duke Colliery was also operated by a series of ground-frames.

What now remains of the line to Gwaun-cae-Gurwen is under the control of a travelling shunter who operates points and gates where required.

Carmarthen Branch
The line was always single throughout with passing loops and had block posts at Carmarthen Valley Junction, Golden Grove, Llanarthney, Nantgaredig and Abergwili Junction. Llandilo Bridge was also a block post, although two trains could not cross there. This provision was due to the station being located next to the cattle market held fortnightly on Mondays, as on these days, a special train arrived from Llandeilo at 1.50pm and departed to Llanelli at 4.30pm.

From its opening in 1864, the line was operated by the train staff system and by 1871, at which time the branch was in the hands of the LNWR, it was controlled by absolute block telegraph and this system was replaced by electric train staff in 1896 and electric token in 1938.

Mountain Branch
This line was controlled by ground-frames and was operated on the OES system (One Engine in Steam) using wooden train staff, the key on which enabled unlocking of hand levers which operated all the points on the line.

Llanmorlais Branch
This line which was always single track with passing loops, commenced at Gowerton. After closure of Gowerton No. 2 box in 1964, the Elba Steelworks box became Gowerton No. 1. Sidings were controlled by a series of ground-frames.

Signal Boxes

Nigel Wassell of The Railway Club of Wales comments:

'It is unlikely that the LNWR inherited very much in the way of signalling equipment when they took over

Carmarthen Valley Junction signal box. The box was closed on 20 March 1955 as were Llandeilo North and South boxes, all three being replaced by a new Llandeilo box. (HMRS/G. M. Perkins collection)

Gowerton No. 1 box. This was Elba Steelworks Sidings Box until 1926.
(Courtesy Dr A. L. Power)

the line between 1868 and 1871. Much improvement work such as the provision of extra passing loops was undertaken in the late 1860s/early 1870s and it seems sensible to conclude that interlocked frames and signal boxes were provided at most locations as part of this work. The earliest design of signal box provided at many locations was that known by the Signalling Record Society (SRS) as Saxby & Farmer Type 2a.

Saxby & Farmer undertook most of the LNWR's signalling work under contract until 1873/4 and naturally supplied equipment to their own designs. The S&F2a type box was current between about 1868 and 1974.

After 1874 the LNWR undertook most of its signalling work itself and between 1874 and 1923 produced signal boxes to three distinct designs, referred to by the SRS as LNWR Types 3, 4 and 5.

LNW3 was hipped roof design, built between 1874 and 1876. The CWL having only been recently signalled by Saxby and Farmer, few, if any of these boxes were built on the line. One example, however, is Gowerton No.1, (formerly Elba Steelworks Siding), on the Penclawdd branch.

LNW4 was the most common type of LNWR signal box, built between 1876 and 1904. This type was characterised by a gabled roof with bargeboards set directly over the boarding and finials set into the boarding, often also an external walkway to allow the signalman to clean the windows.

Examples were widespread and the surviving (preserved) box at Llandrindod Wells is of this type. Severn Bridge Junction Box at Shrewsbury is of a modified Type 4 design, sometimes referred to as 'Type 4 Special'.

LNW5 was a refinement of LNW4 with larger windows and a roof overhang at each end, with conventional 'free' bargeboards. Built after 1904 and into the LMS period, boxes of this type usually replaced earlier boxes, although the box at Howey was probably a Type 5, being a new installation in 1912.

LNWR boxes were normally of 'brick-to-floor' construction. ie the lower storey (locking room) was built of brick, whilst the upper portion (operating floor) was constructed in timber. Virtually all the boxes on the CWL were of this pattern, but one possible exception was Glasbrook's Colliery Siding box at Gowerton which, being built on the side of an embankment, may have been timber throughout (excavations on the site in the early 1990s, when the embankment was being removed revealed some massive timber piles and baulks which were probably the foundations of the box).

After Grouping in 1923, the LMS did not develop its own signal box design for some years and, where new or replacement boxes were required, used pre-Grouping designs (chiefly from the LNWR or Midland Railway) more or less indiscriminately, resulting in two Midland-type boxes appearing at Cynghordy and Garth in 1929 and 1933, respectively.

The installation at Cynghordy was new, in connection with the creation of a passing loop there, but that at Garth replaced an earlier (probably S&F) box. Eventually, the LMS did produce its own design, of somewhat utilitarian outline, which was something of a hybrid between the LNWR and MR designs. The old S&F box at Hopton Heath was replaced by one of these new boxes in 1945.

The foregoing remarks apply only to boxes in the purely LNWR portion of the line. Boxes on the GWR-owned section (Pontarddulais to Llandeilo and the southern portion of the Vale of Towy) were naturally of that company's design, which were not as standardised as those of the LNWR, whilst many of the boxes on the Shrewsbury & Hereford section north of Craven Arms, which was joint LNWR/GWR property, were brick-built to a low-pitched hipped roof design unique to this line (and the Shrewsbury & Welshpool Joint) – the surviving boxes at Marsh Brook, Church Stretton and Dorrington are of this design, as were Craven Arms station and Central Wales Junction. (S&H 1 on list).'

Signal boxes

GF=Became a ground-frame
Open=Date of original box where ascertained
N=New box
orig.=originally
R=Re-sited
S&F=Saxby & Farmer

	Box Type	*Open*	*Closed*
Swansea Victoria No. 3 (orig. No. 1)	LNW4	c1881 NR 1889	1964
2		1883 NR 1890 & 1924	1964
(orig. No. 3) 1	LNW5	c1889 NR 1882 & 1907	1964
St Helens (Swansea Bay 2)	orig. S&F2a		
replaced by	LNW5	1868 N 1922	1964
Swansea Bay 1	LNW4	1892	1964
Mumbles Road	LNW5	c1893 N 1912	1964
Mumbles Crossing		1875	c1893
Voilart		1875	1876
Rhydydefed		1893	c1909
Killay	LNW4	1876 GF 1939	1964
Dunvant (2 until closure of Dunvant 1)	LNW5	1875 N 1921	1964
Caergynydd Down (later Dunvant 1)	1876	1908	
Brynmawr and Bishwell	1875	1896	
Gowerton 3 LNWR Ground-frame hut. Not a block post.		c1867 GF 1896	1964
Gowerton 1 (became 2)	LNW4	1875	1964
Gowerton (on Penclawdd Branch)	LNW3	1873	1964
Elba Steelworks box (Gowerton 1 after 1926)			
Glasbrook Sidings		1881 N c1893	1964
Gorseinon 2	LNW4	1875 NR 1892	1964
Gorseinon 1		1893 NR 1920	1964
Grovesend Colliery Siding		1900	1959
Birch Rock Siding		1893/94	1954
Pontardulais Crossing	LMS 11	c1876 NR 1940	1964
Pontardulais Junction	GWR 25	c1876 R	1893
	GF	1967	1974
Pontardulas North		c1876 NR 1915	1964
Glynhir Siding		1911	1964
Tynycerig		c1876 RS 1905	1913
Garnswilt		1875	by 1900
Pantyfynnon South ('South' dropped 1966)	GWR 5	c1876 NR 1892	——
Pantyfynnon North – original box possibly 'Rhos Siding'		c1840 RS 1892	1966
Tirydail (orig. Duffryn) (remained as Gate box until 1985)	GWR 5	1897 GF	1966
Llandebie	GWR 3	c1884 GF 1966	1985
Limestone Branch (replaced by Cilyrychen X Box)		c1884 NR 1892	1913
Cilyrchen Crossing	GWR 28	1913 GF 1966	1985
Derwydd Road	GWR 2	1876	1966
Ffairfach	GWR Type 31	1880 NR	1935
(remained as Gate box until 1985)		GF 1966	
Carmarthen Valley Junction	GWR SRS 23	1880s	1955
Llandilo South (GWR boxes replacing)			1955
Llandilo North (an original box c 1880)			1955
All three above replaced by new box at Llandilo North 20. 3.1955			
Llandilo (North omitted) Later 'Llandeilo'		1955	1986
Llangadog	GWR	by 1884	1978
Llanwrda	LNW4	late 1880s	1962
Llandovery 2		late 1880s	1986
Llandovery 1	LNW4	late 1880s	1986
Cynghordy	Midland	1929	1965
Sugar Loaf Summit	LNW4	1872	1965
Llanwrtyd	LNW5	1868	1986
Garth	Midland	1867 NR 1933	1965
Builth Road 2	LNW4	1860s	1965
Builth Road 1	LNW4	1860s	1965
Howey Possibly	LNW5	1912	1962
Llandrindod 2		1864	1960s
Llandrindod 1	LNW4	1876	1986
Penybont Station	LNW5	1876	1964/5
Penybont Junction	LNW5	1871	1964
Dolau	LNW4	1871	1965
(Remained as Gate box until 1976)			
Llanbister Road (loop opened 1871)	LNW4	1871	1964
Llangunllo (Block instruments were in station building – No box)			
Knighton 2	S&F2a	1868/73	1964
Knighton 1		c1870	1964
Bucknell	S&F2a	1868/73	1965
replaced by	LNW5		
(Remained as Gate box until 1970s)			
Hopton Heath	S&F2a	1860 N 1945	1965
replaced by	LMS11c		
Broome		1860	1965
Craven Arms Central Wales Junction	S&H1	1851	1965

(Until 26.3.1956 when it became Craven Arms Jcn)			
Craven Arms Stn North End box	S&H1	pre 1880	1956
Craven Arms Crossing (Formerly Long Lane Crossing)			
(Still open)	GWR34	mid 1800s N 1950-	
Stretford Bridge Junction		c1866	1940
(Bishops Castle line)			
Marsh Farm Junction		c1867	1951
(Wenlock Line)			
Marsh Brook (Still open)	S&H1	1850s	-
Church Stretton (Still open)	S&H1	1850s	-
for repair work)			
Leebotwood		c1870	1958
Dorrington (Still open 1994)	S&H1	c1870	-
Condover		c1870	1963
Bayston Hill			
Sutton Bridge Junction (Still open)		-	
Coleham			
Severn Bridge Junction (Still open)		1903	-
Shrewsbury Central		mid 1800s	1909
Swansea (High St)		c1878	1926
Swansea N. Dock Jcn		1877 N 1915	1973
(Renamed High St. 1926)			
Swansea Loop East Jcn		1906 R 1907	1973
Swansea Loop West Jcn		1906 GF	1973
Landore 1 (East by 1914)		c1878	1936
Landore 2 (West by 1914)		c1878	1973
Cwmfelin Sidings (Renamed Cwmfelin &		1896	1962
Cwmbwrla 1906)			
Cwmbwrla Sidings		c1878 R 1896	1906
Cockett East		1899	1935
Cockett		pre 1882 NR 1882	1966
Cockett West		1911	1926
Mynydd Bach y Glo		1874	1884
Gowerton 1 (Became Gowerton East 1894)		1876 NR 1912	1969
Gowerton Jcn 2 (West)		1876 NR 1881	1953
Gowerton Jcn 1		1899	1903
Cae Duke		1893	1933
Loughor		1880	GF 1961
Loughor Bridge		1908	
Yspitty Sidings		by 1884	
Duffryn Crossing		1906	1933
Llandilo Junction East (Llandilo Jcn from 1966)		c1889 N 1912	1973
Llandilo Junction West		1889 N 1908	1966
Llanelly 1		c1877	1901
Llanelly Dock Jcn Box		1901	1969
Llanelly 2 (replaced by Llanelly Dock Jcn Box)		c1877	1901
Llanelly 3 (Llanelly East 1901)		c1878	GF 1973
Genwen Junction		1875 NR 1889	
		& 1907	1966
Bynea		1839	1966
Llangennech Siding		c1886	1966
Llangennech Station		c1880	1966
Morlais Junction		c1909	1970s
Morlais Siding		c1899	1913
Morlais Colliery		1886	1895
Hendy Junction		1913	1973

Brynamman Branch

	Open	Closed
Pantyffynon South (became Pantyffynnon in 1966)	1892	——
Garnant Branch box	c1876 NR 1892	1968
Ammanford	c1893	1990
(Replaced by temporary box/re-sited 10/90 and then closed – barriers operated by train crew)		
Ammanford Coll Halt	1905	1964
Glynmoch Coll Sidings	1874	1897
Middle Ammanford South	c1880	1902
Middle Ammanford North	c1880	1901
Glanamman	c1880	1964
Garnant	c1878 NR c1907	1964
Brynamman	1886	c1958
Garnant to Gwaun-cae-Gurwen		
Gwaun-cae-Gurwen	1908	GF 1964

Llanmorlais Branch

	Open	Closed
Gowerton 1 (became 2)	1875	1964
Gowerton (Elba Steelworks – became 1 after 1926)	1873	1964

Carmarthen Branch

	Open	Closed
Llandilo Bridge	1885	1963
Golden Grove	1864	1963
Llanarthney	1864	1938
Nantgeredig	1864	1963
Abergwili Junction	1864	1963

FOR THE USE OF THE COMPANY'S EMPLOYEES ONLY. (B.R. 4.)

Great Western Railway.

Alterations and Additions to the Book of Regulations for Train Signalling on Double and Single Lines.

To come into operation on 1st November, 1939.

REGULATIONS FOR TRAIN SIGNALLING ON DOUBLE LINES BY THE ABSOLUTE BLOCK SYSTEM.

BELL SIGNALS.—Page 4.

The following entries in the list of Bell Signals to be amended to read :—

See Reg.		Beats on Bell.	How to be given.
3 & 4	Express passenger train, newspapers, breakdown van train going to clear the line, or light engine going to assist disabled train or EMPTY COACHING STOCK TRAIN TIMED AT EXPRESS PASSENGER SPEED ?	4	4 consecutively.
3 & 4	AUTO-TRAIN ?	7	3 PAUSE 1 PAUSE 3.

The following additional entries to be inserted :—

See Reg.		Beats on Bell.	How to be given.
3 & 4	EXPRESS DIESEL CAR ?	8	4 PAUSE 1 PAUSE 3.
3 & 4	ORDINARY PASSENGER OR PARCELS DIESEL CAR ?	9	5 PAUSE 1 PAUSE 3.

(B.R.4.—10/39. O.M. 11951.)

REGULATION 5.—SECTION CLEAR BUT STATION OR JUNCTION BLOCKED.—Page 9.

The last sentence of the note preceding clause (a) to be altered to read :—

UNLESS SPECIAL INSTRUCTIONS ARE GIVEN TO THE CONTRARY, THIS SIGNAL MUST NEVER BE USED DURING FOG OR FALLING SNOW EXCEPT FOR THE ACCEPTANCE OF A TROLLEY IN ACCORDANCE WITH REGULATION 9.

(B.R.4.—10/39. O.M. 11952.)

REGULATIONS FOR TRAIN SIGNALLING ON SINGLE LINES BY THE ELECTRIC TOKEN BLOCK SYSTEM.

BELL SIGNALS.—Page 30.

The following entries in the list of Bell Signals to be amended to read :—

See Reg.		Beats on Bell.	How to be given.
3 & 4	Express passenger train, newspapers, breakdown van train going to clear the line, or light engine going to assist disabled train or EMPTY COACHING STOCK TRAIN TIMED AT EXPRESS PASSENGER SPEED ?	4	4 consecutively.
3 & 4	AUTO TRAIN ?	7	3 PAUSE 1 PAUSE 3.

The following additional entries to be inserted :—

See Reg.		Beats on Bell.	How to be given.
3 & 4	EXPRESS DIESEL CAR ?	8	4 PAUSE 1 PAUSE 3.
3 & 4	ORDINARY PASSENGER OR PARCELS DIESEL CAR ?	9	5 PAUSE 1 PAUSE 3.

(B.R.4.—10/39. O.M. 11951.)

REGULATION 5.—SECTION CLEAR BUT STATION OR JUNCTION BLOCKED.—Page 39.

The last sentence of the note preceding clause (a) to be altered to read :—

UNLESS SPECIAL INSTRUCTIONS ARE GIVEN TO THE CONTRARY, THIS SIGNAL MUST NEVER BE USED DURING FOG OR FALLING SNOW EXCEPT FOR THE ACCEPTANCE OF A TROLLEY IN ACCORDANCE WITH REGULATION 9.

(B.R.4.—10/39. O.M. 11952.)

Page 1 GWR Alterations and Additions to the Book of Regulations for Train Signalling on Double and Single Lines, 1939.

9

Passsenger Traffic

At the commencement, passengers were of little consideration. In the early 1840s, the Llanelly company provided open carriages or wagons attached to the rear of the freight trains with no protection from the elements for any who were prepared to take 'pot luck' – there being no timetables or halts for at least another decade. Journeys were taken at passengers' own risk – at a speed not to exceed 8mph.

However, such accommodation as there was appears to have been welcome. The *Cambrian* newspaper dated 17.4.1841 comments as under:

> 'Llanelly Railway. It is with sincere pleasure we announce to our readers that this railway, which was intended merely for the transmission of coals, and was never thought would be able to command a traffic in passengers, and which, therefore, is provided with only two locomotives and two railway carriages to run on its single way, has actually carried 2,523 passengers in four weeks, or at the rate of 631 per week. Such a circumstance is strikingly indicative of the great powers of railways to increase and even to create passenger traffic in localities where it may be supposed it could hardly exist.'

The Llanelly company's Brynamman branch opened from Duffryn for passengers in June 1842 and it is probable that passengers also travelled from Garnant on the original LRDC line which opened the previous year to Gwaun-cae-Gurwen.

By May 1850 passengers were conveyed from Swansea to Pontarddulais by horse-drawn coach or omnibus, continuing to Duffryn (Tirydail) by rail whence they continued their journey by road again to Llandeilo. The last sentence in the following report from the *Cambrian* 8 April 1853 conjures up an amusing picture of conditions for passengers at that period.

> 'Railway Extension. On Friday last, the junction between the Llanelly and South Wales Railways, about half a mile in extent, was opened for general traffic for the first time. The extension is a material public improvement. Passengers now need not traverse the dangerous walk past the docks, shipping, and tramroads which formerly intervened.
> The station of the Llanelly Railway is now contiguous to that of the South Wales Railway, and on this day many hundreds witnessed the first arrival of the swift little steam engine belonging to the Llanelly Railway which has lately undergone thorough repair. One more improvement is required – that the windows of the third class carriages should be constructed of glass, instead of wood, as at present, for, when closed, they give the passenger an idea that he is in some black hole, instead of a railway carriage.'

In the late 1850s, it was possible to travel from Swansea to Llandovery still using a combination of horse-drawn coaches and trains and between Llanelly Town and Llandovery by through train. The fare for the latter was 2s 7d for third class, 4s 8d for second class and 6s 3d for first class. Thereafter the through carriage of passengers by rail gradually increased, reaching Llandilo in 1857 and Llandovery by 1858 by which time there was first, second and third class accommodation and cheap day return fares.

The service from Swansea Victoria consisted of three 'up' trains departing at 8.40am, 12.50pm and 5.10pm. The 'down' trains from Llandovery left at 8.40am, 1.15 pm and 5.20pm. All had connections to and from Llanelly and Carmarthen; the morning and early evening trains with Brynamman. The journey time between Swansea Victoria and Llandovery was approximately two hours.

The Carmarthen branch from Llandeilo opened to passengers in June 1865.

Later, after the LNWR had taken over the Carmarthen line, there were through coaches from London Euston to Carmarthen but these ceased in the early 1900s and the journey necessitated a change at Llandilo.

The *Cambrian* newspaper dated 20 December 1867, announcing the running of the first passenger train on the previous Saturday between Swansea and Pontarddulais over 'the newly made Swansea extension of the Dunvant Valley Railway' (an existing Llanelly company freight line carrying coal from the Clyne Valley), went on to advise the commencement, on 1 January 1868, of a 'good train service between Swansea and Llanelly'. This was deemed to be of 'great public convenience' due, it appears, to the fact that a train leaving Swansea at 1pm and arriving at Llanelly at 2pm would fill the gap left between existing Great Western Railway departures at 11am and 3.30pm.

The fact that the opening was performed without much ceremony was not, according to the newspaper, 'indicative of any want of confidence in the value and importance of the line' which was to confer 'advantages upon the district of which we have now but very faint idea.' The paper went on to point out that when the LNWR had completed its system from Craven Arms to Llandovery, a direct 'narrow gauge' route would be established:

> 'between Swansea on the one hand and Liverpool, Manchester and the whole of the great centres of industry in the North on the other. And this will be entirely independent and distinct from the Great Western system. The new route to the North will be nearly fifty miles, or two hours shorter, than the present journey – the cost of transit will be considerably less and new districts will be opened up – districts which cannot be surpassed for beauty and romantic scenery'

The report continues in this vein, extolling the benefits of the spa towns and the accessibility of Aberystwyth and, while admitting that the primary object was 'unbroken narrow gauge communication with the North', it cannot resist the prediction that the three mile branch from Gower Road station to Penclawdd 'for the accommodation of the copper works' will open up a district which will 'prove a favourite spot for many a summer picnic'.

It points out:

> 'From Pontardulais at present the passenger changes for Llanelly, Carmarthen, Llandilo and Llandovery but on and after the 1st of January next this will be obviated, the present line now being worked as a branch but such will not be the case at the commencement of the new year. From Pontardulais

Tickets for journies to Gowerton. (Courtesy J. Britton)

the passenger travels through scenery of almost unequalled beauty and grandeur, the charms of which have often been justly dilated upon but which must be seen to be appreciated.'

Faced with such purple prose, who could resist. It makes BR slogans like 'Let the train take the strain' seem tame by comparison.

However, Swansea's lot was not such a happy one. In 1875, the Chamber of Trade sent a delegation to London to try to get something done about the position in which the rivalry between the Midland, GWR and LNWR companies had placed the travelling public.

Later, too, until the loop was finally built in 1906, passengers travelling into Swansea High Street were inconvenienced by the fact that the main line ended at Landore where they often had to change and frequently waited a long time for a train into the city. December 14, 1867 saw the commencement of the passenger service to Penclawdd, extending to Llanmorlais in 1877.

Meanwhile, at the northern end, from 6 March 1861, three passenger trains per day operated on weekdays between Knighton and Craven Arms. With the opening of the whole line in June 1868, there were four trains per day from Swansea Victoria to Liverpool Lime Street (via Manchester London Road) and three in the southward direction, with a fourth commencing at Shrewsbury. These had connections at Pontarddulais to and from Llanelly. It is

LLANELLY RAILWAY.

IMPORTANT
ALTERATION
OF
TRAINS
On and after NOVEMBER 2nd, 1868.

DOWN TRAINS.

The 9.5 p.m. Train from LLANDOVERY to SWANSEA will be discontinued.

The 5.40 p.m. Train from LLANDILO to CARMARTHEN will start at 6.50 p.m.

The 7.30 p.m. Train from LLANDILO to CARMARTHEN will be discontinued.

The 4.32 p.m. Train from PONTARDULAIS to LLANELLY will be discontinued.

On Saturdays, a Train will leave LLANELLY at 8.0 a.m. for Swansea and Penclawdd, leaving Penclawdd for Swansea at 8.50 a.m., arriving at Swansea at 9.25 a.m.

The present Train from PONTARDULAIS and PENCLAWDD to SWANSEA on Saturdays will be discontinued.

UP TRAINS.

The 6.30 a.m. Train from SWANSEA, and 6.25 a.m. from LLANELLY, will be discontinued between these points and Llandilo; the 6.45 a.m. Train from CARMARTHEN to LLANDOVERY will be slightly altered.

The 4.0 p.m. up Train from SWANSEA and LLANELLY, and the 4.15 p.m. from CARMARTHEN will be discontinued.

The 5.50 p.m. train from SWANSEA, the 5.55 p.m. from LLANELLY, and the 6.35 p.m. from CARMARTHEN will be discontinued, and a New Train will leave SWANSEA at 5.15, LLANELLY at 5.30, and CARMARTHEN at 5.5 p.m.

The 5.30 p.m. train from SWANSEA to Penclawdd on Saturdays will start at 6.15 p.m.

The 6.50 p.m. train from PANTYFFYNON to Garnant will start at 6.20 p.m.

Several of the other Trains will be slightly altered: for Particulars see Time Bills.

Llanelly, October 20, 1868. BY ORDER.

Passenger timetable, Llanelly Guardian *29 October 1868.*

The Llanelly Railway.—The last train from Llandovery last night proceeded direct to Swansea without rendering a change of carriage at Pontardulais necessary. After the 1st of January a goods train service will be established between Llandilo and Llanelly, passengers leaving Swansea at one o'clock arriving at Llanelly at two o'clock, and as there is no train on the G.W.R. between eleven and half-past three, this will prove of great convenience to the passengers. The stations along the extension are comfortably fitted up, and all the arrangements are satisfactory. We may remark that persons entering Swansea by the new line are likely to form a far higher opinion of the town than if they entered it by the G.W.R. line, the approaches to the town in the former instance being all that could be desired, but in the latter case wretchedly bad. Too much praise cannot be given the indefatigable manager, Mr. W. D. Phillipps, to whom much of the success which has attended the exertions of the company is to be attributed.

LNWR Llandovery to Swansea, Llanelly Guardian *2 February 1868.*

The Knighton Railway.—July, 1866.

Miles.	UP TRAINS.	WEEK DAYS. 1 Goods. 1, 2. A.M.	2 1, 2, 3. A.M.	3 † Goods. A.M.	4 1, 2. P.M.	5 1, 2, 3. P.M.
	Craven Arms ......dep.	5 0	8 5	10 50	2 40	6 45
3	Broome	5 15	8 12	11 5	2 48	6 52
$5\frac{1}{4}$	Hopton Heath	5 25	8 17	11 15	3 0	6 58
$8\frac{1}{4}$	Bucknell	5 35	8 25	11 30	3 8	7 5
$12\frac{1}{2}$	Knighton ....arr.	5 50	8 40	11 50	3 20	7 15
	Do. Depart for Llandrindod	...	8 45	12 5	3 25	...

† No. 3 Up Goods leaves Craven Arms at 11.5 a.m., on Thursdays, and conveys Market Passengers between Craven Arms and Knighton.

Miles.	DOWN TRAINS.	1 1, 2, 3. A.M.	2 1, 2, 3. A.M.	3 Goods. A.M.	4 Cattle. 1, 2. P.M.	5 1, 2, 3. P.M.			
	Knighton, Arrive from Llandrindod.	...	9 40	11 45	3 15	...	...	...	...
...	Do. ....dep.	6 20	9 45	12 0	3 25	8 15	...	...	...
$4\frac{1}{4}$	Bucknell	6 35	9 55	12 15	3 35	8 27	...	...	...
$7\frac{1}{4}$	Hopton Heath	6 47	10 2	12 26	3 43	8 33	...	...	...
$9\frac{1}{2}$	Broome	6 55	10 10	12 35	3 50	8 40	...	...	...
$12\frac{1}{2}$	Craven Arms ......arr.	7 5	10 20	1 5	4 5	8 48	...	...	...

Knighton Railway, July 1866.

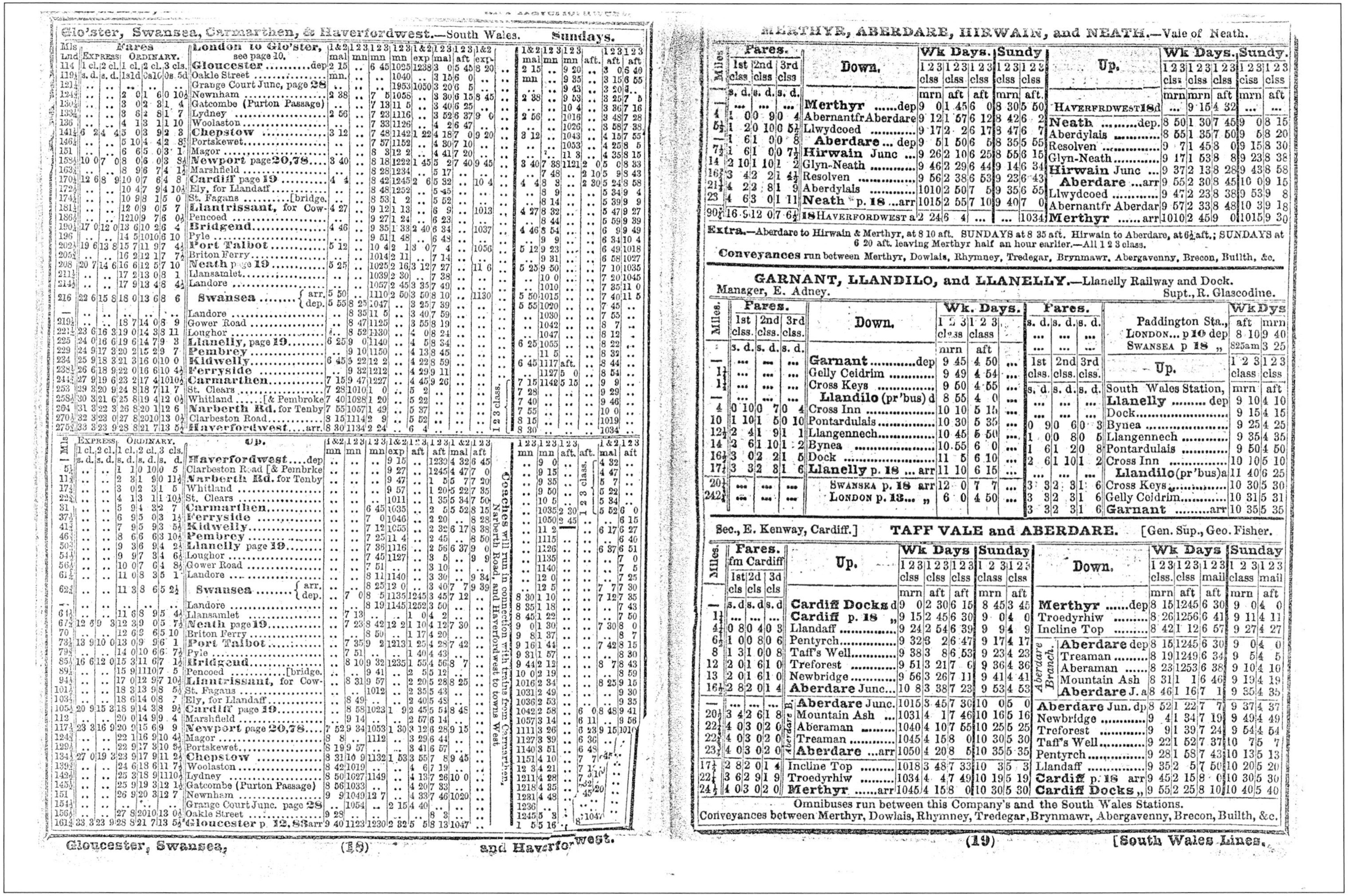

Glo'ster, Swansea, Carmarthen, & Haverfordwest.—South Wales. Sundays.

London to Glo'ster, see page 10.

Coaches will run in connection with trains from Carmarthen, Narberth Road, and Haverfordwest to towns West

Gloucester, Swansea, (18) and Haverfordwest.

MERTHYR, ABERDARE, HIRWAIN, and NEATH.—Vale of Neath.

Miles	Fares 1st clss	2nd clss	3rd clss	Down	Wk Days 1 2 3 clss mrn	1 2 3 clss aft	1 2 3 clss aft	Sunday 1 2 3 clss mrn	1 2 3 clss aft
	s. d.	s. d.	s. d.						
	...	...	...	Merthyr ......dep	9 0	1 45	6 0	8 30	5 50
4	1 0	0 9	0 4	Abernantfr Aberdare	9 12	1 57	6 12	8 42	6 2
5½	1 2	0 10	0 5½	Llwydcoed	9 17	2 2	6 17	8 47	6 7
—	1 6	1 0	0 8	Aberdare ... dep	9 5	1 50	6 5	8 35	5 55
7½	1 6	1 0	0 7½	Hirwain Junc ...	9 26	2 10	6 25	8 55	6 15
14	2 10	1 10	1 2	Glyn-Neath	9 46	2 29	6 44	9 14	6 34
16½	3 4	2 2	1 4½	Resolven	9 56	2 38	6 53	9 23	6 43
21¼	4 2	2 8	1 9	Aberdylais	1010	2 50	7 5	9 35	6 55
23	4 6	3 0	1 11	Neath p. 18 ...arr	1015	2 55	7 10	9 40	7 0
90¾	16 9	12 0	7 6¾	18 Haverfordwest a	2 24	6 4	...	...	1034

Up	Wk Days 1 2 3 clss mrn	1 2 3 clss mrn	1 2 3 clss aft	Sunday 1 2 3 clss mrn	1 2 3 clss aft
Haverfordwest 18 d	...	9 15	4 32	...	...
Neath ....dep.	8 50	1 30	7 45	9 0	8 15
Aberdylais	8 55	1 35	7 50	9 5	8 20
Resolven	9 7	1 45	8 0	9 15	8 30
Glyn-Neath	9 17	1 53	8 8	9 23	8 38
Hirwain Junc ...	9 37	2 13	8 28	9 43	8 58
Aberdare ...arr	9 55	2 30	8 45	10 0	9 15
Llwydcoed	9 47	2 23	8 38	9 53	9 8
Abernantfr Aberdar	9 57	2 33	8 48	10 3	9 18
Merthyr ....arr	1010	2 45	9 0	1015	9 30

Extra.—Aberdare to Hirwain & Merthyr, at 8 10 aft. SUNDAYS at 8 35 aft. Hirwain to Aberdare, at 6½ aft.; SUNDAYS at 6 20 aft. leaving Merthyr half an hour earlier.—All 1 2 3 class.

Conveyances run between Merthyr, Dowlais, Rhymney, Tredegar, Brynmawr, Abergavenny, Brecon, Builth, &c.

GARNANT, LLANDILO, and LLANELLY.—Llanelly Railway and Dock.

Manager, E. Adney. Supt., R. Glascodine.

Miles	Fares 1st clss.	2nd clss.	3rd clss.	Down	Wk. Days 1 2 3 class mrn	1 2 3 class aft
	s. d.	s. d.	s. d.			
—	...	...	...	Garnant ....dep	9 45	4 50
1¼	...	...	...	Gelly Ceidrim	9 49	4 54
1½	...	...	...	Cross Keys	9 50	4 55
—	...	...	...	Llandilo (pr'bus) d	8 55	4 0
4	0 10	0 7	0 4	Cross Inn	10 10	5 15
10	1 10	1 5	0 10	Pontardulais	10 30	5 35
12½	2 4	1 9	1 1	Llangennech.............	10 45	5 50
14	2 6	1 10	1 2	Bynea	10 55	6 0
16½	3 0	2 2	1 5	Dock	11 5	6 10
17½	3 3	2 8	1 6	Llanelly p. 18 ... arr	11 10	6 15
20¼	...	...	...	Swansea p. 18 arr	12 0	7 7
242¼	...	...	...	London p. 13... „	6 0	4 50

Fares 1st class.	2nd class.	3rd class.	Up	Wk Dys 1 2 3 class	1 2 3 class
s. d.	s. d.	s. d.	Paddington Sta.,	aft	mrn
...	...	...	London... p 10 dep	8 10	9 40
...	...	...	Swansea p 18 „	825am	3 25
s. d.	s. d.	s. d.	South Wales Station,	mrn	aft
...	...	...	Llanelly .... dep	9 10	4 10
...	...	...	Dock......................	9 15	4 15
0 9	0 6	0 3	Bynea	9 25	4 25
1 0	0 8	0 5	Llangennech	9 35	4 35
1 6	1 2	0 8	Pontardulais	9 50	4 50
2 6	1 10	1 2	Cross Inn	10 10	5 10
			Llandilo(pr'bus)a	11 40	6 25
3 3	2 3	1 6	Cross Keys	10 30	5 30
3 3	2 3	1 6	Gelly Ceidrim.........	10 31	5 31
3 3	2 3	1 6	Garnant ....arr	10 35	5 35

Sec., E. Kenway, Cardiff.] **TAFF VALE and ABERDARE.** [Gen. Sup., Geo. Fisher.

Miles	Fares fm Cardiff 1st cls	2d cls	3d cls	Up	Wk Days 1 2 3 clss mrn	1 2 3 clss aft	1 2 3 clss aft	Sunday 1 2 3 class mrn	1 2 3 clss aft
	s. d	s. d	s. d						
—				Cardiff Docks d	9 0	2 30	6 15	8 45	3 45
1¼	...	...	...	Cardiff p. 18 „	9 15	2 45	6 30	9 0	4 0
4½	0 8	0 4	0 3	Llandaff	9 24	2 54	6 39	9 9	4 9
6½	1 0	0 8	0 6	Pentyrch..............	9 32	3 2	6 47	9 17	4 17
8	1 3	1 0	0 8	Taff's Well..........	9 38	3 8	6 53	9 23	4 23
12	2 0	1 6	1 0	Treforest	9 51	3 21	7 6	9 36	4 36
13	2 0	1 6	1 0	Newbridge	9 56	3 26	7 11	9 41	4 41
16½	2 8	2 0	1 4	Aberdare Junc...	10 8	3 38	7 23	9 53	4 53
20½	3 4	2 6	1 8	Aberdare Junc. (Aberdare Br.)	1015	3 45	7 30	10 0	5 0
22¼	4 0	3 0	2 0	Mountain Ash	1031	4 1	7 46	10 16	5 16
22½	4 0	3 0	2 0	Aberaman	1040	4 10	7 55	10 25	5 25
22¾	4 0	3 0	2 0	Treaman	1045	4 15	8 0	10 30	5 30
23¼	4 0	3 0	2 0	Aberdare ...arr	1050	4 20	8 5	10 35	5 35
17½	2 8	2 0	1 4	Incline Top	1018	3 48	7 33	10 3	5 3
22	3 6	2 9	1 9	Troedyrhiw	1034	4 4	7 49	10 19	5 19
24½	4 0	3 0	2 0	Merthyr ....arr	1045	4 15	8 0	10 30	5 30

Down	Wk Days 1 2 3 clss. mrn	1 2 3 clss aft	1 2 3 mail aft	Sunday 1 2 3 class mrn	1 2 3 mail aft
Merthyr ......dep	8 15	1245	6 30	9 0	4 0
Troedyrhiw	8 26	1256	6 41	9 11	4 11
Incline Top	8 42	1 12	6 57	9 27	4 27
Aberdare dep (Aberdare Branch)	8 15	1245	6 30	9 0	4 0
Treaman	8 19	1249	6 34	9 5	4 5
Aberaman	8 23	1253	6 38	9 10	4 10
Mountain Ash	8 31	1 1	6 46	9 19	4 19
Aberdare J. a	8 46	1 16	7 1	9 35	4 35
Aberdare Jun. dp	8 52	1 22	7 7	9 37	4 37
Newbridge	9 4	1 34	7 19	9 49	4 49
Treforest	9 9	1 39	7 24	9 54	4 54
Taff's Well	9 22	1 52	7 37	10 7	5 7
Pentyrch	9 28	1 58	7 43	10 13	5 13
Llandaff	9 35	2 5	7 50	10 20	5 20
Cardiff p. 18 arr	9 45	2 15	8 0	10 30	5 30
Cardiff Docks „	9 55	2 25	8 10	10 40	5 40

Omnibuses run between this Company's and the South Wales Stations.

Conveyances between Merthyr, Dowlais, Rhymney, Tredegar, Brynmawr, Abergavenny, Brecon, Builth, &c.

(19) [South Wales Lines.

Garnant–Llanelly April 1855. Also showing South Wales Railway (GWR) timetable Gloucester–Swansea–Carmarthen–Haverfordwest service which necessitated changing at Landore for Swansea.

Shrewsbury and Hereford.] 113 [Knighton, Central Wales, &c.

SHREWSBURY and HEREFORD.—In connection with London and North Western and Great Western.

BISHOP'S CASTLE. [Man., John Craston.

KNIGHTON and CENTRAL WALES.—London and North Western.

Knighton & Central Wales Line April 1867 showing connections with Cambrian Line.

LLANELLY & VALE OF TOWY RAILWAYS.

LLANELLY, LLANDILO, LLANDOVERY & CWMAMMAN

On and after NOVEMBER 15th, 1858.

UP-TRAINS.

Distance	Starting from	1, 2, & 3 Class.	1, 2, & 3 Class.	1, 2, & 3 Class.	Fares 1st Class s.	d.	2nd Class s.	d.	3rd Class s.	d.
	Llanelly ...	8.40	1.45	5.0						
¾	Dock ...	8.45	1.50	5.4	0	3	0	2	0	1
2	Bynea ...	8.50	1.55	5.12	0	9	0	6	0	3
5	†Llangennech ...	8.55	2.0	5.18	1	0	0	8	0	5
7½	Pontardulais ...	9.5	2.10	5.25	1	6	1	2	0	7
	*Garnant depart.	8.50		5.10						
	Cross-Inn "	9.10		5.35						
13	Cross-Inn arriv.	10.0		5.50	2	6	1	10	1	1
17	*Garnant "	10.25		6.15	3	3	2	3	1	5
15	Llandebie ...	9.30	2.35	5.50	3	3	2	3	1	3
6½	†Derwydd Road...	9.40	2.45	5.55	3	6	2	7	1	4½
19	Fairfach ...	9.50	2.55	6.5	4	0	3	0	1	7
20	Llandilo ...	9.55	3.0	6.10	4	0	3	0	1	8
24	†Glanrhyd ...	10.5	3.10	6.20	4	9	3	7	2	0
25½	Llangadock ...	10.10	3.15	6·25	5	2	4	0	2	1½
27½	Lampeter Road ...	10.15	3.20	6.30	5	6	4	3	2	3½
31½	Llandovery ...	10·25	3.30	6·40	6	3	4	8	2	7

DOWN-TRAINS.

Distance	Starting from	1, 2, & 3 Class.	1, 2, & 3 Class.	1, 2, & 3 Class.	Fares 1st Class s.	d.	2nd Class s.	d.	3rd Class s.	d.
	Llandovery ...	8.55	2.40	6.40						
3½	Lampeter Road ...	9·5	2.50	6.50	0	9	0	7	0	3½
5½	Langadock ...	9·10	2.55	6.55	1	2	0	11	0	5½
7	†Glanrhyd ...	9.15	3.0	7.0	1	6	1	2	0	7
11	Llandilo ...	9.25	3.5	7.10	2	3	1	9	0	11
12	Fairfach ...	9.30	3.10	7.15	2	6	1	11	1	0
14½	†Derwydd Road	9.40	3.20	7.25	2	10	2	3	1	2½
16	Llandebie ...	9.45	3.30	7.30	3	6	2	6	1	4
	*Garnant depart.	8.50		7.0 (Saturday only)						
	Cross-Inn ...	9.10		7.25						
20	Cross-Inn arriv.	10.0		7.40	4	3	3	3	1	8
24½	*Garnant ...	10.25		8.5	4	9	3	8	2	0
24	Pontardulais ...	10.15	3.55	7.55	4	9	3	6	2	0
26½	†Llangennech ...	10.22	4.2	8.2	5	3	4	0	2	2
28	Bynea ...	10.28	4.8	8.8	5	6	4	2	2	4
30½	Dock ...	10.36	4.16	8.16	6	0	4	6	2	6½
31	Llanelly ...	10.40	4.20	8.20	6	3	4	8	2	7

** Garnant Passengers will be set down or taken up at Gellyceidrim or Cross Keys, if required.*
Cross Inn Passengers by Middle-day Trains will be set down or taken up at Pantyffynon.

† The Trains will stop at Llangennech, Derwydd Road, and Glanrhyd by signal only; Passengers wishing to alight must give notice to the Guard at the next Station of their intention.

REGULATIONS.

Dogs will be charged Sixpence each.

Children under three years, no Charge; above three years and under twelve, at Half-price.

Tickets issued at intermediate Stations are so issued conditionally upon the chance of there being room in the Carriages, on the arrival of the Train, and if there be no room, the money will be returned for any Ticket produced at the Booking Office, immediately after the departure of the Train for which it had been purchased. Tickets must be shown to the Company's Servants, or delivered up to them when demanded. Parties not producing their Tickets are liable to be charged the Fare from the most distant Station from which the Train shall have started---they are only available on the day of issue. Parties cannot re-book at an intermediate Station by the same Train. No Tickets will be issued after a Train is in sight at an intermediate Station.

Return Day Tickets, *not Transferable*, are issued at a reduction of about one-fourth on the double Journey, to First and Second-Class Passengers. Saturday Tickets will be available on the day of issue, or on the following Monday.

The published Train Bills are only intended to fix the time at which Passengers may obtain their Tickets at the various Stations; it being understood that the Trains will not start from them before the appointed time. Every attention shall be paid to insure punctuality; but the Company Give Notice that they do not undertake that the Trains shall start or arrive at the time specified in the Bills; nor will they be accountable for any loss, inconvenience, or injury which may arise from delay or detention.

Luggage.—First Class Passengers are allowed 100lbs. of Luggage; and Second and Third, 60lbs. of Luggage, Free of Charge, not being merchandize or other articles carried for hire or profit: all excess will be charged for. Passengers are requested to place on each article, their Name and Address; and Notice is Hereby Given that the Company will not be responsible for the care of the same unless booked and paid for accordingly.

Parcels---The Company are not responsible for any Parcel above the Value of £10. unless declared as such at the time of booking, and entered and paid for Insurance at 2½ per cent. upon such declared value. To ensure Parcels being forwarded, they must be delivered at the Booking Offices half an hour before the departure of the Trains.

Parcel Rates	20 miles.		Over 20 miles.	
10lbs. and under	0s.	6d.	0	8d.
10 to 20	0	8	0	10
20 " 30	0	10	1	0
30 " 40	1	0	1	3
40 " 56	1	3	1	6
56 " 84	1	6	2	0
84 " 98	2	0	2	6
98 " 112	2	6	3	0

Incivility---It is requested that any instance of misconduct on the part of the persons employed at the Stations, may be directly reported to the Traffic Manager.

JOHN THOMAS, PRINTER, LLANELLY.

Llanelly and Vale of Towy railways, 15 November 1858.

interesting to compare the journey times with those of the 1990s.

The first train in 1868 departed Swansea Victoria 6.30am arriving Liverpool Lime Street at 2.30pm. (First class single 31s. third class single 13s.) In the 1993-94 Winter timetable, there was a Swansea High Street departure at 06.07 with a connection from Shrewsbury arriving Liverpool Lime Street 13.07. The following summer, passengers on the 06.13 from Swansea, changed at Shrewsbury and Crewe, and arrived at Liverpool at 12.40. In June 1994, a first class single from Swansea to Liverpool cost £58.90.

By 1872, there were connections to and from Scotland (Glasgow and Edinburgh overnight) and Leeds and Carlisle, the latter journey taking ten and a half hours. GWR and LNWR ran through coaches from Pembroke Dock to London (Paddington and Euston respectively) and the latter company's through coaches to Liverpool via the Carmarthen branch, continued until the Second World War.

From 1 January 1908 passengers were carried on the GWR line from Garnant to Gwaun-cae-Gurwen but this closed from 1917, re-opening in 1920 only to be taken off entirely on 4 May 1926. The Pantyffynnon to Brynamman line closed to passengers in 1958 and closure of the Carmarthen branch followed on 6 September 1963.

During their heyday, the spa towns in Mid Wales had through coaches to London Euston, to Manchester, Liverpool and the Midlands and in summer, to Blackpool and Llandudno.

An excellent description of the services on the line in 1912 was given by C. N. Ryan writing in *Railway Magazine*:

> 'Owing to the fact that the Central Wales section is a connecting link between South West Wales and North, via Shrewsbury and Crewe, many of the trains include through vehicles from or to many different destinations. Up and down mails are the fastest, and the latter is made up of through coaches from York, Leeds and Huddersfield, Crewe and Manchester from Swansea. The 3.40am from Shrewsbury connects with the 10pm from Euston the previous evening. The 12.50pm from Shrewsbury often runs in duplicate in the season, and includes through coaches from Manchester and Crewe to Carmarthen, Tenby and Pembroke Dock and Swansea, as also from Liverpool to Swansea. But the most useful train is the 1.50pm from Shrewsbury. This includes through vehicles from Blackpool, Llandudno and Rhyl, Manchester and Liverpool. The 2.40pm is always a heavy train and includes three through coaches from Euston (11am dep.) and one from Birmingham. But the honours for weight usually rest with the 5.10pm from Shrewsbury. This conveys three through coaches from London and one each from Manchester, Liverpool and Hereford. The London departure is by the 1.20pm 'Irish Boat Express'.
>
> A Hereford coach is attached at Craven Arms. By means of the slip carriage detatched at Rugeley from the 2.40pm, ex Euston passengers reach Shrewsbury at 5.55pm and connect with the 6.10pm for Llandovery. In the opposite direction the first train of special interest is the 7.45am from Swansea with three through carriages from Swansea or Llandrindod Wells for Euston, one for Manchester and one for Hereford.
>
> The 10am conveys a Tenby and Pembroke Dock through coach and takes back Blackpool, Llandudno and Rhyl and Liverpool coaches. Included in the 11.25am train is a through carriage from Liverpool, and the 12.25pm conveys vehicles for Euston, Birmingham and Manchester. From Swansea at 3.5pm – with a connection from Carmarthen – vehicles are taken for Manchester and Liverpool. The 'up' mail leaving Swansea at 7pm., is the fastest train by 20 minutes between Swansea and Shrewsbury. It has vehicles for Huddersfield, Leeds and York. In addition to those mentioned there are others completing the service, and providing for the requirements of intermediate stations not served by the more important trains. Most of the local services between Llandilo, Pontardulais and Llandovery are provided by Great Western trains.'

Before the commencement of the Second World War in 1938, a monthly return ticket was available which allowed passengers to travel out from London Paddington (GWR) to Swansea High Street and return from Swansea Victoria via Shrewsbury to London Euston (LMS) or visa versa. The first journey covered a distance of 199 miles and the second 280 miles or even 308 miles if passengers travelled via Crewe which was allowed. Those wanting simply to travel from A to B used the GWR route but as a break of journey was permitted, the Welsh route was useful for access to the Midlands and offered picturesque scenery.

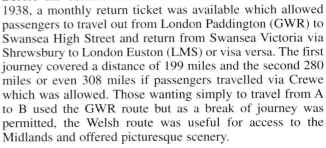

The Shrewsbury to Swansea Victoria train, south of Sugar Loaf Tunnel in 1962.
(Courtesy John Lloyd)

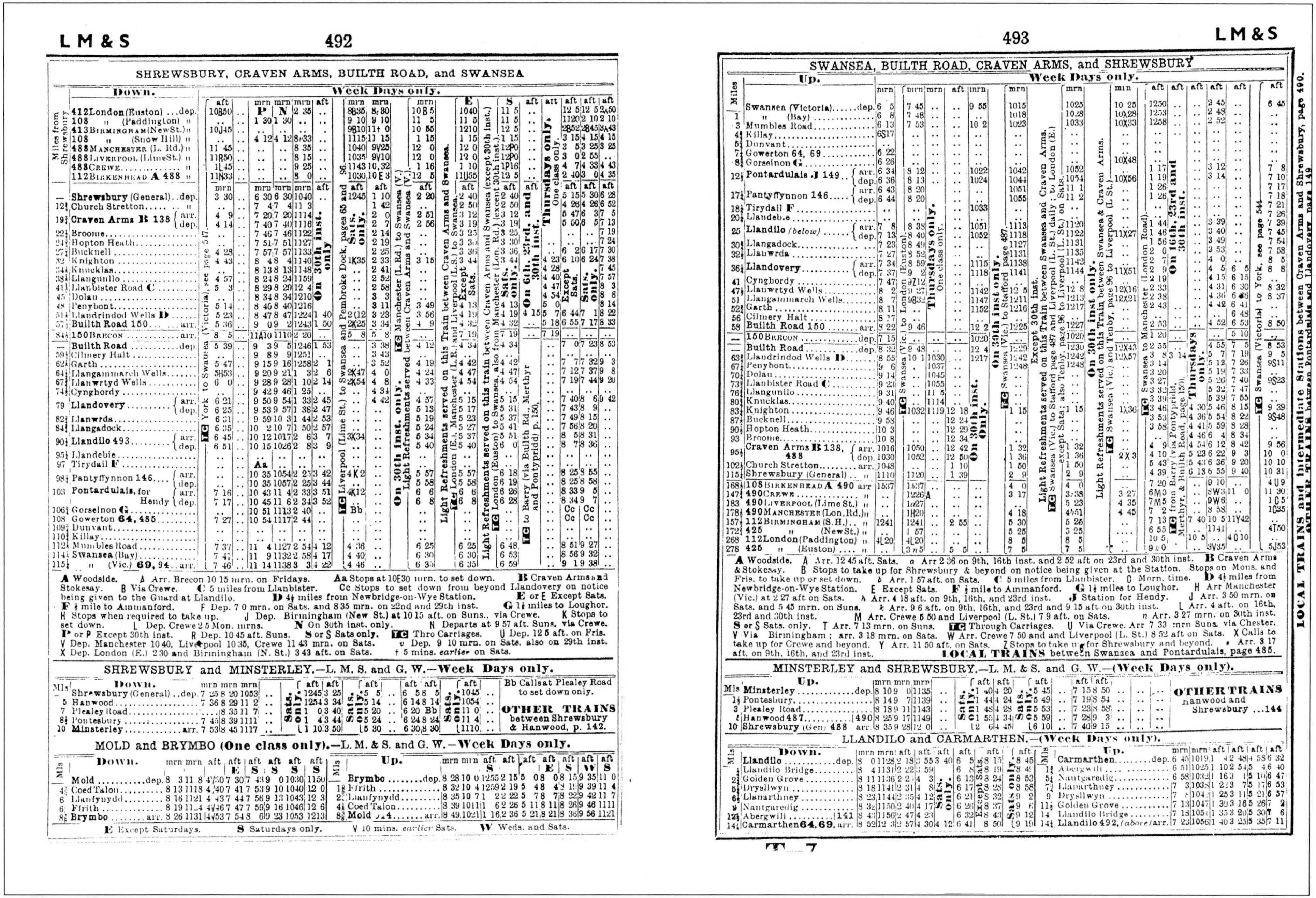
L M & S 492

SHREWSBURY, CRAVEN ARMS, BUILTH ROAD, and SWANSEA

Week Days only.

A Woodside. A Arr. Brecon 10 15 mrn. on Fridays. Aa Stops at 10E30 mrn. to set down. B Craven Arms and Stokesay. B Via Crewe. C 5 miles from Llanbister. Cc Stops to set down from beyond Llandovery on notice being given to the Guard at Llandilo. D 4½ miles from Newbridge-on-Wye Station. E or E Except Sats. F ½ mile to Ammanford. F Dep. 7 0 mrn. on Sats. and 8 35 mrn. on 22nd and 29th inst. G 1½ miles to Loughor. H Stops when required to take up. J Dep. Birmingham (New St.) at 10 15 aft. on Suns., via Crewe. K Stops to set down. L Dep. Crewe 2 5 Mon. mrns. N On 30th inst. only. N Departs at 9 57 aft. Suns. via Crewe. P or P Except 30th inst. R Dep. 10 45 aft. Suns. S or S Sats only. TC Thro Carriages. U Dep. 12 5 aft. on Fris. V Dep. Manchester 10 40, Liverpool 10 35, Crewe 11 43 mrn. on Sats. v Dep. 9 10 mrn. on Sats. also on 29th inst. X Dep. London (E.) 2 30 and Birmingham (N. St.) 3 43 aft. on Sats. † 5 mins. earlier on Sats.

SHREWSBURY and MINSTERLEY.—L. M. S. and G. W.—Week Days only.

Bb Calls at Plealey Road to set down only.

OTHER TRAINS between Shrewsbury & Hanwood, p. 142.

MOLD and BRYMBO (One class only).—L. M. & S. and G. W.—Week Days only.

E Except Saturdays. S Saturdays only. V 10 mins. earlier Sats. W Weds. and Sats.

493 L M & S

SWANSEA, BUILTH ROAD, CRAVEN ARMS, and SHREWSBURY

Week Days only.

A Woodside. A Arr. 12 45 aft. Sats. a Arr 2 36 on 9th, 16th inst. and 2 52 aft on 23rd and 30th inst. B Craven Arms & Stokesay. B Stops to take up for Shrewsbury & beyond on notice being given at the Station. Stops on Mons. and Fris. to take up or set down. b Arr. 1 57 aft. on Sats. C 5 miles from Llanbister. C Morn. time. D 4½ miles from Newbridge-on-Wye Station. E Except Sats. F ½ mile to Ammanford. G 1¼ miles to Loughor. H Arr Manchester (Vic.) at 2 27 aft on Sats. h Arr. 4 18 aft. on 9th, 16th, and 23rd inst. J Station for Hendy. J Arr. 3 50 mrn. on Sats. and 5 45 mrn. on Suns. k Arr. 9 6 aft. on 9th, 16th, and 23rd and 9 15 aft on 30th inst. L Arr. 4 aft. on 16th, 23rd and 30th inst. M Arr. Crewe 5 50 and Liverpool (L. St.) 7 9 aft. on Sats. n Arr. 3 27 mrn. on 30th inst. S or S Sats. only. T Arr. 7 13 mrn. on Suns. TC Through Carriages. U Via Crewe. Arr 7 33 mrn Suns. via Chester. V Via Birmingham; arr. 3 18 mrn. on Sats. W Arr. Crewe 7 50 and Liverpool (L. St.) 8 52 aft on Sats. X Calls to take up for Crewe and beyond. Y Arr. 11 50 aft. on Sats. Z Stops to take up for Shrewsbury and beyond. • Arr. 3 17 aft. on 9th, 16th, and 23rd inst. LOCAL TRAINS between Swansea and Pontardulais, page 485.

LOCAL TRAINS and Intermediate Stations between Craven Arms and Shrewsbury, page 490.

MINSTERLEY and SHREWSBURY.—L. M. & S. and G. W.—(Week Days only).

OTHER TRAINS Hanwood and Shrewsbury ...144

LLANDILO and CARMARTHEN.—(Week Days only).

Bradshaw, *July 1938.*

Refreshment facilities outside Pantyffynnon station in GWR/ LNWR days, and which still exist today. The CWL is on the left and the Brynamman branch is on the right.
(Bernard Matthews collection)

Dining cars were provided until 1939 after which time tea cars remained for a while and there were trolley services until the early fifties. After the Second World War – during which the trains were often full of Army personnel – the services on the Central Wales Line gradually declined: petrol was more readily available for road transport and spas were no longer fashionable.

Records of passengers alighting at Llandrindod Wells station in week ending 21 October 1946 showed 530 on the 'down' trains of whom 53 travelled first class and 487 on the 'up' trains with 14 first class. By 1954, summer figures at Llandrindod (week ending 19 June 1954 when 382 alighted from the 'down' trains and 340 from the 'up') did not compare favourably with those of the off season (October) of 1946. Approximately 20 children per day travelled by train to and from Llandrindod Grammar school where a special bell rang for 'train children' who were allowed to leave earlier than the rest so that they could get to the station on time.

A similar number travelled to school at Llandovery from the south.

During the fifties, only the 'York Mails' and summer Saturday trains to Liverpool and Manchester were operated as through services. The 'York Mail' left Swansea at 6.25pm and combined with the 'Aberystwyth Mail' at Shrewsbury.

June 13, 1964 saw the last regular steam-hauled passenger train but the early morning mail train southwards, departing Shrewsbury at 04.10 instead of the original 03.45 continued well beyond the days of steam as did the Swansea–York mail which did not cease until 1987.

A 1961 passenger survey showed that on Mondays to Fridays, only four stations were used by more than a hundred passengers per day.

Station usage figures for week ending 26 August 1961 produced by British Railways for the TUCC (Transport Users' Consultative Committee) Closure Hearing in 1962 were:

Daily average

Joining	*Mon-Fri*	*(x 5)*	*Sats.*
Llanelli	27	(135)	43
Pontarddulais	166	(830)	219
Llandeilo	130	(650)	318
Llandovery	71	(355)	140
Builth Road	62	(310)	142
Llandrindod Wells	116	(580)	174

A summer Saturday 'extra' at Llandrindod hauled northward by a Class 8F Stanier 2-8-0 No. 48436 in August 1964, after regular steam hauled passenger services had ceased.
(Roy Palmer)

Knighton	65	(325)	113
Craven Arms	53	(265)	68
Church Stretton	44	(220)	53
Shrewsbury	340	(1700)	596

The University College of Wales carried out a similar survey week ending 4 July 1964. In view of the fact that one covers the end of August and the other beginning of July, and that the first is a daily average and the second a weekly, one cannot achieve a strict comparison, but by multiplying the 1961 figures by five, it is possible to arrive at a reasonable one and this shows that passenger traffic over the intervening years had decreased considerably. The increase at Llanelli was due to the fact that with the closure of the passenger service from Swansea Victoria in June 1964, services terminated at Llanelli and passengers to and from Swansea High Street changed there.

Weekly

Joining	*Mon-Fri*	*Sats.*
Llanelli	171	139
Pontdarddulais	40	14
Llandeilo	59	28
Llandovery	81	21
Builth Road	46	21
Llandrindod Wells	130	81
Knighton	72	26
Craven Arms	8	2
Church Stretton	2	1
Shrewsbury	300	165

A general picture of part of the line in 1969 was given by Ernest Kay, whose thesis on transport in Radnorshire included a report on journeys made over a period of two days at the end of February of that year.

Thursday

10.33am Train from Shrewsbury. 2-car dmu. Very comfortable.

Left 22 minutes late after waiting for Liverpool train (announced).

	21 passengers	
Church Stretton	2 alighted	
Craven Arms	2 alighted	2 joined
Broome		1 joined
Hopton Heath		
Bucknell	Nil	Train slowed, did not stop
Knighton	1 alighted	12 mins late (10 made up)

Knighton Station semi derelict. One timetable (not legible).

Same day 15.33 from Knighton

	12 passengers	
	4 alighted	9 joined
Llangunllo	3 alighted	1 joined
Llanbister	Nil	Train stopped
Dolau	2 alighted	
Penybont	Nil	Train stopped
Llandrindod Wells	8 alighted	4 joined

(On time 16.34)

Llandrindod Wells one platform – goods yard derelict

Buildings at all intermediate stations are derelict

Friday

Builth Road (12.05 to Shrewsbury) Train 10 mins late

12 passengers already on

5 joined

Builth Road station has one fallen notice and is semi derelict

Same day

Llandrindod Wells (16.29 to Shrewsbury) Train on time

	14 passengers already on	
	2 alighted	5 joined
Penybont	Nil	
Dolau	3 alighted	
Llanbister Road, Llangunllo, and Knucklas	all Nil	Train stopped at each
Knighton	1 alighted	

Amidst all the statistics, it is interesting to note personal comments of local people. One such, taking part in Mr Kay's survey stated:

'I dislike the removal of the goods services; my coal came by rail.
I changed to oil and this came by rail to Llandrindod – now this has stopped and I expect my next load of oil to cost more'.

And another, 'Our nearest railway station at Builth

A pre-Grouping view of Builth Road High Level.
(HMRS/G. M. Perkins collection)

A 'convenience' for passengers no longer offered at Builth Road; the public toilets situated alongside the former refreshment room on the Low Level. This building now serves as a useful storage place at the end of a garden adjoining the Cambrian Arms, as shown in 1994.

(Rose Coleman)

Road is so sordid that passengers who can get to Llandrindod prefer to board the train there.'

However, the service itself improved. The Ministry of Transport, having refused application for closure in 1969, allocated a grant of £370,000 for two years.

The timetable from 4 May 1970 introduced a through service between Swansea High Street and Shrewsbury with the trains reversing at Llanelli. Cheap fares were offered as an incentive and Sunday excursions on a monthly basis commenced between Newport and Llandrindod Wells.

An article in the *Western Mail* dated 5 March 1978 (complementary to a BBC documentary entitled 'The Sugar Loaf Line') noted that, British Rail had stated that between October 1969 and October 1970, 'custom had increased by 113 per cent' and that there had been some complaints of overcrowding necessitating a third coach.

During the following year, the number of passengers had doubled to 180,000. The first regular Sunday passenger service of any length to be recorded was between Shrewsbury and Llandrindod Wells and ran from 6 July to 14 September 1986 (although in the early 1900s a service operated on Sunday afternoons Llandeilo–Llanelly and return).

Considerable improvements took place in 1987. Having installed the 'No Signalman Key Token' system the previous year, British Rail introduced additional services to the Summer timetable. The forthcoming changes received a great deal of media coverage, albeit confined, for the most part, to the Welsh region.

A Sunday service ran over the whole length of the line:

13.00 Chester to Swansea.

12.15 Pembroke to Shrewsbury (connection from Swansea at Llanelly).

There was also an 11.55 Crewe to Swansea (Mon-Fri) extended to Tenby (Sats) and an 07.16 Swansea to Shrewsbury on Saturdays only.

The 11.50 Saturday departure from Swansea to Shrewsbury was replaced by the 10.30 Pembroke Dock to Crewe.

The various incentives to travel were more positively advertised. These included Circular Saver Tickets, Freedom

A Sunday 'Recreation Rambler' approaches Sugar Loaf halt from the south on 22 July 1990.

(Roy Palmer)

The last early morning 'down' mail was unloaded at Llandrindod on 4 July 1987.
(Roy Palmer)

of Wales Rover Tickets and Heart of Wales Day Ranger Tickets. The 'two for the price of one' scheme also applied to the Central Wales line in the winter of 1986 and 1987.

An important additional summer Sunday service commenced on 21 June 1987 in the form of the 'Recreation Rambler' a joint venture sponsored by the Sports Council for Wales, Dyfed and Powys County Councils and HOWLTA (Heart of Wales Line Travellers' Association). Initially, the train conveyed passengers from Swansea to Llandrindod Wells and then shuttled between the latter and Llandovery to provide facilities for walkers and cyclists. A connecting bus service was available between Llandrindod and the scenic Elan Valley reservoir area. These trains also provide an extra service to and from Mid Wales for passengers seeking to travel farther afield.

One disappointment in the weekday service was the cancellation on 4 July 1987 of the 'Down Mail' 04.00 ex Shrewsbury (mail being carried by Post Office vans). This had been a passenger service although not well used. It continued to run on Saturdays until the end of the summer timetable. Another was the frustrating arrival time at Shrewsbury of the last 'up' train which missed Birmingham and Crewe connections by a few minutes.

Because of the disruption to services at the southern end of the line caused by the Glanrhyd Bridge disaster in October 1987, there was only one Sunday service in the summer of 1988. This ran between Llandrindod Wells and Chester and, according to HOWLTA, its average loading was 20 passengers per week with some 50 or so travelling on certain Sundays.

By 31 October 1988, the bridge had been replaced and a through train service recommenced. (During the intervening twelve months, passengers had been conveyed by connecting bus service between Llandeilo and Llandovery.) In the winter of 1988, until 14 January 1989, British Rail introduced special reductions – some as great as 34% – and special day return prices, in order to win back passengers.

The Recreation Rambler service – renamed 'The Heart of Wales Rambler' recommenced the following summer, its run extending to the northern end of the line and British Rail re-introduced two through Sunday services.

At a meeting between British Rail and HOWLTA representatives in March 1990, it was announced that growth of traffic on the Central Wales Line was only exceeded, for rural lines, by that on the Settle and Carlisle and that since 1983, the 'cost to passenger' ratio had improved by 300%. However, the optimism which this engendered proved to be a little unfounded.

Various changes of timings took place over the next few years. In Summer 1991 the termination at Llandrindod of 06.00 ex Shrewsbury being one example and the later departure at 07.23 of the first 'up' train from Swansea being another. The 1990 Summer timetable had failed to include the 'Shopping service' from Llandovery southwards at approximately 9am which had been specifically promised and in the following Winter timetable, the last two evening trains were limited to Fridays and Saturdays, British Rail blaming stock shortages.

By 1990, Central Government 'Public Service Obligation' grants to British Rail were gradually being reduced and this did not help the situation on the Central Wales Line. In summer 1991, the timings were operated in two parts, the first commencing 13th May and the second on the 8th July.

In the 1992 May–September timetable, the last train from Shrewsbury ran Mondays to Saturdays (as opposed to Fridays and Saturdays only) departing at 19.15, but this terminated at Llandrindod returning as the 20.59 Llandrindod to Shrewsbury so that the last through Shrewsbury–Swansea train was the 16.53. The last train to leave Swansea (Monday to Saturdays) was 17.05 through to Crewe arriving 21.59.

In 1992, the depths of the depression, lack of publicity and an impractical timetable were reflected in numbers and revenue. Excursion traffic over the line was reported by HOWLTA as being at an all time low and passenger numbers had dropped by 8%. This was the year in which the 'Sprinters' were introduced on the CWL on a regular basis.

The summer 1993 timetable was a very piecemeal affair. While having a through train to Crewe and Liverpool Lime Street from Llandrindod at 07.02, there was still no through evening service Shrewsbury to Swansea and in the mornings, a large gap in the service appeared between Llandrindod and Llandovery.

Fortunately, passenger figures improved again in Summer 1993 and with 'specials' plying back and forth to Builth

Table W 144

Table 144 SWANSEA, LLANELLY, CARMARTHEN, BUILTH ROAD, CRAVEN ARMS and SHREWSBURY

WEEK DAYS ONLY

Miles from Swansea (V.)		pm	am	pm	am	am	am		am	am	am	am	am		am	am	am	am	am	am
	104London (Pad.) dep	9C25		9C25															10 55	11L55
	104Cardiff (General) "	2e35		2e35											8 0			10D 0	1 32	2L50
	104Swansea (High St.) ¶ arr	4‡17		4§ 5											9 26			11D22	2 40	4L25
—	Swansea (Victoria) dep			6a15	7 20	7 20			7 45					TC Swansea to Manchester on Saturdays 11th July to 29th August	10 25			12p25	4p15	
1	" (Bay)				7 23	7 23			7 48									12 29	4 19	
3	Mumbles Road			6 21	7 28	7 28			7 53		8 38				10 32			12 34	4 24	
4¾	Killay				7 33	7 33					8 43								4 29	
5¾	Dunvant				7 37	7 37					8 46								4 32	
7¼	Gowerton South				7 42	7 42					8 50							12 44	4 37	
8¾	Gorseinon A			6 37	7 47	7 50					8 58							12 49	4 42	
12½	Pontardulais W arr			6 46	7 56	8 0			8 11		9 7				10 49			12 58	4 55	
—	Mls Llanelly dep	5a37				Except Saturdays 18th July to 15th August inclusive	7 48									Saturdays only TC to Shrewsbury			Except Saturdays	5p 0
—	2¾ Bynea Halt	5 43					7 54													5 5
—	4¾ Llangennech Halt						7 58													5 14
—	7 Pontardulais W arr	5 51					8 3													5 18
—	Pontardulais W dep	5 53		6 47	7 57				8 12	8 43					10 50			1 4		5 20
17	Pantyffynnon arr	6 0		6 55	8 4				8 19	8 50								1 12		5 27
	Pantyffynnon dep	6 3		6 56	8 5				8 20	8 53					10T56			1 13		5 29
18¼	Tirydail H	6 6		6 59					8 23	8 58					11 0			1 16		5 36
20	Llandebie	6 16							8U26	9 3										5 44
24¼	Ffairfach	6 27								9 20										6 0
25	Llandilo arr	6 30		7 22	8 23				8 38	9 32					11 15			1 32		6 8
—	104Fishguard Harbour dep				Sats. only. Runs 18th July to 15th August inclusive							7 50	7 50				10 20			
—	104Pembroke Dock "											7 30	8 30			9 30	10 20			
—	104Tenby "											8 3	9 3			10 3	11 3			
—	Mls Carmarthen dep		6 30									10 20	10 20			11 18	12p30			
—	2 Abergwili		6 36									10 25	10 25				12 36			
—	5¼ Nantgaredig		6 43									10 33	10 33				12 43			
—	8 Llanarthney Halt		6 48									10 39	10 39				12 49			
—	9½ Drysllwyn		6 53									10 44	10 44				12 53			
—	11½ Golden Grove		6 59									10 49	10 49				12 58			
—	14½ Llandilo Bridge		7 7									10 54	10 54				1 3			
—	15¾ Llandilo arr		7 12									10 59	10 59			11 59	1 8			
—	Llandilo dep	6 31		7 24	8 24				8 39	9 40		Saturdays only	Except Saturdays		11 17	12p 2		1 34		6 10
30¼	Llangadog	6 49		7 34					8 48	9 55								1 43		6 21
32¾	Llanwrda	6 54		7 38					8 53	10 5								1 47		6 25
36	Llandovery arr	7 1		7 45	8 46				8 59	10 15					11 36	12 22		1 54		6 33
	Llandovery dep			7 47	8 47				9 3						11 40	12 25		1 58		
40¾	Cynghordy			7 57														2 9		
47½	Llanwrtyd Wells			8 12					9 30						12p 5	12 54		2 26		
51	Llangammarch Wells			8 17					9 35						12 10			2 30		
52¾	Garth			8 21	9 17				9U40									2 35		
56	Cilmery Halt																			
58¼	Builth Road, H.L. arr			8 31	9 29				9 50						12 23	1 13		2 46		
—	185Brecon dep								8 15						10 25			1 25		
—	Builth Road, H.L. dep			8 34	9 32				9 52						12 26	1 15		2 47		
64	Llandrindod Wells M			8 46	9 45				10 5						12 39	1 29		3 0		
67½	Penybont			9 1					10 10									3 6		
70½	Dolau			9 10														3 14		
74	Llanbister Road F			9 20														3 22		
77	Llangunllo			9 27														3 29		
80¾	Knucklas Halt			9 34														3 36		
83½	Knighton			9 43	10 20				10 38						1 12	2 12		3 45		
87¾	Bucknell			9 50											1 18			3 53		
90¾	Hopton Heath			9 55														3 59		
93½	Broome			10 0														4 4		
95¼	Craven Arms and Stokesay arr			10 8	10 40				10h56						1 30			4 12		
	Craven Arms and Stokesay dep			10 14	10 42				10h57						1 32			4 14		
102½	Church Stretton arr			10 31											1 45			4 31		
115¼	Shrewsbury "			10 55	11 17				11h30						2 4	2 57		4 56		
158	152Chester (General) arr								1J11						3gg47	5t22		7 15		
173	Birkenhead G "								2 5						4gg25	6t 0		7 52		
147¾	Crewe "				12 16				12bb37						3zz19	4 23		6Y20		
183	Liverpool (L. St.) "				1 35				3bb7						4cc33	6 9		7Y48		
178½	Manchester (L. Rd.) "				1c22				1 47						4vv33	5 23		7Y38		
157½	152Birmingham (S.H.) "			12 41					2Z42						3 55	5ee23		7 15		
268	152London (Pad.) "								5Z15						6xx0	8 35		10 15		

For Notes, see page 195

Table W 144

Table 144— SWANSEA, LLANELLY, CARMARTHEN, BUILTH ROAD, CRAVEN ARMS and SHREWSBURY
continued

WEEK DAYS ONLY—*continued*

	am		pm	pm		pm	pm		pm	
104London (Pad.) dep	1155			12P55			1S50		3 45	
104Cardiff (General) "	2b50			4 20		4 5	4f30		6 46	
104Swansea (High St.) ¶ arr	4b15			5 40		5 15	5f52		7 55	
Swansea (Victoria) dep	5p35			6 30		6 30	7 5		8 35	
" (Bay)	5 39			Saturdays only		Except Saturdays	7 8		8 38	
Mumbles Road	5 44						7 13		8 43	
Killay	5 49									
Dunvant	5 52									
Gowerton South	5 57						7 26		8 56	
Gorseinon A	6 2						7 31		9 1	
Pontardulais W arr	6 10			6 53		6 53	7 40		9 10	
Llanelly dep										
Bynea Halt										
Llangennech Halt										
Pontardulais W arr										
Pontardulais W dep	6 12			6 55		6 55	7 41		9 12	
Pantyffynnon arr	6 20						7 50		9 20	
Pantyffynnon dep	6 22						7 53		9 21	
Tirydail H	6 30			7 4		7 4	7 58		9 25	
Llandebie	6 40						8 3			
Ffairfach										
Llandilo arr				7 22		7 22				
104Fishguard Harbour dep	Runs Saturdays only and each weekday 6th July to 28th August inclusive		4†25	TC Swansea (V.) to York arr. 3 37 am on Sundays		TC Swansea (Victoria) to York, arr. 3 40 am			Runs Saturdays only and each weekday 6th July to 29th August inclusive	
104Pembroke Dock "			3†50							
104Tenby "			4†33							
Carmarthen dep			6 20							
Abergwili			6 28							
Nantgaredig			6 40							
Llanarthney Halt			6 46							
Drysllwyn			6 50							
Golden Grove			6 55							
Llandilo Bridge			7 0							
Llandilo arr			7 5							
Llandilo dep				7 25		7 30				
Llangadog				7 37		7 40				
Llanwrda				7 40						
Llandovery arr				7 48		7 53				
Llandovery dep				7 52		7 56				
Cynghordy				8K 7						
Llanwrtyd Wells				8 30		8 30				
Llangammarch Wells				8 35		8 35				
Garth				8K40		8U40				
Cilmery Halt										
Builth Road, H.L. arr				8 49		8 49				
185Brecon dep										
Builth Road, H.L. dep				8 52		8 52				
Llandrindod Wells M				9 6		9 6				
Penybont				X						
Dolau				9 20						
Llanbister Road F				9 25						
Llangunllo										
Knucklas Halt										
Knighton				9 43		9 41				
Bucknell				X		X				
Hopton Heath										
Broome										
Craven Arms and Stokesay arr				10 3		10 3				
Craven Arms and Stokesay dep				10 4		10 4				
Church Stretton arr										
Shrewsbury "				10 36		10 36				
152Chester (General) arr				12B41		12B41				
Birkenhead G "										
Crewe "				11 28		11 28				
Liverpool (L. St.) "				1a44		1a44				
Manchester (L. Rd.) "				2a 2		1a38				
152Birmingham (S.H.) "				12a32		12a32				
152London (Pad.) "				5a10		5a10				

- A 1½ miles to Loughor
- *a* am
- B Via Crewe
- *b* On Saturdays dep Cardiff (General) 3 8 pm and arr Swansea (High Street) 4 37 pm
- bb On Saturdays arr Crewe 12 30 and Liverpool (Lime Street) 1 35 pm
- C Sunday to Friday nights
- *c* Mayfield Station
- cc On Saturdays 11th July to 29th August inclusive arr 4 32 pm. On other Saturdays arr 5 5 pm
- D On Saturdays dep Cardiff (General) 9 55 am and arr Swansea (High Street) 11 25 am
- *e* am. On Mondays dep 2 45 am
- ee On 12th September arr 5 36 pm
- F 5 miles to Llanbister
- *f* On Saturdays dep Cardiff (General) 5 8 pm and arr Swansea (High Street) 6 40 pm
- G Woodside
- gg On Saturdays arr Chester (General) 4 10 and Birkenhead (W) 4 48 pm. On Saturdays 11th July to 5th September inclusive arr Chester (General) 3 31 and Birkenhead (W) 4 10 pm
- H ½ mile to Ammanford
- *h* 8 minutes later on Fridays 17th July to 14th August inclusive
- J On Saturdays arr 5 minutes later
- K Calls if required to set down on notice to the Guard at Llandovery
- L On Saturdays dep Paddington 11 35 am, Cardiff (General) 2 40 pm and Swansea (High Street) 4 8 pm
- M 4½ miles to Newbridge-on-Wye Station
- P Runs Saturdays 25th July to 22nd August inclusive only
- *p* pm
- Q Calls if required on Wednesdays only to set down on notice to the Guard at Llandovery
- S Saturdays only
- T Calls on Saturdays only to take up
- t On Saturdays 4th July to 29th August inclusive arr Chester (General) 4 46 and Birkenhead (W) 5 44 pm
- TC Through Carriages
- U Calls to take up for Shrewsbury and beyond. Notice to be given at the station on the previous day
- vv On Saturdays 11th July to 29th August inclusive arr Manchester (Mayfield) 4 5. On other Saturdays arr Manchester (L.Rd.) 5 10 pm
- W Station for Hendy
- X Calls if required to set down from Llandovery or beyond on informing Guard at Llandovery
- xx On Saturdays arr 7 40 pm
- Y On Saturdays arr Crewe 6 7 pm, Liverpool (Lime Street) 7 18 and Manchester (London Road) 7 27 pm
- Z On Saturdays arr Birmingham (S.H.) 1 6, and Paddington 3 25 pm
- zz On Saturdays 11th July to 29th August inclusive arr 3 3 pm. On other Saturdays arr 3 42 pm
- † On Saturdays dep Fishguard Harbour 4 10 pm, Pembroke Dock 3 55 pm and Tenby 4 40 pm
- ‡ Departure time. On Mondays dep 4 13 am
- § am. On Mondays arr 4 7 am
- ¶ Distance between Swansea (High St.) and Swansea (Vic.) ½ mile. Passengers cross the town at their own expense

LOCAL TRAINS and intermediate Stations between Craven Arms and Shrewsbury, see Table 164

Central Wales Line, August 1959.

Table 62 — Weekdays — NOT on Saturdays 19 June to 4 September / Saturdays 19 June to 4 September

Llanelly, Builth Road, Craven Arms and Shrewsbury

Miles	Station		Weekdays	Weekdays	Weekdays	Weekdays	Saturdays	Saturdays	Saturdays B	Saturdays	Saturdays
3	FISHGUARD HARBOUR	d	04k35	08 10	..	16v00	04 35	08 10	..	..	16 00
3	MILFORD HAVEN	d	..	07 55	10 05	16 55	..	07 55	..	10 10	17 05
3	PEMBROKE DOCK	d	..	07 40	09 45	16 30	..	07 40	08 40	09 05	16 35
3	CARMARTHEN	d	05 45	09 24	11 25	18 21	05 45	09 24	09 40	11 25	18 20
3	SWANSEA	d	05 50	09 00	11 10	18 15	05 50	09 00	..	11 30	18 15
—	**LLANELLY**	d	06 25	09 55	11 55	18 55	06 25	09 55	10 55	11 55	18 55
2¾	BYNEA HALT	d	06 31	..	12 01	..	06 31	..	..	12 01	..
4¾	LLANGENNECH HALT	d	06 36	..	12 05	..	06 36	..	..	12 05	..
7	FONTARDULAIS	a	06 41	10 07	12 11	19 08	06 41	10 07	11 09	12 11	19 08
—		d	06 42	10 10	12 12	19 12	06 42	10 10	11 10	12 12	19 12
11¾	PANTYFFYNNON	d	06 49	..	12 19	..	06 49	..	..	12 19	..
13	AMMANFORD AND TIRYDAIL	d	06 54	10 24	12 24	19 23	06 54	10 24	..	12 24	19 23
14¾	LLANDEBIE	d	06 59	..	12 29	..	06 59	..	..	12 29	..
18¼	FFAIRFACH HALT	d	07 19	..	12 43	..	07 19	..	..	12 43	..
19½	LLANDILO	a	07 22	10 46	12 46	19 43	07 22	10 46	11 32	12 46	19 43
—		d	07 23	10 47	12 47	19 46	07 23	10 47	11 33	12 47	19 46
25¼	LLANGADOG	d	07 31	10 55	12 55	19 54	07 31	10 55	..	12 55	19 54
27	LLANWRDA	d	07 36	..	13 00	..	07 36	..	..	13 00	..
30¾	LLANDOVERY	a	07 42	11 05	13 06	20 03	07 42	11 05	11 52	13 06	20 03
—		d	07 43	11 07	13 07	20 06	07 43	11 07	11 54	13 07	20 06
35½	CYNGHORDY	d	07 52	..	13 16	c	07 52	..	..	13 16	e
42¼	LLANWRTYD WELLS	d	08 06	11 31	13 29	20 28	08 06	11 31	12 20	13 29	20 28
45½	LLANGAMMARCH WELLS	d	08 12	11 38	13 35	20 34	08 12	11 38	..	13 35	20 34
47½	GARTH	d	08 16	..	13 40	20h39	08 16	..	..	13 40	20e39
50¾	CILMERY HALT	d	b	..	13e42	20b41	b	..	..	13e42	20b41
52¾	**BUILTH ROAD HIGH LEVEL**	a	08 27	11 50	13 50	20 48	08 27	11 50	12 38	13 50	20 48
—		d	08 28	11 52	13 52	20 50	08 28	11 52	12 39	13 52	20 50
58½	LLANDRINDOD WELLS	d	08 41	12 04	14 06	21 05	08 41	12 04	12 51	14 06	21 05
62	PENYBONT	d	08 46	..	14 11	c	08 46	..	..	14 11	e
65	DOLAU	d	08 54	..	14 19	21f17	08 54	..	..	14 19	21 17
65½	LLANBISTER ROAD	d	09 00	..	14 25	21f24	09 00	..	..	14 25	21 24
71½	LLANGUNLLO	d	09 07	..	14 32	..	09 07	..	..	14 32	..
75½	KNUCKLAS HALT	d	09 14	..	14 40	..	09 14	..	..	14 40	..
78	KNIGHTON	d	09 20	12 37	14 47	21 44	09 20	12 37	13 22	14 47	21 44
82¼	BUCKNELL	d	09 27	12 44	14 53	h	09 27	12 44	..	14 53	h
85¼	HOPTON HEATH	d	09 32	..	14 58	..	09 32	..	..	14 58	..
87½	BROOME	d	09 37	..	15 03	..	09 37	..	..	15 03	..
90¼	**CRAVEN ARMS & STOKESAY**	d	09 48	12 59	15 13	22 04	09 48	12 59	13 42	15 13	22 04
97	CHURCH STRETTON	d	09 58	13 09	..	..	09 58	13 09	..	..	..
110¼	**SHREWSBURY**	a	10 15	13 26	15 38	22 32	10 15	13 26	14 13	15 38	22 32
5	LONDON PADDINGTON	a	14g00	17p00	19 00	05 05	14 10	17 05	..	20 15	05 05
10	CREWE	a	11 08	14 41	17 23	23 31	11 35	14 41	15 16	17 23	23 31
10	MANCHESTER	a	12t01	15 44	18 57	01 29	12 30	15 57	16 13	18 31	01 47
10	LIVERPOOL	a	12 33	16 08	19 24	01 34	12 33	16 15	16 15	18 26	01 34

Heavy figures denote through carriages; light figures denote connecting services
For general notes see page 3

B 17 July to 28 August inclusive

b Stops to pick up only on notice being given at Llanwrtyd Wells
c Stops on Saturdays only to set down on notice to guard at Llandovery
e Stops to set down only on notice to guard at Llandovery
f Saturdays only
g On Saturdays arr 14 10
h Stops to set down on Wednesdays and Saturdays only on notice to guard at Llandovery
k Not on Mondays
p On Saturdays arr 17 05
t On Saturdays from 11 September arr 12 06
v Until 25 September

Table 62 — Weekdays — NOT on Saturdays 19 June to 4 September / Saturdays 19 June to 4 September

Shrewsbury, Craven Arms, Builth Road and Llanelly

Miles	Station		Weekdays MO	Weekdays MX	Weekdays	Weekdays	Weekdays	Saturdays	Saturdays	Saturdays [illegible]	Saturdays B	Saturdays
10	LIVERPOOL	d	00 15	00 15	..	09 45	16 20	00 15	..	10 05	12 45	16 20
10	MANCHESTER	d	00 45	00 45	..	10 00	16 30	00 45	..	10 25	12 25	16 35
10	CREWE	d	02 33	02 25	05 58	10 53	17 22	02 25	05 58	11 18	13 55	17 31
5	LONDON PADDINGTON	d	..	..	00 15	08 20	15p10	..	00 15	08 20	10 10	14 10
—	**SHREWSBURY**	d	03 52	04 00	07 10	11 50	18 30	04 00	07 10	12 25	15 00	18 30
12¾	CHURCH STRETTON	d	..	..	07 30	12 12	18 50	..	07 30	12 47	15 27	18 50
20	**CRAVEN ARMS & STOKESAY**	d	04 25	04 34	07 42	12 25	19 02	04 34	07 42	12 59	15 39	19 02
22	BROOME	d	..	..	07 50	12 33	..	..	07 50	13 07	..	..
25	HOPTON HEATH	d	..	..	07 56	..	19 16	..	07 56	..	..	19 16
28	BUCKNELL	d	04 42	04 50	08 01	12 43	19 22	04 50	08 01	13 17	..	19 22
32¼	KNIGHTON	d	04 57	05 01	08 10	12 52	19 30	05 01	08 10	13 26	15 58	19 30
35	KNUCKLAS HALT	d	..	..	08 15	..	..	..	08 15	..	..	..
38¾	LLANGUNLLO	d	..	..	08 24	13 06	19 44	..	08 24	13 38	..	19 44
41¾	LLANBISTER ROAD	d	..	..	08 31	13 12	19 50	..	08 31	13 44	..	19 50
45¼	DOLAU	d	..	..	08 38	13 19	19 57	..	08 38	13 51	..	19 57
48¼	PENYBONT	d	05k27	05k29	08 49	13 26	20 05	05k29	08 49	13 58	..	20 05
51¾	LLANDRINDOD WELLS	d	05 38	05 39	08 58	13 33	20 12	05 39	08 58	14 09	16 35	20 12
57½	**BUILTH ROAD HIGH LEVEL**	a	05 48	05 49	09 09	13 43	20 23	05 49	09 09	14 19	16 45	20 23
—		d	05 51	05 51	09 12	13 52	20 24	05 51	09 12	14 21	16 46	20 24
59½	CILMERY HALT	d	..	..	j	k	..	..	j	k	..	..
62¾	GARTH	d	..	..	09 23	14 02	20 40	..	09 23	14 31	..	20 40
64½	LLANGAMMARCH WELLS	d	06u05	06u05	09 28	14 06	20 45	06u05	09 28	14 35	..	20 45
68	LLANWRTYD WELLS	d	06 12	06 12	09 35	14 13	20 52	06 12	09 35	14 42	17 04	20 52
74¾	CYNGHORDY	d	..	..	09 49	14 26	g	..	09 49	14 55	..	..
79½	LLANDOVERY	a	06 31	06 31	09 57	14 34	21 11	06 31	09 57	15 04	17 24	21 11
—		d	06 35	06 35	10 00	14 35	21 13	06 35	10 00	15 05	17 26	21 13
83	LLANWRDA	d	06 42	06 42	10 06	14 41	21n19	06 42	10 06	15 10	..	21n19
85	LLANGADOG	d	06 48	06 48	10 11	14 46	21v24	06 48	10 11	15 16	..	21v24
90½	LLANDILO	a	06 56	06 56	10 19	14 54	21 32	06 56	10 19	15 24	17 43	21 32
—		d	07 00	07 00	10 22	14 55	21 34	07 00	10 22	15 25	17 44	21 34
91¼	FFAIRFACH HALT	d	..	..	10 25	14 58	..	..	10 25	15 28	..	..
95¼	LLANDEBIE	d	..	..	10 44	15 12	21n49	..	10 44	15 42	..	21n49
97	AMMANFORD AND TIRYDAIL	d	07 19	07 19	10 50	15 18	21 54	07 19	10 50	15 45	..	21 54
98¼	PANTYFFYNNON	d	07 25	07 25	10 57	15 23	..	07 25	10 57	15 53	18 03	..
103	PONTARDULAIS	a	07 32	07 32	11 04	15 29	22 07	07 32	11 04	16 00	18 11	22 07
—		d	07 34	07 34	11 05	15 30	22 09	07 34	11 05	16 01	18 12	22 09
105¼	LLANGENNECH HALT	d	..	..	11 12	15 36	..	..	11 12	16 07	..	..
107¼	BYNEA HALT	d	..	..	11 17	15 42	..	..	11 17	16 12	..	..
110	**LLANELLY**	a	07 50	07 50	11 23	15 48	22 22	07 50	11 23	16 18	18 27	22 22
3	SWANSEA	a	08 39	08 39	12 10	16 19	22 57	08 30	12 10	17 07	19 18	22 57
3	CARMARTHEN	a	08 33	08 33	12 01	16 47	23 03	08 33	12 03	16 52	19 07	23 03
3	PEMBROKE DOCK	a	10 17	10 17	13 56	18 20	..	10 30	13 35	18 35	20 55	..
3	MILFORD HAVEN	a	09 50	09 50	13 30	18 12	..	09 53	..	18 24	20 28	..
3	FISHGUARD HARBOUR	a	..	..	13b28	..	..	..	13 28	..	..	..

Heavy figures denote through carriages; light figures denote connecting services
For general notes see page 3

B 17 July to 28 August inclusive

b Until 25 September
g Stops on Fridays only to set down passengers
j Stops on notice to the guard at Builth Road H.L. or on giving hand signal to the driver
k Stops to set down only on notice to the guard at previous stopping station
n Stops to set down from Craven Arms and beyond on notice to the guard
p On Saturdays depart 14 10
v Stops to set down only on notice to the guard at Llandovery

Centtral Wales Line, 14 June 1965–17 April 1966.

CRAVEN ARMS, LLANDOVERY, LLANDILO, PONTARDULAIS, GOWERTON, and SWANSEA.—L. & N. W.

Craven Arms, Llandrindod, Llandovery, 460 Llandilo, and Swansea.

Miles from Craven Arms	Down.	Week Days. mrn	aft	mrn	mrn	mrn	mrn	mrn	mrn	aft	aft	aft	mrn	mrn		aft	aft	aft	mrn	aft	aft	aft	aft	aft	aft	Sn aft
	Euston Station, 456 London ......dep.		10 0										5 0	7 10					1037			1 20		2r40		
	404 Birmingham * ... "		11 0d										7 20	9 15					1115			2 55		3 30		
	523 Leeds (New) ... "		1040										6 0	7 55					1042			1 50				
	456 Liverpool † ... "		1155b				2 35						8 15	9h10					12 0			2 40				
	456 Manchester ‡ ... "		12 5n										8 25	9h25					1215			3 0				
	456 Crewe ... "		1 40				5 30						9 30	1017h					1 12			3 55		4 40		
	456 Birkenhead § ... "		10 0				1120q						7 45	9 5					1115			1t35		3 38		
	456 Chester (Gen.) ... "		11 2				2 7						8 40	9 38					1217			2v15		4 25		
	456 Shrewsbury ... "		3 30				6 45						1030	1130					2 15	2 25		5 10		6 10		
—	Craven Arms ** ..dep.		4 15				8 0						1115	12 5					2 51	3 15		5 45		7 10		
2½	Broome						8 6						1122							3 23				7 16		
5	Hopton Heath						8 11						1128							3 30	Thursdays only.	p		7 22		
8	Bucknell		4 28				8 18						1135							3 37	3 cl.			7 29		
12¼	Knighton		4 35			1st and 3rd class between Llandovery and Llanelly.	8 25						1142	1225					3 11	3 45	4 20	6 5		7 36		Sunday Train.
14¾	Knucklas			Saturdays only.			8 33						1150							Stop	4 26			7 44		
18	Llangunllo		4 52		1st and 3rd class between Llandilo and Llanelly.		8 45		1st and 3rd class between Llandovery and Llanelly.				12 0								4 38			7 54		
21½	Llanbister Road ††		4 58				8 51						12 7								4 46			8 3		
25¼	Dolau						8 57						1216								4 53			8 10		
28¾	Penybont		5 9				9 3						1223						3 46		5 0			8 16		
31¾	Llandrindod Wells ‖		5 14				9 11						1233	1 2					3 54		5 10	6 40		8 25		
37¼	Builth Road 468		5 28				9 25						1246	1 15					4 9		Stop	6 55		8 37		
64¾	468 Brecon ... arr.		7 45				11 8						2 25						5 38							
39¼	Cilmery						9 33							1 23					i							
42¾	Garth		5 42				9 38							1 28					4 23			Sig.				
44½	Llangammarch Wells						9 48							1 32					4 27			7 16				
48	Llanwrtyd Wells		5 53				9 54							1 38					4 33	n	aft	7 22				
54½	Cynghordy			3 cl.			1010							1 52						aft	1&3	Sig.				
59¼	Llandovery		6 18	7 5		8 40	1018		1035					2 3					4 59	5 25	6 45	7 46				
63	Llanwrda		6 24	7 12		8 48			1042					2 9					Sig.	5 34	6 54	7 52				
64¾	Llangadock		c	7 22		8 55			1048					2 13					5 8	5 39	6 59	7 57				
66½	Glanrhyd		c			9 3			1053											5 46	7 4					
68¼	Talley Road					9 8			1058											5 51	7 9					
70¼	Llandilo 463 ... arr.		6 44	7 37		9 12			11 4					2 22					5 18	5 55	7 14	8 9				
84¾	463 Carmarthen arr.		8e20	8 40		s1015			12 0			1&3		3 23				3 cl.	6 28			9 10				1&3
—	Llandilo ... dep.		6 49	7 40	8 0	9 18			1110			2 0		2 25				4 30	5 22	6 0	7 20	8 14				4 45
71½	Ffairfach			7 45	8 4	9 22			1113			2 4			Except Saturdays.			4 33		6 4	7 25					4 49
74¼	Derwydd Road			7 52	8 13	9 31		Saturdays only.	1121			2 13						4 42		6 12	7 34					4 58
75¾	Llandebie			7 57	8 18	9 36			1126			2 18				Saturdays only.		4 47		6 18	7 42	g u			Saturdays only.	5 3
77¼	Tirydail ‡‡	Saturdays only.		8 1	8 23	9 41			1131	Saturdays only.	1&3	2 23		h			1&3	4 52		6 23	7 47				1&3	5 8
78¼	Pantyffynnon 92			8 8	8 30	9 47			1140		1 5	2 32	Saturdays only.	2 44			4 5	4 57	m	6 30	7 52	g u			1015	5 12
83¼	Pontardulais §§ ..arr.		7 18	8 16	8 38	9 55			1148		1 13	2 41		2 52			4 13	Stop	5 47	6 38	8 0	8 39			1024	5 23
—	Pontardulais ..dep.				8 42	9 58			1154		1 16	2 45					4 14			6 43	8 2				1045	5 25
85½	Llangennech				8 48	10 4			1159		1 22	2 51					4 20			6 48	8 8				1051	5 31
87¼	Bynea				8 52	10 9			12 5		1 26	2 57					4 25			6 53	8 12				1057	
90	Llanelly 58, 62 arr.				9 0	1015			1215	3 cl.	1 35	3 5					4 32	aft		7 0	8 20				11 5	5 45
—	Pontardulais ...dep.		7 23	8 18	8 50	1010			12 0	1 40		Stop		2 55	2 55	3 15		4 55	5 48	6 55		8 41	9 0			
—	Grovesend				8 54	1014			12 4	1 44					2 59	3 19		4 59		6 59			9 4			
86¼	Gorseinon ‖‖	3 cl.		8 24	8 57	1017		3 cl.	12 7	1 47					3 2	3 22		5 2		7 2			9 7			
—	Mls Llanmorlais ¶ dp.	6 40			8 35			1140							2 45	3 5				6 40			8s50			
—	1¾ Penclawdd	6 44			8 39			1144							2 49	3 9				6 44						
—	4¾ Gowerton 461 arr.	6 55			8 50			1155							2 57	3 18				6 54			9s0			
88¾	Gowerton 62, 461	7 0	7 33	8 29	9 2	1022		12 0	1212	1 52					3 7	3 27		5 7	k	7 7			9 12			
89¾	Dunvant	7 5		8 37	9 10	1028		12 5	1218	2 0					3 13	3 35		5 13		7 13			9 18			
90¾	Killay	7 10		8 42	9 14	1032		1210	1222	2 4					3 17	3 39		5 17	k	7 17			9 22			
92¼	Mumbles Road 663	7 16	7 44	8 46	9 18	1036		1215	1226	2 8		aft			3 21	3 43		5 21	6 5	7 21		g	9 26			
94¼	Swansea (Bay)	7 21	7 48	8 50	9 22	1040		1219	1230	2 12		2e20		3 13	3 25	3 47		5 25	6 9	7 25		8 59	9 30			
95¼	" (Vic.) 62, 71	7 30	7 55	9 0	9 30	1048		1225	1233	2 20		2e25		3 20	3 33	3 55		5 33	6 15	7 33		9 5	9 38			

¶ One class only. ** Craven Arms and Stokesay. §§ Station for Hendy. †† 5 miles from Llanbister. ‖‖ 1¼ miles to Loughor. ‡‡ ¼ mile to Ammanford.

* New Street. † Lime Street. ‡ London Road. § Birkenhead (Woodside). ‖ This Station is 4½ miles from Newbridge-on-Wye Station, on the Cambrian Line.

NOTES.

- **a** 1st and 3rd class only to Llanelly.
- **b** Leaves at 11 aft. on Sundays.
- **c** Stops to take up for Carmarthen or Swansea on notice being given at the Station.
- **d** Leaves at 10 15 aft. on Sundays.
- *e* Except Saturdays.
- **g** Stop to set down from North of Llandovery on informing Guard.
- **h** Stops to set down from beyond Llandilo on informing Guard, and to take up for Swansea Line on notice being given at the Station.
- *h* 1st and 3rd class.
- **i** Stops to set down on informing the Guard.
- **k** Stops to set down from Shrewsbury and beyond on informing the Guard.
- **m** Stops to set down from Shrewsbury or beyond on informing the Guard, and to take up for Mumbles Road or Swansea on notice being given at the Station.
- **n** Leaves at 11 55 aft. on Sundays.
- **p** Sets down from London on informing Guard.
- *q* Except Sunday ngt.
- *r* From Euston in carriage slipped at Rugeley.
- *s* Saturdays only.
- *t* Leaves at 2 35 aft. on Saturdays.
- **u** Takes up for Swansea on notice being given at the Station.
- *v* Leaves at 3 5 aft. on Saturdays.

SWANSEA, GOWERTON, PONTARDULAIS, LLANDILO, LLANDOVERY, and CRAVEN ARMS.—L & N. W.

Dist. Traff. Supt., G. T. Phizackerley, Victoria Station, Swansea.

Swansea and Craven Arms.] 461 [L. & N. W.

Mls	Up.	Week Days. mrn	mrn	mrn	mrn	mrn	mrn	mrn	mrn	mrn	aft	aft	3 cl.	aft	aft	aft	aft	aft	aft	3 cl.	aft	aft	aft	3 cl.	aft	aft	aft	Sn mrn
—	Victoria Station, Swansea ...dep		6 0	7 35	8 0				9 55		1230		1245	1 10	1 50	2 15	3 0	4 5		5 10	5 50	6 5	7 0	8 0	9 20	10 0	11 0	Sunday Train.
1	" (Bay)		6 5	7 39	8 4				9 59		1234		1249	1 13	1 53	2 18	3 4	4 9		5 14	5 54	6 8	7 4	8 4	9 24	10 4		
2¼	Mumbles Road		6 10	7 43	b				10 3		1238		1254		2 1	2 22		4 13			5 58			8 9	9 28	10 9		
4¼	Killay			7 49					10 8				1 0	Except Saturdays.	2 6			4 19			6 3			8 14	9 34	1014	1113	
5¾	Dunvant		6 17	7 53					1012				1 5		2 11			4 23			6 8			8 19	9 38	1020	1120	
7¼	Gowerton		6 21	7 59					1016		1249		1 10		2 16	2 35		4 30		5 27	6 12	6 20		8 24	9 44	1024	1125	
—	Gowerton ¶ ...dep.			8 5					1030	Sats.					2e27	2 37					6e17	6 22		8 35				
10¼	Penclawdd ¶			8 15					1040						2e35	2 45					6e27	6 30		8 43				
12	Llanmorlais ¶ arr.			8 20					1045						2e39	2 50					6e32	6 34						
9	Gorseinon ‖‖		6 27	8 3					1022		1254		1 15		2 22	Stop		4 34		5 32	6 17			8 30	9 48	1030	1131	
—	Grovesend ... [460		6 33	8 7					1026				1 21		2 26			4 38			6 22			8 36	9 52	1036	1136	
12¼	Pontardulais §§ ..arr.	1&3	6 37	8 11	8 20	1&3		1&3	1029	1&3	1 1	1&3	1 25		2 30		3 20	4 42	1&3	5 38	6 26		7 20	8 40	9 56	1040	1140	1&3
—	Ms Llanelly ....dep.	5 20				8 15		9 50		11 5		1250			2 10			Stop	4 25		6 15					10 0		6 55
—	2¼ Bynea	5 29				8 23		9 58		1113		1257			2 17				4 33		6 23					10 8		
—	4¼ Llangennech [460	5 35				8 28		10 3		1118		1 2			2 23				4 38		6 28	Saturdays only. Third class only between Swansea and Gowerton.				1015		7 10
—	6¼ Pontardulais §§ a	5 40				8 33		10 8		1123		1 8			2 30				4 43		6 33					1020		7 14
—	Pontardulais ...dep.	5 42	6 38		8 21	8 38		1010	1031	1126	1 2	1 10	Saturdays only.		2 35	Saturdays only.	3 21		4 46	5 39	6 37		7 21	Saturdays only.		1045	Saturdays only.	7 16
17¼	Pantyffynnon 92	5 55	6 48		8 29	8 49		1018	1039	1139	1 11	1 18			2 52		3 29		4 56	5 48	6 48					1054		7 26
18¾	Tirydail ‡‡	6 0				8 53		Stop		1143					2 56				5 0	5 53	6 52					Saturdays only. Third class only between Swansea and Pontardulais, and 1st and 3rd class between Llanelly and Pantyffynnon.		7 30
20¼	Llandebie	6 5	6 56			8 58				1148	1 19				3 1				5 5	5 58	6 57							7 35
21¾	Derwydd Road	6 10				9 3				1153					3 6				5 10	6 13	7 2							7 40
24¼	Ffairfach	6 17				9 11				12 1					3 14				5 17	6 20	7 10							7 48
25	Llandilo 463 ...arr.	6 20	7 8		8 47	9 14			1057	12 5	1 31				3 18		3 47		5 20	6 23	7 13		7 45					7 51
—	463 Carmarthen dep.		6 15			8s25			1010		1245						2 55		4 35				6 55					
—	Llandilo ...dep.		7 13		8 48	9 19			11 5		1 36				3 22		3 51		5 25	6 27	7 16		7 50					
27	Talley Road		7 17			9 24									3 27				5 30	6 32	7 21							
29	Glanrhyd		7 22			9 29									3 32				5 35	6 37	7 26							
30¾	Llangadock		7 27		g	9 35	Thursdays only.		1115		1 46				3 36				5 41	6 42	7 32		d					
32¼	Llanwrda		7 31		g	9 41			1119		1 51				3 45			aft	5 48	6 50	7 37		d					
36¼	Llandovery		7 40		9 9	9 50			1128		2 5				3 53		4 12	6 35	5 55	7 5	7 45		8 12					
41	Cynghordy		7 50								Sig.							6 45										
47¼	Llanwrtyd Wells		8 3		9 31				1151		2 27				1st and 3rd class between Llanelly and Llandovery.		4 34	6 58		Saturdays only.	1st and 3rd class between Llanelly and Llandovery.		8 34					
51	Llangammarch Wells		8 12		g				1158		2 34						4 46	7 5					f h					
52¾	Garth		8 17		g				12 3		2 39							7 9										
56	Cilmery		8 23															7 15										
—	468 Brecon ... dep.		7 25						1040		1 20							5 53										
58	Builth Road 468		8 41		9 54		3 cl.		1215		2 51						5 2	7 30					8 55					
63¾	Llandrindod Wells ‖		8 53		10 4		1145		1227		3 3						5 14	7 42					9 6					
67¼	Penybont		9 4				1150		1237		3 13						5 24	7 52					f					
70¼	Dolau		9 11				1157				3 19							7 59										
74	Llanbister Road ††		9 18				12 4				3 25							8 6										
77¼	Llangunllo		9 25				1214				3 31							8 13										
80¼	Knucklas		9 35				1224	aft			3 40					aft		8 21										
83¼	Knighton		9 50		1034		1230	1235	1 2		3 44					5 5	5 53	8 27					9 38					
87¼	Bucknell		10 0					1242	1 11							5 12		8 37					f					
90¼	Hopton Heath		10 8					1248			a					5 18		8 44					f					
93	Broome ... [458, 491		1015					1255								5 25		8 51					f					
95¼	Craven Arms ** 103		1025		1054			1 5	1 24		4 5					5 35	6 15	8 59					9 59					
115¼	458 Shrewsbury arr.		1113		1128				2 5		4 35						7 4	9 47					1030					
154	458 Chester (Gen.) "				1 30				3 37		7 11						9 4						1234c					
168¼	458 Birkenhead § "				2 31				4 16		8 27						9 46						3 15c					
147¼	458 Crewe "				1238				3 22		6 17						8 2	11 1					1135					
178¼	458 Manchester ‡ "				1 35				4 40		7 10						8 57						1h10c					
182	458 Liverpool † "				1 35				5 8		7n20						9 10						h1240c					
215¼	520 Leeds (New) "				2 37				6 17		8 13						1020						2 38c					
172¼	412 Birmingham * "				1 57				4 52		7 24						1135	2 [illegible]										
278¼	458 London (Eus.) "				3 15				7 0		9 5							3h50										

NOTES.

- **a** Stops to take up for London (Euston) on notice being given at the Station.
- **b** Stops to take up for Pantyffynnon and beyond on giving notice at the Station.
- **c** Morning time.
- **d** Stops to set down from Carmarthen and beyond on informing the Guard.
- *e* Except Saturdays.
- **f** Stops to set down from South of Llandovery on informing the Guard.
- **g** Stops to take up for Shrewsbury and beyond on notice being given at the Station.
- **h** Stops to take up for beyond Shrewsbury on notice being given at the Station.
- *h* 1st and 3rd class.
- *n* Arrives at 7 25 aft. on Thursdays.
- *s* Saturdays only.
- * New Street.
- † Lime Street.
- ‡ London Road.
- § Birkenhead (Woodside).
- ‖ This Station is 4½ miles from Newbridge-on-Wye Station, on the Cambrian Line.
- ¶ One class only.
- ** Craven Arms and Stokesay.
- †† 5 miles from Llanbister.
- ‡‡ ¼ mile to Ammanford.
- §§ Station for Hendy.
- ‖‖ 1¼ mls. to Loughor.

Bradshaw, *April 1910.*

SWANSEA (VICTORIA), MORLAIS JUNCTION, CARMARTHEN AND

Up Trains.

STATIONS.	B	F		B		G	A		A		B	E	
	Pass.	Harlescott Sidings Freight.		Leeds Passenger.		Light Engine.	York Passenger.		York Passenger.		Pass.	Cattle.	
	dep.	arr.	dep.	arr.	dep.	dep.	arr.	dep.	arr.	dep.	dep.	arr.	dep.
				F	O		S	O	S	X	SO	R	R
	p.m.	p.m.	p.m.	p.m.	p.m.	p.m.	p.m.	p.m.	p.m.	p.m.	p.m.	p.m.	p.m.
SWANSEA (Victoria)	..	—	5 40	—	5 55	..	—	6 30	—	6 30	..	..	..
Swansea Bay	..	—	—	—	—	..	—	—	—	—	..	..	..
Mumbles Road	..	—	—	—	—	..	—	—	—	—	..	..	..
Rhydydefed Siding	..	—	—	—	—	..	—	—	—	—	..	..	..
Killay	..	—	—	—	—	..	—	—	—	—	..	..	..
Dunvant	..	5	58	—	—	..	—	—	—	—	..	..	..
Gowerton	..	6	4	6	9	..	6	44	6	44	..	..	..
Glasbrook's Siding	..	—	—	—	—	..	—	—	—	—	..	..	..
Gorseinon	..	6 10Y	6 25	—	—	..	—	—	—	—	..	..	..
Grovesend	..	Y—Calls at Gorseinon on Saturdays only. Pontardulais arrive 6.40 p.m.		—	—	..	—	—	—	—	..	..	..
Birch Rock Siding	..			—	—	..	—	—	—	—	..	..	..
Cambria Siding	..			—	—	..	—	—	—	—	..	..	..
Morlais Junction	..			..	..	..	..	..	..	..	..	..	..
Hendy Junction	..			..	..	..	..	..	..	..	..	..	..
Hendy Siding	..			..	..	..	..	..	..	..	..	..	..
PONTARDULAIS	..	6Y22	7 3	6 18	6 19	..	6 53	6 55	6 53	6 55	7 17	..	..
Glynhir	..	—	—	—	—	..	—	—	—	—	—	..	..
PANTYFFYNNON	..	7	16	6	26	..	7	2	7	2	7 25	..	..
Ammanford	..	..	..	July 15th to August 26th (inclusive). SUSPENDED		..	..	..	..	..	July 23rd to Aug. 27th (incl.)	..	..
Ammanford Coll. Halt	..	..	..			..	..	..	..	..		..	..
Glanamman	..	..	..			..	..	..	..	..		..	..
Gellyceidrim Coll. Sdg	..	..	..			..	..	..	..	..		..	..
GARNANT	..	..	..			..	..	..	..	..		..	..
Raven Junction	..	..	..	..	..	..	..	..	..	..	..	..	..
New Cawdor Siding	..	..	..	..	..	..	..	..	..	..	..	..	..
Gwaun-cae-Gurwen C.	..	..	..	..	..	..	..	..	..	..	..	..	..
BRYNAMMAN	..	..	..	..	..	..	..	..	..	..	..	..	..
Pantyffynnon North	..	—	—	—	—	..	—	—	—	—	—	Regular Wednesdays only.	
Parcyrhun Halt	..	—	—	—	—	..	—	—	—	—	—		
Tirydail	..	7	20	—	—	..	7 4	7 6	7 4	7 6	7 29	..	..
Llandebie	..	7	28	—	—	..	—	—	—	—		..	..
Cilyrychen Crossing	..	7 30X	7 46	—	—	..	—	—	—	—	..	..	..
Derwydd Road	..	7	50	6	36	..	7	15	7	15	SUSPENDED	..	..
Ffairfach	..	—	—	—	—	..	—	—	—	—		..	..
CARMARTHEN	6 25	..	..	..	..	..	..	..	..	..		—Z	7 35
Abergwili Junction	6 29	..	..	..	..	..	..	..	..	..		7	40
Abergwili	6 34	..	..	..	..	..	..	..	..	..		—	—
Nantgaredig	6X46	..	..	..	..	..	..	..	..	..		7	53
Llanarthney	6 52	..	..	..	..	..	..	..	..	..		—	—
Drysllwyn	6 56	..	..	..	..	..	..	..	..	..		—	—
Golden Grove	7 1	..	..	..	..	..	..	..	..	..		8	15
Llandilo Bridge	7 6	..	..	..	..	..	..	..	..	..		8	22
Carmarthen Valley Jct.	7 8	8	2	6	42	After assisting 3.55 p.m. Stafford to Swansea (Vic.).	7	21	7	21	..	8	24
LLANDILO	7 10	8 4	8 33	6 46	6 47		7 23	X7 28	7 23	X7 32	..	8 26	—
Talley Road Halt		—	—	—	—		—	—	—	—	..	..	..
Glanrhyd Halt	..	—	—	—	—		—	—	—	—	..	..	..
Llangadock	..	8 48	X8 53	6	57		7 37	7 38	7 41	7 42	..	..	..
Llanwrda	..	—	—	7 1X	7 4		—	7 42	7	46	..	..	..
LLANDOVERY	..	9 11 X	9EO36	7 10	7 15		7 48	7 54	7 52	7 58	..	Z—Carmarthen Goods Yard.	
Cynghordy	..	9	54	7	25		8	5	8	9	..		
Sugar Loaf Summit	..	1014 X	P1019	7	35		8	16	8	20	..		
Llanwrtyd Wells	..	1028X	P1033	7 39	7 40		8 20	8 22	8 24	8 26	..	..	..
Llangammarch Wells	..	—	—	—	7 46	..	—	8 27	—	8 31	..	..	..
Garth	..	10	44	7 49X	7 55	..	8	30	8	34	..	..	..
Cilmery Halt	..	—	—	—	—	..	—	—	—	—	..	..	..
BUILTH ROAD	..	1058O	W11 3	8 4	8 8	..	8 39	8 43	8 43	8 47	..	..	..
Howey	..	11	16	8	14	..	8	49	8	53	..	..	..
LLANDRINDOD WELLS	..	1124C	T1129	8 19	8 22	..	8 54	8 59	8 58	9 3	..	..	..
Penybont	..	11	37	8	28	..	9 5	9 6	9	9	..	..	..
Penybont Junction	..	11	39	8	30	..	9	8	9	11	..	..	..
Dolau	..	—	—	—	—	..	—	—	—	—	..	..	..
Llanbister Road	..	11	51	8	39	..	9 16	9 18	9	20	..	..	..
Llangunllo	..	122O	WP126	8	44	9‖ 0	9	23	9	25	..	..	..
Knucklas	..	Continued on pages 164 and 176.		—	—	—	—	—	—	—	..	..	..
KNIGHTON	..			8 54	8 57	9‖12	9 33	9 38	9 35	9 38	..	..	..
Bucknell	..			—	9 4		Z	9 45	Z	9 45	..	..	..
Hopton Heath	..			—	—	..	..	..	—	—	..	..	..
Broome	..	..	..	—	—	..	—	—	—	—	..	..	..
CRAVEN ARMS	..	..	..	9 20	9 22	..	10 1	10§ 3	10 1	10§ 3	..	..	..
Shrewsbury	..	..	..	9 55	10 5	..	10 36	10 45	10 36	10 45	..	..	..

Z—Calls at Bucknell to set down from Llandovery and beyond on notice being given to the Guard at Llandovery.
§—Advertised 10.2 p.m.

GWAUN-CAE-GURWEN, BRYNAMMAN, CRAVEN ARMS.

Week Days.

STATIONS.	F		B	B	K		F		B	F		F	
	Harlescott Sidings Freight.		Motor.	Motor.	Local Freight. No. 23.		Stafford SX Shrewsbury (Abbey Foregate) SO Freight.		10.5 p.m. Llanelly Pass.	Harlescott Sidings SX Crewe SO Freight.		Shrewsbury Freight.	
	arr.	dep.	dep.	dep.	arr.	dep.	arr.	dep.	dep.	arr.	dep.	arr.	dep.
									SO			S	X
	p.m.	p.m.	p.m.	p.m.	p.m.	p.m.	p.m.	p.m.	p.m.	p.m.	p.m.	p.m.	p.m.
SWANSEA (Victoria)	—	6 45	7 30	8 25	..	..	—	8 55	..	—	9 45	—	11 20
Swansea Bay	—	—	7 34	8 29	..	..	—	—	..	—	—	—	—
Mumbles Road	—	—	7 39	8 34	..	..	—	—	..	—	—	—	—
Rhydydefed Siding	—	—	—	—	..	..	—	—	..	—	—	—	—
Killay	—	—	7 44	8 39	..	..	—	—	..	—	—	—	—
Dunvant	7	3	7 47	8 42	..	..	9	13	..	10	3	11	38
Gowerton	7	9	7 52	8 47	..	..	9	19	..	1011B	E1016	1146B	E1151
Glasbrook's Siding	—	—	—	—	..	..	—	—	..	—	—	—	—
Gorseinon	7 15	7 27	7 57	8 52	..	..	9 25	9 35	..	10 22	10 37	11 57	12 7
Grovesend	—	—	—	SUSPENDED	..	..	—	—	..	—	—	..	..
Birch Rock Siding	—	—	—		..	..	—	—	..	—	—	..	..
Cambria Siding	—	—	—		..	..	—	—	..	—	—	..	..
Morlais Junction	..	..	..	..	..	..	..	..	10 21	..	..	Continued on page 165.	
Hendy Junction	..	..	..	..	9	10	..	..	—	..	..		
Hendy Siding	..	..	..	..	—	—	..	..	—	..	..		
PONTARDULAIS	7 42●	8 15	8 6	9 0	9	12	9 50	10 5	10 24	10 52	11 8	..	..
Glynhir	—	—	—		—	—	—	—	—	—	—	..	..
PANTYFFYNNON	8	28	8 14	..	9 23	11 15	10	18	10 33	11	21	..	..
Ammanford	..	..	8 17	..	..	..	..	..	10 37	..	..	..	..
Ammanford Coll. Halt	..	..		..	..	..	..	..	10 39	..	..	..	..
Glanamman	..	..	..	..	..	..	..	..	10 45	..	..	..	..
Gellyceidrim Coll. Sdg	..	..	..	..	..	..	..	..	—	..	..	..	..
GARNANT	..	..	..	..	..	..	..	..	10 49	..	..	..	..
Raven Junction	..	..	..	..	..	..	..	..	..	..	..	..	..
New Cawdor Siding	..	..	..	..	..	..	..	..	..	..	..	..	..
Gwaun-cae-Gurwen C.	..	..	..	..	..	..	..	..	..	..	..	..	..
BRYNAMMAN	..	..	..	..	..	..	..	..	10 54	..	..	..	..
Pantyffynnon North	—	—	..	..	..	..	—	—	..	—	—	..	..
Parcyrhun Halt	—	—	..	..	..	..	—	—	..	—	—	..	..
Tirydail	8	32	..	..	..	..	10	22	..	11 33	X11 40	..	..
Llandebie	8	40	..	..	..	..	10	30	..	—	—	..	..
Cilyrychen Crossing	—	—	..	..	..	..	—	—	..	11	46	..	..
Derwydd Road	8	46	..	..	..	..	10	36	..	—	—	..	..
Ffairfach	—	—	..	..	..	..	—	—	..	..	..	..	..
CARMARTHEN	..	..	..	..	..	..	..	..	..	..	..	..	..
Abergwili Junction	..	..	..	..	..	..	..	..	..	..	..	..	..
Abergwili	..	..	..	..	..	..	..	..	..	..	..	..	..
Nantgaredig	..	..	..	..	..	..	..	..	..	..	..	..	..
Llanarthney	..	..	..	..	..	..	..	..	..	..	..	..	..
Drysllwyn	..	..	..	..	..	..	..	..	..	..	..	..	..
Golden Grove	..	..	..	G	..	..	..	..	..	..	..	..	..
Llandilo Bridge	..	..	..		..	..	..	..	..	..	..	..	..
Carmarthen Valley Jct.	8	58	..	Light Engine.	..	..	10	48	..	11	58	..	..
LLANDILO	9 0 O	WX97	..		..	..	10	X50	..	12 1O	W12 6	..	..
Talley Road Halt	—	—	..		..	..	—	—	..	Continued on pages 165 and 176.		..	..
Glanrhyd Halt	—	—	..	dep.	..	..	—	—	..			..	..
Llangadock	9	22	..		..	..	11	5	..			..	..
Llanwrda	9	29	..	p.m.	..	..	11	12	..			..	..
LLANDOVERY	9 40E	O1025	..		..	..	11X23	12EO5	..	..	..	..	..
Cynghordy	10	X43	..	After assisting 7.40 p.m. Coleham to Swansea (Vic.).	..	..	Continued on pages 165 and 176.		..	..	..	..	..
Sugar Loaf Summit	11 3X	P11 8	..		..	..			..	..	..	..	..
Llanwrtyd Wells	11 17	P11 22	..		..	..			..	..	..	..	..
Llangammarch Wells	—	—	..		..	..	..	..	..	..	..	..	..
Garth	11	34	..		..	..	..	..	..	..	..	..	..
Cilmery Halt	—	—	..		..	..	..	..	..	..	..	..	..
BUILTH ROAD	1149O	W1220	..		..	..	..	..	..	..	..	..	..
Howey	Continued on pages 165 and 176.		..		..	..	..	..	..	..	..	..	..
Llandrindod Wells			..		..	..	..	..	..	..	..	..	..
Penybont			..		..	..	..	..	..	..	..	..	..
Penybont Junction			..		..	..	..	..	..	..	..	..	..
Dolau	..	..	..		..	..	..	..	..	..	..	..	..
Llanbister Road	..	..	..	..	..	..	..	..	..	..	..	..	..
Llangunllo	..	..	..	10‖42	..	..	..	..	..	..	..	..	..
Knucklas	..	..	..	—	..	..	..	..	..	..	..	..	..
KNIGHTON	..	..	..	10‖54	..	..	..	..	..	..	..	..	..
Bucknell	..	..	..		..	..	..	..	..	..	..	..	..
Hopton Heath	..	..	—	..	—	..	..	..	..	..	..	..	..
Broome	..	..	..	..	..	..	..	..	..	..	..	..	..
CRAVEN ARMS	..	..	..	..	..	..	..	..	..	..	..	..	..
Shrewsbury	..	..	..	..	..	..	..	..	..	..	..	..	..

BR (WR) 1949/50 Winter timetable Swansea Victoria–Carmarthen and Gwaun-cae-Gurwen–Brynamman–Craven Arms.

Road for the National Eisteddfod and the Royal Welsh Show and an increase in excursions generally, four of which were steam hauled, a much healthier picture was presented. Ever-watchful HOWLTA reported an encouraging increase in those using the Sunday Rambler services from the southern end.

As a general rule, the average through passenger working over the whole of the Central Wales Line (Swansea–Shrewsbury–Swansea) throughout most of its existence seems to have been approximately five trains per day in each direction Mondays to Fridays, but in the past with considerable variations for Saturdays and peak season requirements, through coaches to London, the Midlands and the North West and with a great many additional local services, particularly in the south. (In 1911, there were 18 'up' and 19 'down' on parts of the line.)

In contrast, the 1993/94 Winter timetable showed four trains per day in each direction, necessitating two changes to achieve connections to Euston due to through trains from Swansea to Crewe being taken off and an InterCity service direct from Shrewsbury to Euston having been withdrawn previously. However, through early evening trains re-appeared on the Central Wales Line itself with a 19.00 Shrewsbury to Swansea and an 18.15 Swansea to Shrewsbury. In spite of all attempts at persuasion, the Sunday services were once again taken off for the winter.

With the withdrawal of suitably timed early morning and late afternoon commuter trains in October 1993, a new bus service was introduced by Shropshire CC to replace it. On Mondays to Saturday leaving Knighton at 07.10, via Craven Arms and arriving Shrewsbury at 08.40, returning from Shrewsbury at 17.15 and arriving Knighton at 18.40.

The Summer 1994 timetable showed little change other than that the first train from Shrewsbury departed nearly an hour earlier, at 05.57, arriving Swansea at 10.05 in order to improve the service at the southern end of the line for day trippers into Swansea, and the winter one 1994/95, followed the same pattern, without of course, the long hoped for winter Sunday service. By the end of 1995 the line still had only four services in each direction, but although these were not increased, a more commuter-friendly timetable was introduced in 1996 and passenger numbers improved.

These days Llandrindod Wells is the only station between Llanelli and Shrewsbury at which tickets can be purchased. (Open 07.15–14.45 Mon–Fri and until 13.30 Sats.). Passengers joining at other points obtain their tickets from the conductor. Travel is usually in single-car Class 153 'Sprinters' with a buffet trolley service originally provided by HOWLTA volunteers on Saturdays and special occasions (See Chapter 12, HOWLTA) and now by Cherry Tree

Sunday Rambler services continue to be successful; one August Sunday in 1994 saw 230 passengers, 70 of whom took advantage of the Elan Valley coach trip from Llandrindod, necessitating an additional bus. HOWLTA are pressing for the 'Rambler Season' to be extended for the duration of the Summer timetable in 1997. In June of 1994, the following announcement appeared in the *Brecon and Radnor Express*:

Hopes of Direct London-Llandrindod trains

'A boost for Mid-Wales as a holiday centre, with tourists travelling direct from London to Llandrindod and other stations on the Heart of Wales Line is in prospect, with the first high speed train using the track on Saturday. This follows extensive work on the line which has made it suitable for heavier locomotives, John Owen, Chairman of the Engineering Working Group of the Heart of Wales Line Committee told the Express.

Mr Owen, Senior Assistant County Surveyor for Powys, said that previously only light rolling stock had been able to use the line. But because of investment in signalling and crossing improvements over the past two years, the Line could now take the high speed trains. This meant that trains could run direct from Paddington to Swansea, and up to Shrewsbury, instead of passengers having to change, he said, adding:

"This would bring a large number of tourists into the area. We have always suffered in the past because British Rail was unable to run excursion trains into Mid-Wales because of the practical problems.'

Meanwhile private express trains making fast connections between north and south Wales from Cardiff to Holyhead via Hereford and Shrewsbury are a project of John Davies, former Regional Railways Manager for Wales, who took early retirement from British Rail and has started his own consultancy. Commenting on this Mr Owen said, "We must all hope that it doesn't endanger existing services". The present connections via Hereford or Shrewsbury to towns such as Manchester and Leeds were very useful to local people. The proposal would not help to bring tourists into Mid-Wales, he said but he added "Any additional transport – and speedier transport – in this area is to be welcomed".

This resulted in a great many calls to Llandrindod station to enquire when this wonderful new express service would commence. One caller assumed it would be the following week. The key words in the newspaper report were, alas, 'prospect', 'project' and 'proposal'. But hope, as they say, springs eternal and meanwhile, travellers on the line are benefiting by less exciting but useful facilities like the installation of a recorded telephone information service in the summer of 1996. This is updated by the staff of Pantyffynnon signal box and is of considerable help to passengers in the remote regions which the railway serves.

10

Excursions and Special Trains

Excursions were being run on the Central Wales Line by the end of the 19th century. In 1862 the Knighton Railway offered trips to Rhyl and to the Isle of Man at a price of 20s and 21s respectively and in the same year, there was a special service to the Great Exhibition in London. The latter journey, via Shrewsbury and Stafford, took 9½ hours, leaving Knighton at 7am and arriving in London at 4.30pm. The price was 20s plus 10s if a closed carriage was required. By the following year, passengers from Llandrindod were also able to avail themselves of the Knighton excursions, there being a horse-drawn carriage *The Railway Queen,* which plied back and forth to connect with the Knighton trains.

The LNWR advertised:

> 'On Saturday September 14th 1895 – An Express Half day trip to Knighton (one of the sites of Birmingham New Water Works) and Llandrindod Wells Fare there and back – third class 2/6.'

This left Birmingham New Street at 12.55pm and returned from Llandrindod Wells at 8.35pm. Passengers were invited to apply to Mr. A. Entwistle, District Superintendent, New Street, Birmingham for information on LNWR excursion trains. LNWR posters at Gowerton in 1880/90 period advertised a '1/3 Day Trip (an Express Excursion) to Belle Vue Manchester for 6/-' and a '1 or 3 Day trip to Manchester, Liverpool and the Isle of Man' also for 6/-.

There was also an 'every Saturday cheap weekend ticket to Llandilo for 3/-'.

There were local specials on fair days to races and other events.

The LNWR Swansea Division General Working Notice for week ending 22 April 1898 'Special Trains and Excursion Arrangements' mentions:

Friday, 15 April Carmarthen Fair
Saturday, 16 April Newcastle Emlyn Fair and Builth Fair
Monday, 18 April Llandovery Fair
Tuesday and Wednesday, 19 and 20 April Ludlow Races
Wednesday, 20 April Maenclochog Fair
Thursday, 21 April Knighton Fair

In the case of Builth, Llandovery and Knighton Fairs it is stated that 'Market Tickets will be issued from stations usually obtained.

The Ordinary Trains to be suitably strengthened.'

In the case of the first two 'Any Live Stock from this Fair to be worked on 9.15am Goods from Swansea'

There was a special cattle train from Knighton Fair which departed at 2.30pm to Craven Arms, Church Stretton and Shrewsbury (Coleham) arriving at 4.35pm.

By the 1930s, from the catchment area in Mid Wales, there were 15-coach Sunday school excursions to the coast including Rhyl, Southport and Swansea. From these small beginnings excursion traffic grew and continued in popularity into the mid-1960s Rugby excursions like that in 1961 from Swansea to Edinburgh were very popular. A lot of traffic was involved with stock brought in from far afield. Some had sleeping cars and all trains had attendants for which there was no shortage of volunteers from local staff anxious for a free trip to Edinburgh.

However, when steam finished on the line in 1964, the number of excursions dropped considerably and was not to revive until the 1970s. In 1972 there were 18 and a noticeable recovery began. In the next four years over 90 excursions ran over the line.

There were 31 specials in 1977, including eight Women's Institute charter trains to Llandrindod during May and June, each usually with a ten coach loading.

The latter included, upon arrival, a bus trip around the Elan Valley reservoirs necessitating transfer to the coach park via the station bridge. During the course of the fourth trip, the representative from the local tourist office who was overseeing the exercise, noticed that the bridge was beginning to vibrate alarmingly under the stampede to acquire a good seat on the buses: at subsequent arrivals the ladies were directed via the barrow crossing!

There followed 25 excursions in 1978, 22 in 1979 and 29 in 1980, seven of which were to Gowerton for the National Eisteddfod. A weekend trip from Leeds to Llandrindod Wells ran on 20/21 December 1980 hauled by diesel

An Edinburgh excursion stands at the 'down' platform of Llandovery station in the 1930s.
(Dorothy Bound)

C.W. & S.D. No. 17.

L. & N. W. Ry.—SWANSEA DIVISION. GENERAL WORKING NOTICE.

For Week ending Friday, April 22nd, 1898.

SPECIAL TRAINS AND EXCURSION ARRANGEMENTS.

For Regulations for working Special Passenger Trains, see Appendix to Working Book.

EXPLANATION OF REFERENCE T—Collect Tickets. E—Examine Tickets. L—Stops if required for Locomotive purposes. F C—Fitted with Cord. P—Stops to pick up or set down Pilotmen R—Stops if required for Refreshments. C R—Calls if required. R S—Roadside duties only.

THURSDAY, APRIL 14th.

2-43 p.m. Passenger Train—Craven Arms to Swansea.

To be run in two portions, if required. The second portion, if run, to be worked by Engine and Men of 5-45 pm "C" Cattle Train from Carmarthen, on Wednesday, April 13th. Locomotive Department to provide a vacuum engine. Inspector HANCOCK to arrange connections to Carmarthen off both portions.

FRIDAY, APRIL 15th.

Carmarthen Fair.

Special Passenger Train, Carmarthen to Llandilo.

No. 1	arr. am	dep. am	
Swansea	..	11 30	Cross 11-15 a.m. Passenger Train from Llandilo at Nantgaredig.
Nantgaredig	11 42	x 11 45	
Llandilo	12 5		

Special Cattle Train No. 2

		arr. pm	dep. pm	
	Carmarthen	..	2 0	
	Llanarthney	C.R.		
	Llandilo	2 40	2 45	
	Llandovery	3 10	3 15	
Shunt at Builth Road for 2-50 p.m. from Swansea.	Sugar Loaf Summit	3 40	x 3 45	9-0 am Local Goods from Craven Arms to cross special at Sugar Loaf.
	Llanwrtyd Wells		x 3 55	
	Garth	4 10	x 4 15	
	Builth Road	4 30	x 5 5	Cross 2-43 pm passenger from Craven Arms at Garth.
	Llangunllo Tunnel	5 55	6 0	
	Knighton	6 25	6 30	
	Craven Arms	7 0	7 10	
	Church Stretton	7 35	7 40	
	Shrewsbury (Coleham)	8 15		

Engine for working this train from Llandilo to Salop, to leave Llandovery at 1-45 pm Engine working train. Carmarthen to Llandilo, to return at once to Carmarthen. The 3-30 pm Conditional Cattle Train, Carmarthen to Salop, will also run on this date. For times see Working Book. Engine for working this train. Llandilo to Salop, to leave Llandovery at 3-0 pm. Engine working train, Carmarthen to Llandilo, to return to Carmarthen at once.

FRIDAY, APRIL 15th.

The 7-35 am Mixed Train, Llandilo to Carmarthen to run as a Passenger Train, and a Special Goods Train to follow as under:—

No. 3	arr. am	dep. am
Llandilo	..	8 5
Golden Grove	8 15	8 20
Abergwili	CR	
Carmarthen	9 0	

SATURDAY, APRIL 16th.

Newcastle Emlyn Fair.

The 5-45 pm Conditional Cattle Train, Carmarthen to Shrewsbury will run on this date For times see Working Book. Cattle Specials must stop at Church Stretton. Engine working this train from Llandilo to Shrewsbury, to leave Llandovery at 5-50 pm. Engine working train from Carmarthen to return from Llandilo to Carmarthen at once. The Special will run from Llandilo to Shrewsbury in the times of the 3-30 pm "C" Goods and Cattle Train from Swansea. For times see April Working Book.

2-43 p.m. Craven Arms to Swansea. To be divided as shewn in Easter Notice C.W. & S.D. No. 15.

Builth Fair.

Market Tickets will be issued from stations where usually obtained. The Ordinary Trains to be suitably strengthened.

Any Live Stock from this Fair to be worked on 9-15 a.m. Goods from Swansea. Inspector WHITFORD to arrange.

MONDAY, APRIL 18th.

Llandovery Fair.

The 9-15 am Goods from Swansea, to convey any live stock from this Fair. The Ordinary Passenger Trains to be suitably strengthened, and Market Tickets to be issued. Inspector WHITFORD to arrange.

TUESDAY & WEDNESDAY, APRIL 19th & 20th.

Ludlow Races.

Cheap Tickets will be issued as per C.W. & S.D. Bill No. 18

Passengers from Stations Builth Road to Knucklas inclusive travel by 6-30 a.m. Ordinary Train from Swansea, and return from Ludlow by 6-5 pm Ordinary Train.

Special Passenger Trains.

No. 4	arr. am	dep. am
Knighton	..	11 35
Bucknell	..	11 43
Hopton Heath	..	11 50
Broome	..	11 57
Craven Arms	12 5 T	12 10
Bromfield (Empty Coaches)	12 18	12 21
Ludlow (Empty Coaches)	12 25	

No. 5	arr. pm	dep. pm
Ludlow (Empty Coaches)	..	4 40
Bromfield (Empty Coaches)	4 45	4 50
Craven Arms	4 58	5 3
Broome	..	5 10
Hopton Heath	..	5 16
Bucknell	..	5 22
Knighton	5 30	

Engine and Men for working No. 4 special to leave Craven Arms 10-45 a.m. for Knighton. Engine and Men working No. 5 special to return to Craven Arms at once. The Ordinary Trains concerned to be suitably strengthened. Inspector WHITFORD to arrange.

WEDNESDAY, APRIL 20th.

Maenclochog Fair.

The 6-30 pm Conditional Cattle Train, Carmarthen to Shrewsbury, will run on this date. For Times see Working Book. Cattle Specials must stop at Church Stretton. Engine working this train from Llandilo to Shrewsbury, to leave Llandovery at 6-20 pm. Engine working train from Carmarthen, to return from Llandilo to Carmarthen at once.

THURSDAY, APRIL 21st.

Knighton Fair.

Special Cattle Train. No. 6

	arr. pm	dep. pm
Knighton	..	2 30
Craven Arms	3 5	3 30
Church Stretton	3 55	4 0
Shrewsbury (Coleham)	4 35	

All Ordinary Trains to be suitably strengthened, and the usual Market Tickets to be issued.

Crewe Permanent Way Engineer's Stores Train.

This Train will run from Crewe and deliver materials for relaying, etc., Central Wales Main Line and Branches as required until further notice.

GENERAL INSTRUCTIONS.

Through Goods Trains—Swansea to Shrewsbury.

Breaksmen working above trains must inform the Foreman at Llandovery whether they have any traffic to detach on the loop at Builth Road, and a wire must be sent the latter station giving this information. (T. 180,380).

PERMANENT WAY AND OTHER WORKS.

Necessitating the Blockage of Lines or running of Trains at slackened speed.

From Friday, April 15th, to Friday, April 22nd, 1898, inclusive.

IMPORTANT NOTICE.—*Engine Drivers, Firemen, Guards, Breaksmen, &c. must keep a good look-out for Hand Signals, which will be exhibited at the various localities in accordance with the General Regulations. It must, however, be understood that Repairs of Lines may be necessary at other places besides those mentioned below, and of which owing to their urgency, it has not been possible to give previous notice; and Engine Drivers, must therefore be always on the look-out, and prepared to stop or run at reduced speed wherever and wherever Hand Signals are exhibited.*

The Permanent Way Department will be engaged as under:—

Central Wales Line.

Between Broome and Hopton Heath—Both Lines—Painting Bridges. 3 and 3¼ mile posts.

Between Bucknell and Knighton—Down Line—Relaying. 9¼ and 10 mile posts.

Between Sugar Loaf Summit and Cynghordy—Single Line—Resleepering. 52 and 52¼ mile posts.

LNWR special trains and excursion arrangements, week-ending Friday, 22 April 1898.

locomotive No. 40030 after which there was an almost total ban on loco-hauled excursions due, allegedly, to the condition of the track and lack of finances. This was not only a sad state of affairs for the line but also a blow to Llandrindod and Llanwrtyd Wells, the hotels and traders of which had benefited from large pre-Christmas and other off-peak weekend excursions from the North for about five years (as had secondary destinations to which the visitors were coached during their stay).

A great deal of work had been put in to arrange those large weekend specials. This involved the hosting of railway executives, the meetings for whom were usually based at one of Llandrindod's larger hotels and before they took place, there was a great deal of work done in the form of packaging the number of beds available in both towns for various off-peak weekends and agreement on, by how much the first suggested price could be reduced once the bargaining began. The meetings were attended by railway managers from across the country, the majority from the North, the rapport with Leeds being particularly good.

The accommodation sector all contributed towards the hosting costs according to their size and, although there were official workshops, the real business often took place in the early hours when a lot of good natured wheeling and dealing was done.

The results meant that trains with as many as 500 passengers arrived for weekends at extremely off peak times, those leading up to Christmas and in January and February. In those days the cost of running these excursions was very high, involving the stock being hauled on the CWL by locomotives equipped with spotlights and the special opening of the line on a Sunday (before the days of NSKT). The prices for accommodation, therefore, had to be honed down to a minimum but everyone made a profit.

After the introduction of the locomotive ban, a compromise was tried which involved transferring the excursion passengers to chartered bus services at Shrewsbury to continue their journey by road to the resorts. This was far from satisfactory, depriving the travellers of the enjoyment of an entire journey by rail and on one occasion, the Central had the last laugh when the visitors had to return in a dmu on the ordinary weekday service. The local press described the event:

15.12.1981. British Rail Excursion. Saturday 12th/13th.

Due to the blizzard conditions which coincided with plans for their departure after lunch Sunday by coach to Shrewsbury to pick up the excursion train, the 275 passengers had to spend an extra night in Llandrindod. They left at about 10.30am on Monday packed into three carriages sent up specially on the local railway line to take them as far as Shrewsbury. A somewhat ironic sequel in that, after all the alternative arrangements, they ended up by using the Central Wales line after all.

They reached their destination at Sheffield and Nottingham areas at about 4.45pm. Overall, they were very cheerful and many said they hoped to come back next December.

Over a hundred stood outside in the Town Hall Gardens singing carols in the freezing conditions late Saturday afternoon. It was so cold that the town band had to cram into the Information Office and play with the window open because their instruments were freezing up. The singers stood around the window on the outside. Several shops opened specially on Sunday morning.

The cost of the extra nights stay is being born by British Rail but hoteliers involved are being as co-operative as possible about price.

The determination of these visitors to enjoy themselves whatever the weather was most impressive.'

The paper omitted to mention the surprise of the local vicar who, having cancelled a carol service on Sunday evening due to the appalling weather, turned out, in the company of his dog, to perform the compulsory ritual of Evensong and to lock the church, only to find it full of the excursion passengers who had crossed the road from the Hotel Metropole in the hope of whiling away an hour before dinner by singing carols.

These specials acted as a shop window for the area; many people returning on indiviudal holidays to travel on the CWL. Unfortunately, during the period in which the line was closed to heavy excursions, managerial power in British Rail was centralised and the old contacts lost. There were only five excursions in 1981.

In 1982 there were six dmu excursions plus one 10-coach loco-hauled from Pontarddulais to Paddington on the southern end and a steam-hauled trip, Hereford–Craven Arms–Carlisle on the northern section. One of the dmu specials, (2 June 1982) was to Swansea/Cardiff for Pope John's visit, the return working of which did not run, there being only one passenger forward from Llandovery.

There were eleven excursions in 1983 and on 13 June, the first revenue earning loco-hauled passenger train since the ban in January 1981 ran over the line. This was an 8-coach Pullman hauled by No. 37300 on a round trip from Paddington via Hereford and Craven Arms.

HOWLTA (Heart of Wales Line Travellers Association) ran a 10-coach charter to Llandudno on 2 July 1983. This also was hauled – on the Central Wales line – by a Class 37. On 5 November 1983, No. 47590 *Thomas Telford* hauled two InterCity coaches and eight RailFreight wagons to Sugar Loaf Summit. The purpose of this 'special' is unknown, but was probably something to do with a military operation.

Among the 17 excursions in 1984 – twelve of which were loco-hauled – was a Llanelli–Blackpool excursion with ten coaches on the foward journey and twelve on the return. This was hauled by No. 37266 to and from Crewe (the heaviest single engine load for this class to date). The Crewe–Blackpool–Crewe legs were hauled by a Class 47.

The 15 excursions in 1985 (all but four loco-hauled) included a 9-coach VSOE ('Venice Simplon Orient Express') Pullman charter from Ealing Broadway hauled by two Class 33s on 19 April and on 30 November an 11-coach excursion, 'The Valley Trekker' from Plymouth to Abernant and the Valley lines hauled by Nos 25325 and 33012 with 37306 and 37234 assisting between Pantyffynnon and Gwaun-cae-Gurwen.

The next two years saw 31 specials on the Central Wales line, 14 of which were dmu excursions plus No. 37426 *Vale of Rheidol* on 3 September 1986 hauling three RailFreight vans and one brake van from Llandovery to Longtown – another mystery trip attributed to the military. With the collapse of Glanrhyd Bridge in October 1987 there was only limited traffic during the following year. This did include a 3-coach VSOE charter on 1 July 1988 Salop–Llandovery hauled by No. 37425 and a HOWLTA 3-car dmu charter from Llandovery to Llandudno on 21 August.

After the new bridge at Glanrhyd was completed in October 1988, the first special train to run over the line was the 'Welsh Cobbler' tour on 25 February 1989. This was a 10-coach Northampton–Reading–Northampton excursion via Cardiff and Shrewsbury with 550 passengers and was hauled by No. 47612 *Titan*. There followed, that year, another 14 excursions, one a pair of 3-car dmus and the rest hauled by Class 47s, the latter including an 'Orient Express' special.

One of the first InterCity trains on the line in the mid 1980s, at Llandrindod 'down' platform looking south.
(Courtesy Tony Williams)

The bookings for the VSOE excursions were disappointing. Only one of several scheduled for 1988 ran – on 15 July. The train, from London, was touring the Principality for a week and stopped at Llangammarch before continuing to North Wales. There were only twelve occupants of the two passenger coaches and the cost of the journey was about £1,700 per head.

The success rate was no better in 1989 when out of the four 'Orient Express' trips which were planned, only that on 7/8 July actually materialised and this ran into problems. Locomotive No. 47824 *Glorious Devon* failed in the sidings at Llandrindod. There was some difficulty locating a relief engine, there being nothing at Swansea and, having arranged for one to come up from Carmarthen, the Pantyffynnon signalman also had the task of finding a path for it. The difficulties did not end there for, on the previous night, just north of Builth Road, a lorry had collided with a road bridge which had been knocked out of alignment. Local trains had been crossing the bridge at a speed of 5 mph but there were doubts about the wisdom of allowing the relief No. 47526 *Northumbrian* to cross it and this, having started up the line, returned to Llandovery, leaving the 3-coach load of VSOE passengers marooned in Llandrindod, where they were taken for a tour of the town and bused around the Elan Valley dams. Local trains continued to creep over the bridge and eventually No. 47526 also ventured northwards, picking up the surprisingly cheerful passengers and hauling the 'Orient Express' safely down the line. The train had been delayed for eight hours.

There followed three years with a marked reduction in excursion traffic; seven in 1990, eight and in 1991 – all hauled by 47s. In 1992, there were only two; one in June consisted of four 153s – the first time so many 'Sprinters' had run on the line coupled together: the other train in November was a round trip, Derby to Cardiff, with eight coaches hauled by two Class 31s.

In 1993 however, the Central Wales Line was able to boast 20 specials, albeit some of them local. Ten of these were in July, Carmarthen–Builth Road–Carmarthen for the Royal Welsh Show and National Eisteddfod.

A triumph was the return of steam to the line to celebrate its 125th anniversary as a through route. The BR press release stated:

> 'A unique programme of steam trains has been organised during May and June to celebrate the 125th anniversary of the Heart of Wales Line.
> And additional steam excursions have been organised in West Wales, so that local people, visitors and enthusiasts alike cannot only experience the nostalgia of a bygone age, but also sample the beautiful scenery of Central and West Wales.
> This exciting and varied steam programme has been

Class 47 No. 47612 Titan *with a Welsh Land Cruise Excursion, the 'Welsh Mountain Cobbler', organised by Hertfordshire Railtours, at Llandrindod on 25 February 1989. This was the first loco-hauled excursion over the line after Glanrhyd Bridge had been re-instated. The train comprised ten coaches in Network SouthEast livery.*
(Roy Palmer)

No. 47824 Glorious Devon *hauling a diminutive 'Venice Simplon Orient Express', failed at Llandrindod on 8 July 1989, resulting in an eight-hour delay.* (Roy Palmer)

organised by Regional Railways, Flying Scotsman Services and The Steam Locomotives Operators' Association, with sponsorship from local district councils. Two steam locomotives will be used on the special excursions; the BR Standard Class 4 tank No. 80079 based at the Severn Valley Railway, Kidderminster and the 'Black Five', locomotive No. 44767, named *George Stephenson*, based on the North Yorkshire Moors Railway. Both types were associated with the Heart of Wales Line in its steam operating years.'

The enthusiasm which greeted these excursions was tremendous. The first, hauled by BR Standard 2-6-4T No. 80079 with six coaches and fully booked weeks in advance, ran Shrewsbury to Carmarthen on 16 May 1993, the return journey being made behind diesel No. 37414.

The weather was appallingly wet and as it continued south the train was running late. Nevertheless, people stood in the pouring rain, not only at the stations through which it passed but in fields as well, and police were called out to control the road traffic.

The second trip, on 23 May was, as promised, LMS 4-6-0 'Black 5' No. 44767 *George Stephenson* hauling seven coaches, Shrewsbury to Carmarthen (Coventry to Carmarthen excursion). The return journey was diesel hauled.

On 6 June 1993 the third excursion saw both the 2-6-4T, No. 80079 and the 4-6-0 No. 44767 double-headed, hauling nine coaches on the 'Central Wales Anniversary Ltd', Carmarthen to Shrewsbury.

On 9 October, a Nottingham to Carmarthen excursion (load 9) ran behind a Class 47 to Shrewsbury and was then double-headed by steam locomotives Nos 80079 and 80080 to Carmarthen, arriving Llandovery in the afternoon as a part of the town's celebration of the 125th anniversary of the opening of the line as a through route.

These steam locomotives returned to the line again on 23 October 1993 when an InterCity Charter ran from Paddington to Shrewsbury, being hauled to Pantyffynnon by Class 47 No. 47822 and then changing locomotives to continue to Shrewsbury behind the two 2-6-4Ts. (Load nine to Pantyfynnon and ten thereafter, including one support coach.)

Early April of 1994 saw an unusual and colourful site in the form of a telecommunications train conveying officials on an inspection tour and a High Speed Train set appeared at the end of May chartered by Hertfordshire Railtours.

'The Sugar Loafer', a Hertfordshire Railtours' excursion hauled by No. 33109 *Captain Bill Smith RNR*, seven InterCity coaches ran on 19 November 1994. A round trip from Paddington, this was intended to be double-headed but the second locomotive had failed. There was a decline in excursions in 1995/6 but these are expected to increase in 1997 with charter trains booked for late spring, early summer and October.

Royal Trains

20 July 1904 Conveyed HM King Edward VII and Queen Alexandra from Swansea Victoria to Builth Road en route to opening the Elan Valley Water Works, near Rhayader. Double-headed with two 2-4-2 tank locomotives. (It comprised five coaches and a brake van, in LNWR livery.)

An InterCity 125 'High Speed Train' heads south of Llandrindod in February 1993. (Roy Palmer)

BR Standard Class 4MT 2-6-4T No. 80079 is greeted with enthusiasm and pouring rain at Llandrindod Wells as it heads the first 'return of steam' excursion (Shrewsbury–Carmarthen) on 16 May 1993.
(Brijid Doughty)

The Royal train travelled up the line from Swansea, stopped at Llandeilo and then continued to Builth Road No. 2 signal box where it was able to transfer to the Mid Wales Line without entering the station. Engines were changed and the train ran on to Rhayader. It returned to Euston via Moat Lane Junction, Welshpool and Shrewsbury having, between Shrewsbury and London, made up a delay of an hour incurred travelling over the single track on the first part of the homeward journey.

In 1921, HM George V, en route to open Talgarth Hospital, transferred via a specially built gangway at Builth Road loop from an LNWR to a Cambrian Railways Royal train which was standing in a siding.

23 October 1952
HM Queen Elizabeth II and Duke of Edinburgh were conveyed to Llandrindod Wells en route to opening the Claerwen Dam in the Elan Valley complex. Eleven coaches hauled by two GWR 'Castle' class locomotives, Nos 7030 *Cranbrook Castle*' and 7036 *Taunton Castle*. The train was preceded by No. 6971 *Athelhampton Hall*.

6 August 1955
HM Queen and Duke of Edinburgh were conveyed to join Royal Yacht *Britannia* at Milford Haven after the opening of Usk Reservoir, near Trecastle. The journey was made from Paddington to Brecon by train and the empty stock went from Brecon via Builth Road to Llandovery while the Royal party were at the reservoir whence they continued to Llandovery by road to rejoin the train to proceed to Neyland. Hauled on the Central Wales Line, Builth Road–Llandovery–Llandeilo by LMS Stanier 2-8-0s Nos 48309 and 48707.

1957
Conveyed Duke of Edinburgh en route Bangor to Cardigan, hauled by Stanier 'Black 5' No. 45406.

22 July 1975
The Duke of Edinburgh travelled from Shrewsbury to Builth Road to open the Royal Welsh Show. Four coaches hauled by Nos 37177 and 37180.

23 October 1979
HRH Prince of Wales and party were conveyed from Llandrindod to Genwen Junction (Llanelli) after attending the Welsh Trade Fair. Four coaches hauled by No. 47555 *Commonwealth Spirit*.

29 October 1981
HRH Prince and Princess of Wales travelled from Genwen Junction (Llanelli) to Builth Road during a three-day tour of Wales. Nine coaches hauled by No. 47511 *Thames* (restricted to 30mph on Central Wales Line north of Pantyffynnon).

21 July 1983
The Royal Train conveyed by HM Queen and Duke of Edinburgh to Builth Road for the Royal Welsh Show. Eleven coaches hauled by Nos 47555 *Commonwealth Spirit* and 47513 *Severn* (locomotives 'top-and-tailing' while on CWL).

29 November 1985
HRH Prince of Wales went to Builth Road to open new buildings at Royal Welsh Showground. Five coaches hauled by No. 47555 *Commonwealth Spirit* (leading) and No. 47600 *Dewi Saint* (rear).

14 July 1989
HRH Prince of Wales was conveyed to Llandrindod Wells to visit the Centre for Mentally Handicapped at Howey and to a nature reserve in the Rhayader area. Seven coaches hauled by No. 47624 *Cyclops* arrived Llandrindod 05.45 and was left in the sidings. The Prince of Wales left the train at 10am to travel by road.

25 July 1989
Duke of Edinburgh conveyed to Builth Road for a visit to the Royal Welsh Show.

Seven coaches hauled by Nos 47818, with 47831 *Bolton Wanderers* at the rear.

BR 2-6-4T No. 80079 and LMS 'Black 5' 4-6-0 No. 44767 double heading the 'Central Wales Anniversary Ltd', Carmarthen–Shrewsbury excursion on 6 June 1993.

(Roy Palmer)

Passengers off the 'Sugar Loafer' arrive in Llandrindod.

(Rose Coleman)

Leading Porter

NOTICE No. 60.

PRIVATE.—For use of the staff concerned only

BRITISH RAILWAYS
(WESTERN OPERATING AREA)

NOTICE
OF
ROYAL TRAINS

PADDINGTON
TO
LLANDRINDOD WELLS

LLANDRINDOD WELLS
TO
SHREWSBURY

SHREWSBURY
TO
PADDINGTON

22nd, 23rd and 24th OCTOBER, 1952

☞ THIS NOTICE, WHICH WILL BE DISTRIBUTED BY THE DISTRICT OPERATING SUPERINTENDENTS CONCERNED TO ALL STAFF AFFECTED IN THEIR RESPECTIVE DISTRICTS, MUST BE ACKNOWLEDGED TO THE DISTRICT OPERATING SUPERINTENDENTS IMMEDIATELY ON RECEIPT BY TELEGRAM AS FOLLOWS :—" ARNO GROVE 60."

TIME TABLE OF ROYAL TRAIN—PADDINGTON TO STABLING POINT BETWEEN MARSH FARM JUNCTION AND HARTON ROAD (ON MUCH WENLOCK BRANCH), EARLY THURSDAY MORNING, 23rd OCTOBER, 1952—*continued.*

Distances from Paddington. Mls.	Chs.	PRINCIPAL STATIONS AND INTERMEDIATE SIGNAL BOXES.	TIMES. a.m.	REMARKS.
142	17	Stafford Junction .. pass	—	
142	50	Wellington .. .. „	2.25	To run via Down Main Line.
143	7¾	Market Drayton Junction „	—	
—	—	Belvidere Signals .. „	—	Intermediate Block Signals—Down Distant and Down Home.
152	28	Abbey Foregate.. .. „	2.40	
152	30	Abbey Foregate Junction „	—	
152	56	English Bridge Junction „	—	
152	73	Coleham .. .. .. „	2.44	The 1.25 a.m. Crewe to Cardiff must run punctually and leave Shrewsbury at 2.22 a.m. (advertised time).
153	13	Sutton Bridge Junction „	—	
156	48	Condover .. .. „	—	
158	56	Dorrington .. .. „	—	
161	45	Leebotwood .. .. „	—	
—	—	Dudgeley Signals .. „	—	Intermediate Block Signals—Down Distant and Down Home.
165	5½	Church Stretton .. „	3. 7	The 2.0 a.m. Crewe to Penzance to be held at Church Stretton until the " Train out of Section " signal has been received from Marsh Brook for the Royal Train.
167	55	Marsh Brook .. .. „	—	
169	2	**MARSH FARM JCT. .. arr. (Down Starting Signal) dep.**	**3.20 3.40**	**Change Engines. Train Reverses.** Engine No. 7913 to work the Royal Train Marsh Farm Junction to Stabling Point to leave Coleham Shed 2‖0 a.m., Marsh Farm Junction arrive 2‖45 a.m. For detailed instructions for dealing with the Royal Train at Marsh Farm Junction, see page 16.
169	62	**STABLING POINT .. arr. (Between Marsh Farm Junction and Harton Road)**	**3.50**	For detailed instructions for dealing with the Royal Train at Stabling Point, see page 16.

TIME TABLE OF ROYAL TRAIN—STABLING POINT BETWEEN MARSH FARM JUNCTION AND HARTON ROAD (ON MUCH WENLOCK BRANCH) TO LLANDRINDOD WELLS, THURSDAY, 23rd OCTOBER, 1952.

The formation of the Royal Train leaving Stabling Point will be similar and the order of the vehicles the same as from Paddington (see page 2).

The Engine, or where more than one is used, the Leading Engine, to carry FOUR HEAD LAMPS, viz. one at the foot of the chimney, one at each end of the buffer beam, and one in the centre of the buffer beam. (Important.—See paragraph 1 of R.E. Circular O/RR, dated December, 1950.)

The Train will carry TWO TAIL LAMPS. (Important.—See paragraph 2 of R.E. Circular O/RR, dated December, 1950.)

The Head Lamps and Tail Lamps must be lighted before leaving the Stabling Point.

The Train will run on the Main Line from Marsh Farm Junction to Llandrindod Wells.

WORKING OF TRAIN ENGINES.

The engines (Nos. 7030 and 7036) to work the Royal Train from Stabling Point to Llandrindod Wells to leave Coleham Shed, chimneys leading, at 7‖30 a.m., Marsh Farm Junction arrive 8‖15 a.m., reverse, depart 8‖17 a.m., Stabling Point arrive 8‖22 a.m.

THE PERMANENT AND TEMPORARY SPEED RESTRICTIONS MUST BE STRICTLY OBSERVED.

Distances from Stabling Point. Mls.	Chs.	PRINCIPAL STATIONS AND INTERMEDIATE SIGNAL BOXES.	TIMES. a.m.	REMARKS.
—	—	**STABLING POINT .. dep. (Between Marsh Farm Junction and Harton Road)**	**8.55**	For detailed instructions for dealing with the Royal Train at Stabling Point, see page 16.
—	60	Marsh Farm Junction .. pass	9. 4	
3	76	Craven Arms & Stokesay „	9.10	The 7.50 a.m. Shrewsbury to Hereford } Must run The 7.28 a.m. Hereford to Shrewsbury } punctually.
6	42	Broome .. .. .. „	—	
12	0	Bucknell.. .. .. „	9.23½	
16	19	Knighton .. .. „	C9.31S	The 6.15 a.m. Swansea (Victoria) to Craven Arms to be held at Llangunllo and cross the Royal Train at that place.
18	64	Knucklas .. .. „	—	
21	75	Llangunllo Tunnel .. „	—	R.E. Circular O/RR (clause 16) in regard to the examination and protection of Tunnels must be observed. (See local Notice issued by District Engineer.)
22	54	Llangunllo .. .. „	C9.48S	
25	51	Llanbister Road .. „	C9.53S	
29	22	Dolau .. .. .. „	9.58	
31	56	Penybont Junction .. „	C10.2S	
31	66	Penybont Tunnel .. „	—	R.E. Circular O/RR (clause 16) in regard to the examination and protection of Tunnels must be observed. (See local Notice issued by District Engineer.)
32	17	Penybont .. .. „	C10.5S	
35	67	**LLANDRINDOD WELLS arr. (Down Platform)**	**10.15**	The 7.55 a.m. Swansea (Victoria) to Shrewsbury to be held at Howey until the Royal Train has been cleared from the Down Platform at Llandrindod Wells to the Up and Down Refuge Siding and the two Royal Train engines have passed Howey *en route* to Llandovery. For detailed instructions for dealing with the Royal Train at Llandrindod Wells, see page 16. **The Royal Train to be stabled at Llandrindod Wells on the Up and Down Refuge Siding with Engine No. 6971 attached.**

Working timetable for the Royal Train Paddington–Llandrindod. Llandrindod–Shrewsbury. Shrewsbury–Paddington. 22, 23 and 24 October 1952.

TIME TABLE OF ROYAL TRAIN—LLANDRINDOD WELLS TO STABLING POINT BETWEEN MARSH FARM JUNCTION AND HARTON ROAD (ON MUCH WENLOCK BRANCH), THURSDAY, 23rd OCTOBER, 1952.

The Engine, or where more than one is used, the leading Engine, to carry FOUR HEAD LAMPS, viz. one at the foot of the chimney, one at each end of the buffer beam, and one in the centre of the buffer beam. (Important.—See paragraph 1 of R.E. Circular O/RR, dated December, 1950.)

The Train will carry TWO TAIL LAMPS. (Important.—See paragraph 2 of R.E. Circular O/RR, dated December, 1950.)

The Head Lamps and Tail Lamps must be lighted before leaving Llandrindod Wells and Marsh Farm Junction.

The Train will run on the Main Line Llandrindod Wells to Marsh Farm Junction.

WORKING OF TRAIN ENGINES.

The engines (Nos. 7030 and 7036) to work the Royal Train from Llandrindod Wells to Marsh Farm Junction to leave Llandovery, chimneys leading, at 3‖10 p.m. for Llandrindod Wells, arrive 4‖45 p.m.

FORMATION (*FROM ENGINES*) **LEAVING LLANDRINDOD WELLS:—**

L.M.R. Stock.	BRAKE FIRST	No. 5155	482 tons.
	SALOON	" 45005	
	H.M. THE QUEEN'S SALOON	" 799	
	SALOON	" 798	
	DINING SALOON	" 76	
	SALOON	" 807	
	SLEEPING SALOON	" 495	
	SALOON	" 806	
	DINING SALOON	" 77	
	SLEEPING SALOON	" 477	
	BRAKE FIRST	" 5154	

Length of Train (excluding Engines) .. .. 727 feet 10½ inches.

The distance from the centre of the footplate of the leading engine to the centre of the principal door of H.M. The Queen's Saloon No. 799 is approximately 279 feet 9¾ inches. The distance from the centre of the principal door of H.M. The Queen's Saloon No. 799 to the buffer of the rear coach (Brake First No. 5154) is approximately 535 feet 10¼ inches.

THE PERMANENT AND TEMPORARY SPEED RESTRICTIONS MUST BE STRICTLY OBSERVED.

Distances from Llandrindod Wells. Mls.	Chs.	PRINCIPAL STATIONS AND INTERMEDIATE SIGNAL BOXES.	TIMES. p.m.	REMARKS.
—	—	**LLANDRINDOD WELLS dep. (Down Platform)**	5.30	For detailed instructions for dealing with the Royal Train at Llandrindod Wells, see page 17.
3	50	Penybont .. .. pass	C5.38½S	
3	62½	Penybont Tunnel .. "	—	R.E. Circular O/RR (clause 16) in regard to the examination and protection of Tunnels must be observed. (See local Notice issued by District Engineer.)
4	11	Penybont Junction .. "	C5.41½S	
6	45	Dolau .. .. .. "	5.46	
10	16	Llanbister Road .. "	C5.53S	
13	13	Llangunllo .. .. "	C5.58S	

TIME TABLE OF ROYAL TRAIN—LLANDRINDOD WELLS TO STABLING POINT BETWEEN MARSH FARM JUNCTION AND HARTON ROAD (ON MUCH WENLOCK BRANCH), THURSDAY, 23rd OCTOBER, 1952—*continued.*

Distances from Llandrindod Wells. Mls.	Chs.	PRINCIPAL STATIONS AND INTERMEDIATE SIGNAL BOXES.	TIMES. p.m.	REMARKS.
13	42½	Llangunllo Tunnel .. pass	—	R.E. Circular O/RR (clause 16) in regard to the examination and protection of Tunnels must be observed. (See local Notice issued by District Engineer.)
17	3	Knucklas .. .. "	—	
19	48	Knighton .. .. "	C6. 9S	The 5.30 p.m. Shrewsbury to Swansea (Victoria) must run punctually in order to pass the Royal Train on the Double Line Section between Central Wales Junction and Knighton.
23	67	Bucknell .. .. "	6.16	
29	25	Broome .. .. .. "	—	
31	71	Craven Arms & Stokesay "	6.31	
35	7	**MARSH FARM JCT.** { arr. dep.	6.39 7. 0	**Change Engines. Gas and Water as required.** Engine No. 7913 to work the Royal Train Marsh Farm Junction to Stabling Point to leave Coleham Shed 5‖10 p.m. and arrive Marsh Farm Junction 5‖50 p.m. For detailed instructions for dealing with the Royal Train at Marsh Farm Junction, see page 17. The 6.26 p.m. Shrewsbury to Hereford to be held at Church Stretton until the "Blocking Back outside Home Signal" for the Down Line is cleared by Marsh Farm Junction.
35	67	**STABLING POINT .. arr. (Between Marsh Farm Junction and Harton Road)**	7.10	For detailed instructions for dealing with the Royal Train at Stabling Point, see page 17.

TIME TABLE OF ROYAL TRAIN—STABLING POINT BETWEEN MARSH FARM JUNCTION AND HARTON ROAD (ON MUCH WENLOCK BRANCH) TO SHREWSBURY, FRIDAY, 24th OCTOBER, 1952.

The formation of the Royal Train leaving Marsh Farm Junction will be similar and the order of the vehicles the same as from Llandrindod Wells (see page 8).

The Engine, or where more than one is used, the Leading Engine, to carry FOUR HEAD LAMPS, viz. one at the foot of the chimney, one at each end of the buffer beam, and one in the centre of the buffer beam. (Important.—See paragraph 1 of R.E. Circular O/RR, dated December, 1950.)

The Train will carry TWO TAIL LAMPS. (Important.—See paragraph 2 of R.E. Circular O/RR, dated December, 1950.)

The Head Lamps and Tail Lamps must be lighted before leaving the Stabling Point and Marsh Farm Junction.

The Train will run on the Main Line from Marsh Farm Junction to Shrewsbury (Up and Down Platform).

WORKING OF TRAIN ENGINES.

The engines (Nos. 7030 and 7036) to work the Royal Train from Marsh Farm Junction to Shrewsbury, to leave Coleham Shed, tenders leading, at 8‖5 a.m., via Long Lane Crossing, and arrive Marsh Farm Junction at 9‖0 a.m.

THE PERMANENT AND TEMPORARY SPEED RESTRICTIONS MUST BE STRICTLY OBSERVED.

Distances from Stabling Point. Mls.	Chs.	PRINCIPAL STATIONS AND INTERMEDIATE SIGNAL BOXES.	TIMES. a.m.	REMARKS.
—	—	**STABLING POINT .. dep. (Between Marsh Farm Junction and Harton Road)**	9.25	For detailed instructions for dealing with the Royal Train at Stabling Point, see page 17. Engine No. 6976 to work the Royal Train from Stabling Point to Marsh Farm Junction to leave Coleham Shed 7‖45 a.m., Marsh Farm Junction arrive 8‖25 a.m. Reverse. Depart 8‖27 a.m., Stabling Point arrive 8‖35 a.m.
—	60	**MARSH FARM JCT.** { arr. dep.	9.35 9.55	**Change Engines. Train Reverses.** For detailed instructions for dealing with the Royal Train at Marsh Farm Junction, see page 17. The 7.28 a.m. Hereford to Shrewsbury } Must run The 7.50 a.m. Shrewsbury to Hereford } punctually.
2	7	Marsh Brook .. .. pass	—	
4	56½	Church Stretton .. "	10. 6	
8	17	Leebotwood .. .. "	—	
11	6	Dorrington .. .. "	—	
13	14	Condover .. .. "	—	
16	49	Sutton Bridge Junction "	—	
16	69	Coleham .. .. .. "	10.26	The 8.55 a.m. Birkenhead to Paddington to be held at Coton Hill South until the Royal Train has arrived at the Up and Down Platform at Shrewsbury and the Royal Party has left the Station. The 9.49 a.m. Welshpool to Shrewsbury to be held at Hookagate until the Royal Train has arrived at the Up and Down Platform at Shrewsbury and the Royal Party has left the Station. The 8.8 a.m. Solihull to Birkenhead to be held at Upton Magna until the Royal Train has arrived at the Up and Down Platform at Shrewsbury and the Royal Party has left the Station.
17	41½	**SHREWSBURY .. .. arr. (Up and Down Platform)**	10.30	For detailed instructions for dealing with the Royal Train at Shrewsbury, see page 18. **Train to be turned via Abbey Foregate, English Bridge Junction and Coton Hill North in accordance with instructions shewn in the Chester District Operating Superintendent's Notice. The Royal Train to be stabled at Coton Hill (No. 1 Up Siding).**

Working timetable for the Royal Train Paddington–Llandrindod. Llandrindod–Shrewsbury–Paddington. 22, 23 and 24 October 1952–continued.

TIME TABLE OF ROYAL TRAIN—SHREWSBURY TO PADDINGTON, FRIDAY, 24th OCTOBER, 1952.

The Engine, or where more than one is used, the Leading Engine, to carry FOUR HEAD LAMPS, viz. one at the foot of the chimney, one at each end of the buffer beam, and one in the centre of the buffer beam. (Important.—See paragraph 1 of R.E. Circular O/RR, dated December, 1950.)

The Train will carry TWO TAIL LAMPS. (Important.—See paragraph 2 of R.E. Circular O/RR, dated December, 1950.)

The Head Lamps and Tail Lamps must be lighted before leaving Shrewsbury.

The Train will run on the Main Line throughout the journey; via the Up Middle Line at Birmingham (Snow Hill), Leamington Spa, Ardley, Bicester North, Brill & Ludgershall, Haddenham, Princes Risborough, High Wycombe, Beaconsfield, Gerrards Cross, Denham and Greenford.

WORKING OF TRAIN ENGINES.

The engines (Nos. 7030 and 7036) to work the Royal Train from Shrewsbury to Paddington, to leave Coleham Shed, chimneys leading, at 2||0 p.m., via Abbey Foregate, and arrive Shrewsbury Station Up Main Siding 2||15 p.m.

FORMATION (*FROM ENGINES*) LEAVING SHREWSBURY:—

	BRAKE FIRST	No. 5155	
	SALOON	„ 45005	
	H.M. THE QUEEN'S SALOON	„ 799	
	SALOON	„ 798	
	DINING SALOON	„ 76	
L.M.R. Stock.	SALOON	„ 807	482 tons.
	SLEEPING SALOON	„ 495	
	SALOON	„ 806	
	DINING SALOON	„ 77	
	SLEEPING SALOON	„ 477	
	BRAKE FIRST	„ 5154	
	Length of Train (excluding Engines)	727 feet 10½ inches.	

The distance from the centre of the footplate of the leading engine to the centre of the principal door of H.M. The Queen's Saloon No. 799 is approximately 279 feet 9¾ inches.

THE PERMANENT AND TEMPORARY SPEED RESTRICTIONS MUST BE STRICTLY OBSERVED.

Distances from Shrewsbury. Mls.	Chs.	PRINCIPAL STATIONS AND INTERMEDIATE SIGNAL BOXES.	TIMES. p.m.	REMARKS.
—	—	**SHREWSBURY .. dep. (Up Main Line Platform)**	**3.20**	For detailed instructions for dealing with the Royal Train at Shrewsbury, see page 18. The 2.35 p.m. Shrewsbury to Paddington must run punctually. The 3.10 p.m. Shrewsbury to Stafford (L.M.R.) to be held at Shrewsbury to follow the Royal Train. The 1.10 p.m. Birkenhead to Shrewsbury to be held at Coton Hill South until the Royal Train has cleared Abbey Foregate. The 2.35 p.m. (Parcels) Crewe to Pontypool Road to be held at Harlescott Crossing until the Royal Train has cleared Abbey Foregate.
—	20	Severn Bridge Junction pass	—	
—	43	Abbey Foregate.. .. „	—	
—	—	Belvidere Signals .. „	—	Intermediate Block Signals—Up Distant and Up Home.
9	65¼	Market Drayton Junction „	—	
10	23	Wellington .. .. „	3.37	To run via Up Main Line. The 2.55 p.m. Wellington to Wolverhampton must run punctually. The 3†35 p.m. Empty Stock Wellington to Cosford to be held at Wellington until the Royal Train has cleared Oakengates.
10	56½	Stafford Junction .. „	—	
13	32¾	Oakengates Tunnel .. „	—	R.E. Circular O/RR (clause 16) in regard to the examination and protection of Tunnels must be observed. (See local Notice issued by District Engineer.)

WORKING OF EMPTY ROYAL TRAIN, FRIDAY, 24th OCTOBER, 1952.

PADDINGTON TO L.M.R. via KENSINGTON (OLYMPIA).

The Empty Train must be worked from Paddington to Kensington (Olympia) as shewn below:—

THE TRAIN TO CARRY "A" HEAD CODE and be given a clear run.

PRINCIPAL STATIONS AND INTERMEDIATE SIGNAL BOXES.	TIMES. p.m.	REMARKS.
PADDINGTON (No. 8 Platform).. dep.	7†50	To run via the Down Carriage Line to Subway Junction. Absolute Block Working to be maintained for the passage of this train.
Subway Junction .. .. .. pass	**RL**	
Old Oak Common East .. arr. / dep.	8† 0 / 8†15	To be dealt with on the Down Relief Line at Old Oak Common East. Shunter to be provided. Engine to be detached at Old Oak Common East Down Relief Starting Signal, run to Old Oak Common West (Down Northern Line), thence via Up Relief to Old Oak Common East. Empty Train to work direct from Old Oak Common East to Kensington (Olympia). The 7.55 p.m. (Parcels) Kensington (Olympia) to Penzance to run to and be dealt with on the Down Goods Avoiding Line at Old Oak Common.
North Pole Junction .. .. pass	8†17	
KENSINGTON (OLYMPIA) .. arr.	8†25	

L.M.R. take forward from Kensington (Olympia) at 8†55 p.m. en route to Wolverton (arrive 10†45 p.m.).

BREAKDOWN VANS, CRANES AND GANGS.

The Breakdown Vans and Gangs must be held in readiness as under:—

Depot.	To be in readiness:— From	To
Wednesday night/Thursday morning, 22nd/23rd October.		
Old Oak Common	8.30 p.m.	12. 0 night
Banbury	10.30 p.m.	1.30 a.m.
Stafford Road	11.30 p.m.	3. 0 a.m.
Coleham	12.30 a.m.	4.45 a.m.
Thursday, 23rd October.		
Craven Arms	9.30 a.m.*	7.45 p.m.
Swansea (Paxton Street)	9. 0 a.m.	3. 0 p.m.
Friday, 24th October.		
Coleham	7. 0 a.m.	5. 0 p.m.
Stafford Road	3. 0 p.m.	6. 0 p.m.
Banbury	4. 0 p.m.	7.15 p.m.
Old Oak Common	5. 0 p.m.	8.30 p.m.

* Breakdown Vans, Crane (in steam) and Gang to be available at Coleham from 8.30 a.m. and proceed at 8.45 a.m. to Craven Arms, arrive 9.30 a.m., on 23rd October.

STAND-BY ENGINES.

Suitable engines to be held in readiness as under:—

Wednesday night/Thursday morning, 22nd/23rd October.
At Old Oak Common, Banbury, Tyseley, Stafford Road and Coleham.

Thursday morning, 23rd October.
At Craven Arms.

Thursday afternoon, 23rd October.
At Llandrindod Wells and Coleham.

Friday morning, 24th October.
At Coleham.

Friday afternoon, 24th October.
At Coleham, Stafford Road, Tyseley and Banbury.

INSTRUCTIONS IN CONNECTION WITH THE WORKING OF THE ROYAL TRAIN.

Note.—The intimation to the Guard that all is in order for the loaded Royal Train to start from any point must be given by the Operating Superintendent's Chief Inspector accompanying the train, who must also take charge of any other movements required to be made with the train.

JOURNEY, PADDINGTON TO MARSH FARM JUNCTION.
WEDNESDAY/THURSDAY, 22nd/23rd OCTOBER, 1952.

WOLVERHAMPTON.

1. The Royal Train drawn by Engines Nos. 7030 and 7036 will call at Wolverhampton for water, etc., and fifteen minutes before it is due to arrive Points Nos. 47 and 49 at Wolverhampton South Box and Nos. 43 and 44 at Wolverhampton North Box must be clipped and padlocked in the normal position.

2. The Royal Train must be brought to a stand at the Wolverhampton North Down Main Home Signal, which will be in the "off" position. As soon as the train has been brought to a stand the Signalman at Wolverhampton South Box must set Points No. 66 for the Down Goods Loop and they must be clipped and padlocked in that position. After the Guards have applied their hand brakes Engines Nos. 7030 and 7036 must be detached by the Fireman of Engine No. 7036 and proceed to the water column. A Shunter must be in attendance, and after water has been taken he must handsignal the engines back to the train, to which they must be attached by the Fireman of Engine No. 7036.

MARSH FARM JUNCTION.

1. The Royal Train will be stabled between 176m. 64c. and 176m. 50c. on the former Marsh Farm Junction–Much Wenlock Branch Line. A rail will be removed from the line at 175m. 0c. near Harton Road, converting the line to a siding.

2. Thirty minutes before the Royal Train is due to arrive at Marsh Farm Junction, Engine No. 7913 to draw the train to the stabling point must be placed on the Stabling Siding clear of Points No. 18. All points which become facing for the movement of this engine must be clipped and padlocked. Points No. 16 must be clipped and padlocked in the normal position and so remain until the Royal Train has left for Llandrindod Wells.

3. The Royal Train worked by Engines Nos. 7030 and 7036 will arrive on the Down Main Line at Marsh Farm Junction and must be brought to a stand at the Down Main Starting Signal. The Guards must apply the hand brakes. Points No. 17 must then be set, clipped and padlocked for the Stabling Siding and Points No. 18 clipped and padlocked in the normal position. Engine No. 7913 must then be piloted from the Stabling Siding to the Down Main by the District Operating Inspector, where it must be attached to the Royal Train by the Fireman. Engines Nos. 7030 and 7036 must then be detached from the train by the Fireman of Engine No. 7036 and remain at a stand until instructed to move by the District Operating Inspector.

4. The Royal Train must then proceed to the Stabling Point and be brought to a stand with the centre of the footplate gangway of the engine opposite a white post with white light affixed, situated on the Driver's side at 176m. 52½c. As soon as the train has been brought to a stand the Guards must apply the hand brakes. Engine No. 7913 will remain attached to the Royal Train throughout the night.

5. As soon as the Royal Train has proceeded into the Stabling Siding clear of Points No. 18, Points No. 17 must be restored to normal and be clipped and padlocked in that position. The keys of all padlocks must be handed to the Operating Superintendent's Chief Inspector accompanying the train.

JOURNEY—STABLING POINT, MARSH FARM JUNCTION TO LLANDRINDOD WELLS.
THURSDAY, 23rd OCTOBER, 1952.

MARSH FARM JUNCTION.

1. The keys of all padlocks must be obtained from the Operating Superintendent's Chief Inspector at 7.30 a.m. and conveyed to Marsh Farm Junction. Engines Nos. 7030 and 7036 to work the Royal Train to Llandrindod Wells will arrive on the Down Main Line from Coleham at 8.15 a.m. and must be brought to a stand in advance of Points No. 17. These points must then be unclipped and set, clipped and padlocked for the Stabling Siding and Engines Nos. 7030 and 7036 must be piloted to the Royal Train by the District Operating Inspector.

2. Engines Nos. 7030 and 7036 must be attached to the Royal Train by the Fireman of Engine No. 7036, after which Engine No. 7913 must be detached by the Fireman of that engine and remain at a stand until instructed to move by the District Operating Inspector.

LLANDRINDOD WELLS.

1. The public road level crossing at Llandrindod Wells No. 1 Box must be closed to all road traffic 15 minutes before the Royal Train is due to arrive.

2. Thirty minutes before the Royal Train is due to arrive Engine No. 6971 must be placed in the Up and Down Refuge Siding at Llandrindod Wells No. 2 Box and all points which become facing for the movements of this engine must be clipped and padlocked.

3. Points No. 9 at Llandrindod Wells No. 2 Box must be set for the Down Main and be clipped and padlocked in that position before "Line Clear" is obtained from Howey for the Royal Train. Fifteen minutes before the Royal Train is due to arrive Points Nos. 10, 16 and 17 must be clipped and padlocked in the normal position.

4. The Royal Train worked by Engines Nos. 7030 and 7036 will arrive at the Down Platform and must be brought to a stand with the centre of the footplate gangway of the leading engine opposite a white post situated on the Driver's side 62¼ yards in advance of the Llandrindod Wells No. 2 Box Down Main Starting Signal. The Guards must apply the hand brakes.

5. After the Royal Party has left the Station, Points No. 10 must be unclipped, and those points and Points No. 11 must be set, clipped and padlocked for Engine No. 6971 to be piloted to the rear of the Royal Train, to which it must be attached by the Fireman. Engines No. 7030 and 7036 must then be detached by the Fireman of Engine No. 7036 and proceed "light" to Llandovery.

6. The Empty Royal Train must then be drawn to the Up and Down Refuge Siding. All points which become facing for movements of the Empty Royal Train and the engines in connection therewith must be clipped and padlocked. After the engine has run round and has been attached at the Swansea end, Points Nos. 9 and 11 (Llandrindod Wells No. 1 Box) and Nos. 10, 11 and 17 (Llandrindod Wells No. 2 Box) must be clipped and padlocked in the normal position.

Working timetable for the Royal Train Paddington–Llandrindod. Llandrindod–Shrewsbury. Shrewsbury–Paddington. 22, 23 and 24 October 1952–continued.

JOURNEY—LLANDRINDOD WELLS TO MARSH FARM JUNCTION STABLING POINT.

THURSDAY, 23rd OCTOBER, 1952.

LLANDRINDOD WELLS.

1. Engines Nos. 7030 and 7036 to work the Royal Train forward will arrive at Llandrindod Wells No. 2 at 4.45 p.m. and must stand on the Up Main Line in advance of Points No. 17.

2. The Royal Train will start from the Down Platform and after the departure of the 3.5 p.m. Passenger train Shrewsbury to Swansea (Victoria) Points No. 9 must be set for the Down Main Line and be clipped and padlocked in that position. An Electric Train Token for the Llandrindod Wells–Howey Section must be withdrawn and handed to the Driver of Engine No. 6971. The "Blocking Back outside Home Signal" must also be sent to and acknowledgment received from, Llandrindod Wells No. 1 Box, after which Points No. 11 and 10 at Llandrindod Wells No. 2 Box must be set, clipped and padlocked for the train to be drawn by Engine No. 6971 from the Up and Down Refuge Siding to the Down Main Platform, where it must be brought to a stand with the centre of the footplate gangway opposite a Handsignalman exhibiting a red handsignal on the Driver's side 42 yards in advance of Llandrindod Wells No. 2 Box Down Main Starting Signal. The Guards must apply the hand brakes. Points Nos. 10 and 11 must then be restored to normal and be clipped and padlocked. Points No. 17 (slip in crossover road) must be clipped and padlocked in the normal position and Crossover Points Nos. 16 and 17 must be set, clipped and padlocked for Engines Nos. 7030 and 7036 to be piloted by the District Operating Inspector from the Up Main Line to the Royal Train, to which they must be attached by the Fireman of Engine No. 7036. Engine No. 6971 must then be detached by the Fireman of that engine and remain at a stand until instructed to move by the District Operating Inspector. Points No. 10 and Crossover Points Nos. 16 and 17 must remain clipped and padlocked until the Royal Train has proceeded to the Up Main Line through the crossover road.

3. The keys of the padlocks must be held by the Operating Superintendent's Chief Inspector accompanying the train, while it is at Llandrindod Wells.

MARSH FARM JUNCTION.

1. Engine No. 7913 to work the Royal Train from Marsh Farm Junction to the Stabling Point must be placed on the Stabling Siding clear of Points No. 18 thirty minutes before the Royal Train is due to arrive and those points must then be clipped and padlocked in the normal position. All points which are not provided with facing point locks and bars and which become facing for the movements of this engine must be clipped and padlocked.

2. Gas and water tanks must be placed at the stop block of the spur on the Up Loop, at the Craven Arms end at 5.45 p.m., after which Points No. 14 at Marsh Farm Junction must be clipped and padlocked in the normal position.

3. The Royal Train worked by Engines Nos. 7030 amd 7036 will arrive on the Up Main Line at Marsh Farm Junction and must be brought to a stand with the centre of the footplate gangway of the leading engine opposite a white post with white light affixed, situated on the Driver's side 42¼ yards in advance of the Up Inner Home Signal. The Guards must apply the hand brakes. Engines Nos. 7030 and 7036 must then be detached by the Fireman of Engine No. 7036 and must draw ahead to the Up Main Starting Signal and remain at a stand until the Royal Train has proceeded to the Stabling Point. Any necessary gassing and watering of the Royal Train will be carried out from the gas and water tanks in the Up Loop. Points Nos. 18 and 16 must be set, clipped and padlocked for Engine No. 7913 to be piloted to the Royal Train by the District Operating Inspector and it must be attached to the train by the Fireman.

4. The Royal Train must then proceed to the Stabling Point and must be brought to a stand with the centre of the footplate gangway of the engine opposite a white post with white light affixed, situated on the Driver's side at 176m. 52¼c. The Guards must apply the hand brakes.

5. As soon as the Royal Train has proceeded into the Stabling Siding clear of Points No. 18, those points and Points No. 16 must be restored to normal and be clipped and padlocked in that position. Points No. 17 must be clipped and padlocked in the normal position. The keys of all padlocks must be handed to the Operating Superintendent's Chief Inspector accompanying the train.

JOURNEY—STABLING POINT, MARSH FARM JUNCTION TO SHREWSBURY.

FRIDAY, 24th OCTOBER, 1952.

MARSH FARM JUNCTION.

1. At 8.0 a.m. the keys of all padlocks must be obtained from the Operating Superintendent's Chief Inspector accompanying the train by the District Operating Inspector, who must then proceed to Marsh Farm Junction. Engine No. 6976 to draw the Royal Train from the Stabling Point to the Up Main Line at Marsh Farm Junction will arrive from Coleham at 8.25 a.m., and after Points No. 17 have been unclipped and set for the Stabling Siding and clipped and padlocked, the engine must be piloted to the Royal Train by the District Operating Inspector. As soon as Engine No. 6976 has cleared Points No. 18, Points No. 17 must be restored to normal and be clipped and padlocked in that position.

2. At 9.0 a.m. Engines Nos. 7030 and 7036 to work the Royal Train from Marsh Farm Junction to Shrewsbury will arrive from Long Lane Crossing and must be brought to a stand on the Up Main Line on the Shrewsbury side of the Up Loop Points No. 21, which must be clipped and padlocked in the normal position. The "Blocking Back outside Home Signal" must be sent to, and acknowledgment received from, Marsh Brook and Long Lane Crossing Boxes. Points No. 14 must be clipped and padlocked in the normal position and Points No. 16 must be set, clipped and padlocked for the Stabling Siding. Points No. 18 must be set for the Up Main Line and be clipped and padlocked in that position. A Handsignalman exhibiting a green handsignal must be provided at Signal No. 32, which will be passed in the "On" position for the movement of the Royal Train from the Stabling Point to the Up Main Line.

3. Engine No. 6976 must be attached to the Royal Train by the Fireman and Engine No. 7913 must then be detached by the Fireman of that engine and remain at a stand until instructed to move by the District Operating Inspector. The train must be drawn to the Up Main Line and be brought to a stand with the centre of the footplate gangway of the engine opposite a white post situated on the Driver's side 18 yards on the Craven Arms side of the Up Main Home Signal. The Guards must apply the hand brakes.

4. Points No. 16 must then be restored to normal. Engines Nos. 7030 and 7036 must be piloted to the Royal Train by the District Operating Inspector and be attached to the train by the Fireman of Engine No. 7036. Engine No. 6976 must then be detached from the train by the Fireman and must remain at a stand until instructed to move by the District Operating Inspector.

Journey—Stabling Point, Marsh Farm Junction to Shrewsbury, Friday, 24th October, 1952—*continued.*

SHREWSBURY.

1. Fifteen minutes before the Royal Train is due to arrive Points Nos. 8 and 24 in the Up and Down Platform Line at Shrewsbury Central Box must be clipped and padlocked in the normal position. Points No. 36 at Crewe Junction set for the Down Main Line must be clipped and padlocked in that position and Points No. 29 must be set for the Up Main Line and be clipped and padlocked in that position. Points Nos. 59 and 67 at Crewe Junction must be clipped and padlocked in the normal position. Points No. 46 at Abbey Foregate Box must be clipped and padlocked in the normal position and Points No. 48 must be set for the Down Bay Line and be clipped and padlocked in that position.

2. The Royal Train drawn by Engines Nos. 7030 and 7036 must run to the Up and Down Platform Line (Platforms 5 and 6) and must be brought to a stand with the centre of the footplate gangway of the leading engine opposite a white post situated on the Driver's side at the foot of the platform ramp 33 yards in advance of the Banner Repeating Signal for Crewe Junction Down Home Signal. The Guards must apply the hand brakes.

3. No movement of the Empty Royal Train or engines in connection therewith must be made until after the Royal Party has left the platform. The Empty Royal Train will be turned via the triangle, Severn Bridge Junction—Abbey Foregate—English Bridge Junction, and then be stabled in the Up Siding at Coton Hill North (see the Chester District Operating Superintendent's special notice for details of working). All points not provided with facing point locks and bars, or track circuits in lieu of bars, which become facing for the movement of the Empty Royal Train, or engines in connection therewith, must be clipped and padlocked.

JOURNEY—SHREWSBURY TO PADDINGTON.

FRIDAY, 24th OCTOBER, 1952.

SHREWSBURY.

1. The Royal Train will leave from the Up Main Platform at Shrewsbury and before the Empty Royal Train is drawn to the Up Main Platform from Coton Hill the Signalman at Crewe Junction must send the "Blocking Back outside Home Signal" to, and receive acknowledgment from, Crewe Bank Box. Points Nos. 49 and 58 in the Up Main Platform Line at Shrewsbury Central Box must be clipped and padlocked in the normal position and so remain until the Royal Train has left for Paddington.

2. All points which become facing for the movements of the Empty Royal Train and the engines in connection therewith and which are not provided with facing point locks and bars, or track circuits in lieu of bars, must be clipped and padlocked. (See Chester District Operating Superintendent's Special Notice for details of working of the Empty Royal Train and engines in connection therewith.)

3. As soon as the Empty Royal Train has been placed in position at the Platform and Engines Nos. 7030 and 7036 have been attached, Points No. 59 at Crewe Junction must be set for the Up and Down Platform Line and be clipped and padlocked in that position. Points Nos. 29 and 34 must be clipped and padlocked in the normal position.

4. At Severn Bridge Junction Points Nos. 55, 117, 107 and 136 must be clipped and padlocked in the normal position and Points No. 149 must be set for the Bay Line and be clipped and padlocked in that position. The keys of the padlocks must be handed to the Operating Superintendent's Chief Inspector accompanying the Royal Train.

PADDINGTON.

1. The Station Master, Paddington, must arrange for the platforms and approaches to be cleared of all unauthorised persons 30 minutes before the Royal Train is due to arrive.

2. The Royal Train will run to No. 8 Platform Line and must be brought to a stand with the centre of the footplate gangway of the leading engine opposite a Handsignalman exhibiting a red handsignal on the Driver's side. The Guards must apply the hand brakes.

Instructions for Signalling the Royal Train—*continued.*

Journey—Paddington to Marsh Farm Junction, Wednesday, 22nd October, 1952 —*continued.*

Instructions for Signalling the Royal Train through Short Sections—*continued.*

Name of Signal Box affected.	Signalman to return "Line Clear" for the Train to the Box in the rear when he has received	Signalman to return "Train out of Section" for the train preceding the Train referred to in this Notice and for the Train itself, provided it is complete with tail lamp, when he has received
Leebotwood	The Signalman at Leebotwood must obtain "Line Clear" from Church Stretton and lower Dudgeley Intermediate Block Signals before allowing the train to enter the Advanced Section. "Train entering Section" signal to be sent to Church Stretton when the Train passes the Box. **Note.**—Special attention is directed to the instructions on page 61 of the L.M. & S. and G.W. Joint Sectional Appendix to the Working Time Tables (pages 25 and 26 of Supplement No. 4). A Handsignalman to be stationed at Dudgeley Down Intermediate Block Home Signal 30 minutes before the Royal Train is due to pass. A Signal Fitter specially to examine the signal fittings before the Royal Train is due and to remain in attendance until after it has passed.	
Marsh Brook	—	For the Royal Train when he has received "Train out of Section" from Marsh Farm Junction.
Marsh Farm Junction ..	"Line Clear" from Long Lane Crossing.	For the train preceding the Royal Train when the train has passed a quarter of a mile beyond the Home Signal and is continuing its journey. For the Royal Train when the Train has drawn clear on to the Stabling Siding, the points have been re-set for the Main Line and Engines Nos. 7030 and 7036 have proceeded to Long Lane Crossing. *See Special Instructions, page 16.*

JOURNEY—MARSH FARM JUNCTION TO LLANDRINDOD WELLS.

THURSDAY, 23rd OCTOBER, 1952.

Note.—The instructions given below are supplemental to the General Instructions, *and will apply in clear weather and during fog or falling snow.*

SPECIAL OPENING OF SIGNAL BOXES:—

Broome.—To open at 8.30 a.m.

Hopton Heath.—To open at 8.30 a.m. and remain open until the Royal Train has cleared.

Knighton No. 1.—To open at 8.30 a.m. and remain open until the Royal Train has cleared.

Dolau.—To open at 8.45 a.m.

ASKING "IS LINE CLEAR?"—The Signalman at Marsh Farm Junction to ask "Is Line Clear?" for the Royal Train five minutes prior to the booked time of departure of the Train.

INSTRUCTIONS FOR SIGNALLING THE ROYAL TRAIN THROUGH SHORT SECTIONS.

Name of Signal Box affected.	Signalman to return "Line Clear" for the Train to the Box in the rear when he has received	Signalman to return "Train out of Section" for the train preceding the Train referred to in this Notice and for the Train itself, provided it is complete with tail lamp, when he has received
Marsh Farm Junction ..	**Note.**—Before asking "Is Line Clear?" the Signalman at Marsh Farm Junction must send the "Blocking Back outside Home Signal" to, and receive acknowledgment from, Marsh Brook. *See Special Instructions, page 16.*	
Long Lane Crossing ..	"Line Clear" from Craven Arms Station.	"Train out of Section" from Craven Arms Station.
Craven Arms Station ..	"Line Clear" from Central Wales Junction.	"Train out of Section" from Central Wales Junction.
Central Wales Junction	**Note.**—The Signalman at Central Wales Junction must send the "Blocking Back outside Home Signal" to, and receive acknowledgment from, Onibury before returning "Line Clear."	

Note.—Between Central Wales Junction and Llandrindod Wells No. 2, to avoid delay to the Royal Train the "Is Line Clear?" signal must, provided the "Train out of Section" signal has been received for the previous train and the block indicator is in the normal position, be sent forward as soon as the "Is Line Clear?" signal has been acknowledged and before the "Train entering Section" signal has been received.

Working timetable for the Royal Train Paddington–Llandrindod. Llandrindod–Shrewsbury. Shrewsbury–Paddington. 22, 23 and 24 October 1952–continued.

Instructions for Signalling the Royal Train—*continued.*

Journey—Marsh Farm Junction to Llandrindod Wells, Thursday, 23rd October, 1952—*continued.*

Instructions for Signalling the Royal Train Through Short Sections—*continued.*

Name of Signal Box affected.	Signalman to return "Line Clear" for the Train to the Box in the rear when he has received	Signalman to return "Train out of Section" for the train preceding the Train referred to in this Notice and for the Train itself, provided it is complete with tail lamp, when he has received
Knighton No. 1 ..	"Line Clear" from Knighton No. 2	"Train out of Section" from Knighton No. 2.
Knighton No. 2 ..	"Line Clear" from Llangunllo ..	When the Train has passed a quarter of a mile beyond Home Signal and is continuing its journey.
	Note.—The Signalman at Knighton No. 2 to ask "Is Line Clear ?" for the Royal Train and withdraw a token for the Knighton No. 2–Llangunllo Section fifteen minutes before the Royal Train is due to pass.	
Llangunllo	**Note.**—The Signalman at Llangunllo to ask "Is Line Clear ?" for the Royal Train and withdraw a token for the Llangunllo–Llanbister Road Section fifteen minutes before the Royal Train is due to pass.	
Penybont Junction ..	**Note.**—The Signalman at Penybont Junction to ask "Is Line Clear ?" for the Royal Train and withdraw a token for the Penybont Junction–Penybont Section fifteen minutes before the Royal Train is due to pass.	
Penybont Station ..	"Line Clear" from Llandrindod No. 1.	When the Train has passed a quarter of a mile beyond Home Signal and is continuing its journey.
Llandrindod No. 1 ..	"Line Clear" from Llandrindod No. 2.	"Train out of Section" from Llandrindod No. 2.
Llandrindod No. 2 ..	"Line Clear" from Howey	For the Train referred to in this Notice when the Royal Party has left the Station, Engines Nos. 7030 and 7036 have left for Llandovery and the Empty Train has been drawn clear into the Down Sidings.
	Note.—The Signalman at Llandrindod No. 2 to withdraw a token for the Llandrindod No. 2–Howey Section fifteen minutes before the booked time of arrival of the Royal Train. *See Special Instructions, page 16.*	

JOURNEY—LLANDRINDOD WELLS TO MARSH FARM JUNCTION.

THURSDAY, 23rd OCTOBER, 1952.

Note.—The instructions given below are supplemental to the General Instructions, *and will apply in clear weather and during fog or falling snow.*

SPECIAL OPENING OF SIGNAL BOXES:—

Dolau.—To remain open until the Royal Train has cleared.

Knighton No. 1.—To open at 4.45 p.m. and remain open until the Royal Train has cleared.

Hopton Heath.—To open at 5.0 p.m. and remain open until the Royal Train has cleared.

Broome.—To remain open until the Royal Train has cleared.

ASKING "IS LINE CLEAR ?"—The Signalman at Llandrindod No. 2 to ask "Is Line Clear ?" for the Royal Train fifteen minutes prior to the booked time of departure of the Train.

SPECIAL INSTRUCTIONS FOR SIGNALLING THE ROYAL TRAIN.

Note.—Between Llandrindod Wells No. 2 and Central Wales Junction, to avoid delay to the Royal Train the "Is Line Clear ?" signal must, provided the "Train out of Section" signal has been received for the previous train and the block indicator is in the normal position, be sent forward as soon as the "Is Line Clear ?" signal has been acknowledged and before the "Train entering Section" signal has been received.

INSTRUCTIONS FOR SIGNALLING THE ROYAL TRAIN THROUGH SHORT SECTIONS.

Name of Signal Box affected.	Signalman to return "Line Clear" for the Train to the Box in the rear when he has received	Signalman to return "Train out of Section" for the train preceding the Train referred to in this Notice and for the Train itself, provided it is complete with tail lamp, when he has received
Penybont ..	"Line Clear" from Penybont Junction.	"Train out of Section" from Penybont Junction.
	Note.—The Signalman at Penybont to ask "Is Line Clear ?" for the Royal Train and withdraw a token for the Penybont–Penybont Junction Section fifteen minutes before the Royal Train is due to pass.	
Penybont Junction ..	"Line Clear" from Dolau	When the Train has passed a quarter of a mile beyond Home Signal and is continuing its journey.

Instructions for Signalling the Royal Train—*continued.*

Journey—Llandrindod Wells to Marsh Farm Junction, Thursday, 23rd October, 1952—*continued.*

Instructions for Signalling the Royal Train through Short Sections—*continued.*

Name of Signal Box affected.	Signalman to return "Line Clear" for the Train to the Box in the rear when he has received	Signalman to return "Train out of Section" for the train preceding the Train referred to in this Notice and for the Train itself, provided it is complete with tail lamp, when he has received
Llanbister Road ..	**Note.**—The Signalman at Llanbister Road to ask "Is Line Clear ?" for the Royal Train and withdraw a token for the Llanbister Road–Llangunllo Section fifteen minutes before the Royal Train is due to pass.	
Llangunllo	**Note.**—The Signalman at Llangunllo to ask "Is Line Clear ?" for the Royal Train and withdraw a token for the Llangunllo–Knighton No. 2 Section fifteen minutes before the Royal Train is due to pass.	
Knighton No. 2 ..	"Line Clear" from Knighton No. 1	"Train out of Section" from Knighton No. 1.
Knighton No. 1 ..	"Line Clear" from Bucknell ..	When the Train has passed a quarter of a mile beyond Home Signal and is continuing its journey.
Central Wales Junction	"Line Clear" from Craven Arms Station.	"Train out of Section" from Craven Arms Station.
	Note.—The Signalman at Central Wales Junction must send the "Blocking Back outside Home Signal" to, and receive acknowledgment from, Onibury before returning "Line Clear."	
Craven Arms Station ..	"Line Clear" from Long Lane Crossing.	When the Train has passed a quarter of a mile beyond Home Signal and is continuing its journey.
Marsh Farm Junction ..	"Line Clear" from Marsh Brook ..	For the Royal Train when Engines Nos. 7030 and 7036 have cleared towards Marsh Brook and the Royal Train has proceeded into the Stabling Siding, has cleared Points No. 18, and Points No. 16 have been set, clipped and padlocked in the normal position.
	Note.—The Signalman at Marsh Farm Junction to send the "Blocking Back outside Home Signal" to, and receive acknowledgment from, Marsh Brook on the Down Line before returning "Line Clear." **Note.**—As soon as the Royal Train has been brought to a stand the "Cancelling" signal must be sent to Marsh Brook, and "Line Clear" obtained for light engines coupled when ready to proceed. *See Special Instructions, page 17.*	

JOURNEY—MARSH FARM JUNCTION TO SHREWSBURY.

FRIDAY, 24th OCTOBER, 1952.

Note.—The instructions given below are supplemental to the General Instructions, *and will apply in clear weather and during fog or falling snow.*

ASKING "IS LINE CLEAR ?"—The Signalman at Marsh Farm Junction to ask "Is Line Clear ?" for the Royal Train five minutes prior to the booked time of departure of the Train.

The "Is Line Clear ?" signal must be arrested at Bayston Hill until the "Train Approaching" signal is received from the box in the rear.

On receipt of "Train entering Section" from	"Train Approaching" Signal to be sent by	To be repeated through to
Church Stretton	Leebotwood	Bayston Hill.

INSTRUCTIONS FOR SIGNALLING THE ROYAL TRAIN THROUGH SHORT SECTIONS.

Name of Signal Box affected.	Signalman to return "Line Clear" for the Train to the Box in the rear when he has received	Signalman to return "Train out of Section" for the train preceding the Train referred to in this Notice and for the Train itself, provided it is complete with tail lamp, when he has received
Sutton Bridge Junction	"Line Clear" from Coleham ..	"Train out of Section" from Coleham.
	Note.—The Signalman at Sutton Bridge Junction must send the "Blocking Back outside Home Signal" to, and receive acknowledgment from, Hookagate, before returning "Line Clear" and must also withdraw the token for the Sutton Bridge Junction–Berrington S.V. section in accordance with E.T.T. Regulation 13, and must not restore it until "Train out of Section" has been received for the Royal Train.	
Coleham	"Line Clear" from English Bridge Junction.	"Train out of Section" from English Bridge Junction.
English Bridge Junction.	"Line Clear" from Severn Bridge Junction.	"Train out of Section" from Severn Bridge Junction.

Instructions for Signalling the Royal Train—*continued.*

Journey—Marsh Farm Junction to Shrewsbury, Friday, 24th October, 1952—*continued.*

Instructions for Signalling the Royal Train through Short Sections—*continued.*

Name of Signal Box affected.	Signalman to return "Line Clear" for the Train to the Box in the rear when he has received	Signalman to return "Train out of Section" for the train preceding the Train referred to in this Notice and for the Train itself, provided it is complete with tail lamp, when he has received
Severn Bridge Junction	"Line Clear" from Shrewsbury Central.	"Train out of Section" from Shrewsbury Central.
	Note.—The Signalman at Severn Bridge Junction must send the "Blocking Back outside Home Signal" on the Down Main Line to, and receive acknowledgment from, Abbey Foregate before returning "Line Clear."	
Shrewsbury Central ..	"Line Clear" from Crewe Junction	"Train out of Section" from Crewe Junction.
Crewe Junction ..	"Line Clear" from Coton Hill South	—
	Note.—Before returning "Line Clear" the Signalman at Crewe Junction must set Points No. 36 for the Down Main Line and must send the "Blocking Back outside Home Signal" to, and receive acknowledgment from, Coton Hill South, and to, and receive acknowledgment from, Shrewsbury Central Box for the Down Main and Down Platform Lines. *See Special Instructions, page 18.*	

JOURNEY—SHREWSBURY TO PADDINGTON.

FRIDAY, 24th OCTOBER, 1952.

Note.—The instructions given below are supplemental to the General Instructions, *and will apply in clear weather and during fog or falling snow.*

SPECIAL OPENING OF SIGNAL BOXES.

Walcot	To remain open until after the Royal Train has cleared.
Albrighton	To open at 2.30 p.m. and remain open until the Royal Train has cleared.
Dunstall Park	To open as directed and remain open until after the Royal Train has cleared.
Swan Village Junction South	To open as directed and remain open until after the Royal Train has cleared.
Tyseley North	To open as directed and remain open until after the Royal Train has cleared.
Acock's Green	To open as directed and remain open until after the Royal Train has cleared.
Widney Manor	To open as directed and remain open until after the Royal Train has cleared.
Knowle & Dorridge ..	To open as directed and remain open until after the Royal Train has cleared.
Rowington Junction ..	To open as directed and remain open until after the Royal Train has cleared.
Hatton North	To open as directed and remain open until after the Royal Train has cleared.
Warwick North	To open as directed and remain open until after the Royal Train has cleared.
Warwick (Avon Bridge) ..	To open as directed and remain open until after the Royal Train has cleared.
Greaves Siding	To open as directed and remain open until after the Royal Train has cleared.
Knighton	To open as directed and remain open until after the Royal Train has cleared.
King's Sutton Junction ..	To open as directed and remain open until after the Royal Train has cleared.
Blackthorn	To open at 5.0 p.m. and remain open until 6.15 p.m.
High Wycombe North ..	To remain open until the Royal Train has cleared.
Northolt Junction West ..	To open at 5.30 p.m. and remain open until the Royal Train has cleared.
Perivale	To open at 5.45 p.m. and remain open until the Royal Train has cleared.

ASKING "IS LINE CLEAR ?"—The Signalman at Shrewsbury Severn Bridge Junction Box to ask "Is Line Clear ?" for the Royal Train five minutes prior to the booked time of departure of the Train.

The "Is Line Clear ?" Signal must be arrested at the following Signal Boxes until the "Train Approaching" signal is received from the Box in the rear:—Admaston, Shifnal, Oxley North Junction, Bilston Central, Handsworth Junction, Bordesley North, Solihull, Lapworth, Budbrook, Fosse Road, Fenny Compton, Cropredy, King's Sutton Junction, Bicester, Ashendon Junction, Saunderton, Beaconsfield, West Ruislip, North Acton Junction.

On receipt of "Train entering Section" from	"Train Approaching" Signal to be sent by	To be repeated through to
Severn Bridge Junction ..	Abbey Foregate ..	Admaston.
Allscott Sugar Works ..	Admaston ..	Shifnal.
Shifnal ..	Cosford ..	Oxley North Junction.
Codsall ..	Oxley North Junction ..	Bilston Central.
Bilston Central ..	Wednesbury North ..	Handsworth Junction.
Handsworth Junction ..	Handsworth Station ..	Bordesley North.
Bordesley North ..	Bordesley South ..	Solihull.
Solihull ..	Widney Manor ..	Lapworth.
Lapworth ..	Rowington Junction ..	Budbrook.
Budbrook ..	Warwick North ..	Fosse Road.
Fosse Road ..	Southam Road & Harbury ..	Fenny Compton.
Fenny Compton ..	Claydon Crossing ..	Cropredy.
Cropredy ..	Ironstone Branch ..	King's Sutton Junction.
King's Sutton Junction ..	Aynho Junction ..	Bicester.
Bicester ..	Blackthorn ..	Ashendon Junction.
Haddenham ..	Princes Risborough North ..	Saunderton.
Saunderton ..	West Wycombe ..	Beaconsfield.
Wilton Park ..	Gerrards Cross ..	West Ruislip.
West Ruislip ..	Northolt Junction West ..	North Acton Junction.

Working timetable for the Royal Train Paddington–Llandrindod. Llandrindod–Shrewsbury. Shrewsbury–Paddington. 22, 23 and 24 October 1952–continued.

NOTICE No. 40.

PRIVATE.—For use of the staff concerned only

BRITISH RAILWAYS
(WESTERN OPERATING AREA)

NOTICE
OF
ROYAL TRAINS

PADDINGTON
TO
BRECON (via Talyllyn)

LLANDOVERY
TO
HAVERFORDWEST

HAVERFORDWEST
TO
NEYLAND

5th/6th AUGUST, 1955

THIS NOTICE, WHICH WILL BE DISTRIBUTED BY THE DISTRICT OPERATING/TRAFFIC SUPERINTENDENTS CONCERNED TO ALL STAFF AFFECTED IN THEIR RESPECTIVE DISTRICTS, MUST BE ACKNOWLEDGED TO THE DISTRICT OPERATING/TRAFFIC SUPERINTENDENTS IMMEDIATELY ON RECEIPT BY TELEGRAM AS FOLLOWS :—" ARNO GROVE 40."

WORKING OF EMPTY ROYAL TRAIN, SATURDAY, 6th AUGUST, 1955

BRECON TO LLANDOVERY.

THE PERMANENT AND TEMPORARY SPEED RESTRICTIONS MUST BE STRICTLY OBSERVED.

PRINCIPAL STATIONS AND INTERMEDIATE SIGNAL BOXES.		TIMES.	REMARKS.
		a.m.	
BRECON (Up Main Platform)	dep.	10.45	**To carry " A " Head Code and be signalled accordingly To be given a clear run.** For detailed instructions for dealing with the Empty Royal Train at Brecon, see page 15. Dining Saloon No. 77 to be gassed and watered. Worked by Engines Nos. 46503 and 46508, Brecon to Builth Road Exchange Sidings and assisted coupled at rear by Engine No. 46516 Brecon to Builth Road (Low Level). The 10.32 a.m. Brecon to Builth Wells to start at 10.55 a.m. and run at amended times shewn in the Oswestry District Traffic Superintendent's Notice. The 11.6 a.m. Three Cocks Junction to Hereford to start at 11.28 a.m. and run at amended times shewn in the Chester District Operating Superintendent's Notice.
Talyllyn Tunnel	pass	—	
Talyllyn North Junction	"	10.58	
Trefeinon	"	—	
Talgarth	"	—	
Three Cocks Junction	"	11.15	
Boughrood & Llyswen	"	—	
Erwood	"	—	
Builth Wells	"	11.45	
Builth Road (Low Level)	arr.	11.50 noon	For detailed instructions for dealing with the Empty Royal Train at Builth Road (Low Level), see page 15
	dep.	12. 0	A White Post to be provided on the driver's side (left-hand side), 27 yards in advance of the Builth Road (Low Level) Up Starting Signal. The Royal Train to come to a stand with the centre of the footplate of the leading engine opposite the white post. Detach Assistant Engine No. 46516 from rear. **Train Reverses.** To be propelled by Engines Nos. 46503 and 46508 from Builth Road (Low Level) to Exchange Sidings.
		p.m.	
Exchange Sidings	arr.	12. 5	**Change Engines.** Attach Engine No. 48309.
	dep.	12.20	Detach Engines Nos. 46503 and 46508. For detailed instructions for dealing with the Royal Train at Exchange Sidings, see page 15.
Builth Road (High Level)	pass	12.25	The 10.15 a.m. Relief Swansea (Victoria) to Shrewsbury; The 10.25 a.m. Swansea (Victoria) to Manchester (Mayfield) } Must work punctually
Garth	"	12.36	
Llanwrtyd Wells	"	12.49	
Sugar Loaf Summit	"	12.59	
Cynghordy	"	1. 7	
LLANDOVERY (Down Platform)	arr.	1.20	For detailed instructions for dealing with the Empty Royal Train at Llandovery, see page 16. Train to be stabled and re-serviced in No. 1 Siding. Gas Tanks, etc., to be positioned in No. 2 Siding. The 12.30 p.m. Carmarthen to Llandilo must work punctually. The 1.10 p.m. Llandilo to Shrewsbury must work punctually. The 12.25 p.m. Swansea (Victoria) to Shrewsbury; The 11.57 a.m. Shrewsbury to Swansea (Victoria) } Must work punctually

8

TIME TABLE OF ROYAL TRAIN—LLANDOVERY TO HAVERFORDWEST— SATURDAY, 6th AUGUST, 1955—*continued.*

Distances from Llandovery		PRINCIPAL STATIONS AND INTERMEDIATE SIGNAL BOXES.		TIMES.	REMARKS.
Mls.	Chs.			p.m.	
14	34	Golden Grove	"	4.49	
20	63	Nantgaredig	"	5. 2	
23	77¼	Abergwili Tunnel	"	—	R.E. Circular O/RR (clause 16) in regard to the examination and protection of Tunnels must be observed. (See Local Notice issued by District Engineer.)
24	76	Abergwili Junction	arr. dep.	5.18 5.20	**Change Drivers.**
26	26	Carmarthen Town	pass	5.26	The 10.55 a.m. Paddington to Pembroke Dock; The 3.35 p.m. Swansea (High Street) to Carmarthen } Must work punctually The 11.35 a.m. Paddington to Neyland to leave Swansea (High Street) at 4.15 p.m. and run thence at amended times shewn in Swansea District Operating Superintendent's Notice. The 11.55 a.m. Paddington to Pembroke Dock to leave Swansea (High Street) at 4.55 p.m. and run thence at amended times shewn in Swansea District Operating Superintendent's Notice. The 5.45 p.m. Carmarthen to Aberystwyth to start at 6.0 p.m. and run at amended times shewn in Notices of District Operating Superintendents concerned. The 3.50 p.m. (Fish) Milford Haven to Severn Tunnel Junction must work punctually at amended times shewn in Swansea District Operating Superintendent's Notice. The 5.20 p.m. Carmarthen to Swansea (High Street) to start at 4.45 p.m. and run at amended times shewn in Swansea District Operating Superintendent's Notice. The 3.20 p.m. (Fish) Milford Haven to Carmarthen must work punctually at amended times shewn in Swansea District Operating Superintendent's Notice. The 5.15 p.m. (Parcels) Carmarthen to Llandilo to start at 5.45 p.m. and run at amended times shewn in Swansea District Operating Superintendent's Notice. The 4.45 p.m. (Fish and Parcels) Swansea (Victoria) to Crewe to run from Llandilo at amended times shewn in Notices of District Operating Superintendents concerned. The 6.15 p.m. Llandilo to Carmarthen to start at 6.18 p.m. and run at amended times shewn in Swansea District Operating Superintendent's Notice. The 6.20 p.m. Carmarthen to Llandilo to run at amended times shewn in Swansea District Operating Superintendent's Notice. **Speed not to exceed 15 miles per hour at Carmarthen Bridge Junction.**
26	71	Carmarthen Bridge	"	5.28	**Speed not to exceed 30 miles per hour between Carmarthen Bridge and Llanstephan Crossing from 245 miles 32 chains to 245 miles 34 chains over River Towy Bridge.**
34	54	St. Clears	"	—	**Speed not to exceed 60 miles per hour between St. Clears and Whitland from 256 miles 40 chains to 257 miles 20 chains.**
38	40¼	Whitland Tunnel	"	—	R.E. Circular O/RR (clause 16) in regard to the examination and protection of Tunnels must be observed. (See Local Notice issued by District Engineer.)
40	33	Whitland	arr. dep.	5.48 5.58	**Engine to take water.** The 6.15 p.m. Whitland to Milford Haven to start at 7.5 p.m. and run at amended times shewn in Swansea District Operating Superintendent's Notice. The 6.20 p.m. Whitland to Cardigan to start at 7.20 p.m. and run at amended times shewn in Swansea District Operating Superintendent's Notice.
52	30½	Clarbeston Road	pass	6.20	**Speed not to exceed 55 miles per hour between Clarbeston Road and Haverfordwest.** The 6.43 p.m. Clarbeston Road to Fishguard Harbour to start at 7.33 p.m. and run at amended times shewn in Swansea District Operating Superintendent's Notice.

10

Working timetable for the Royal Train Paddington–Brecon. Llandovery–Haverfordwest. Haverfordwest–Neyland 5 and 6 August 1955.

JOURNEY—TALYLLYN STABLING POINT TO BRECON, SATURDAY, 6th AUGUST, 1955.

TALYLLYN

1. At 8.30 a.m. the District Traffic Superintendent's Chief Inspector must obtain the key of the padlock of Points No. 12 from the Chief Operating Superintendent's Chief Inspector accompanying the Train.

2. Engines Nos. 2225 and 2284 to work the Royal Train to Brecon will arrive on the Single Line from Brecon at 8.25 a.m., and must be brought to a stand opposite Talyllyn East Signal Box, where they must remain until 9.0 a.m. At 9.0 a.m. the Signalman at Talyllyn East must restore the Token to the instrument and send " Train out of Section " to the West Box, after which the Signalman at Talyllyn East must ask " Is Line Clear ? " to West Box for the Royal Train and withdraw a Token for the Talyllyn East—Talyllyn West Section and hand it to the Driver of Engine No. 2225. The two engines must then draw forward into the Talyllyn East—Talyllyn West Section and stand at a point 50 yards to the rear of Talyllyn East Brecon Line Down Home Signal No. 15 to await the Royal Train being withdrawn from the Loop on to the Single Line. A Handsignalman exhibiting a hand danger signal must be stationed at the Down Home Signal until it is in order for the engines to proceed to the Royal Train.

3. An Electric Train Token must be withdrawn by Talyllyn East for the Talyllyn East—Talybont-on-Usk Section in accordance with E.T.T. Regulation 13, and after the clip and padlock have been removed from Points No. 12, and these points have been restored to normal, Engine No. 2219 will draw the Royal Train from the Loop Line on to the Single Line and will come to a stand with the centre of the footplate of the engine opposite a white post situated on the Driver's side 313 yards beyond Talyllyn East Box. The Guards must apply the hand brakes.

4. Engines Nos. 2225 and 2234 must then be piloted to the Royal Train by the District Traffic Superintendent's District Inspector and be attached by the Fireman of engine No. 2284, after which engine No. 2219 must be detached by the Fireman of that engine and remain at a stand until instructed to move by the Talyllyn Station Master.

5. As soon as the Royal Train has passed the Signalman at Talyllyn West Box must place three detonators on the line opposite Starting Signal No. 5, and they must be maintained in that position until " Train out of Section " is received from Brecon for the Royal Train.

BRECON.

1. No engine or vehicle must be allowed to stand in the Down Main, Down Loop or Up Bay Platforms for thirty minutes before the Royal Train is due to arrive.

2. Sixty minutes before the Royal Train is due to arrive, Engines Nos. 46503 and 46508, which are to work the Empty Royal Train from Brecon to Builth Road (Low Level) must be placed in the Up Spur clear of Catch Point No. 38, which must be scotched in the open position, and lever collars must be placed on the levers working Catch Point No. 38 and Signal No. 39.

3. Sixty minutes before the Royal Train is due to arrive, Engine No. 46516, which is to assist coupled in rear of the Empty Royal Train from Brecon to Builth Road (Low Level) must be placed in Mount Street Siding clear of Catch Point No. 7, which must be scotched in the open position, and lever collars must be placed on the levers working Catch Point No. 7 and Disc No. 6.

4. Sixty minutes before the Royal Train is due to arrive, Points No. 36 must be set, clipped and padlocked for the Royal Train to run from the Single Line to the Up Main Platform. Points Nos. 32 and 13 must be clipped and padlocked in the normal position and Points No. 10 must be set, clipped and padlocked for the Single Line. The keys of the padlocks must be held by the Brecon Station Master.

5. A Handsignalman must be stationed at the Down Home Signal No. 45 thirty minutes before the Royal Train is due to pass, and he will be instructed by the Signalman over the telephone provided at the signal to handsignal the Royal Train to pass the signal at Danger.

6. A Handsignalman must be stationed at the Down Inner Home Signal No. 44, and he will be authorised by the Signalman by written instruction to handsignal the Royal Train to pass the Signal at Danger.

7. The Royal Train must be brought to a stand with the centre of the footplate of the leading engine opposite a white post situated on the Driver's side 37 yards beyond the Neath end of the Up Platform. The Guards must apply the hand brakes.

8. As soon as the Royal Train has cleared Points No. 36 they must be restored to normal.

WORKING OF EMPTY ROYAL TRAIN, BRECON TO LLANDOVERY, SATURDAY, 6th AUGUST, 1955.

BRECON

1. After the Royal Party has left the Approach Road the Empty Royal Train will be drawn forward and must be brought to a stand 15 yards before reaching Points No. 10.

2. After Catch Point No. 38 has been closed, clipped and padlocked and Signal No. 39 lowered, engines Nos. 46503 and 46508 will be piloted by the District Traffic Superintendent's District Inspector from the Up Spur to the Empty Royal Train and coupled by the Fireman of engine No. 46508.

3. After engines Nos. 46503 and 46508 have been coupled to the Empty Royal Train, the two engines which worked the Train into Brecon will be detached by the Fireman of Engine No. 2284 and run forward on to the Single Line, thence to Sheds via the Loop Line.

4. The clip and padlock will then be removed from Points No. 10, and after Catch Point No. 7 has been closed, clipped and padlocked and Disc No. 6 lowered, engine No. 46516 will be piloted by the District Traffic Superintendent's District Inspector from Mount Street Siding to the rear of the Empty Royal Train and attached by the Fireman of that engine.

5. The Empty Royal Train will leave from the Up Main Platform.

BUILTH ROAD.

1. Before returning " Line Clear " for the Empty Royal Train to Builth Wells the Token for the Builth Road—Newbridge-on-Wye Section must be withdrawn in accordance with E.T.T. Block Regulation 13 and Up Starting Signal No. 7 lowered.

2. The Empty Royal Train must be brought to a stand with the centre of the footplate of the leading engine opposite a white post situated on the Driver's side (left-hand side), 27 yards in advance of Builth Road Up Starting Signal No. 7.

3. After the Empty Royal Train has come to a stand Engine No. 46516 will be detached from the rear of the Train by the Fireman of that engine and will proceed on to the Down Line, thence to depot.

4. After engine No. 46516 has cleared on to the Down Line and Points Nos. 31 and 28 have been reversed, engines Nos. 46503 and 46508 must slowly propel the Empty Royal Train on to the Exchange Siding (ex L.M.R. Loop). The Drivers must keep a sharp look out and be prepared to stop on a handsignal being exhibited. The Instructions for " Working Loop between Low Level and ex-L.M.R. Lines " on the footnotes and on page 83 of No. 16 Appendix must be strictly complied with and the propelling movement must be carried out under the supervision of the Chief District Inspector.

5. When the Train has been brought to a stand in the Exchange Siding, ex-L.M.R. Engine No. 48309 must be attached at the Llandovery end, and engines Nos. 46503 and 46508 detached. After the ex-L.M.R. engine has been attached to the Empty Royal Train the automatic brake must be released throughout the Train and the vacuum afterwards re-created by the ex-L.M.R. engine.

6. Before the Signalman at Builth Road (High Level) No. 2 Box asks " Is Line Clear ? " for the Empty Royal Train, Points No. 7 must be set for the Train to leave the Exchange Siding and be clipped and padlocked at both ends.

15

WORKING OF EMPTY ROYAL TRAIN, BRECON TO LLANDOVERY, SATURDAY, 6th AUGUST, 1955—*continued*.

LLANDOVERY.

1. Before returning " Line Clear " for the Empty Royal Train the Signalman at Llandovery South Box must withdraw an Electric Train Token for the Llandovery South—Llanwrda Section in accordance with E.T.T. Regulation 13.

2. The Empty Royal Train must be brought to a stand at Llandovery South Down Home Signal No. 2. The engine must be detached upon instructions being given by the Chief Operating Superintendent's Chief Inspector, and proceed to Shed. A special pilot engine must then be attached and the Train drawn forward clear of Points No. 23, and then be propelled into No. 1 Up Siding.

3. After the special pilot engine has been detached and sent to Shed, ex-L.M.R. engine No. 48309, which is to work the Royal Train to Neyland, must be piloted by the District Operating Superintendent's District Inspector to the Llandilo end of the Empty Royal Train and be attached by the Fireman.

4. After the departure of the 11.57 a.m. Shrewsbury to Swansea, the Signalman at Llandovery South must send the " Blocking Back Outside Home Signal " signal to Llandovery North, and the Signalman at the latter Box must withdraw the Electric Train Token for the Llandovery North—Cynghordy Section, in accordance with E.T.T. Regulation 13. The " Blocking Back Outside Home Signal " signal must then be acknowledged to Llandovery South. A Wrong Line Order Form " D " must be issued by the Signalman at Llandovery North and be countersigned by the Signalman at Llandovery South. The Empty Royal Train must be drawn from No. 1 Up Siding on to the Single Line clear of Points No. 23, which must then be restored to normal and the Empty Royal Train propelled along the Down Main Line to the Down Platform.

5. On receiving " Train out of Section " from Llanwrda for the 11.57 a.m. Shrewsbury to Swansea (Victoria), the Signalman at Llandovery South must withdraw an Electric Train Token for the Llandovery South—Llanwrda Section in accordance with E.T.T. Regulation 13.

6. All points not provided with facing-point locks and bars, or track circuits in lieu of bars, must be clipped and padlocked for movements of the Empty Royal Train and engines in connection therewith.

7. Detailed instructions in regard to dealing with the Empty Royal Train at Llandovery are shewn in the District Operating Superintendent's local notice.

JOURNEY—LLANDOVERY TO NEYLAND, SATURDAY, 6th AUGUST, 1955.

LLANDOVERY.

1. Fifteen minutes before the Royal Train is due to depart the Signalman at Llandovery South Box must restore the Electric Train Token withdrawn under E.T.T. Regulation 13 and obtain " Line Clear " for the Royal Train.

2. The Electric Train Token for the Llandovery North—Cynghordy Section must not be restored by the Llandovery North Signalman until " Train out of Section " has been received for the Royal Train.

ABERGWILI JUNCTION.

For the purpose of changing Enginemen the Royal Train must be brought to a stand at the Down Starting Signal No. 6, which will be in the " off " position and where a Handsignalman will be provided to repeat the signal.

ST. CLEARS.

As soon as the Royal Train has passed the Signalman must arrange for three detonators to be placed on the Down Main Line opposite the Box, and these must be so maintained until " Train out of Section " signal is received for the Royal Train.

WHITLAND.

1. Fifteen minutes before the Royal Train is due to arrive, Points Nos. 4 and 7, worked from Whitland East Signal Box, must be clipped and padlocked in the normal position.

2. The Royal Train must be brought to a stand at the Down Platform with the engine opposite the water column situated 20 yards to the rear of the West Box Down Home Signal (No. 2), which will be in the " off " position.

CLARBESTON ROAD.

Before returning " Line Clear " for the Royal Train, Points No. 54 must be clipped and padlocked in the normal position. As soon as the Royal Train has passed the Down Branch Starting Signal No. 12, facing points No. 49 must be set for the direction of Fishguard and clipped and padlocked in that position. These points must be so maintained until " Train out of Section " is received for the Royal Train.

HAVERFORDWEST.

1. Fifteen minutes before the Royal Train is due to arrive Points Nos. 15 and 23 must be clipped and padlocked in the normal position.

2. A Handsignalman exhibiting a red hand signal will be stationed on the Driver's side (left-hand side), 69 yards in rear of the Down Starting Signal No. 54, and the Train must be brought to a stand with the centre of the footplate of the engine opposite the Handsignalman. The Guards must apply the hand brakes.

3. Immediately the Train has come to a stand Points Nos. 41 and 39 must be reversed, clipped and padlocked. The keys must be handed to the Chief Operating Superintendent's Chief Inspector. These points must be maintained in this position until the Royal Party has left the Station.

4. After the Royal Party has left the Station, Points No. 41 must be unclipped and restored to normal for Assistant Engine No. 6629 (Bunker leading) to be piloted by the District Operating Superintendent's Chief Inspector to the rear of the Train, to which it will be attached by the Fireman, after which Points No. 41 must again be reversed, clipped and padlocked.

5. All points which become facing and which are not provided with facing-point locks and bars, or track circuits in lieu of bars, must be clipped and padlocked for movements of the Assistant Engine.

NEYLAND.

1. Thirty minutes before the Royal Train is due to arrive, Points Nos. 26, 30 and 33 must be clipped and padlocked in the normal position.

2. The Train will run to the Down Platform and must be brought to a stand with the centre of the footplate of the Train engine opposite a white post with white light affixed situated on the Driver's side (left-hand side), 16 yards to the rear of the stop block.

3. As soon as the Train has been brought to a stand the Guards must apply the hand brakes and Points No. 6 must be restored to normal.

4. See District Operating Superintendent's local notice for instructions for dealing with the Empty Royal Train at Neyland.

16

INSTRUCTIONS FOR SIGNALLING THE ROYAL TRAIN

JOURNEY—LLANDOVERY TO NEYLAND.

SATURDAY, 6th AUGUST, 1955.

Note.—The instructions given below are supplemental to the General Instructions, *and will apply in clear weather and during fog or falling snow.*

ASKING " IS LINE CLEAR ? "

The Signalman at Llandovery North to ask " Is Line Clear ? " for the Royal Train fifteen minutes prior to the booked time of departure of the Train.

The Signalman at Haverfordwest to ask " Is Line Clear ? " for the Royal Train fifteen minutes prior to the booked time of departure of the Train.

RELEASE OF ELECTRIC TRAIN STAFF OR TOKEN.

The Electric Train Staff or Token for the Section ahead must be withdrawn fifteen minutes before the Royal Train is due to pass.

All persons engaged in Electric Train Staff or Token working must exercise the utmost care in the operations so as to avoid any interruption in the working.

Name of Signal Box affected.	Special Instructions.
Llandovery	**Note.**—See special instructions for dealing with the Royal Train at Llandovery, page 16.
Llandilo	**Note.**—The Signalman at Llandilo must send the " Blocking Back " signal in accordance with Electric Train Token Regulation 16 to, and receive an acknowledgment from, Ffairfach before returning " Line Clear ". The Signalman at Ffairfach, on receipt of the " Blocking Back " signal from Llandilo, must send the " Blocking Back " signal to, and receive an acknowledgment from, Derwydd Road. The Signalman at Llandilo must not send the " Obstruction Removed " signal until the " Train out of Section " signal is received for the Royal Train from Llandilo Bridge.
Abergwili Junction ..	**Note.**—The Signalman at Abergwili Junction to ask " Is Line Clear ? " for the Royal Train when " Is Line Clear ? " is received from Nantgaredig and this signal must be repeated through to Sarnau. Before returning " Line Clear " the Signalman must obtain " Line Clear " from Carmarthen Goods Yard and withdraw a Token for the Abergwili Junction–Conwil Section in accordance with Electric Train Token Regulation 13. The Token must not be restored until the " Train out of Section " signal has been received from Carmarthen Goods Yard for the Royal Train.

EXCHANGING OF ELECTRIC TRAIN STAFFS OR TOKENS.

In all cases where the exchange of Staffs or Tokens has to be made by hand, the exchange must be made from the Station Platform where provided and, if neither " Setting Down " nor " Picking Up " posts are provided, two men must be employed, one to receive the Staff or Token for the Section in the rear, and the other to deliver the Staff or Token for the Section in advance, the two men standing at a distance of not less than 40 yards apart.

The " Is Line Clear ? " Signal must be arrested at the following Signal Boxes until the " Train Approaching " Signal is received from the Box in the rear :—

Sarnau.

Cardigan Junction.

On receipt of " Train entering Section " from	" Train Approaching " Signal to be sent by	To be repeated through to
Abergwili Junction	Carmarthen Goods Yard	Sarnau.
Sarnau	St. Clears	Cardigan Junction.

INSTRUCTIONS FOR SIGNALLING THE ROYAL TRAIN THROUGH SHORT SECTIONS

Name of Signal Box affected.	Signalman to return " Line Clear " for the Train to the Box in the rear when he has received	Signalman to return " Train out of Section " for the train preceding the Train referred to in this Notice and for the Train itself, provided it is complete with tail lamp, when he has received
Abergwili Junction ..	" Line Clear " from Carmarthen Goods Yard. (See also above.)	" Train out of Section " from Carmarthen Goods Yard.
Carmarthen Goods Yard	" Line Clear " from Carmarthen Crossing.	" Train out of Section " from Carmarthen Crossing.
Carmarthen Crossing ..	" Line Clear " from Carmarthen Station.	" Train out of Section " from Carmarthen Station.
Carmarthen Station ..	" Line Clear " from Carmarthen Bridge. **Note.**—The Signalman at Carmarthen Station must send the " Blocking Back outside Home Signal " to, and receive an acknowledgment from, Myrtle Hill Junction before returning " Line Clear ". The Signalman at Myrtle Hill Junction, on receipt of the " Blocking Back outside Home Signal " from Carmarthen Station, must send the " Blocking Back outside Home Signal " to, and receive an acknowledgment from, Carmarthen Junction Station.	" Train out of Section " from Carmarthen Bridge.

24

Working timetable for the Royal Train Paddington–Brecon. Llandovery–Haverfordwest. Haverfordwest–Neyland. 5 and 6 August 1955–continued.

Class 47 No. 47555 The Commonwealth Spirit *hauls the Royal Train conveying HRH Prince of Wales to attend the Wales Craft Fair at Llandrindod on 23 October 1979.*
(Courtesy Tony Williams)

Extracts from Special Trains List – Central Wales Line 1972-1993
(Courtesy of Glyn Watson)

1972				
Date	*From*	*To*	*Engine*	*Notes*
Mar 4	Llandrindod	Paddington		Heavy snow
Mar 4	London	London	6887	
		Llandrindod	471857	(Engine failure at
	Llandrindod	Salop	471853	Berthddu Crossing)
Mar 11	London	Caerphilly	6884/6889	Charter
Jun 11	Newport	Llandrindod	DMU	
Jun 22	York	Llandrindod	6888	+ 7 coaches
Jun 25	Llandrindod	Paignton	6889	Mystery
Jul 9	Newport	Llandrindod	DMU	
Aug 6	Llandrindod	Portsmouth		Mystery
Aug 6	Newport	Llandrindod	DMU	
Aug 19	Milford Haven	Shrewsbury		Charter/Flower Show
Aug 20	Weston-S-Mare	Shrewsbury		Mystery
Aug 27	Newport	Llandrindod	DMU	
Sep 2	Euston	Llandrindod		Merry Maker charter
Sep 16	Nottingham	Swansea		
Sep 24	Pantyffynnon	Blackpool		Illuminations
Sep 24	Newport	Llandrindod	DMU	
Oct 14	Manchester	Rtn via CWL		Steam Salop to Newport
Oct 14	Bristol	Hereford	DMU	Lunch Stop Llandrindod
Dec 9	Llandrindod	Paddington		ADEX Excursion
Dec 9	Crewe	Carmarthen & Branches		WRC Charter
1973				
Mar 3	Watford	Barry		Loco failed Llandovery
May 5	Llandrindod & CWL Stns	Paddington		Only 140 passengers
May 19	Euston	Llandrindod		Merry Maker – Load 9
Jun 2	Manchester	Swansea		Delayed – derailment N of Shrewsbury
Jun 13	Builth Rd	Chester		School Exc. Load 10
Jun 17	Pantyffynnon	Rhyl		ADEX Load – 10
Jun 17	Loughborough	Welshpool fwd via Cardiff		Charter Load – 10
Jun 30	Nottingham	Llandrindod	DMU	Attached to ordinary services
Jul 15	Bath/Bristol/ Newport	Llandrindod	3+2 DMU	Delay due to points failure
Jul 24	Milford Haven	Builth Road	37	Charter Royal Welsh Show. Load – 5
Jul 29	Bucknell & CWL Stns	Tenby	2+3+3 DMU	(Sunday) ADEX 360 passengers
Jul 29	Bristol/Newport	Llandrindod	2+3 DMU	ADEX Excursion
Jul 29	Clapham Jcn	Llandrindod & Hereford	37	ADEX Load – 10
Jul 29	Portsmouth	Hereford & Llandrindod	37	ADEX Load – 10
Aug 12	Llandrindod & CWL Stns	Dawlish/ Teignmouth	37	Mystery. Load – 9
Aug 12	Bristol/ Newport	Llandrindod	DMU	
Aug 12	Weston-S-Mare	Shrewsbury Rtn via CWL	37	Mystery. Load – 10
Aug 26	Milford Haven	Shrewsbury		Charter Shrewsbury Flower Show. Load – 7
Sep 1	Euston	Llandrindod	6888	Merry Maker Load – 10
Sep 2	Paddington/ Reading	Shrewsbury Rtn via CWL	6888	Load – 10
Sep 22	York/Leeds	Llandrindod	6877	Weekend Charter Load 10
Sep 22	Wolverhampton/ Worcester	Pembroke Dock	68 +68 Double Hd	Severn Valley Rail Tour Load – 10
Sep 29	Weston-S-Mare	Shrewsbury Rtn via CWL	6877	Load – 10
Oct 20	Llanelli + CWL Stns	Blackpool N.	6889	ADEX Load – 9
Dec 8	Llandrindod + CWL Stns	Paddington	6888	ADEX Load – 9
Dec 13	Llandrindod	Kings Norton	2 car DMU	Auto Palace Charter
1974				
Mar 2	Watford	Barry Rtn via CWL	6888	LNER Charter. Load – 10
Apl 6	Mexborough	Llandrindod/ Cardiff	6888	ADEX Load – 10
Apl 20	Liverpool	Newport	6888	LCGB Charter

Class 47 locomotives 'top-and-tailing' the Royal train conveying HRH Prince Phillip to Builth Road to visit the Royal Welsh Show on 25 July 1989.
(Roy Palmer)

Apl 20	Euston	Fwd via CWL Newport Rtn via CWL	37192 37192 6888	Load – 11 LCGB Charter Load – 11
Apl 27	Llanelli + CWL Stns	Leeds/York	37190	Sunday. ADEX Load – 10
May 20	Llanelli	Llandovery off return charter	2 car DMU	Special connection Southampton-Carmarthen
May 25	St.Pancras	Llandrindod	37192	Merry Maker Load 10
Jun 3	Llangadog + Llandovery	Chester	37190	Schools Exc Load 10
Jun 19	Builth Road & CWL Stns	Oxford via Carm-Newport	37190	WI charter Load 10 Eng. worked to Oxford
Jun 29	London	Carmarthen	37192	LNER Soc. Load 10
Jun 29	Brighton	Llandrindod	37189	Weekend Charter Load 10
Jul 14	Newport Cardiff	Llandrindod	2+3 DMU	ADEX
Jul 14	Pembroke Dock	Llandrindod	3+2 DMU	ADEX
Jul 23	Milford Haven	Builth Road	37192	Royal Welsh Show Charter Load 5
Jul 28	Newport Cardiff	Llandrindod	3+2 DMU	ADEX
Jul 28	Milford Haven	Llandrindod	3+2 DMU	ADEX
Aug 4	Bucknell & CWL Stns	Tenby	37192	ADEX Load 9
Aug 4	Plymouth District	Llandrindod via Cardiff	37188	ADEX Load 10
Aug 11	Llanelli & CWL Stns	Morecambe	37192	Mystery Load 10
Aug 16	Milford Haven	Shrewsbury	37190	Charter Load 7
Aug 18	Poole & Bournmouth	Llandrindod Rtn via Hereford	37190	Load 10
Aug 25	Newport Cardiff	Llandrindod	3+3 DMU	ADEX
Sep 1	Weston-S-Mare	Llandrindod and Shrewsbury	37192	Load 10 MK II B InterCity stock
Sep 1	Paddington	Llandrindod and Shrewsbury	37189	Land-Cruise Load 10
Sep 14	Leicester	Swansea	37192	ADEX Load 9
		via Shrewsbury		
Oct 12	Llanelli & CWL Stns	Blackpool		ADEX
Oct 27	Yatton via Cardiff	Llandrindod and Shrewsbury	3 car DMU	Clevedon Rotary Charter
Nov 23	Llandrindod & CWL Stns	Paddington		ADEX
1975				
Mar 1	Watford	Cardiff & Barry	37180	LNER Soc. Load 10
Mar 29	Llandrindod & CWL Stns	Paddington	37190	ADEX from Cardiff
Apl 19	Southend	Llandrindod	37177	Weekend Break Load 9
May 31	York	Llandrindod	37177	Weekend Break Load 10
Jun 8	York	Llandrindod	37190	Mystery. Load 10
Jun 28	Croydon & Redhill	LLandrindod	37180	Weekend Break Load 9
Jul 13	Bucknell & CWL Stns	Tenby	2x3 DMU	Light Load Supervisors Work to Rule
Jul 22	Shrewsbury	Builth Rd.	37177 37180	HRH Duke of Edinburgh See 'Royal Trains'
Jul 27	LLanelli & CWL Stns	Southport	37190	Mystery Load 10
Jul 27	Newport/Cardiff & Swansea	Llandrindod	3+2 DMU	ADEX
Jul 29	Batley	Llandrindod	37180	Mystery Load 10
Aug 10	Newport/Cardiff & Llanelli	Llandrindod	3+3 DMU	ADEX
Aug 15	Milford Haven	Shrewsbury	37180	Charter Flower Show Load 10
Aug 24	Newport/Cardiff & Swansea	Llandrindod	3+2 DMU	ADEX
Sep 13	Leicester	Swansea	37190	ADEX Load 10
Oct 11	Leeds	Llandrindod	37190	Weekend Break York WI Load 10
Oct 25	Llanelli & CWL Stns	Blackpool	37177 + 47252	ADEX Load 10
Oct 25	West Wales	Crewe	37177	WRC 'Pembroke Coast Express' Load 10

11

Promotion and Tourism

The Central Wales Line was originally constructed to carry freight; for some time passengers boarded and travelled in a way which was unbelievably haphazard, little being done for about ten years for their comfort and convenience.

Even when passenger traffic was established and excursions began and, although the LNWR made considerable efforts to promote the mid-Wales spas, tourism as a concept and certainly not as a word, was not considered as vital to the economical stability of the line.

There is no longer any freight north of Pantyffynnon so the line's continuance – to state the obvious – can only be justified by its necessity for passenger traffic and it is not an exaggeration or the sentimental burblings of the enthusiasts to say that the Central is a life line for local communities.

However, no matter how much future services might be improved and fares reduced, it would be unrealistic to expect passenger numbers to be increased to a very impressive level if only regional usage is sought. Tourism is big business. In every small town on the CWL between Llandeilo and Shrewsbury it plays a role and even in the south, enterprise is encouraging visitors to sample Industrial Heritage Trails and similarly named 'experiences'. Llanelli, for instance – an unlikely candidate one might think – spends a lot on marketing its tourist facilities and could easily add railway history to its interests for visitors.

The spa towns, whose stations used to bustle with the thousands who came to take the waters, are still there. Llandrindod, the largest (a relative term for a population of five thousand) has a thousand visitor beds within walking distance of the station.

Those who publicise the Central Wales Line today find they have to target the tourism market – even though British Rail have been quoted as saying that 'leisure activities' do not count in connection with grant allocations.

Promotion is uphill work, stretching the resources, ingenuity and energies of the Heart of Wales Line Travellers' Association to the limit. There is little doubt that, since its formation, HOWLTA, concerned as it is solely with CWL, has been the most consistent organisation in the production and distribution of publicity material. British Rail have made spasmodic efforts to promote the line, presumably as finances dictate.

In 1976 Mike Tedstone was appointed by BR as Central Wales Line Development Officer and quite a lot was done to boost the Central during the period of his employment. In the 1970s Golden Rail holidays included Llandrindod and Llanwrtyd Wells in their scheme and the appearance of these two resorts in their widely distributed brochure was of considerable benefit, not only to the towns but to the line as well. The first Golden Rail passengers to Llandrindod were greeted by a champagne reception and the town ceremoniously welcomed its 1,000th visitor on the scheme in 1979. Subsequently, the numbers decreased and, in spite of strong representation by the hoteliers involved, particularly the Metropole whose manager had been involved in the original negotiations, the resorts lost the business during the 1980s. Besides those connected only with rail, there have been other sources of publicity. One began in the 1980s when an organisation responsible for marketing the Mid Wales area, the Heart of Wales Tourist Association, promoted Super Ted Holidays. These were based on a popular cartoon character on Welsh television and families with young children arrived by train to be greeted and entertained at hotels in the Llandrindod area by someone dressed in suitable costume. Super Ted breaks – which brought the additional benefit of business during the quiet season – were successful on a regional basis.

In 1985, the HOWLTA Newsletter published a letter from an ex Llanwrtyd man in Germany who had heard on the local Bavarian radio at peak time what he termed as a 'lengthy piece' extolling the beauties of the Central Wales Line, summarised as '50km of delightful scenery with pretty stations'. Enquiries about the various travel packages on offer were to be made to the BBC in Berlin.

For some reason, it was thought that the name 'Heart of Wales Line' would enhance tourist potential. This, while having a common identity with other marketing bodies which were subsequently similarly named, seems a doubtful move and its validity is questionable and, given that the line serves South Wales as well, a title acknowledging this fact might have been better.

After an investment of £644,000 was made in the line in 1986, BR made strong efforts to promote it although the HOWLTA Newsletter in autumn of that year commented on the lack of publicity given to the first regular Sunday train service between Shrewsbury and Llandrindod. The association had itself distributed 15,000 leaflets and followed this with several thousand more the following winter to promote the half price travel scheme which operated until the end of March, as well as a poster and handbills to advertise the improved summer service in 1987.

However, in the same year, British Rail launched various fare incentives and produced a very good full-colour brochure on the line. In 1989, HOWLTA was responsible – with funding from Mid Wales Development – for 2,000 full-colour A3 posters showing an outline of the route and six photographs for distribution throughout the county. Another BR brochure followed in 1990 and its national poster advertising Senior Citizen Railcards carried a photograph of a couple alighting at Llanwrtyd Wells. At a meeting of the Central Wales Line Forum in July 1991, BR's comments were:

> 'Regional Railways had indicated that the line had been heavily advertised nationally and that the line was publicised whenever the opportunity was available including national newspapers. There was some fear that there may be an overlapping of publicity or lack of publicity in certain areas and it was suggested that a small marketing group be set up.'

A working group was duly set up comprising local authority officers, Wales Tourist Board and HOWLTA. In 1993, the Heart of Wales Line was featured on BR's 'Britain's Scenic Railways' poster with a photograph of a Class 153 'Sprinter' climbing the Sugar Loaf. In that year two publications on the line appeared in commemoration of the 125th anniversary of its opening as a through route. One was a 60-page book containing memoirs and articles produced by Nigel and Sue Bird in conjunction with HOWLTA and the other of 24 pages, was produced by the Breconshire Railway Society.

These were of course, saleable publications at £3.50 and £1.30 respectively, and did not have the wide circulation which would have been achieved had there been a full-colour brochure available.

The appointment by the Heart of Wales Line Forum of Mike Wilson as a Development and Liaison Officer took place in 1994. He is based at Llandrindod County Hall/Rail Station/Town Hall and the post is to be renewable annually *subject to funding* and annual performance assessment. The Objectives on the job description were:

The 1,000th Golden Rail Passenger (a family of three) welcomed at Llandrindod by the Tourist Officer, Chairman of Local Tourism Committee, Manager of Hotel Metropole, the BR Marketing Officer for the line and the Mayor of Llandrindod.
(Courtesy Marina Gallery)

General
a) To implement the appropriate County Council public transport policies and Forum's Marketing Strategy for countryside recreation in relation to railways.
b) To maintain a close relationship with the appropriate Railway Managers and to ensure initiatives are in line with the Regiona Railways strategy plans.
c) To foster links between the rail project and its sponsors.
d) To work and liaise with HOWLTA.
e) To foster and promote use of the Line by the local community and visitors.
Marketing
f) To develop interpretation/promotional needs for the Line and to ensure the efficient and cost effective distribution of leaflets and promotional publications.
g) To encourage tourism related businesses and others to promote the rail transport facilities that are available, and improve the viability of the line.
Facilities
h) To identify, develop and improve links with the railway: to include walks, cycle routes, trails and bus links to present a package in an attractive and simple form – the package must be complete and allow for choice.
i) To encourage public facilities adjacent to or at rail stations:- cycle hire outlets, refreshments, interpretation points/centres, park and ride and associated activities.
j) To improve signing to and from the attraction and facilities in that area in relation to rail transport.
k) To identify links with public transport including use of Regional Railways services that will ease traffic congestion and the effect of the car on rural infrastructure.
l) To encourage station sponsorship/adoption scheme projects.

It was not clear what funds would be available to the officer and as the County Councils and other organisations appear to be bearing the cost of the salary, it may be that they hope to be eligible for various grants.

The Wales Tourist Board has contributed to a variety of projects on the Central Wales Line in the past but they have widespread responsibilties and probably can only afford to act as a catalyst in promotional schemes such as hosting journalists. This latter is a useful exercise as travel writers do not usually turn up of their own accord, and need persuading.

Those who work on the nationals tend to be, of necessity, a tough lot, are usually tired out by the time they arrive, having probably just returned from their previous assignment and expect – and genuinely need – a good meal and a comfortable bed. The Tourist Board is good at establishing contacts and setting such things up, hoteliers who know their job will usually co-operate with a free bed and meal and with the issue of free train tickets; useful articles will normally be the result.

There is no denying the power of the press; one good article in a national paper can be worth thousands spent in buying advertising space.Julian Critchley, MP for Aldershot and now a Vice-President of HOWLTA, wrote an excellent piece about the Central called 'The last train to Arcadia' which appeared in *You* magazine in the *Mail on Sunday* on 31 December 1989. The paper had the forethought to telephone the Radnor District Council Tourist Office in Llandrindod which remains open all year and ask permission to quote them as a contact. Only the telephone number was given – no address – and the result was that the office was inundated with calls which continued non-stop for weeks. The office's stock of leaflets on the CWL was soon exhausted, as were those from Llandrindod station who then obtained more from Llandovery. Packs were made up by staff after closing, ready to service the next day's enquiries. Finally the office had to resort to sending out the previous year's brochures.

It was interesting to note that calls continued well into the summer and a few until the following Christmas which means that that particular magazine is in circulation a long time – presumably in surgery waiting rooms and the like. In the end the number of enquiries reached four figures, the District Council, without really being aware of the fact, having picked up the postage bill.

There have, of course, been other excellent articles – one by Matthew Engel in the *Guardian* on 28 February 1994 – which certainly engendered considerable interest but that by Julian Critchley is mentioned particularly because the machinery happened to be in place to monitor the response.

In 1995 the BTA travel guide *Getting Around Britain* gave good coverage of the line and a free *Travellers Guide to the Heart of Wales Line* was commissioned by the Heart of Wales Forum in 12-page magazine format and issued in 1997. The 1996/7 timetable took the form of a colourful brochure. During 1996 some marketing was placed in the hands of a public relations agency, and there was wide distribution of brochures and promotion on television and radio. Applications are being made in 1997 by the Forum for funds from the Millennium Commission and to the European Regional Development Fund.

12

HOWLTA (The Heart of Wales Line Travellers Association)

The decision to form a support group was taken during a train journey over the line on 23 June 1981. Two members of the Cambrian Coast Line Action Group, Mike Watson and Chris Magner, were joined by Alec Prior of Knighton and Glyn Watson of Llandrindod and the result was a public meeting on 7 November of that year.

The support group was to be, in the words of Chris Magner, ' . . . an organisation to try to foster more traffic on the line and to act as a co-ordinating voice for all those anxious to see this very valuable social route retained'. The use of the initials of 'Central Wales Line Travellers Association' would have meant a clumsy acronym and it was therefore decided to use the name Heart of Wales Line Travellers Association (HOWLTA) reflecting the use of the term 'Heart of Wales Line' in BR publicity.

After the public meeting, those involved lost no time and the first committee meeting was held within three weeks.

In the winter of 1981-82 the first Newsletter was published:

NEWSLETTER NO. 1

What's in a name?

If you attended the inaugural meeting in Llandrindod on 7th November, you will know that the name 'Heart of Wales Line Promotion Group' was provisionally adopted. However, at the first committee meeting the title 'Travellers Association' was preferred – it makes the purpose of the organisation more obvious, i.e. to protect the interests of those who use the line, by trying to keep it open and suggesting improvements to services.

Newsletters and other Activities

1. The committee hopes to produce several newsletters during the year.

We certainly cannot afford a glossy magazine – all available funds and effort should be directed to supporting the line – but members must be kept informed of what we are trying to do on their behalf. At first, of course, there may not be much to report – it is going to take some time to establish ourselves in the eyes of B.R., local authorities, etc. – but you can be sure that we will be doing our best to support YOUR railway.

2. The idea is to fit the newsletters into an overall programme of activities covering the year. You will see from the report below of our first committee meeting, that such a programme is beginning to take shape.

Membership Campaign

Of course, we cannot make any progress at all without a large number of members because:

1. A small association will just be ignored by B.R. and their political masters.

2. If there are only a small number of subscriptions coming in, they will be used up running the association (newsletters, notepaper, postage, etc.). There would be nothing left to use in activity promoting the Heart of Wales Line.

3. At the moment there is far more work to be done than can be achieved by a few committee members working in their very limited spare time – more help is urgently needed if we are to move at more than a snail's pace.

So the answer must be : RECRUIT MORE MEMBERS!!!

It has taken time to prepare for a membership campaign – fixing subscription levels, finding a membership secretary, getting membership cards ready, etc. But now we must get as many members as we can. If each one of you can recruit ten new members, we shall be over 300 strong – but every single new name is important – who knows where potential committee members may be lurking?

A membership leaflet is being prepared, but any new recruits can send their subscriptions (£1.00 minimum for individuals, £5.00 minimum for organisations, local councils etc.). . .

HOWLTA is born – by Chris Magner and Mike Watson

As this is our first newsletter, it seems a good idea to explain how the association came to be formed.

You are all aware that at the end of 1980 B.R. announced that, in view of their serious financial problems, they were postponing track renewals on the Heart of Wales Line, and heavy main line locos would be banned to prevent further deterioration of the track.

This news was seen by many as 'the beginning of the end'. In the short term it is now much more difficult to run excursion trains, either *onto* the line or *from* stations along it. This has hit the tourist trade at towns like Llandrindod, in what was already a difficult year for tourism. But the long term effects could be far more serious – obviously if the track renewals are not carried out a backlog of work will accumulate, and the line will have to close for safety reasons.

To us it seemed that something must be done. Other rural railways have long had supporters' groups – 'The Cambrian Coast Line Action Group' is probably the best known – but no such group existed for the Central Wales line from Shrewsbury to Swansea. One evening in June 1981 we travelled down from Shrewsbury on the 18.48 to Swansea and were joined by Alec Prior of Knighton. We three decided that a public meeting should be held to see if a supporters' group could be formed.

Some may say 'Why wait until November for a meeting?' One answer is that by now it was near to the summer holidays, and we reckoned that few people would be able to change their holiday arrangements to attend such a meeting. Moreover, our own commitments, and those of others who would be attracted to such a meeting, continued to push the date further into the autumn. In the end November 7th 1981 was chosen and the hall booked.

Launched in Llan'dod! The summer and early autumn were taken up with what seemed endless letter writing. We aimed to attract railway enthusiasts from all over the country as well as local people, as we were sure we could learn from those having previous experience of fighting for other lines.

Therefore we alerted railway journals, as well as the press, radio and TV. As we had no funds, and we both lived away from the line, a poster and leaflet campaign was impossible. However the local press carried news of the meeting, as did the *Western Mail*, *Liverpool Post* and even the *Daily Telegraph*. Chris was also interviewed on Radio Wales.

In the event our aim was achieved – the meeting was attended by 30 or so people, and from this relatively small number a committee was selected to plan for the future. And, of course, we made headlines again.'

As well as being attended by the general public, the

meeting was supported by representatives from other action groups, among whom were John Rogers (Cambrian Line Action Group), a seasoned campaigner for rural railways, Mr Mervyn Matthews (Welsh Rail Action Group).

Mr Bakarlaski (Wirral Rail Circle) and Dr George Penn (West Wales Railway Action Committee).

This first newsletter continues to report on the committee meeting held on 28 November 1981, the election of officers, general business, etc. necessary at such first meetings. It acknowledges a 'donation of £10 from the Cambrian Coast Line Action Group which has always held a 'watching brief' for lines such as ours which have lacked their own groups'.

Paragraphs 7 and 8 include the following:

'It was agreed in principle to organise rail trips to increase traffic on the line; e.g. Llanelli to Blackpool illuminations, and North Wales to the Royal Welsh Show in Builth Wells.

The secretary would contact BR to see if a meeting could be held with their officers to discuss the future of the line and ideas for developing traffic.'

The newsletter ended by urging that, 'people in every town and village served by the line should act as representatives' and with what has become the HOWLTA slogan for the line, 'Use it – don't lose it!'

From these very small beginnings grew an enormously successful group. The 'magazine type' newsletter which they could not at first afford, made an appearance in 1985 and published quarterly, has now reached its 60th issue.

The Association, which has members all over Britain and beyond, does its utmost to publicise the line, printing and distributing many thousands of leaflets, taking advertising space in newspapers, selling promotional goods and encouraging and organising every sort of activity likely to attract people to the CWL and providing couriers for special excursions when required. It also ran a buffet service on most Saturdays and for special trains.

The dedication of the volunteers who manned this refreshment trolley during its first days, was a wonder to behold, involving boiling up kettles at various stations en route and using thermos flasks until in December 1985, they were able to acquire a new trolley with adequate 'brewing up' facilities. This service, which was run entirely by volunteers, was greatly appreciated by passengers. In 1996 Cherry Tree, a commercial enterprise, took over the trolly service. This showed confidence in the line, relieved HOWLTA of the responsibility of providing volunteers but also an income of about £700 per year.

HOWLTA acts as an excellent liaison service with the various authorities. Above all, the association is to be congratulated on its dealings with British Rail, working, as it has done, on the principle that co-operation and understanding of the problems is the best way forward, polite persistent pressure taking priority over protest, unless the latter is likely to produce any benefit when it will always take a strong stance.

The enthusiasm of some members is boundless – one was actually found cleaning the doors and windows of a particularly grubby Class 108 dmu and more recently another regularly gives a quick 'wipe over' to any dirty 'Sprinter' that happens to be on the platform. An example for such dedication was set by founder member, the late Alec Prior, a founder member, who lived in Knighton and who used to offer to go to one of the staffed stations (Llandrindod and Llanwrtyd in those days) at his own expense to buy tickets for local people as an incentive to travel.

At the end of 1996, the number of HOWLTA members stood at 1,332. Subscription rates are £3.00 for individuals, £5.00 for families and £6.00 for corporate membership.

The Membership Secretary is – Miss P. Thomas, Frankville, Broad Street, Llandvoery, Dyfed SA20 0AR.

13

The Workforce

The first major workforce to appear on the CWL, as on any railway line, were the gangs of navvies, mostly Irish and joined by agricultural labourers who were equally strong and were tempted by the pay. Until the introduction of basic machines, sometime after 1860, the navvies worked with pick and wheelbarrow. When commencement of the building of the Central Wales Extension Railway was celebrated in November 1860, they took part in the procession at Llandovery carrying the tools of their trade; one with a ceremonial wheel barrow and, to add to the sense of occasion, another carried a model of a locomotive.

As the traffic on the line increased, all the stations had a full complement of staff and employment was provided for thousands. Today, at stations like Llandovery with its proximity to the main road, those of the spa towns of Llandrindod and Llanwrtyd Wells and at Knighton, it is not difficult when surveying the station buildings to conjure up an image of the days when they were dignified with a station master and a considerable workforce.

It is less easy to imagine the time when the tiny halts also had a station master. These included isolated places like Garth, from whose Mr Morton we have a graphic account of the day he took up duties when the station was opened.

> 'In March 1867, I acted as relief-clerk at Shrewsbury under the LNWR Superintendent, Mr Henry Plews, who instructed me to hold myself in readiness to take up duty on the new Central Wales line. On March 7, I left Shrewsbury by the 7.10am train and on arrival at Craven Arms I was met by Mr Bentley (Mr Joseph Bishop's chief clerk) from Abergavenny and Mr James Bishop and a Mr Allum, both of Ludlow. The four of us settled down in a cosy first class compartment with two footwarmers, and we wanted them as the morning was bitterly cold and snow falling heavily.
>
> We left Craven Arms at 8.5am on our journey to the Wilds of Wales, and on arrival at Llandrindod I met my

A track laying gang at Mumbles Road station, pre 1923.
(City of Swansea Archives)

A permanent way gang in front of Gowerton station, c1880. Posters advertise excursions to the Isle of Man, Belle Vue, Manchester and cheap weekend fare of 3s to Llandilo.
(Courtesy Peter S. Jones)

A gang plus 'extra gang' at the mouth of Llangunllo Tunnel c1926.

(Courtesy Douglas Jones)

old friend Mr Bayldon whom I knew at Shrewsbury. About four inches of snow had fallen on the platform and a wooden structure, about the size of a sentry box, stood there to do duty as a railway station. At Builth Road we met Mr Pierce, another Shrewsbury man. We then proceeded by special train until we arrived at Cilmery, where Mr Allum was dropped out. Not a soul was visible, not even a footprint in the snow could be seen.

My turn came next. We arrived at Garth about 11am with ticket case, tickets, books, stationery, etc. and on Monday, I opened the station. Hundreds of people availed themselves of the opportunity of having their first ride in the train to attend Builth market. The whole country was in a mantle of spotless white snow six inches deep. It was the severest late winter in memory. I succeeded Mr Bayldon at Llanwrtyd on October 30 1870 and remained there until October 30 1877.'

The Central Wales Line is no longer a major employer. With the cessation of freight, introduction of NSKT system and the de-staffing of all but two stations excluding the termini, the CWL is now reduced, south of Craven Arms, to the signalmen at the latter box and that at Pantyffynnon and the staff at Llanelli and Llandrindod stations.

In early 1994 Llandrindod station was manned by former signalman Tony Williams and relief Robin Powell, who also transferred from the signal box. In the spring of that year, the latter retired leaving the station to be run six days a week by Tony Williams without assistance. It was hoped that this situation would be remedied and that a second man would again be employed, a suggested alternative being to close the station office on Mondays but by December 1994, the solution was deemed to be to shorten the daily hours worked.

In 1994 the responsibility for running the Central Wales Line fell between Retail Manager Michael Hurley, based in Carmarthen and Regional Railways in Swindon. The Permanent Way Department consisted of 16 men in three gangs based at Llangadog, Llandrindod and Knighton, with the addition of the Section Manager, Assistant Section manager and Time Keeper at Llandrindod making a total of 19.

Train crews were based at Swansea and Shrewsbury. Drivers from Swansea have route knowledge of the southern section and those from the latter know the route as far as Llandovery or Llanwrtyd. At one time, crews were also

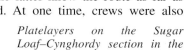

Platelayers on the Sugar Loaf–Cynghordy section in the early 1930s.

(Dorothy Bound)

Chrieste Amundsen at the turn of the century.
(The late V. Amundsen, courtesy M. Amundsen)

based at Llandovery and often worked lodging turns to Shrewsbury, returning the following day.

During the Second World War, all duties on the route were 'change overs' as men from Swansea did not want to be away from their families due to the bombing there and Shrewsbury men did not want to be in Swansea for the same reason.

A 'mileage turn' was introduced after the war, so in working trains the length of the line and back in one day, more than the basic 200 miles were covered (236 miles in fact) and this entitled the men to extra pay.

The rivalry which existed between the workforces of the two large companies is well known and there are still people on the CWL who feel an allegiance to the GWR or LMS. Some are not old enough to remember them, let alone to have worked for either, but their fathers and grandfathers did and the old loyalties remain. It soon became difficult to relate to any particular operating company, so complex was the naming and the division of responsibilities.

The train service was provided by Regional Railways South Wales and West (South Wales and West Train Operating Unit) until December 1994 and thereafter by South Wales and West Railways, and later by Prism, the infrastucture being owned by Railtrack Great Western and Railtrack Midland zones. Train crews from Shrewsbury to Llandrindod or Llanwrtyd were provided by Regional Railways (Central Train Operating Unit) and crews for Swansea to Llandrindod by Great Western Trains Company (formerly InterCity Great Western). New South Wales and West Railway crews from Crewe began on the Northern section in 1996, the Southern end being worked by drivers from Carmarthen and conductors from Swansea depot, the latter sometimes working the whole line. Some Shrewsbury drivers switched allegiance to join SW&WR at Crewe.

Such changes are hardly the stuff from which loyalties are forged and the sense of 'belonging' can no longer apply, but there is still dedication to the job. The following are just a few representatives of the hundreds of dedicated men who have worked the line.

Chrieste Amundsen
He began work on the Central Wales Line in the 1890s. Originally from the Knighton area, he moved to Swansea, became a guard and for some time worked at Builth Road, retiring from Swansea LMS locomotive depot in 1938. He is reputed to have turned down the chance of promotion to station master at some stage in his career, not wanting the responsibility. His workmates presented him with a clock engraved with a brass plate upon his retirement.

Sid Brooks
A track man on the CWL for 39 years and started work on the Sugar Loaf–Cynghordy Viaduct section. His father was a signalman at Sugar Loaf and he was born in No. 1 of the five cottages built for the railwaymen there. Later, he lived in No. 3 and recalls how the houses shook with the vibration of the goods trains pounding up the line. Due to his wife's health, he later moved to Llanwrtyd and cycled the steep three miles to Sugar Loaf. Still interested in the line, he can now be found caring for the area around Llanwrtyd station and is seen below weeding out grass from the cobbles.

David Thomas Davies
A signalman at Pantyffynnon, known affectionately to his colleages as Davy Tom, started work on the railway at Tirydail in 1945, went on to Llangennech and Derwydd Road and became signalman at Pantyffynnon in 1960 where he still works. He received the BEM in the Queen's 1992 Birthday Honours list, the medal being presented by the Lord Lieutenant of Dyfed, David Mansel Lewis. On 19 August 1992, David Davies, with relief signalman John Rowe, was present at the unveiling of a plaque at Pantyffynnon box commemorating its centenary.

Sid Brooks meticulously weeding the cobbled entrance to Llanwrtyd station in Autumn 1994.
(Rose Coleman)

Signalman D. T. Davies in a rare moment of relaxation in Pantyffynnon box, September 1994.

(Rose Coleman)

Albert Edwin Delahaye, station master of Builth High and Low Level in the 1930s.

(Courtesy Noel Trigg)

Station Master Albert Delahaye at Builth High and Low Levels on his retirement day, 31 October 1936, saying farewell to a guard on the lower station (GWR).

(Courtesy Noel Trigg)

A period postcard view of Glanrhyd in 1910 showing David Griffiths and his two daughters. He started work on the railways at 19 in 1881 as porter/guard and became a station master ten years later and was the father-in-law of John Alan Thomas. His father was a platelayer on the Llanelli-Llandovery line. (Courtesy Douglas Thomas)

Albert Edwin Delahaye

An unusual position was held by a GWR man, Albert Edwin Delahaye who, in 1929, was the first to take up a post of station master of both the GWR and LMS railways at Builth Road. He was born at Talgarth station where his father had been station master for 38 years and was one of eight sons. (The total railway service of the family was over 300 years).

Mr Delahaye started work as a porter at Talgarth in 1889, was transferred to Rhayader as signalman and later to Llanidloes. After Grouping, he became station master at Trefeinon where he stayed for 19 years and then at Llansaintffraed for a further six. In spite of being a GWR man, he showed no favouritism and his tact earned him respect and affection from the men of both companies.

When he left on 31 October, 1936 after 47 years service, a combined presentation of a solid oak chiming grandfather clock and an armchair was made by both GWR and LMS staff.

David Griffiths

Started on the CWL in 1881 at the age of 19, as porter/guard and worked at Glanrhyd. He became a station master ten years later. His father was a platelayer on the Llanelli–Llandovery section.

Bill Matheson 'The Pigeon' in 1994.

(Rose Coleman)

The naming of Class 37 No. 37431 Sir Powys County of Powys *on 17 June 1987 at Llandrindod showing station staff Tony Williams and Robin Powell with former relief signalman Jim Smout.* (Courtesy Tony Williams)

Bill Matheson 'The Pigeon'

Bill Matheson started work on the Central just after Nationalisation in 1948 as a 'track' or 'length' man. When the line was singled, he became a track inspector but due to a disability necessitating a hip replacement, he was later transferred to Knighton and was responsible for the delivery of the Craven Arms to Swansea worksheets.

Bill, or 'the Pigeon' as he was then called, had a handy arrangement with the guard who saved him going up the line to Knighton by handing him the worksheets when he boarded the train at his local station, Llanbister Road. By leaving the latter at 7.30am on the 'down' train he had time for a leisurely breakfast in Swansea and could return to Llanbister Road by 3pm.

Bill continued his 'Pigeon run' until he retired in 1978. In the meantime, he took over the 18th century Greyhound Inn in Llangunllo. In 1959, it was, as the brewery explained, only a 'barrel and a half a week' affair and in order to make a living he would need his job as well. Thus, the Pigeon/Publican continued for 19 years, his wife attending to the lunch time trade and he to the evening, even though he had to get up early to catch the 7.30am 'down'.

In 1994, at the age of 81, Bill still ran the Greyhound and the adjacent petrol pump and was found by the writer filling a tumbler from a bottle marked 'Rum' but which, in fact, contained rhubarb wine.

He recalls that when the line was singled, the sleepers were purchased by dealers for local farmers and he himself bought a telephone pole for a shilling piece. The steel rail was carted away by Wards of Sheffield. Bill looks up from his rhubarb wine, 'Must have made an awful lot of razor blades' he says.

John Price

In 1990 he received first prize for the most courteous member of railway station staff in Wales in a competition run by the Transport Users' Consultative Committee for Wales. Originally employed at Knighton station, he had been working at Llandovery for five years, having been transferred from Llanwrtyd in 1985.

Jim Smout

He commenced at Penybont as a porter in 1948, just before Nationalisation, and became Rest Day Relief Signalman in 1951. He retired in 1985 but still interests himself in events

Signalman John Alan Thomas standing by the 'down' line at Llandovery in the 1950s, facing north.
(Courtesy Douglas Thomas)

John Alan Thomas
Started work as porter/signalman at Garnant GWR c1920, he was promoted to Llandovery North box, controlling crossing gates. A severe gas leak occurred in the signal box and he suffered such ill effects that he was forced to retire. In spite of the fact that he was 'gassed' through no fault of his own, he received neither compensation nor commendation–not even a gold watch to mark his 39 years of service.

Glyn Watson
A leading porter at Llandrindod from December 1949 until October 1965, he is now Assistant Publicity Officer of the Heart of Wales Line Travellers' Association of which he was a founder member. He has a very great interest in the line and not only counts passengers on the Rambler services each summer Sunday but records information on every 'Special' running on the CWL. It is said that on the none-too-frequent occasions when Railway authorities carry out a passenger count, if their number differs from that recorded by Glyn, his is usually accepted as correct.

Tony Williams
Began work as junior porter at Builth Road High Level in the late 1950s and later became a signalman in Builth Road No. 2 box which controlled the connecting loop between High and Low Level stations. Having worked in most of the boxes north of Builth Road, he is now in charge of Llandrindod Wells station.

Glyn Watson at Llandrindod station in November 1994.
(Rose Coleman)

Tony Williams at Llandrindod No. 1 signal box in wooden staff and ticket days.
(Courtesy Tony Williams)

14

Tales of the Line

Contributors: D. T. Davies, Douglas Jones, Michael Lewis, Jim Smout, A. Thomas, Douglas Thomas, Mike Watson and Penry Wilson.

John Alan Thomas, later a signalman at Llandovery, was coming home on leave from the forces. He had to alight at Llangadog and then cycle back to Glanrhyd as the train was not stopping at the latter but he decided to throw his case out as he passed Glanrhyd to save him carrying it on his bike. The catch came undone and its contents went flying through the air, much to the dismay of his future father-in-law, the station master who, standing on the platform, found himself surrounded by socks and underwear.

★★★

The last man to stay in the Swansea lodging house was a Stockport guard, a cheery soul who always began the journey by saying in a broad Cheshire accent, 'Hallo driver. We'll have a good trip today. Just remember, do your best and the LMS will do the rest.'

★★★

One passenger wrote to the Heart of Wales Line Travellers' Association in 1985 praising the staff on the line and recalling the time when, on travelling to Gatwick, he realised that he had unintentionally taken with him a pair of large boots which would have been a considerable nuisance to carry around. The station master at Llandeilo took charge of them and delivered them to the house of the passenger's parents on his way back from work.

★★★

Quote from HOWLTA Newsletter September 1989
'PSUL To our more knowledgeable railway readers, this is the commonly used term in railway parlance for passenger services over unusual lines. This applied to one of our service trains in April of this year when the Swansea departure from Shrewsbury was found by the driver to have a leaking roof, which was allowing rain to enter his cab. To overcome the problem the train left Shrewsbury in the Wolverhampton direction and then reversed on to the southern section of the triangular junction so that the other end of the train was facing south. He then transferred to the other cab and could proceed to Swansea without getting a soaking.'

★★★

In 1925, a fox jumped off the Heyope end of the 69ft high Knucklas Viaduct. Having been pursued by the hunt from Vron Rocks, Dutlas, over Beacons Hill it started across the viaduct towards Craig-y-Don woods. The local vicar at that time, Reverend Frank Evans, wrote that it was not unusual to see a fox walking the parapet, crossing from Castle Hill to the wood and that on a moonlight night, to stop and bark. However, this unfortunate animal found itself ambushed by workmen who happened to be walking over from the one end and huntsmen following behind it. Thus trapped, it leapt, the leading hounds only just being restrained from following it. The story varies. Some say that the fox was killed on impact, others that it was uninjured but was finished off by the hounds. It is more likely that it was, in fact, badly injured and thus an easy target for the latter.

Whichever is true, the poor animal met its death and its passing was commemorated by the word 'fox' scored into a viaduct lintel at the point from which it jumped.

The incident aroused considerable feeling amongst some members of the community. An article by the headmaster of a nearby school appeared in the press and a local lady, Mary Bowen, incensed by the cruelty, wrote a poem entitled 'Blackguards Bridge'. By 1964, the event was still remembered and in June of that year a ceremony was performed by Reverend Proctor, and attended by organisations and individuals, at the viaduct to commemorate it.

★★★

In the early 1900s attempts were made to derail trains on the

Knucklas Viaduct, from which great height the fox jumped. (Rose Coleman)

Llanbister Road section. The gist of 86 year old Mr Penry Wilson's description of the events written in 1994, is as follows:

'It would be about 86-87 years ago when my father was salesman at Llanbister Road for the Radnorshire Company. (My oldest brother who would be 96 now could recall their talking about it). The man was putting rail chairs on the track and he always came on moonlit nights. Detectives and police tried to catch him but failed. One day when discussing it with the police and the signalman, my father suggested that it was probably some lunatic who had been reading books about such things and the police agreed. A likely suspect of this type was interviewed but was cleared by the local schoolmaster and suspicion was then turned on someone from the Penybont area.

One night, my brother and a companion were standing on the bridge and saw the man coming half way down White House Garden. He then climbed over the hedge and threw something at the signal box. However, they still failed to catch him. In order to ensure the safety of the line, the ganger had to patrol night and day and it is said that the latter encountered the culprit under a bridge not far from Cwm-y-Guest but he got away.'

It appears that the vandal was never apprehended although it is understood that some of the local inhabitants who are now in their nineties could – but would not – put a name to him.

★★★

The lift between Builth High and Low Level stations was for luggage only and staff were not allowed to use it. In the mid 1930s, a porter with a wheel trolley disobeyed the rules to his cost and travelled on it. His arm was caught between the lift and the framework and he was trapped for hours, quite a portion of the contraption having to be dismantled before he could be released.

★★★

In the 1960s, transportation of a ram provided a good two hours entertainment at Builth Road when it escaped between High and Low Level stations. Someone unkindly remarked that the porters had more exercise that day than they had had all month.

★★★

On one occasion, a local enthusiast, noticing the driver 'hooting' much more than usual at Knucklas Viaduct, was alerted to the fact that there were sheep on the track. He 'phoned the nearest farmer who, on asking how long he had to clear them, was told '45 minutes'. The latter subsequently rang up saying that he had had a 'devil of a job' to round up the sheep – and then discovered that they weren't his!

★★★

On 8 August 1982, a tractor was left across the line north of Llandrindod and was hit by a pair of 2-car dmus forming the 11.55 Crewe to Tenby. Although, fortunately, no one was seriously hurt, there was severe damage to the second man's side of the front unit including broken windows. The driver was able to run the train into Llandrindod station but, due to the damage, there was insufficient clearance to cross with the 'up' train. The passengers alighted, were given refreshments and their injuries treated by BR staff and HOWLTA members while the front unit was moved into the 'up' siding north of the station. The remaining single-car unit continued to Whitland and due to the late running, passengers transferred to a Swansea–Pembroke Dock train to continue to Tenby. Despite the shock, the driver of the damaged unit, continued to work his roster by taking the 'up' train to Shrewsbury.

★★★

Very personal service was accorded to Douglas Jones when he lived in Stanage during the war. When he returned home on leave, the train would stop and drop him off at the bottom of his garden which adjoined the railway embankment. The staff would be told on which train he intended travelling when he had to return, the driver would give an arranged short blast and a long blast – and pick up their passenger who climbed into the cab and was then transferred to one of the coaches at Penybont. The only thanks the train crew would ever accept was a bottle of warm tea and the empties would be left at the bottom of the garden with a message 'Many thanks and Good luck'.

★★★

A line running through such remote and unspoiled countryside abounds with wildlife which is visible from the train. A well-known ornithologist, Tom Ammonds of Shobden, was a regular traveller on the Central. His companion on many expeditions, Douglas Jones, comments that he combed the streams and hills from the heights of Sugar Loaf to the shores of Swansea Bay and that, aided by binoculars, steadied by a foam pad on the top of his walking stick, he could identify birds at a great distance from a moving train. Bed and breakfast accommodation along the line usually amounted to just 'bed' with an egg sandwich to ensure they wasted no time in getting out at first light.

Douglas Jones describes this knowledgeable man as a pioneer of the use of the railway train as a convenient 'armchair moving hide', pointing out such a concept as being useful for the disabled who need not leave the train to study wildlife. Tom Ammonds died in October 1984 from injuries sustained in a car accident on his way home from a presentation to commemorate his 25 years as Chairman of the Herefordshire Ornithological Club.

★★★

A tramp seeking a warm place to spend the night bedded down on top of the Cilyrychen Lime Kilns which were served by a line from the CWL and can still be seen from the train. The poor fellow was discovered to be dead the next day, having been killed by the fumes.

★★★

From the *Cambrian* 27 August 1863

> 'Railway Accident – On Saturday evening last, a shocking accident happened to a young man named John Williams, near the Dyffryn station, Llanelly Railway. It appears he was stationed there in order to learn the telegraph. When the goods train arrived, he jumped up, and took a ride up the Mountain branch; and on his way back, near the station, he jumped off, but not far enough from the waggons, to prevent an accident, and we are sorry to say, that one of the waggon wheels passed over his leg. He was removed to the Dyffryn House, and an engine was immediately despatched to Llandilo for medical aid. Doctors Prothero and Lewis, of Llandilo, and Dr Davies of Cross Inn, were soon in attendance. They saw that it was necessary to amputate the leg, which was very skilfully done; and the sufferer gets on now as well as can be expected.'

★★★

The vexed problem of insufficient space for bicycles on the 'Sprinters' had its lighter side when a plan to make a point during a local election in 1994 failed due to kindly co-operation. The idea was that a woman with a bicycle was to attempt to board the 'up' train at Builth Road and travel to Llandrindod, knowing full well that a 'plant' with his bicycle en route to Shrewsbury, was already on board and that there would be no room for her machine. Media coverage was set up to film her distress but the guard seeing that there was room to accommodate her and the bike to travel just one station up the line, helped her aboard. Not only was the point not made – which was, of course, a pity – but the would-be damsel in distress had let herself in for a seven mile cycle ride back to Builth Road which she had not anticipated.

★★★

On 7 April 1990, the body of regular Central Wales Line user and rambler, Graham Nuttall, was found in the remote hills above Llanwrtyd, where it had lain for eleven weeks. His faithful cross border collie, Ruswarp, who always accompanied him, had stayed by his owner and though starving, weighing only eight pounds and too weak to walk, was nursed back to health by a local vet. The dog died in the autumn of 1991, aged about 16 years. A Rowan tree to commemorate man and dog was planted in the pleasant garden at Llanwrtyd station in 1995.

★★★

Short and Tall Stories

(For the authenticity of which, the author takes no responsibility whatsoever. Some – but not all – should be taken with a very large 'fistful' of salt!)

★★★

One of the drivers based at Llandovery in the 1960s, who was often short of beer money, took advantage of the absence of his wife for a few days, to kill one of their pigs and sell it to supplement his funds. Naturally, he could not own up to his deed so he told his wife that one had inexplicably died and showed her the little mound of earth behind the house where it was buried. Fortunately for him, the good lady did not attempt to investigate it.

★★★

They used to say that if you could hear the trains clearly in Llandovery as they went up the Sugar Loaf, it was going to rain.

★★★

They also used to say that if you could hear the trains clearly on Llandrindod platform as they went past Howey, it was going to rain.

★★★

It is said that mock water tanks were erected at Knighton during the Second World War as a decoy for enemy aircraft looking for a target. The Germans declined the invitation.

★★★

When the line was constructed through Llandrindod, the Irish navvies, finding the nearest hostelry a little too far for convenience, had a house near the track converted into a pub. The fact that the downstairs room needed knocking into one to accommodate this facility, posed no problem. They cut 10ft off one of the rails to use as a lintel and once all was propped and plastered no one was any the wiser, even though the missing section of rail caused some scratching of heads among those in authority. Thus – so it is said – was the Middleton Inn born!

★★★

An unfortunate goat consigned by her owner to travel to Scotland to mate, instead remained tethered under the signal box at Cynghordy for two weeks because the station master was unfamiliar with the forms necessary for her transportation. She was duly collected at the end of the fortnight, but her owner, unaware of her sexual frustration, subsequently wondered why she produced no offspring.

★★★

In the heyday of Llandrindod Wells as a spa, there were freelance luggage porters as well as those sent from the hotels. One of the tricks of the trade, should the passenger decide to accompany the luggage, was to charge by the distance covered and conduct them to their destination by a very circuitous route. It was reckoned that the journey to the Hotel Metropole – a mere 45 seconds walk from the station – could be stretched to 10 minutes or even more if visitors arrived on the 'up' line which could entail, if they were gullible, a pleasant detour via the upper part of the Rock Park. (It is believed that the sons of these porters moved to London and became taxi drivers!)

★★★

A farmer in the Knucklas area was very puzzled and not a little suspicious when he took delivery of some ferrets at the local station. Not only were they later than expected but they were also extremely muddy. The reason was that upon their arrival the guard had 'borrowed' them to have a little sport with some of his friends but had encountered a problem in retrieving them – it was a couple of days before he succeeded in digging them out of the rabbit holes.

★★★

If you stand on Llangunllo station looking down the line, you will notice that the track has a slight 'kink' to the right. According to a signalman who once worked at Llanbister Road, this is because the line of the original route isolated a spring from a local farm. The farmer, unwilling to be deprived of a useful source of water, moved the pegs to curve around the spring and the gangers laid the track accordingly.

★★★

When fish arrived in Llandrindod Wells by train it was bedded in ice crystals. The latter, once the fish were removed, could be mixed with a good supply of ordinary custard and sold as ice cream. No one ever detected anything 'fishy' about it.

15

Survival in the 1990s

With the re-election of the Conservatives in 1992, the line faced another threat when, the following year, the government pushed ahead with its plan for privatisation. Promises that this would not endanger the line were viewed with suspicion.

Unease was fuelled in 1993 by the M.P. for Brecon and Radnor, Jonathan Evans, when he stated that the annual running costs of the line amounted to £4½m against an income of approximately £500,000 p.a. Many question the accuracy of these figures.

With suitably timed services, realistic fares and adequate publicity, the line would no doubt increase its revenue but not to such an extent as to cover a deficit of £4m – if indeed the amount is correct. The line qualifies for funding under the 1968 Transport Act which committed the government to allocate grants to ensure the continuous running of socially necessary lines. This grant which, in 1975, became the Public Service Obligation (PSO) grant is limited and government policy is to reduce it gradually.

At the beginning of 1991 the Central Wales Line Forum was formed at the instigation of Powys County Council to monitor developments on the line in view of the reduction of the PSO, the position being highlighted by British Rail's withdrawal – without consultation – of the last train in each direction on Mondays to Thursdays. Initially, county councils along the line, the Development Board for Rural Wales, the Sports Council for Wales and HOWLTA were invited to send representatives and the first Forum meeting was held in February 1991. The meeting on 25 July of that year was attended by representatives from Dyfed, Powys, West Glamorgan and Shropshire County Councils, South Shropshire District Council, Welsh District Councils, the Transport User's Consultative Committee for Wales, the Wales Tourist Board, the Development Board for Rural Wales, British Rail and the Minister of State for Wales.

The social needs were itemised as:

That there is little alternative transport particularly for long distance travelling. There seems to be difficulty for trainees attending Shrewsbury College and that there ought to be an early and late train in and out of Mid- Wales.

There is need for commuter transport into Swansea, Llandrindod Wells and Shrewsbury. That promotion of leisure activities should receive substantial encouragement.

That access from Knighton into Llandrindod Wells for the magistrates' court should be considered.

There should be appropriate connections into the InterCity Service Network.

Railways have a beneficial environmental effect upon Mid-Wales.

The Railways should enhance the infrastructure, particularly in the South where there are prospects of increasing manufacturing industry and that in Dyfed a consultants report on all three railways in the area is due in January and this should be taken into consideration. There should be additional parking facilities to encourage park and ride.

There is a deterioration in the standard railway stations and that improvements would do much to enhance the image. The problems of passengers requiring access to and egress from Swansea beyond Llandovery needs greater recognition.

The response from British Rail to this list was not particularly positive but it did state that there were no plans to close the Central Wales Line and that 'Regional Railways are committed to keeping the line open with all the assistance that it can receive from local authorities and other bodies'.

On 18 February 1993 a public meeting in Llandrindod was called by Powys County Councillor, Chris Mann, to discuss the effect which privatisation would have on the line.

John Stewart, a representative from Transport 2000 explained how privatisation would work and expressed the view that the CWL as a non profit making line would be unlikely to attract many bidders and could well be one with which BR would have to struggle on. The County Surveyor confirmed the commitment of Powys County Council in

A Class 153 'Sprinter' approaches Llandrindod in the snow on the 'down' line 1993. (Roy Palmer)

giving grants towards the running costs but was concerned at the anticipated reduction of 20 per cent in government grants.

A petition which, at the date of the meeting, already bore more than 4,500 signatures would be presented to the House of Commons before the third reading of the Bill for Privatisation. In the summer of 1993, efforts seem to have been made to allay fears of closure. On 27 July a number of top ranking officials travelled up the line. These included the Minister of Transport, Roger Freeman, the Member of Parliament for Brecon and Radnor, Jonathan Evans, the Secretary of State for Wales, John Redwood and important representatives from British Rail.

They received a barrage of searching questions from HOWLTA, the press – both national and local – and from television reporters. Jonathan Evans re-iterated his statement that the line would stay open if use did not decline. Thus returning the questioner to the vicious circle. While the minimum amount possible is spent on publicity and the timetables and services are inconvenient, passenger usage will not increase. On the other hand, as no fairy godmother is lurking in the wings with £4m, the financial situation is not likely to improve without an increase in passengers.

The reassurances are still forthcoming. An article in the *Western Mail* on 4 April 1994 stated:

> 'British Rail says it has no plans to close the Heart of Wales Line. From April 1st it will simply be run by one of BR's successors, the Regional Railways South Wales and West Train Operating Company.'

This scenic route lies permanently under the 'Sword of Damocles' having fought off threats of closure in 1962 and 1967. When asked about its future in the 1960s, one railway official said that it had to be faced that the papers were 'always in the pigeon hole'. A fact which is probably just as true today.

Some feel that the CWL would fair better with a mini-franchise of its own or sub-contracted from the cumbersomely named 'Regional Railways South Wales and West Train Operating Company' in order to obtain the necessary management attention and effort.

Meanwhile one can only hope that RRSW&W TOC will make an effort towards more positive achievements.

Paul Fielding, Marketing Manager of the latter at a meeting of the Heart of Wales Line Forum in November 1994, said that 'this year there is no particular threat', but added that if grant money was reduced it would be near the top of the hit list. The line, according to Mr Fielding, cost £2m pounds a year to operate and passengers contributed only half a million.

By the spring of 1996 the line's rolling stock had been bought by ROSCO (Angel Rolling Stock Leasing Company), Railtrack owned the track and was responsible for the infrastructure and HOWLTA was told by South Wales and West Railway that every aspect of the line was 'currently timetabled to be sold by the end of 1996'.

In that year, Prism won the franchise for the SW&W trains and by October the company took over the operation of the line. Some degree of apprehension was apparent that the firm's reputation was that of a successful bus company. However, by the commencement of 1997, it was being stressed that, to quote a HOWLTA newsletter, 'Prism is a train operator' and, it would appear, a train operator prepared to do its best for the line. As one heads towards the millennium, with the 'Forum', HOWLTA, Prism and other interested parties working together and Railtrack committed to station repairs to the tune of some £300,000, there are grounds for cautious optimism.

However, complacency is dangerous and it must be born in mind that this scenic route lies permanently under the 'Sword of Damocles' having fought off threats of closure in 1962 and 1967. When asked about its future in the 1960s period, one railway official said that it had to be faced that the papers were 'always in the pigeon hole'. A fact which is probably just as true today.

Statistics are various and confusing but it is obvious that the more passengers the line can attract, with timetables better tailored to the needs of the community, good connections, efficient service and competitive fares, the more tourists it can encourage (and, some would say, the longer it runs through marginal constituencies) the greater are its chances of survival.

Bibliography

Welsh History Review Vol. 7. No. 1 June 1974 'Impact of Railways on Agricultural Improvement on 19th century Wales' David W. Howell

A Passenger Survey 1964 'University of Wales Dept. of Economics'

Working with Steam H. C. H. Burgess

Railways of Shropshire Richard K. Morris

Welsh Coal Mines Dr W. Gerwyn Thomas, Dept. of Industry, National Museum of Wales 1976

Railway and Canal Traffic Cases Vol. II. R. Neville & W. H. MacNamara (Lond 1876)

Shrewsbury to Swansea D. J. Smith, Town and Country Press Ltd 1971

Epitome of Agreements (LMS 1925)

British Railways Journal No. 32 1990

The Central Wales Line Tom Clift, Ian Allan 1982

Track Layout and Diagrams of GWR and BR Western Region. Section 54 1994, *Section 57* 1985, *Section 55* 1984. R. A. Cooke

Forgotten Railways South Wales James Page, David & Charles 1979

British Railway Signalling O. S. Nock, George Allen & Unwin Ltd

A Regional History of the Railways of Great Britain Vol. 11 North and Mid Wales Peter E. Baughan, David & Charles 1980

History of the Great Western Railway Vol. 1 E. T. MacDermot MA, Great Western Railway Co. 1927

A Regional History of Railways of Great Britain Vol. 12 South Wales D. S. M. Barrie, David & Charles

Western at Work Series No. 3 OPC 1981

Western at Work Series No.7 British Rail (Western) and Avon Anglia Publications 1987

HOWLTA Newsletters 1985-1996

Railway History Sources C. R. Clinker, Avon-Anglia Publications & Services 1976

Railway Magazine: 'The Central Wales Railway' Herbert Rake. May and June 1906

'The London and North Western Railway in Central Wales' C. N. Ryan 1912

'London–Swansea via L.M.S.R, – 1' John D. Hewitt & Charles E. Lee September 1938

'London–Swansea via L.M.S.R, – II' John D. Hewitt October 1938

'Welsh reprieve Part 1' J. M. Dunn May 1964

'Taking the Waters in Rural Wales' Geoffrey F. Bannister BA. September 1972

'Class 9 to Llandovery' Malcolm Roughley January 1982

Signal Box Directory 1987

Clinkers' Register of Closed Passenger Stations and Goods Depots Avon-Anglia Publications 1978

The Signal Box OPC 1986

British Railway Signalling G. M. Kitchenside & A. Williams, Ian Allan 1963

Index